PELICAN BOOKS

MAN AND ENVIRONMENT

Robert Arvill is the pen-name of one of the few
exponents of conservation planning and development to have detailed, practical knowledge and
experience on local, central and international
levels. After serving for seven years in the army,
being demobbed as a major (1946), he had two
years (1946–8) on the development staff of a
large county borough and six years in one of the
leading county planning and development departments (1948–54), before, as he puts it,
'getting immersed' in conservation with national
and international bodies. In this work he has
made important contributions as a member of
teams which have produced many publications
and has himself given numerous papers to many
national and international conferences.

ROBERT ARVILL

MAN AND ENVIRONMENT

Crisis and the Strategy of Choice

*

FOURTH EDITION

PENGUIN BOOKS

Penguin Books Ltd, Harmondsworth, Middlesex, England
Penguin Books, 625 Madison Avenue, New York, New York 10022, U.S.A.
Penguin Books Australia Ltd, Ringwood, Victoria, Australia
Penguin Books Canada Ltd, 41 Steelcase Road West, Markham, Ontario, Canada
Penguin Books (N.Z.) Ltd, 182–190 Wairau Road, Auckland 10, New Zealand

—

First published 1967
Second edition 1969
Reprinted 1970, 1971
Third edition 1973
Reprinted with revisions 1974
Fourth edition 1976

—

Copyright © Robert Arvill, 1967, 1969, 1973, 1974, 1976

—

Made and printed in Great Britain
by Richard Clay (The Chaucer Press) Ltd,
Bungay, Suffolk
Set in Monotype Imprint

CONTENTS

APPENDICES

SUPPLEMENTS

LIST OF FIGURES AND TABLES

PREFACE

THIS book is about people; about their impact on land, air, water and wildlife, and the environment they create; about the damage and destruction they cause and the measures they take as a society to remedy this. Above all it is about the possibilities they now have to reshape and create an environment that fits their highest aspirations.

Environmental problems are being mentioned more and more frequently in the press and journals, and on television and radio. Such interest reflects man's dissatisfaction with what he is doing to natural resources and his search for knowledge on which to base his 'value' judgements.

Perhaps most important, this quickening interest – this recognition of the wrongs done and the groping attempts to prevent a recurrence of them – is an evolving acceptance by man of his personal responsibility for the state of this planet.

The great potentialities of modern science and technology and the new approaches in administration, education and information, offer man the ways and means for creating a high-quality environment. He will, however, often have to forgo short-term self-interest and take satisfaction instead from acting as a trustee for man's heritage.

Achievements in this field require planning – a much abused word for a good idea: forethought plus teamwork. Planning can be truly successful only if it is done for the people and carried out with the approval of the people. There must be a process of continual involvement: the planners and the people they are planning for must settle together the objectives to be sought, the limits to which the plans should go, what society should do and what is best for the individual.

Planning for posterity must be based on a full understanding of the interaction of human activities and natural forces, and of the ability of nature to sustain and to renew herself. Ecology is the science which seeks to elucidate the principles governing the interactions of the natural processes of land, air, water and living things. Conservation involves the application of these scientific principles and a policy of trusteeship. Conservation requires planning of the factors of supply and demand and can itself be meaningful only if it is borne in mind when *all* human activities are considered.

This book seeks to give enough information about man's numbers and his impact on land, air, water and wildlife to show the range of choices open to him. It stresses the interdependence of town and country but, because of the vast range of problems involved, does not deal to any extent with the detail of town planning and urban renewal. It suggests that increasing government emphasis ought to be laid on conservation philosophy, principles and strategy rather than the detailed, negative, restrictionist planning which at present often bedevils individual freedom and irks so many. It proposes that what is essentially a process of reconciliation should be arranged between competing claims and individuals, between the forces of nature and our power to guide them, between man's baser and his finer capacities.

But so much depends upon the individual. Will he devote just that degree of personal interest and the few hours a year necessary to ensure that he does have a choice, that he can contribute to the strategy of choice, and that he will leave some choice for posterity?

I believe man can and will do this. He is concerned for the future of his children. But time is short. And posterity is with us now.

*

The major issues dealt with in this book have been kept under close review. Recent data and reports confirm the main trends and features and show that action is already under way on some of the proposals in the book. The text has been brought up to date with the latest readily available material, and new Supplements deal with issues of worldwide importance.

ACKNOWLEDGEMENTS

FOR this fourth edition, I would like to emphasize my continuing gratitude to those whose helpful observations were acknowledged in earlier editions.

I owe a special debt of gratitude to Dr Robin Best for the data and guidance he has generously given me on urban land and related matters for all editions of this book; in particular, the revision of Urban Land in Chapter 4 is based on his latest work. I am also grateful to the Editor of *The Planner* for allowing me to refer to the data in an article by Dr Best for his Royal Town Planning Institute Journal in advance of publication in 1976. My thanks are also due once more to the Chief Librarian (Miss S. M. Penny) and her colleagues in the library of the Nature Conservancy Council. And I am much indebted to Miss Sonia Kostromin for invaluable secretarial help. As always, I owe a great deal to my wife.

I should also express my appreciation of all those people who in numerous reports, papers and conferences provided sources of material for this book and would like to draw special attention to the wealth of material in the Annual Reports of the U.S.A. Council on Environmental Quality, on which I have drawn for the Supplement on Environmental Impact Assessments.

For permission to reproduce the tables and illustrations in this book I am very grateful to the persons and organizations noted in the text. The permission of the Controller of Her Majesty's Stationery Office was obtained to reproduce the maps of Dorset and of statutory conservation in Britain.

CHAPTER I

INTRODUCTION

I will show you fear in a handful of dust.
T. S. Eliot, *The Waste Land*

FROM primitive times man has been making an assault on his environment with fire, water and tools. Until a century or so ago, this attack took place over limited areas and in most cases at a relatively slow pace. Today there is a danger that man may use up the habitable and cultivable land. His activities increasingly outstrip the capacity of natural processes to restore the fertility of the land and water which has taken thousands of years to create. And through errors and misuse of his powers he is ruining or degrading vast areas of the globe.

The great driving force behind this new fierce assault is the population explosion. It took 200,000 years for man to reach his first thousand million, but only 100 years to reach his second. The world population in 1976 was over 4,000 million. By the year 2000 it is expected to be over 6 thousand million. If present trends continue, 50 years from now, when many of today's children will still be alive, the figure could well be 12 thousand million.

Already we can see the devastation spreading, but what few people seem to realize is that the devastation to come may be so great that its scale will give it an entirely new quality – just as air-raids changed when the atom bomb replaced T.N.T.

There is no doubt that the spectacular increases in world population which have been forecast are inevitable except under two conditions: either a major catastrophe occurs – a pandemic, a plague, an all-out nuclear war – or man introduces severe population control. Since 1945, for example, the expectancy of life in India has risen from twenty to forty years. Its population increases by one million a month. Man has

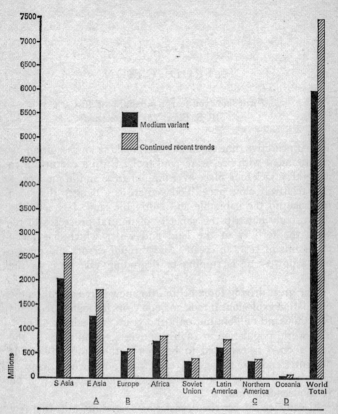

A Includes mainland China, Japan, Mongolia, Korea and China (Taiwan) B Outside the Soviet Union and Turkey C Includes Hawaii D Not including Hawaii

Figure 1. Populations in A.D. 2000 based on main trends – see Chapter 15 (United Nations)

introduced 'death-control'; now he must find a replacement for the normal regulating processes of nature.

All animal populations have a direct relationship to their environment, not only in connection with food supply but also for living space. Man is no exception; but, unlike other animals, he has the power consciously to regulate his own numbers. Many techniques are becoming available to do this, but for the great masses of people in the underdeveloped countries modern methods of birth-control are still either unknown or too expensive. Then, too, in many countries religious sensibilities inhibit effective action by the State. So we are faced with the dismal prospect that there may be within our lifetime a substantial debasement of living standards and of the environment.

Furthermore, the very pace of population growth poses major problems of adjustment for man as a social animal. When, during the nineteenth century, Europe's population increased rapidly, tension there led to nearly sixty million emigrating, notably to the U.S.A. A similar emigration today from, say, China or India, would be almost unthinkable; the suggestion alone could create dangerous international problems. Even the numerically minor emigrations from the East now create great difficulties, but for the mass of Asiatic peoples the problem is far worse: there is no place for them to go to.

Expectations

The impacts of this sheer weight of numbers are increasingly intensified by a range of forces which can be summed up in one word – expectations. Worldwide communications reveal how poor are the poor – and this disturbs the conscience of the richer peoples. And the poor have glimpsed the material wealth of the developed nations and they are no longer content with the 'natural order'.

The effects of the world's first century of mass education – however inadequate – are now manifesting themselves in demands by individuals to determine their own political systems and to shape their own destinies. The developed countries rage with claims for participation in decision-making and expression for cultural minorities. Third World countries strive to escape from poverty, illiteracy and squalor, seek self-reliance and demand national independence. Power-sharing becomes everyone's concern, locally and globally.

The Indian Prime Minister told the United Nations' (U.N.) First World Conference on the Human Environment in 1972 that poverty is the greatest pollutant, stressing that a third of the world's population should not be condemned to live undernourished, illiterate in slums and without work. The individual's problem of survival in a world of misuse and maldistribution of resources is self-evident; but the whole community of man could be engulfed if these lead to war or pandemic.

The U.N. World Conferences in 1974 on Population (Bucharest) and Food (Rome) made it clear beyond doubt that the development of the earth's resources, its population numbers and the levels of consumption of its peoples are inextricably interwoven. These are immense shifts in thought – rapidly pervading the world scene. Self-centred attitudes will persist among many countries, but this recognition of the fundamental bases of world problems now motivates expectations as no other force in man's history. Other major expectations affecting the environment arise over shelter, energy and movement. Everywhere, there is an inflation of claims and desires, too often incompatible with the existing capacity of individuals and systems to attain, and possibly beyond the resources of the biosphere to sustain.

These forces also press for international cooperation and towards a convergence between the precepts governing man's physical and moral conditions; existing systems of thought are challenged everywhere; and the expectation grows that man can and must reshape his way of life and environment to provide equity and justice.

Food

Estimates by the U.N. World Food and Agriculture Organization (F.A.O.) suggest that one fifth of the population is well fed, two fifths are on a diet just adequate for subsistence and two fifths are starving. U.N. expert surveys have concluded that up to one half of the world's population may be suffering from hunger or malnutrition or both. The urgent calls for wheat in recent years from the developing countries, in order to prevent famine conditions, show that much of the world is one harvest away from starvation. The alarmingly frequent famines in these poorer countries are one of the world's greatest challenges. The U.S.S.R. and China cannot survive without grain imports. And, paradoxically, North America is the only region in the world with a large unused capacity for export. This maldistribution of the world's food production may itself be a factor menacing the peace of the world. A starving man is often a desperate one.

F.A.O. stated in the mid-seventies that the world food situation was more difficult than at any time for 30 years. Agricultural and fishery production had dropped slightly per person, as world population continued to grow. Surplus stocks of food in the major exporting countries, which have 'cushioned' the the world against adversity, had nearly gone; in particular, cereal stocks were the lowest for 20 years. The recent vast increase in oil prices intensifies world food problems, especially in the poorer countries. Probably 60 out of 100 developing countries have a deficit in food/energy supplies.

At the Rome Conference a World Food Council was set up under the U.N. to coordinate the policies of U.N. Agencies on food production, security and aid and related matters. An International Fund for Agricultural Development and two Committees on Food Aid and Food Security were also formed. These four bodies together comprise the essential elements of a possible World Food Authority. And the Conference resolved not only that every effort should be made to grow and distribute food to give all human beings an adequate diet, but proposed, as a longer-term solution, rational population policies. By the mid seventies, the exploding appetites and over-consumption by the rich countries, especially of protein, made them increasingly vulnerable. The poor have so little to lose.

The increasing demands for food have led inevitably to over-exploitation of the better quality and more accessible land. The Dust Bowl disaster of the U.S.A., the problems arising from the cultivation of the great plains of Kazakhstan in the U.S.S.R., the agricultural settlement failures in Kenya and,

on a smaller scale, the shrinking peat fens of England, are all
recent illustrations of man's mishandling. We are now faced,
too, with a great increase in the numbers of pests capable of
ruining a crop. Pests in such numbers are largely the outcome
of man's agricultural systems, particularly the concentration
on single crops in large areas, which create conditions favourable to certain forms of animal and plant life.

Yet the paradox, both of demand and production, is that in
Western countries agriculture has reached such relative
efficiency that in the U.S.A. many farmers have been paid not
to produce food but to conserve their soil – the 'soil bank'.
Despite such extra productive capacity, despite the prospect of
utilizing the relatively untapped resources of the sea and
despite the continuing achievements of science and technology,
the global food situation appears likely to get worse.

To feed the population of the year 2000 will require a
spectacularly increased production. The U.N. surveys indicated that the food supplies of the developing countries must be
quadrupled. Overall, world production of cereals must be
doubled and that of animal products trebled; in some of the
presently under-fed areas food outputs, especially of protein,
will need to increase four to six fold.

It is difficult to predict the long-term effects of these various
factors and trends. On the one hand, total food demand may
lead to a concentration on food production from every available hectare. On the other hand, if population numbers can be
controlled, an increase in agricultural productivity may release
considerable quantities of land for other purposes, for example,
afforestation and recreation.

But there is little doubt that in either case the environment
will change. Intensive farming may imperil the fertility of the
land; to maintain it is now the task of the great chemical
industry. The use of chemicals on land and water is further
extended by the need to keep down pests. Replacing traditional
practices of agriculture by the use of chemicals, factory farming, spray irrigation and the development of large fields without hedgerows and copses will remove much that has led to an
attractive landscape.

Many people today regard the countryside as unchangeable. They do not know that there are very few natural areas, certainly in Britain, and fail to realize that much of what they see is the result of man's activities over the centuries, particularly his search for food.

Shelter

In the case of man's basic need of shelter the effect on the environment is more obvious. Vast proliferations of dwellings are to be found in every continent as the tide of population rises. In Europe, the annual natural increase of population to A.D. 2000 is expected to be around seven per cent. Since this increase is also accompanied by a desire for smaller family groupings, separate houses for different age-levels, and higher general standards of accommodation and living space, the effects will be tremendous.

The great sprawl of bricks and mortar, ironically dubbed subtopia, and the constant battle over land for development, green belts and new towns, make daily headlines in press, radio and television. It is prophesied that in a century Europe will be a continuous conurbation from Manchester to Milan. In the U.S.A., the east and west coasts are developing into walls of bricks and mortar greater than any built by China or Rome. And all over the world the giant cities of the twentieth century continue to spread remorselessly. In 1800 the world had fifty cities of over 100,000 people; today there are over 1,600. The U.N. consider that two thousand cities, each of one million people, are needed for the world's urban population by the turn of the century.

Once the land is sealed over with steel and concrete man cannot do much to restore it – his powers do not at the moment stretch that far. Even worse, within these expanding towns, factory sites, motorways and airfields, there are often large areas of neglected land and many sites are left degraded or derelict.

In the underdeveloped countries, although the living standards are low, pressures on the land and water are more intense as their populations increase at breakneck speed. In many of

the urban centres of the world, in cities such as Hong Kong or
Rio de Janeiro, vast ant heaps of people cling tenaciously to life
in conditions so crowded and so primitive as to be beyond
description – and all this very close to skyscrapers and other
symbols of twentieth-century development. In these areas, the
nineteenth-century lesson that public health is everyone's
business – for example, that disease is no respecter of persons –
has yet to be learnt. The twentieth-century lesson, the need for
planning and development directed to creating a healthy
environment, is not yet on the curriculum.

But by whatever standards these areas of West and East are
judged, they are symptoms of a general disease: man is degrading his own environment on a scale without historic
parallel. Slums make no sense, they are not necessary, and
their perpetuation is a sad reflection on man.

Energy

Even the waste in the slums is often exceeded by the devastation which man creates in his quest for the sources of fuel and
power. Whole landscapes have been changed as men cleared
forests to provide timber for fuel. Scotland grimly illustrates
this, with its barren moors and bogs and eroded mountains –
often the still-visible results of forests being felled in the
seventeenth and eighteenth centuries to provide charcoal for
iron smelting. The enormity of the impact of man's search for
coal can be seen in the torn and scarred valleys of Wales, the
great opencast mining cuts in the Appalachians of eastern
U.S.A. and the vast lignite areas of Czechoslovakia. Here
the workings stretch for miles and have created a scene of
devastation and pollution aptly described as 'the garden of
Hell'.

More recent sources of power, such as oil, natural gas or
electricity, do not so obviously degrade the landscape but their
effect is still great. The countryside becomes a 'wirescape' for
electricity and a conduit for pipelines. In just over a decade,
3,000 km of large pipelines for oil have been laid in Europe
and more are under construction. The skyline is dominated by
massive power stations; coastlines are the site for nuclear

'temples of power', which may become monuments as lasting as the pyramids.

The twentieth-century quest for power is urgent. Nations have been frightened by current assessments of the known resources of power. At present rates of consumption (and more coal and oil have been used up this century than in all recorded history), several of the existing usable supplies of major fuels will last only for decades and not for centuries. Hence, vast numbers of scientific and technical staff and huge amounts of capital are locked up to locate, devise and exploit new supplies of energy.

All this was given great urgency in the seventies as the oil-producing countries exposed the worldwide imbalance between energy supply and material expectations.

Nations intensified their efforts to find and develop new and old sources of energy: solar power; geothermal resources; nuclear power; underseas oil and gas; opencast, strip-mining, and deep coal; shale and tar beds for oil; ocean currents, tidal bores, barrage schemes, rivers, reservoirs, and wind-power. All have an impact on the environment.

Energy exploitation may disrupt communities, eliminate good soils and agricultural land, and diminish or destroy great scenic and amenity areas and wildlife habitats; its production and by-products can pollute and waste; and its infra-structure may pervade the environment. Intensive agriculture depends on many oil products, such as some pesticides and fertilizers, and relies, with industry everywhere, on oil for its machinery and on power generally for its operations. And, overridingly, the energy resource itself may be burned up, without serving as the source of other products capable of being recycled.

The priorities of individuals are altered as energy costs affect every activity of society, and an energy-needy nation gives priority to energy production.

Most nations must soon formulate a national policy for the production, use and conservation of energy in all its forms. This is vital to the capacity to manage and enhance the environment and its resources. As the world moves into an energy strategy under the pressure of political and social forces, so energy, economics and environment become permanently intertwined in everything to do with the welfare of mankind.

Movement

But without question the most talked of, written about and glamourized of man's activities in the second half of the twentieth century are those relating to movement – his mobility on and off the planet. In the 1960s, its main feature was the space race between the U.S.A. and U.S.S.R., a race that created enormous new industries and devoured vast resources, as well as impairing the environment.

Historically, population movements have taken many forms: a search for new pastures and new lands; a flight from scourges and persecutions; invasions of one nation by another. Nearly always these movements have had lasting effects on the natural environment. Today's movement, based largely on motor transport, is having an all-pervasive impact. More than any other factor, motor transport has led to the sprawl of suburbs and to the relentless erosion of the countryside. It has led to the decay of many old urban forms and the merging of town and village into conurbations. In the U.S.A. in particular, the problem is causing great concern. The pressures arising from the arrival of a new baby every 12 seconds and a new car every 5 seconds are estimated to lead to the loss of 1 hectare (ha) of countryside every minute.

Today, a new scale has been given to man's restlessness by his pursuit of leisure. A foretaste of what was to come was seen in the nineteenth century when much of Scotland was turned into a playground for the wealthy. The advent of the railway and the accumulation of wealth from the Industrial Revolution led to whole areas being devoted to pastimes like grouse shooting and deer hunting. The landscape was transformed within a few decades.

The rapid growth of travel by rail, sea and air during the past two centuries is now being surpassed in one generation. Enormous numbers of people possess a motor scooter or car and the money to travel at home and abroad. On public holidays, huge populations surge to and from the coast and the countryside is bestrewn with cars. Millions of people migrate from country to country in search of sun and sand or sight-seeing. The tourist industry is one of the world's largest. It dictates the economy of whole countries and demands ever-increasing numbers of roads, buildings and services.

These mass movements are like a floodtide in their impact on the environment. They are creating a wear and tear never before known. Probably hardest hit is the coastline. All over the world it is being developed and disfigured, primarily to cater for holiday-makers. In England, Wales and Northern Ireland already about a quarter of the 5,200 km of coast is recorded as developed. In continental Europe, many believe it to be too late to save the coasts of Italy, Spain and Portugal. Those of Scandinavia seem likely to become the next victims. In many other areas sheer pressure of numbers has destroyed the original attraction. Once-remote spots are being degraded by the pervasive forces of human erosion. Nature gets no chance to recuperate.

Prospect

So, what is the outlook for the future? What is the lesson to be learnt about the impact of man's demands for food, shelter, power and mobility? It is that the natural environment can no longer survive without positive action by man to conserve it.

Changes in nature arising from man's activities over past centuries have been relatively gradual. Had there been satellites and modern photographic techniques in past centuries, they would have shown a pattern of continuous change in the countryside. Occasional flurries of activity, such as the de-forestation of Roman times, were, until recently, the exception to the slow and apparently deliberate movement of zones of vegetation. For example, looked at from a satellite, the forests of the Mediterranean would have been seen steadily shrivelling in face of cropping by goats and sheep, erosion, burning and development by man. But today, films from satellites would show a succession of arable lands being rapidly transformed into bricks and asphalt. Everywhere change is swifter and more drastic.

Many features of the 'natural' environment are threatened. The chalk grasslands of southern England are disappearing with changes in agricultural practice. The wetlands of Europe and North America, reservoirs of wildfowl and valuable for science and recreation, are being eliminated by drainage. In Africa and Asia, animals once found in great numbers are now on the list of rarities. And wildlife everywhere is affected by the loss of habitats.

Change is, of course, inherent in the relationship of man and the rest of nature. What is now required is a purposive and regulated change to a design consciously formulated and reflecting man's highest aspirations. Has man the capacity for this? Do not 5,000 years of experience, since the days of the first pastoralists, suggest that he cannot live on this planet without degrading it? And, in any event, would not his efforts be in vain in view of the population explosion?

The answer is that to survive man must reject a counsel of despair. He must control his numbers; he has the capacity to do so. He has sufficient knowledge and means now, not merely to avoid debasing his environment but also to enhance and enjoy it more fully. He must assert his will to do so, and replace a generally *laissez faire* attitude towards his environment by positive, substantial and sustained intervention to manage all his resources.

Action

How must man prepare this grand design? He must make his approach simultaneously on three fronts: political; organizational and administrative; and professional and scientific.

Politicians themselves need to become aware of the unity of the environment: that measures affecting it often have consequences beyond their immediate aims. They must cope with a public that cannot, or will not, perceive the long-term effects and values of environmental policies. Of course it is difficult to get the public's cooperation. Knowledge of the many factors involved in any decision on land or water use is rarely available to the citizen. Often only the politician in power can have access to the knowledge and possibilities on which to make value judgements and take decisions. Yet, if a healthier environment is to be achieved, it is essential that the public become informed, aware of the issues, with attitudes and ideas based more fully on scientifically diagnosed facts. Leadership in politics must, therefore, be increasingly concerned with telling people and, in the broadest sense, with educating them about the implications of policies.

It is ironic that in this century – the age of the 'organization man' – there should be so many problems arising from faulty or inadequate organization. Without subscribing to Pope's view

> For forms of government let fools contest,
> Whate'er is best administered is best

there is, nevertheless, vast scope for improvement in the structure and content of central and local government; in the size of areas, membership of governing bodies and the quality of staff; in delegation at all levels; in the arrangements for cooperation between public and private enterprise; and, perhaps above all, in the ways of getting citizens to participate in decision-making.

For example, much of the twentieth-century industrial development is concentrated in extensive conurbations, often based on estuarine and tidal-water sites, as at Rotterdam and on the Thames. Water is a vital resource for industry and where it is not locally adequate reservoirs have to be constructed, usually in upland valleys far beyond existing administrative boundaries. The resulting problems are complex and wasteful of resources. Nearly all these conurbations urgently need a structure of government related to their economic and physical hinterland.

Administration particularly requires new attitudes and ideas. New techniques for measuring the social cost and benefits of public projects and for assessing the value of amenity areas, open spaces and countryside must be developed if the money is to be found to manage them effectively for modern requirements. The social benefits to be derived from improving derelict and degraded land must be assessed, and the cost shared in an enlightened partnership between civic authorities and commercial firms. These and many other fields call for an administration capable of solving problems in a positive way, of bridging or eliminating the gaps between bureaucracy, technocracy and democracy, and of providing better inter-communication at all levels of society.

One of the major problems of our times in every sphere is the collation, retrieval and dissemination of information. Failure here leads to waste of the most vital resource – man's intellect. All over the world progress is delayed, research and studies are unnecessarily repeated, mistakes recur, because information is not spread effectively. Yet 40,000 scientific journals are published annually and the number is growing rapidly; communication sometimes breaks down under the weight of its own processes.

Although scientists and technologists have provided the computer and are working with administrators to deal with this information-exchange problem, there are others very special to science and the professions which machines cannot resolve. The great specialization required in many subjects is leading to barriers between the disciplines and a failure 'to talk the same language'. The relationships of scientists with politicians, administrators and especially the public call for urgent and continuous attention. Scientists – and there are more of them alive today than existed in all history – must make a bigger effort to clarify and project their ideas to all sectors of society.

People who work in the environmental sciences and professions connected with the use and management of land, water and wildlife must pay particular attention to the problem of how to spread their knowledge. Long-established and well-tested practices – for example, intensive irrigation to avoid soil erosion, and limitation of pests by growing mixed crops – are insufficiently known and acted upon. More advanced concepts, such as land capability, multi-purpose use, biological productivity and wildlife farming, and how to apply them, are not yet part of the practices of the average landowner and farmer. And one of the main reasons is the inadequate relationship between the man on the job and the scientists and professionals.

Of outstanding importance and urgency is the application of science to harvesting the natural resources of the sea. This could make a great contribution in food, minerals and energy, but prior ecological studies of fish and appropriate controls are essential to avoid denudation of stocks. Major barrage projects to provide power are already working successfully and their use could be extended to many parts of the world. Further research and development could rapidly bring the extraction of minerals and desalination of salt water within normal economic values and use.

Even now, in all these fields, there is sufficient knowledge and first-hand experience to effect a great improvement in the quality of the environment. Man has many successes to his credit – the Tennessee Valley Scheme, the agricultural settlements of Israel, and the recent exploitation of the mineral resources of the Sahara. During the past two decades substantial efforts have been made to cleanse rivers, to eliminate oil pollution of the seas, to prevent the misuse of pesticides and to safeguard wildlife and landscape.

If the best policies and practices from these cases could be made widely known and acted upon, many lands could be radically transformed. The spur to action may be the great pressure of population itself. And developments in education have revealed a wealth of untapped human talent to be harnessed to the problems of production and distribution, to the wise exploitation of existing resources, and to the discovery of new ones.

Despite these promising lines of improvement, man must create for himself a better relationship within nature if he is not to have an irretrievably adverse impact on the environment. He must resolve the uncertainty and ignorance about the social factors of his habitat. He must exert the control over his physical environment which he now has in his power. And he must give greater priority to maintaining the long-term supply of land, air, water and wildlife which are essential ingredients in the high-quality environment which posterity will expect. Time runs out rapidly. The future starts today.

CHAPTER 2

LAND

Any landscape is a condition of the spirit.
Henri-Fréderic Amiel

THROUGHOUT history land has been the most sought-after and yet one of the least understood of the earth's phenomena. Nearly always it has been regarded as wealth and something to satisfy a demand for food or living-space. Rarely has it been treated both as a living entity and a resource in very limited supply.

Land covers approximately one quarter of the earth's surface. But half of this is at present uninhabitable because it is in the polar regions or in mountainous or desert terrain. Man cannot do very much about the structure and disposition of the rocks underlying the land. He is able to alter the form of the land surface but only on a fairly small scale. He cannot yet transmute the vast deserts, such as the Sahara or the Gobi, into fertile and habitable country, despite the pioneer work of Israel in the Negev and projects such as those of the Food and Agriculture Organization in Tunisia. Much of today's degraded land (like the dry wastes of North Africa, the arid, purple mountains of Greece and the wet moorlands of Britain) is, in fact, the result of previous misuse.

At present, the earth has many million square km of habitable and cultivable land, but vast areas of this, especially near the great cities, are being taken out of cultivation for urban expansion, mineral working and roads and by erosion. It has been calculated that every human requires the product from at least 1 ha per annum to support him. It is obvious, therefore, that with his rocketing population and the decline in the quality of his environment, man cannot afford to squander or misuse the land. What makes caution more necessary than ever is that the world's population is distributed so unevenly: for each citizen in the U.S.A. there are 5 ha, in France 1·3, and in Britain ·4 ha.

The term land includes soil and topography, in fact, all the physical features of a given location. It reflects the interaction of physical conditions, natural processes, and man's response to them in social and economic terms. Very often it is the economic situation which dictates the planning and use of land. Sometimes in areas where labour and capital are readily available medium-quality soils are made highly productive, while elsewhere better soils produce poor crops because no one can afford to farm them efficiently.

Over the centuries man has tended to find and to settle on the land with the best combination of qualities. Today it is even more essential that he finds and conserves the areas with the greatest value for food production. This may mean that in order to give the best soils special consideration, thousands of people, perhaps whole towns and cities, will have to be re-settled in less productive areas. Modern society has the mobility and means to do this.

One of the great problems about soil is that not enough is known about it – the distribution of the best soil, its quality and scope for improvement, and its suitability for various types of crops. The F.A.O. and the United Nations Educational, Social and Cultural Organization (U.N.E.S.C.O.) have prepared soil maps of the world to pinpoint the areas most suitable for food production and those where faulty agricultural policies and practices prevail. Some countries have maps of the potential vegetation cover of their land – that is, the vegetation that would develop, given present flora, fauna and climate, if human intervention were to cease. These maps now show the areas which would respond to agriculture or forestry, and should facilitate the conservation of soil, water and other resources. In particular, significant progress has been made in Canada with its Land Inventory, described in Supplement 4, which is firmly based on soil capability classifications.

But though our knowledge is inadequate, we fail to make full use of what we do know. To help remedy this situation, the Council of Europe has prepared a Soil Charter, which sets out clear guidelines for the wise use of soil. Once this is widely acted upon – and educators as well as land managers should make good use of it – then long-term soil conservation becomes a real prospect. But how is man treating soil now?

SOIL

From our point of view, the most vital element in land is its wafer-thin outer layer of soil and sub-soil – a layer which is on average only 60 to 250 cm deep. The productive top-soil itself is little more than 25 cm thick over most of the earth.

What we call 'soil' is a highly complex and dynamic entity. It is composed of many substances and harbours an infinite number of living organisms; in fact, the weight of animals below the surface of a field usually greatly exceeds that of the cattle grazing upon it.

Soil is the end-product of a continuing and intricate inter-relationship and interaction between living things and dead matter, water, air and light. It takes nature centuries to create the productive soil which is the main feeding zone for plants and on which all life ultimately depends. Man cannot yet make soil in any quantity, and his fertilizers can only supplement or partly restore depleted soils. The primary importance of soil conservation to man *should* not, therefore, require further argument.

But, unfortunately, it does. For instance, it has been estimated that in England and Wales, if present trends continue, the remaining years of this century will see about ·7 million ha of farmland developed for urbanization, and as much derelict land will have been produced from mineral workings as in the previous two centuries. In or near most of the great urban centres of the world, the amount of ill-managed and neglected rural land increases as agriculturalists work under the threat of urban encroachments. Some of it is in green belts, and some is not yet ripe for development. Its existence brings out unpleasant features of human behaviour – trespassing, allowing dogs to interfere with cattle, the dumping of litter and old cars – and the landowner finds that working this land becomes increasingly uneconomic. It is a zone of 'rural twilight'.

Much of the earth's cultivable land has soil unfavourable to many crops; it suffers from adverse climate, a shortage or surplus of water, and much natural erosion. To mitigate these conditions and to enhance soil fertility in such areas requires expert management. Alas, this is often lacking, and many of man's activities only make the situation worse. Two special problems merit fuller study: these are soil erosion and pesticides.

Erosion

Soil erosion is a continual process in nature. Over the centuries weather and rocks interact to replace worn-out soil, much as man renews his outer layer of skin. But the accelerated soil erosion created by man often destroys faster than nature can renew. It usually results from rapid and thoughtless exploitation, an attempt to obtain the maximum product as quickly as possible. This attitude has led to excessive cultivation, deforestation, overgrazing, a failure to consider the nature of the soil and its environment, and a reluctance to devote labour and finance to maintaining its qualities. The results are seen in the barren lands of North Africa, the Middle East and South China. And soil erosion has been a factor in the downfall of past civilizations.

Perhaps the most frequently quoted example of soil erosion is that of the American Dust Bowl. This covers a large area of the Middle West – Colorado, Kansas, Oklahoma and Texas. Originally grassland in a semi-arid climate, its natural equilibrium was upset and the land reduced to near-desert conditions by over-cultivation and wind erosion accentuated by a succession of dry years. From this land, short of cover and of water, vast quantities of grain were produced earlier in this century. With the advent and rapid spread of farm machinery in the 1920s, the soil soon became worn and depleted. As its stability and holding capacity disappeared, it was swirled away in dust storms which left behind a degraded land and a defeated human population.

But there are many areas of the U.S.A. which have been similarly subject to wind erosion. Others have felt the impact of water erosion on land which, through misuse, had lost its porosity and coherence. Fertility in these areas dwindled at increasing speed.

The publicity given to erosion undoubtedly helped to develop a more conservation-minded leadership in the U.S.A. The graphic pictures of vast dust storms blackening the horizon, of derelict farms and silted-up rivers, awakened the conscience of the nation. Nevertheless, America's wasted land, difficult as it is to restore, is not now as a serious a problem as the continuing active soil erosion in other parts of the world, especially in Africa.

A number of measures which help to conserve soil have been in use for centuries in many parts of the world. Their primary aim is to make the best use of rain. They include terracing, contour farming and strip ploughing, which control the quantity and pace of water run-off. Over the years, many of the best soils have been developed under grass. The soil itself must have a good biological content of minute organisms to circulate the nutrients and to maintain a healthy structure. With some crops soil conservation is facilitated by allowing weeds to grow or by cultivating leguminous crops. These help to protect the soil from wind and water erosion and can be ploughed back as manure. (It is ironic that the great increase in the use of heavy machinery in agriculture is giving rise to a new problem, the 'compacting' of soils on the wetter lands. This and other effects on soils of the techniques of modern farming are reviewed in a U.K. report (see page 45).)

To restore vegetational cover to barren lands is a slow process, but the scientific and technical problems are far outweighed by those arising from man's legal, social and economic institutions, and his use of domestic animals, notably goats and sheep. These animals have caused soil erosion in many areas and it is urgently necessary to have more control over them. Quaintly dubbed 'nature's lawnmowers', goats* and sheep have grazed large areas of Mediterranean countries into subsistence farming or desert; they prevent tree growth and have

---

*But see F.A.O. report 'Observations on the goat', Agricultural Study No. 80.

reduced the average tree-line by 300 m in four centuries. Unfortunately, they and cattle are still being introduced into areas being cleared of forest in Africa. For example, the cattle of the Masai tribe in Tanzania, which serve as a status symbol, give rise to much erosion in their now restricted territories. In many instances, a far greater yield of protein could be obtained by 'farming' the wild animals in these territories. These animals and the plants on which their life is based have achieved a harmony or balance in their relationship which, history shows, is rarely achieved between the goat, as farmed by humans, and its terrain.

On the other hand, sheep and goats are probably the only practical way of maintaining many lands in their present condition – for example, some of the downland and grasslands of southern England. These well-loved amenity lands are the result of centuries of intervention by man, mainly through his use of grazing animals. With fewer rabbits and the changes in agricultural practice which make 'close' shepherding on them uneconomic, these lands quickly revert to scrub, gorse and bracken. They become inaccessible to humans on foot and horse, and lose their character and charm. Chemicals can achieve some control but they have effects on the soil about which not enough is yet known. They cannot, therefore, be used to the extent necessary to control the natural succession of vegetation, which, in Britain, tends to cover many areas with scrub or forest, without unforeseeable effects.

Pesticides

Pesticides are part of the great chemical revolution of recent decades. Without them, world standards of food, health and hygiene would be incomparably lower. But they pose major problems and have created controversy the world over.

The great impetus to the use of pesticides was the discovery of the insecticidal properties of D.D.T. in the Second World War. This insecticide, and others based on the same element – chlorine – made fantastic inroads on the insect-carried diseases, like malaria and sleeping sickness, and on such scourges of the world as locusts. Thus, as a major factor in 'death-control', pesticides accelerate the population explosion. They are indispensable until effective and economic alternatives are found, as crops must be protected and the spectacular yields of recent years maintained if we are to feed the world's growing population. But strains of insects have emerged which are resistant to pesticides. F.A.O. scientists report that during the past twenty years in approximately two hundred species of pests resistance has developed to the products devised to kill them. So new formulations are required.

Some chemicals persist in the soil of fields for a day or two, others for many years. Some chemical residues change in the soils: a very potent one, aldrin, is readily converted into a more persistent one, dieldrin. Chemicals can be taken from the soil by plants and animals and by physical action, such as leaching, and by run-off. They have been found in fields, rivers and oceans many miles from their point of application.

Chemicals are stored in the fat of animals. Some species of predatory birds are particularly vulnerable to the harmful effects of this accumulation – their fertility and reproductive capacity have suffered and their numbers have been severely reduced by certain pesticides. And most humans in Europe and the U.S.A. now have at least some D.D.T. in their body fat, about 3 parts per million – probably harmless but worth keeping an eye on!

As man thus contaminates the soil, so he affects the whole environment. Major governmental reviews of persistent organochlorine pesticides in Britain have confirmed that these chemicals represent at least a potential danger to some plants and animals, including man himself. The policy is that the present accumulative contamination of the environment by the more persistent organochlorine pesticides should be curtailed.

Voluntary cooperation in Europe and the U.S.A. between governmental bodies (national and international), wildlife interests and pesticide manufacturers to secure wise use of chemicals is spreading. In Britain it has already proved effective. The uses of the main persistent pesticides have been strictly controlled (some pesticides have been withdrawn from production) and their remaining uses are kept under review so that, wherever possible, they can be replaced by less persistent chemicals. In particular, D.D.T. is not available to the home gardener.

Control of pests by viruses moved nearer to being a practical possibility in the mid seventies with scientists in the U.K. Natural Environment Research Council carrying out safety tests on two insect viruses which can cause high levels of mortality in insect populations. It is probable that in time a balanced solution will emerge which will integrate techniques of rotation and cultivation, biological controls, chemicals and many other methods.

The applications of new scientific discoveries are likely to affect the uses of pesticides and fertilizers. For example, the mid seventies saw experiments on the fixation of nitrogen from the atmosphere by a new variety of maize. Many plants already draw the nitrogen they require for growth from the atmosphere; if this capability can be developed successfully in grasses such as wheat, rice, barley and maize, which provide much of the world's food, it could have a more profound effect than the 'green revolution' in agriculture of the past decade. In particular, it would obviate the need for continuing large applications of nitrogenous fertilizers, with their high cost and dependence on energy resources.

All this will require of farmers and land-users an even higher standard of training and a much wider outlook than is common now. Perhaps the most important need is to treat the soil as a living entity. It requires positive management carried out with an increasing knowledge of the many processes that go to create this vital element. This management should be based on a scientific assessment of how much wear and cultivation the soil can stand while yet maintaining its fertility. If he fails to make the right calculations, man may destroy the soil on which his existence depends; as Henry Wallace said: 'Nations live as long as their humus'.

Equally difficult to renew are all those vast areas which, over the last century, have been denuded of their trees and left to decay. It is the trees which, with the soil, generally determine the character of the landscape.

TREES

> . . . we cannot restore – once it is lost – the
> majesty of a forest whose trees soared upwards
> 2,000 years ago.

President Lyndon B. Johnson, 1966

Trees were once the main cover over most of the land surface. Today very little of the original forest remains except in parts of South America and Africa. For centuries man has stripped the earth of trees to develop land for cultivation and to provide his fuel, homes and ships. In every way man has been prodigal in his use of wood. Often he has been driven to seek new territory and to fight wars because he has denuded the forest and the soil. Wars in their turn consume vast quantities of timber. In the Second World War many forests were destroyed as part of a 'scorched earth' policy adopted by retreating armies. In Greece and Crete the invading troops felled and burned trees as part of their total, scientifically waged warfare. In the Vietnamese war, chemicals were sprayed from the air to defoliate forests.

When the forest has gone the top-soil is soon washed away and deserts are created; floods and avalanches become seasonal; bogs and swamps develop; and the soil is impoverished as its nutrients are leached into the lower strata and water-courses. In many Mediterranean countries the mistakes of 3,000 years ago destroyed the tree cover, hot sun and arid wind did the rest, and the result is barren or degraded land.

But more important in the long term than the uses to which man puts the forest is its place in nature. It contributes substantially to the fertility of land and is the habitat of vast numbers of wild creatures. The root system of a tree is an intricate and incredibly lengthy network of main, secondary and minor roots and spurs – perhaps over 300,000 altogether. Masses of these roots in a wood can retain 2,400 tonnes of water per hectare. A large amount (27 per cent) of rain or snow (precipitation) is held in the top of a tree and a further considerable volume passes from the roots to the top of the tree and is

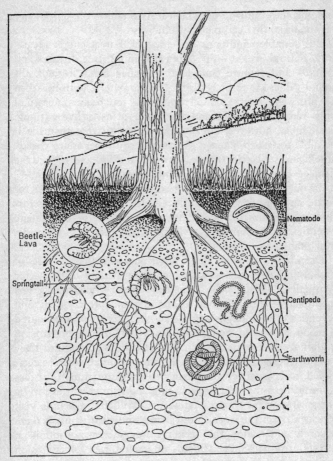

Figure 2. The root system of a tree (B. H. Grimes)

there evaporated. This water 'cycle' is important to water conservation and to climate. The fall of leaves helps to create the humus in the top-soil and reintroduces the minerals and other substances essential to fertility. The tree continually maintains and enriches the land on which it lives and is the only major raw material that can renew itself.

But suitable conditions are essential. Forests suffer greatly from natural events – fire (from lightning), tree diseases and pests – and require considerable management if their all-round values are to be realized. Unfortunately, until less than a century ago, man exploited timber very much as a mineral and only rarely cultivated and harvested it as a living thing. Enough is, however, already known about trees to make it possible for us to manage them and use timber more wisely. Intelligently planted trees can protect the soil and reduce the damage caused by rain and snow. They can act as 'nurses' to favour the growth of young seedlings, serve as shelter for cattle and provide windbreaks to protect crops. Hedgerow timber harbours many insects which can help to pollinate essential plants and which will prey on other, less welcome, inhabitants.

Despite the many synthetic fibres now available, the uses of timber increase and actually include providing cellulose for synthetics. About 5,000 uses can now be identified. The manufacture of paper alone consumes whole forests; in the mid seventies the Sunday issues of the *New York Times* devoured 330,000 tonnes of newsprint, equivalent to the cut from 6 million trees. Forests are immense reservoirs of wildlife. They can provide a direct crop from the sale of animals, such as deer, culled in accordance with a management programme. The fees from licences for hunting, shooting and fishing within forests are an important source of revenue. Millions of people visit forests all over the world, most being content to stroll in them leisurely and enjoy the scenery. For increasing numbers, forests are open-air classrooms or laboratories for education and research. And overall, the forest is a major feature in the landscape.

For these and many other reasons, most countries now have afforestation programmes. For a century the Swiss and Austrians have planted trees systematically in the Alps as a protection against avalanches and erosion. Defence and economics have also influenced tree planting in many countries. In the last sixty years in the U.S.A. and Germany, and since the First World War in Britain and many other countries, timber has been planted and managed scientifically and cropped in a way which favours its renewal. Afforestation is, however, a costly and time-consuming process. The rewards do not usually come within a generation and man does not yet know enough about the wonderful and complex life of the forest to ensure that he always plants every species in the most appropriate soil and situation. From seedling to harvest, a timber crop rarely takes less than thirty years even for some of the quick-growing conifers and poplars. Although the rate of tree growth can be increased for some species and younger and lower-grade trees may be acceptable for some modern industries, plantations designed to give quick results can supply only a part of the total requirements, and do not contribute wholly satisfactorily to the landscape.

Felling trees meets a demand for the uses already mentioned, and provides a cash return; afforestation usually does neither until the next generation has taken over. Hence the tendency is for forests to be destroyed faster than they can be replaced. At the present rate of use, supplies of timber in the world may have been exhausted within a century.

And contrary to popular belief, the great tropical and monsoon forests of South and Central America, Africa, Indonesia and South-East Asia are unlikely to meet the demands of the temperate, populated areas. Commercial exploitation is handicapped by the inaccessibility of much of the timber and its distance from markets; the wood is dense and difficult to season; and the climate creates labour problems. Few of the trees are in much demand apart from special woods, such as teak, mahogany, rosewood and ebony, whose qualities make them worth the extra effort. But if political and economic circumstances were favourable, significant forest industries could be established in areas which have suitable land and climatic conditions.

The great centres of population and industry may, therefore, have to look to their own plantations to meet their vast and seemingly insatiable demands for timber. In Europe, the growth in demand for wood and wood products will be huge, especially for small round wood for the manufacture of wood-pulp and wood-based panel products. Improved utilization of existing forests and forest land will help, but if the bulk of the extra demand is to be met from European supplies, then more land will have to be afforested and more intensive systems of management employed.

Additionally, the prospects for importing timber into Europe could worsen. In the twenty-first century, the U.S.A. may need to import timber, most likely from Canada whose exports elsewhere would probably diminish. Siberia has a vast area of timber, probably exceeding all North America's resources, but for technical reasons this is untapped, while political factors could also affect its development. The utilization of bark has enormous potential, and lignin, a waste product of paper-making which needs a technical break-through to become a major resource for the synthetic wood industry, may also become significant. But greater efforts should be made to develop economic alternatives to the use of timber – such as synthetic plastics and derivatives from minerals – and to recycle paper, if we are to ease the pressure on the world's forests, and to enhance them for wider values.

ETHICS

These main components of the land – soil and trees – are obviously not easy to create or to replace in the desired quality or quantity. They should be regarded as what in fact they are, natural resources vital to all life on earth. To appreciate their full significance requires more, however, than an understanding of their part in the energy cycle, more than a detailed scientific knowledge of their constituents and how to conserve them. It requires what has been called a *land ethic*. The late Aldo Leopold stated in *A Sand County Almanac*, first published in 1949 . . .

That land is a community is a basic concept of ecology, but that land is to be loved and respected is an extension of ethics.

That land yields a cultural harvest is a fact long known, but latterly often forgotten. . . .

A land ethic, then, reflects the existence of an ecological conscience, and this in turn reflects a conviction of individual responsibility for the health of the land. Health is the capacity of the land for self-renewal. Conservation is our effort to understand and preserve this capacity. . . .

The 'key-log' which must be moved to release the evolutionary process for an ethic is simply this: quit thinking about decent land-use as solely an economic problem. Examine each question in terms of what is ethically and aesthetically right, as well as economically expedient. A thing is right when it tends to preserve the integrity, stability and beauty of the biotic community. It is wrong when it tends otherwise.

If such an awareness of the deeper relationships of man and the land were to become widely diffused throughout the community, it would do much to create and maintain the high quality environment man now has the capacity to achieve. And it would conserve the good earth.

But do the policies and practices of governments and the behaviour of peoples give any hope for such an ethic? Britain has many problems typical of those of the developed countries. What are her policies and practices? How do Britons treat their land? And what are the new trends and patterns? These are some of the issues examined in the next three chapters.

CHAPTER 3

LAND IN BRITAIN – I

Ill fares the land, to hastening ills a prey . . .
Oliver Goldsmith

OUT of Britain's total land area of 22·4 million hectares, approximately 11·6 million are under crops and grass; 6·8 million are under rough grazing of little value for agriculture, except for the rearing of hardy sheep and cattle, and are increasingly used for afforestation and recreational pursuits; about 1·6 million are under woodland; and the remaining 2·4 million cover urban and residual uses.

Within these main categories, there are many features, such as wetlands, moors, downs, copses and the pattern of farms, which are the product of man's interaction with nature over the centuries. By the seventeenth century, a considerable part of the woodland had been replaced by agricultural land – in small enclosures, large common fields or open moorland. The eighteenth-century revolution in agricultural techniques led to the disappearance of most open fields so that the lowlands came to be characterized by small fields, separated by hedgerows or stone walls, which are part of the attractiveness of that type of countryside today. A strong corps of landscape specialists, such as the legendary 'Capability' Brown, developed many estates and landscape parks which helped to create new standards of visual beauty.

From Tudor times onwards much oak had been planted for the Navy. John Evelyn was prominent in this work in the seventeenth century. In 1664 he wrote *Sylva, or a Discourse of Forest Trees*, purposely directed to preserve the English woods which were later to provide the ships for Trafalgar. At the end of the eighteenth century, Lord Nelson insisted that the Forest of Dean should be replanted with oak. During and after the Napoleonic Wars there was also some planting of the hardwoods treasured so much today. Generally, much of what is

today regarded as beautiful or 'natural' landscape reflects these
relatively recent developments.

Many of the features which gave rise to the accepted aesthetic
qualities of the countryside are now disappearing, despite their
new values for amenity and recreation. Often changes are taking
place without any thought or consideration of their effect on
the landscape and the ecology of the countryside. New techniques in agriculture and forestry are likely to bring a revolution in our landscape greater than the one experienced in the
eighteenth century. What, then, are the major trends of significance to the countryside?

Trends and Views

Undoubtedly the macro-factors touched on in Chapter 1 are
creating a framework largely beyond the control of individual
national governments. For example, world population numbers and their expectations interacted dramatically with resources in 1972. Then, for the first time in twenty years, world
cereal production, over 1,200m tonnes annually, declined. The
shortfall was the substantial amount of 33m tonnes, whereas to
meet growing world demand, the production of cereals should
increase annually by about 25m tonnes. The U.S.S.R. had then
to purchase grain on the world market on an unprecedently
large scale (a repetition of poor harvests in 1975 led to long-
term purchasing arrangements with the U.S.A.). The spectacular increases in petroleum prices from 1973 directly
affected the costs of fertilizers and energy – vital to the intensive agricultural systems of the developed countries. The effect
of these macro-trends was, and continues to be, inflationary.
The poor everywhere suffer and thought for long-term care
of the environment recedes to lower priority.

Britain's economy and environment are inevitably affected.
The great increases in agricultural yields of the past few
decades are largely dependent on cheap feeding stuffs (much
imported), on the use of chemicals, such as fertilizers and pesticides, and on the use of tractors and other machines for ploughing, irrigation, harvesting and distribution of crops. The total

energy consumed by British agriculture is only three per cent; although this is important to an increasingly energy-conscious nation and will obviously have to be safeguarded to avoid severe dislocation of existing systems of food production, nevertheless its costs mount inexorably. The farmer is thus put under stronger economic constraints than formerly and in the short term can less afford to devote effort to conservation measures, such as those required for landscape and wildlife.

Few alternatives appear feasible in the near future without a tergiversation of attitudes and political upheaval. To bring labour back on to the farms runs counter to all the trends. To utilize more areas of marginal land on a scale much greater than envisaged in the seventies would demand large additional inputs of capital and labour. Changes in the choices of diets were being advocated in the mid seventies; for example, by urging more eating of cereals by humans and less feeding of cereals to animals, and less meat-eating generally by individuals in the developed countries with their protein-rich food. Certainly Britain cannot feed its existing and prospective population by domestic agriculture without significant shifts in the dietary preferences of its peoples. And there can be little doubt that the much-favoured high protein diets affect individual health, balances of payments and the shape of the countryside – adversely, many believe. And quite obviously, Britain's needs increasingly compete with those of the much poorer developing countries.

Some ecologists urge the adoption of agricultural strategies – on a world and national scale – to develop land uses and food production towards self-sufficiency in the staples of day-to-day living – cereals, fat, milk, potatoes and sugar. They contend that the long-term impact of the world macro-factors and inexorable trends demand the use of less energy, less resources devoted to meat production, and much greater economy throughout the food chain. Any of these measures would change the shape of the rural environment, but so will a continuation and extension of intensive agriculture. And as the physical resources of the countryside dwindle and demands increase, what they produce – food, timber, amenity, wildlife and so on –

becomes more valuable and decisions about agriculture, in particular, more and more critical to the environment.

The major features seem to be that Europe will have an intensification of multiple-use farming on the one hand and large-scale farming on the other. Conflict may arise from the often unseen dangers to the soil from modern techniques and the pressure of economic and technological forces. These are brilliantly discussed in a United Kingdom report* by a panel of farmers and scientists. They show that in some areas soil structure between 15 and 90 cm below the surface is impaired where the free movement of water and air to the fine roots of the crop is impeded by the compacting of soils. A dangerous drop in the organic content of some soils was found; heavy machines had damaged others during wet conditions; high stocking densities in areas of heavy rainfall had affected some surface soils; and everywhere there was a need for better drainage. The foreword to the Report states:

It [the soil] has not always had too happy a time. There could be a remarkable response from the soil of this country if all forces combined to treat it 'with respect'.

Thus, agriculture itself may conflict with soil conservation, unless much greater regard to long-term factors is shown by the industry and governments and unless society responds more positively to meet the needs of those living and working in rural areas. All this reminds us that we neglect the soil – perhaps our primary capital asset – at our peril. Increasing production of food from the soils of Europe cannot continue indefinitely without much greater understanding of their ecological capacity and much more harmony between the processes of farming and those of nature. But there are counter trends to those so far discussed which may bring further problems and conflicts.

Some are based on the proposition that changes in world markets will require Britain – and the rest of Europe – to become as near self-sufficient in food as possible. Proponents of this view refer to the F.A.O. statistics. These show that the

* *Modern Farming and the Soil*, H.M.S.O., 1971.

impressive increases in world food production over the past decade have been counterbalanced by the rise in population, which is now outstripping food supplies. If such trends continue Britain would be unwise to rely upon the idea that she can continue indefinitely to import fifty per cent of her food supply. It would be necessary to provide food from every available piece of land, although it seems at present unlikely that Britain could ever be self-supporting in the wide range of produce required by modern standards of living.

Some people, more optimistic about international prospects, consider that Britain should concentrate on those industrial activities in which she can maintain exports adequate to pay for her imports of raw materials and food; such a policy invites an even more selective approach in agriculture and the need for this may be intensified by the freer movement of products within an enlarged European Economic Community.

Overall, there have been two main points of view: the one favouring strong safeguards for the better-quality land, and the other contending that agriculture should not have a prior right over other interests. The arguments are now being intensified and further affected by new developments. Comparatively speaking, modern aids and techniques have made the physical quality of the land for food production less dominant in relation to labour and capital than it was a few decades ago. Although land has acquired new and extended social values, these may be relatively short-term factors. Land is a long-term commodity and the best soils are a vital resource.

There are other viewpoints. One is that agriculturalists and foresters should be encouraged to develop an ecologically healthy and balanced countryside. Some of its proponents favour the term 'sacramental agriculture', believing that the land has special qualities of its own, living and enduring and playing a vital part in all man's relationships. Others regard agriculture as a 'public-service' industry, pointing out that it provides a landscape for amenity and recreation and maintains land for water conservation and multiple uses. Both attitudes seek to prevent land from being used purely for the intensification of food production and would not treat agriculture and forestry solely as economic activities. They aim to conserve a good proportion of the land for traditional vegetational cover and to design and manage the landscape to the highest standards.

Changes in any of the directions proposed will have a substantial effect on the land and its appearance. The spread of large-scale farming and mechanization eliminates hedges and copses and leads to large open fields. Drainage affects meadows, alder and reed. More buildings for 'indoor' farming – for example, chicken broilers or sheds for calves – are being erected. The intensive farming may also give rise to pollution through the organic material produced by pigs and cows (as much as that of three and sixteen people respectively) which it is often uneconomic to spread on the land. This manure gets washed out of buildings into drains and streams and may require special provision on the farm or at a sewage works. And the smell is often penetrating and extensive. Technical aids, such as spray-irrigation, are also now features of many parts of the countryside.

With present policies and Britain's capacity to import, the amount of land which it will not be profitable to farm solely for agricultural produce may increase. No one will bother to manage marginal land adequately unless it is developed for other worthwhile and lucrative uses – for example, game rearing and outdoor recreation.

Change is inherent in all these trends and proposals. Growth and decay are inevitable cycles in nature. The countryside should evolve, but now that man can guide and reshape this process, he should make sure the changes follow conscious and desired patterns. It is particularly essential that agriculture should be developed on a strategic basis, taking account of wide physical and economic conditions and reflecting its predominant place in the countryside.

AGRICULTURE

Agriculture accounts for about 80 per cent of the land surface of Britain. Its gross output in the mid seventies was worth around £5,000m. Despite an average annual loss of 58,300 ha a year in the seventies (urbanization, roads, reservoirs, etc., took 30,360 ha a year and forest and woodland 27,940 ha) and an average annual fall of 6 per cent in the labour force, the agricultural industry increased net output by a third in a decade. Agriculture in Britain employs 3 per cent of the total civilian workforce as compared, for example, with 13 per cent and 7 per cent in France and West Germany respectively. The industry provides about two thirds of all the commodities which can be produced in Britain. Thus agriculture is clearly a vital force in the economic and social life of the nation and of primary importance in shaping the rural environment.

Since 1940 there have been vast changes in agriculture. The major alteration, affecting the whole economy of farming and its operations, has been mechanization, particularly the ousting of the horse by the tractor. The one million horses used in 1918 have been largely replaced by tractors, combine harvesters and a vast quantity of agricultural machinery. A team of two horses could plough on average ·4 ha a day; a tractor will do three or four ha, it can operate on steep slopes and enables more land to be utilized. One of the fundamental results of mechanization was that the discipline of rotational farming was eased. In consequence, the famous Norfolk or 'four-course shift' has been superseded in many areas. Its objectives – to prevent disease and weeds and to maintain fertility – are now largely achieved by fertilizers and herbicides. Intensive crop-rotational systems are practised in the southern and eastern counties of England; on Salisbury Plain barley has been grown in some fields for eleven years in succession. Cash crops – wheat, barley, peas, beet – are interspersed with ley – land temporarily under grass – which provides an income from the cattle which graze it.

The break-up of many large estates and the shortage and high cost of manpower all affect the structure of farming. The spread of owner-occupancy and large capitalized concerns leads to new approaches. Factory production techniques are applied to the rearing of poultry and livestock. Producers are having to follow market requirements closely and to organize themselves so that they can respond rapidly to new needs. Increasing population and higher incomes are leading to a demand for more food. Consumers require better quality and luxury products. Satisfying these demands in turn accelerates the pace of change in agriculture and influences the shape of the new emerging landscape. All these factors are interacting to give an agricultural revolution greater than any before.

Membership of the E.E.C. raises difficult decisions for the whole direction of Britain's agriculture within the framework of the Common Agricultural Policy, its premises disputed by others of the Nine. Should Britain concentrate on the most profitable crops and continue with intensive energy-using techniques and depending on imported phosphates, feeding stuffs for cattle and other essentials to the industry? And what about the overall vulnerability – political and economic – to which Britain is exposed by importing about half of her current food?

Some answers were attempted in 1975 when a White Paper (Cmnd. 6020) set out the Government's appraisal of the prospect and policies for food production from Britain's own resources of land and labour for the following five to ten years. The Government considered that the likely levels of world and E.E.C. prices for major foodstuffs, and the risks of possible shortage and sharp price fluctuation, justified a policy of expansion of food production in the U.K. Most benefit, it was anticipated, would come from higher output of milk (with its by-product of beef from the dairy herd) and sugar beet, with a significant contribution from cereals and sheepmeat. The Government's objective was, therefore, to continue the then-current rate of expansion of the net product of the agricultural industry of about $2\frac{1}{2}$ per cent per year on average.

Clearly, changes in the ratios of home produce to imports directly affect not only agriculture and land use, but also the country's balance of payments; success in achieving the Government's objective would save considerably on imports. The nation's 'antennae' to anticipate and detect factors influencing the level of imports must, therefore, be highly developed if planning is to be effective. But the problem is complex and sophisticated, unlike that in the underdeveloped countries where the primary need is a rapid increase in food production. In Britain, as in other advanced countries, a harmonious relationship of supply and demand is required to ensure stability and adequate returns to farmers, farm workers and investors.

Planning

To make any adjustment in the intricate pattern of agreements and traditions is a complex task. There are many agencies involved in this vital industry: official departments of agriculture, a government research council, an influential association of landowners, a powerful farmers' union, a strong agricultural workers' union and a highly professional body of land agents. There are also several organizations which help to move produce through the distributive chain to the consumer – for example the Milk, Potato, Hops and Wool Marketing Boards; the Home Grown Cereals Authority; the Meat and Livestock Commission; and the Eggs Authority.

Long-term agricultural planning, integrated within overall social and economic objectives, is increasingly part of the pattern of State activity in the developed countries as the need to ensure the wise use of the limited natural resources of the land becomes urgent. But the industry is also increasingly geared to the short-term, wafer-thin margins of the great chains of supermarkets, competing for the housewife's basket.

In Britain, government intervention in agriculture has been particularly pronounced from 1945 onwards. Three major Acts – 1947, 1957 and 1967 – chart its policies and measures, as it has sought to resolve some of the fundamental problems of the industry. One of the toughest is that of the structure of farming. There are now around 350,000 holdings in the United Kingdom, of which about 70 per cent are small or very small, producing just over 30 per cent of total agricultural output. This obviously reduces the overall efficiency of the industry and affects adversely the allocation of land between alternative activities. The Government therefore seeks to increase the size of farms and to promote cooperative enterprises. It gives special grants and promotes farm improvement schemes to speed up the adoption of better techniques and the construction of labour-saving buildings and devices and special measures to encourage greater business efficiency and the training of managers.

On the assumption that British agriculture remains primarily as it is now – a food-producing industry – there are clearly sectors where greater productivity can be obtained: in structural change and farming efficiency, the employment of new technological systems and equipment and the improvement of the quality of land. With developments in these inevitable, agriculture may have little stability in the next few decades. The industry will be under great pressure from economic, technical and social forces and it will be singularly difficult for farmers to take adequately into account other than strictly economic considerations. If, therefore, farmer and forester are to be helped and persuaded to produce the food required in a manner compatible with the enhancement of the landscape, Government intervention in some form is essential.

In the uplands of northern England, Scotland and mid-Wales, some contribution is needed from the State to relate the economic interests of agriculture and forestry to the social values of recreation and amenity. Without this, rural areas will become denuded of people and it is unlikely that there will be much viable community life in the remoter countryside.

Similar trends are found in Continental countries and certainly affect British agriculture. Members of the European Economic Community (the Common Market) increasingly operate within the framework of their plan to harmonize farm prices and to promote agricultural restructuring on the Continent. The E.E.C. seeks to reduce the number of small-holdings, to modernize farming methods, and to retrain those who leave the land. The main premises of the E.E.C. plan are that the farming population in the founder member countries should be halved within about 10 years to become around 5 million and that 5 million ha of the land now farmed should be taken out of agriculture and used for afforestation, recreation and wider social objectives.

The E.E.C. claims legitimately that the plan seeks to meet the trends in a rational manner. The agricultural population in these countries already shrinks at the rate of 5 million every 10 years; despite expensive structural improvements – and perhaps partly because of a price policy which has reflected the politics of agriculture more than its economic and long-term needs – the E.E.C. has had surplus products such as butter and beef; and yet has failed to provide adequate incomes and conditions for the farmers themselves. Perhaps the most immediate task is to ensure that prices move into a better relationship with the needs of farmers and a prosperous industry and the ecological health of rural lands.

Farming and Landscape

The seventies revealed clearly the inexorable effects of intensive agriculture, particularly in lowland England. Mechanized farming has little, if any, need of internal farm hedges; it requires large fields and the increased size reduces the number of boundaries, increasingly demarcated by wire fences. River and road authorities often eliminate hedges for dredging of water courses and for safety. Dutch Elm disease has already affected and, indeed, impoverished the landscape in many areas. Overall, the network of hedges and hedgerow trees inherited in some locations from Saxon times, in others from the enclosures of the eighteenth century, remorselessly diminishes.

Society must soon decide on the landscape it wants – modern prairie (East Anglia or Lincolnshire) or a created new-style based on the planting of trees, hedges, grass or shrubs in a variety of farmland situations where they are compatible with the primary function of food production. New habitats, copses, small ponds, new linear 'corridors' of trees and vegetation – these would not only enhance the amenity of the countryside but, over the years, could develop into reservoirs of wildlife. The need is clear. The challenge is to devise means to encourage owners and occupiers to manage their land to produce the desired landscape. And although they have social responsibilities to contribute to this goal, nevertheless the public should obviously pay for any additional costs solely incurred for the creation of landscape and habitats for wildlife.

FORESTRY

In much of Britain, trees represent what some scientists call the 'climax' type* of vegetation, that which is most likely to emerge in existing physical conditions without human interference. In the South and East, the main tree was the pedunculate oak, forming large forests on the heavier soils; on the lighter soils of the North and West, it was replaced by the sessile oak. With these were associated ash, beech, birch, elm, hornbeam, limes and poplar, with hazel as undershrub, giving typical deciduous broadleaved woodland in many parts of England and Wales. Coniferous forests predominated in the Scottish Highlands, with the Scots pine being found with the deciduous birch.

Heavily wooded until the Norman Conquest, Britain has since lost much of its woodland. Great inroads were made for cultivation, grazing, housing, shipbuilding, charcoal – for use in smelting iron ore and in cottage industries – as well as for fuel. Statutes of the fifteenth and seventeenth centuries disclose the concern of the governments of the time. During these centuries the first major replanting of woodland began, mainly by the large landowners, and this continued until the new uses for capital of the Industrial Revolution diverted effort. Nevertheless, the total area of woodland shrank, particularly when in Scotland further clearing of woodlands took place in the eighteenth and nineteenth centuries, much of it for sheep farming and later for sport. There are now only remnants of the once-great Caledonian Pine forests; some are in nature reserves.

Measures to conserve the hardwoods of southern England and the increasing difficulty and cost of getting fuel undoubtedly contributed to the pressure on industrialists, such as Abraham Darby, to find an alternative to charcoal for

*This concept involves arbitrary judgements and is not acceptable to all ecologists.

smelting iron ore, and thus led to the Industrial Revolution, which was to change the land even further. By the twentieth century, Britain was one of the few major countries in Europe without any large-scale State programme to replenish its vital woodland resources.

Today, about 8 per cent of the land surface of Britain is devoted to trees. Although this is one of the lowest figures in Europe, nevertheless it is clear that woodlands are still important in the British landscape. This area of woodland works out at about 1 ha per 30 citizens; in West Germany it is 1 ha per 7; but in the U.S.A. it is about 1·6 ha to each person.

Just over 60 per cent of British woodland is conifers (the Sitka Spruce dominating with 20 per cent, followed by the Scots Pine with 14 per cent) and just under 40 per cent is broadleaved trees (with the oak having 11 per cent and the birch 9 per cent). The Elm occupied ·4 per cent of the total until the savage impact of Dutch Elm disease in the seventies eliminated 6 million trees in as many years, with the prospect of killing 20 million by the 1980s. This and the increasing loss of hedgerow trees could significantly affect the appearance of the countryside.

The area of conifer high forest has increased greatly and will continue to do so as these trees – mainly larches, pines and spruces – are well-suited to modern needs. Although large areas of these economically important forests are under thirty years old, many of them are now being managed for multiple uses. Some of the woodlands contain deer which provide sport; several species of birds have colonized the rides and fringes; and increasingly these forests become important for amenity and science.

Hardwood high forest consists mainly of oak and beech. Economically these have always been less profitable than conifers because of the very long rotations (100–120 years) and hence the deferment of repayment on capital invested, which is not wholly compensated for by the high prices paid for good quality timber. In recent years this difficulty has been accentuated by the high interest charges on capital and the high costs of establishment.

Coppices are tree crops from stool or vegetative shoots, usually hazel. The standards (trees of seedling origin) with which they are associated are usually oak. The original demand for these products – for sheep hurdles, pea and bean sticks, and thatching, for example – has largely disappeared and the area of these woodlands has dwindled rapidly in recent decades. Many are now neglected and their main interest is often amenity, educational or scientific. Coppice of sweet chestnut is, however, still a commercial proposition – for example, for hop poles and fencing – in the limited areas climatically suitable for it; these are mainly in Kent and Sussex and the South-West.

Special features of British woodlands of considerable importance to the landscape are the hedgerows, park trees and small woodlands of less than ·5 ha (which are additional to the areas already mentioned). They consist mostly of broadleaved species, once chiefly elm, and occur throughout Britain but are most evident on farmland in Central and Southern England.

The Forestry Commission

In 1919 the Forestry Commission – a government agency – was set up to help restore the timber resources of the country depleted by the First World War and to create a national strategic reserve of timber. In the following twenty years the Commission planted about 240,000 ha and private landowners about 51,000 ha. The Second World War led to further depletion of the national timber stock and post-war policy was based on an estimate that by the year 2000 Britain would need two million ha of woodland (about ten per cent of the land surface). Three fifths of this would be provided by the afforestation of bare land, mostly in Scotland. The privately owned areas of the existing woodlands were to be dedicated to forestry or acquired by the Commission. At present, it manages over ·8 million ha of national forests.

Several policy reviews took place in the following three decades. By the mid seventies, the Forestry Commission had two principal functions: one as Forestry Authority to support and control the private sector through grants, research and felling licences, and another as the Forestry Enterprise, to run the national forests (by then around 0·8 million hectares). In general, under the Forestry Act 1967, the Commission have the duty 'of promoting the interests of forestry, the development of afforestation and the production and supply of timber and other forest products in Britain.' They are also charged to ensure adequate reserves of growing trees and to control timber pests and diseases. Considerations of amenity and provision of tourist, recreational and sporting facilities are included in their terms of reference by the Countryside (Scotland) Act 1967 and the Countryside Act 1968.

These wide-ranging duties are at the heart of the Commission's objectives. For its work as Forest Authority, these are specifically stated to be:

(1) to advance knowledge and understanding of forestry and trees in the countryside;
(2) to develop and ensure the best use of the country's timber resources and promote efficiency and development in the home timber industry;
(3) to undertake research relevant to the needs of forestry; to combat forest and tree pests and diseases and to initiate Plant Health Orders when appropriate;
(4) to advise and to assist with safety and training in forestry;
(5) to administer controls and schemes for assisting private woodland owners and, by so doing, encourage the practice of sound forestry, secure good land use and – where relevant – effective integration with agriculture, and ensure the use of forest management systems and practices which safeguard the environment.

The Commission has a wide range of publications, from formal papers and manuals on research and techniques to 'glossy' and attractive informative popular booklets. It has numerous information centres of high quality, runs specialist training courses, fosters interpretative work, and undertakes a wide range of activities in its 'open-door' policy to educate the public to a greater awareness of the nation's forests, their importance and their place in the countryside, and how to enjoy them.

Britain imports 92 per cent of her timber needs – some 40m cubic metres, second only to Japan's 50m – so that it is questionable whether on any basis she has enough trees. The effect of the planting which has been done since 1945 should raise the figure to about 11 per cent (taking account of an increased consumption rate) by the turn of the century. Timber is a bulky cargo and expensive in shipping space – a factor important in peace and war. The nation's forests – public and private – are therefore likely to become increasingly important in economic terms, as the macro-pressures on the world's resources intensify in the next century.

The Commission has been mainly responsible for prescribing the measures to tackle the spread of Dutch Elm disease, and it was their researchers who first identified the new virulent strain. With the greater facility for the passage of disease carriers in trade and transport by other means, the Commission's duties to combat diseases become more and more significant. Its research programme deals with such immediate problems as those of protection and production techniques, which have clearly helped it and private owners in developing the nation's forests, especially on much poor land.

Privately owned woodlands cover over 1·1m ha and over 14,000 ha have been planted in recent years. Of the total volume of timber cut annually in the seventies, of $3\frac{3}{4}$ million cubic metres some 60 per cent comes from private woodlands and hedgerows, including most of the hardwood timber. Thus, the nation continues to depend on private forests and must foster them in various ways. Following a review of policy involving three years of widespread consultation, the Commission started to operate in the mid seventies a new scheme of grant-aid for private forestry. Under this, the woodland owner gets an outright payment* per hectare when approved planting or replanting takes place. In return, the owner accepts a continuing obligation to manage all his woodlands within the ' Dedication' scheme in accordance with plans of operations designed to secure sound forestry practice, effective integration

*£45 in 1976 – £125 is payable where a significant proportion of broadleaved trees are involved.

with agriculture, environmental safeguards, and such opportunities for public recreation as may be appropriate.

Those having rights and obligations under the previous Dedication, Approved Woodlands, and small Wood Planting Schemes, operating up to 1972, could retain them or transfer to the new terms. In addition to such forms of financial help over the past fifty years, the Commission gives expert advice and has helped private owners to plant large areas. The Commission also works closely with the Timber Growers' Organization in England and Wales and the Scottish Woodland Owners' Association in Scotland which look after the interests of private landowners.

The Commission's Regional Advisory Committees were reconstituted following this review and now include representatives of agriculture, local planning and amenity interests, as well as representatives of the forestry industry. These Committees advise both on broad area strategy and individual cases of doubt arising in the administration of grants.

The Commission is also involved in the two statutory controls affecting forestry. It administers the felling licensing system under which it can require areas (outwith the Dedication Schemes) to be replanted. Amenity has now become the primary purpose for this and the Commission normally consults local planning authorities over such licences in areas of particular amenity interest. The second control is that exercised by local authorities to make tree preservation orders and here they consult closely with the Commission over a variety of considerations.

In its role as the Forestry Enterprise, the Commission must strive to produce wood as economically as possible. Here, too, it must pay attention to amenity and landscape and the potential of its properties for nature conservation and recreation. The Commission has, therefore, defined these objectives as follows:

(1) to develop forestry and increase the production of wood for existing industries, or industries yet to be established, by the extension and improvement of the forest estate;

(2) to protect and enhance the environment;

(3) to provide recreational facilities;

(4) to stimulate and support the local economy in areas of depopulation by the development of forests, including new plantations, and of wood-using industry;

(5) in pursuit of these objectives and in the extension of the forest estate, to further the integration of forestry and agriculture and to manage the estate as profitably as possible.

In the Commission's programme of new planting and re-planting of up to 22,000 ha a year, the new planting (of up to 18,000 ha per year) is concentrated mainly in the upland areas of Scotland, Wales and the north of England, where it thus helps to fulfil its remit from the Government to contribute towards the provision of employment. In practice, over 80 per cent of new planting is taking place in Scotland.

The production of timber is the Commission's prime objective as well as its main source of revenue. It aims to earn as much as possible from its sales of wood in the form of sawn timber, pulp wood, mining timber and material for wood-based panel manufacture. Management plans aim at achieving the maximum out-turn of which the forests are capable in the form of wood to specifications matching the needs of industry.

Its environmental goals lead the Commission to accept lower financial returns in order to maintain the predominantly broadleaved character of the typical southern lowland land-scape. The Countryside Acts strengthen the Commission's powers to plant trees for amenity. In the uplands, where often only conifers can be grown, it landscapes wherever practicable. And in this work it has, for over a decade, had advice from a leading landscape architect. Despite this, many people have not looked favourably on the Commission's planting of conifers *en masse*, although, with the rapidly rising demand for softwoods – 90 per cent of the timber used – and the poor quality of land used, much of this was inevitable.

The nation's forests are also important as reservoirs for wildlife. The Commission, therefore, collaborates closely with the Nature Conservancy Council in enhancing the value of them as wildlife habitats. Some have become Forest Nature Reserves, with nature trails and viewpoints. The nation's forests are increasingly a source of recreation and the Commission provides in them a wide range of activities and facilities, particularly for the day visitor. Examples are car parks, picnic places, viewpoints, forest trails, information centres, horse-riding and orienteering. Access to the forest on foot is free and facilities for day visits are provided at a minimal charge; those for longer stays, such as cabins and campsites, depend on resources being available, and are expected to give an economic return. Sporting facilities already provide a useful additional income. All these activities are now integrated through recreational plans tailored to the forest environment.

The British forestry industry as a whole employs 33,000 people, of which 22,000 are with the Commission and private forestry and the rest in the timber, pulp, paper and transport industries. Generally, the economic and ecological balance of the countryside is improved as the nation's forests expand. They make use of poor land, contribute to the economy of farming, play an important, if not yet fully understood, part in water catchment, and provide good recreation areas and sanctuaries for wild life.

As the largest single land-user in Britain, and as one of the organizations best suited to obtain and give out information about tree-planting and afforestation, the Forestry Commission has great responsibilities. In many ways it is now the nation's 'planning' authority for forests and woodlands as well as obviously being the estate manager. It must see that the best possible professional and scientific advice is used when policies are determined that will substantially affect the character and interest of the landscape. In all this it requires the support and goodwill of the people.

MARGINAL AND OTHER LANDS

Large areas of land in Britain fall within three main categories: common lands; the 'minor' sites, such as village greens and roadside verges; and 'true' marginal land. If the pressures on space continue to increase it will be necessary to examine very carefully the management of these lands to ensure their optimum use.

Estimates of common land vary: there may be about ·6 million ha in England and Wales. Although some of it is of poor quality, common land is a heritage of considerable importance. It provides many wooded areas, which with good management could be made more valuable; its open spaces are vital 'lungs' to many towns; its soil and trees, being largely untouched by modern fertilizers and pesticides, should provide good material for scientific and educational studies; and it supports many animals and plants which can no longer flourish in agricultural or urban areas. Fuller details of common land are given in Chapter 13.

The second category, 'minor' lands, could also become important. The area taken up by road verges in England and Wales may be as much as 100,000 ha. Every new motorway adds hundreds of hectares to that total. Even so, the area, however large, does not indicate the real importance of road-side verges. They are a source of pleasure to residents and to the travelling public. Often they are the 'shop window' of the country to tourists. Roadside verges are also a significant reservoir of wildlife and their hedges and vegetation function as wind- and snow-breaks. Intelligent use of modern tech-niques and the application of scientific knowledge, especially about plants, can reduce the destruction of roadside vegetation arising from measures carried out for road safety. Skilful management – planting the right trees and shrubs in lay-bys and selecting plant species – can enhance the appearance of verges. Village greens, semi-urban parks and some of the great estates are obviously precious open spaces. For amenity, recreation and essential living-space they make a valuable contribution. But not all of them are adequately cared for.

The 'true' marginal lands – the areas of low population and deteriorating soil and vegetation – are to be found mainly in the Pennines and Lake District, Wales and Scotland. Many of them are at high altitude, have steep slopes and are in the wetter parts of Britain. Since the original vegetational cover – generally woodlands – has been destroyed by man, these lands have deteriorated badly. Now they are not only inaccessible and awkward to cultivate, but are infertile as well. And the less money that can be wrung from them, the less money people are willing to spend on them. It is this type of marginal land which accounts for most of the rough grazing in Britain (6·8 million ha) and also for some of those areas remaining unclassified. Its main use in farming is as a breeding ground for cattle and sheep and as seasonal pasturage. In these ways many hill and valley areas are complementary and the loss of one often affects the economic value of the other.

The uplands offer scope for forestry, water catchment and recreation. In the Peak District National Park, the uses of the marginal land are summed up as the ' 4 G.s' – that is, grazing, gathering grounds (for water), game (grouse and partridge) and gold awards (the Duke of Edinburgh's Award). The need for coordination of effort in these areas is probably greater than in the more prosperous localities and should be on a large enough scale for proper long-term planning.

Appraisal

Clearly the future development and management of agriculture, forestry and marginal land have to be related to many factors, in addition to the obvious demands for food and timber. They should reflect the greatly increased need for access to land for enjoyment; they must be considered within the visual framework and unity of the landscape; and they must be part of a national policy for the land related to the whole social and economic life of the countryside.

Conflict is inherent in every aspect of these issues – conflict between urban and rural dwellers, conflict between the interests of agriculture and leisure, and conflict between particular forms of conservation.

These conflicts could be reduced by relating demands much more to the most suitable long-term uses for land in terms of its physical qualities – soils, minerals, water, forests, wildlife and so on – and guiding planning and management to support these allocations. In particular, the best soils should be safe-guarded for agriculture, increasingly to be managed in harmony with ecological processes and the maintenance of soil fertility. Marginal and sub-marginal areas should be managed to restore their ecological health and potential for other uses such as afforestation, amenity interests and leisure pursuits. The management of forests should reflect their significance in the landscape and as reservoirs for wildlife, as well as their in-creasing importance for recreation.

The economic returns from food and timber production are obvious; they are essential to the livelihood of the farmer or forester. Those from land management for the wider environ-mental goals now expected by society may not only be difficult to establish and calculate, but may be negative – costs he can ill afford. The impact of modern technology, the structure and problems of ownership and occupation and the pressure of short-term market forces tend increasingly to make farming less sensitive to nature than formerly. Thus production in-centives – price levels, support monies, grants, specialist ad-vice, etc., – should take much greater account of these goals and recompense the farmer and forester for their contribution to the health and appearance of the countryside and its use and enjoyment by society.

CHAPTER 4

LAND IN BRITAIN – II

Britain has not, like Holland, France or America,
developed an urban bourgeoisie which is content
with a luxury flat.

Anthony Sampson, *Anatomy of Britain*

URBAN LAND

BRITAIN for long lacked accurate figures of the land used for
urban development. Local government titles – such as county
and city and urban and rural – were misleading. Towns and
once-rural settlements frequently merged in suburban dif-
fuseness, while some city boundaries contained large areas of
farmland as well as great stretches of rural-looking commons.
The 1974 reforms of local government, discussed in Chapter 18,
have not yet led to any significant improvement in resolving
this position.

Despite the pioneering work of the first Land Utilization
Survey of the 1930s and data from the Ministry of Agriculture,
it was not until results started to flow from the post 1947
planning system that substantive estimates began to emerge.
Inevitably, calculations of the urban extent were also bedevilled by problems in definitions, but urban land has for
some time generally been taken to include the main areas used
for housing and industry, education and open space, roads
and railways and other infrastructures and their related land
uses. All these tend to move in relationship with population
numbers and development densities. The estimates also
include built-up land in the countryside.

The first really usable figure for the composition of the
urban area is that for 1950–51 provided by R. H. Best. His
calculations were deliberately generous to avoid being under-
estimates and led to maximum estimates of 1,458,000 ha for
England and Wales and 190,000 ha for Scotland.

Better data from work for development plans and the 1961

Population Census, improved techniques and further studies by Best and others have led to more accurate totals. The extent of urban land in Britain in 1961 has been assessed to be around 1,700,000 ha, approximately 7·4 per cent of the land surface. The figures for England and Wales were 1,500,000 ha and 10 per cent, and for Scotland 200,000 ha and 2·6 per cent. These figures have been up-dated for 1971 to a grand total for Britain of 1,875,000 ha, of which 1,650,000 ha are for England and Wales and 225,000 ha for Scotland.

Growth

With the 1961 figures as a baseline, calculations by Best show that urban land uses in England and Wales probably doubled from around 5 per cent in 1900 to about 11 per cent in 1971, with the most rapid expansion having occurred between the two world wars. Then, the sprawl of low-density suburbs took some 50 per cent more urban land, from around 854,000 ha to 1,206,000 ha. Undoubtedly, the post 1947 planning system controlled this rate of increase, although expectations for lower densities and improvements in urban living standards inevitably push towards using more land.

The position in the 1970s is that approximately 16,000 ha were being taken annually from agricultural uses for urban purposes. It is difficult to say whether this rate will continue into the twenty-first century in view of the possibility of a lower total population for Britain in A.D. 2000 than that forecast a few years ago. With world pressures driving Britain to wiser use of her natural resources, it may be that the quality of the best soils will be safeguarded as a national priority. And it is unquestionably the quality of the land taken for urban use and its location which are vital in the long term.

Again, we can turn to the work of Best, who shows that there is only about 23 per cent of agricultural land in England and Wales which can be classified as 'good' (Ministry of Agriculture, Fisheries and Food (M.A.F.F.) grades 1 and 2 land). Poor land (grades 4 and 5) accounts for a third of the total, with the remainder being of medium quality. His appraisal of the conversion of agricultural land to urban uses for the two

decades up to 1971 shows that the use of good and medium
quality land was only marginally smaller than in the two previous decades.

In terms of location if all new major urban development
could take place on degraded land in, say, the Pennines or
Scottish Highlands, much best-quality soil would be saved.
But this is not yet practicable on a large scale, and another
complication is that much of this poorer land is important for
amenity and recreation and for wildlife.

Composition and Distribution

Housing absorbs most of the urban area, taking up to 50 per
cent, while open space and education – with its school playing
fields – takes up to 20 per cent of the urban total, although, as
the Table shows, this varies from 23 per cent in important

Table 1. Composition of the urban area in England and Wales,
1961

Land use	1 All urban land	2 Main urban area	3 Large & medium towns	4 Small settle-ments
	per cent			
Housing (N.R.A.)*	49	54	46	79
Industry	5	7	8	4
Open space	12	17	18	11
Education	3	4	5	2
Four main uses	69	82	77	96
Residual uses†	31	18	23	4
Total urban area	100	100	100	100

*Net residential area.
†Including transport land.
1. Total urban area of England and Wales.
2. Including small settlements of under 10,000 population, but excluding isolated dwellings and transport land outside settlements
(the aggregate area of 3 and 4 below).
3. Towns of between 20,000 and 500,000 population – which form the
most typical and extensive part of the whole urban area.
4. Small towns and villages of under 10,000 population, but excluding isolated dwellings.

towns to 13 per cent in small settlements. The residual uses probably include about 6 per cent for railways and a larger proportion for roads, some of which is also included in the figures for other categories. Industry accounts for around 5 per cent, with, expectedly, about 8 per cent in the larger industrial towns of the north.

Urban land is very unevenly spread across Britain. Much is concentrated in the older industrial areas of the North-West and West Midlands, which form, with the newer ones in the South-East, the noted 'coffin' shape from Merseyside to the London conurbation. Elsewhere, the proportion of urban land diminishes rapidly, so that it is as low as 3–6 per cent in peripheral areas of Scotland, Wales and East Anglia.

These features and factors of quality and location strengthen the case for regional strategies. The sections which follow in this chapter on other major land uses – aggregates, derelict land, and so on – further reinforce the need for a regional approach. It is vital to replace the nibblings into the countryside around the towns, and the periodic forays of the larger cities. Land-use planning, especially at regional level, should be related to the qualities of land really required. In particular, a special effort is required to promote the use of the large areas of spoilt, low-grade land or land half-committed to urban use. Making such sites readily available and encouraging their development would reduce the pressures on the better land.

Regional Strategies

All the Economic Planning Councils (referred to also in Chapter 16) for England, Scotland and Wales had produced strategies for their areas by the mid seventies. Unfortunately, the economic recession and the many other pressures discussed earlier inhibited their implementation. This was particularly sad in the case of the South East region, which had been the subject of three major studies leading to a Strategic Plan approved in principle by Government in 1971. Before it could be made operational by the reorganized local government of 1974, Government announced in 1975 that its premises would have to be reviewed. It is, however, worth noting its main features, as it brings into relationship the major factors affecting most regions.

Strategic Plan for the South East. This joint planning study of South East England was commissioned in 1968 by the Government, the Standing Conference on London and South East Regional Planning and the South East Economic Planning Council in order to provide a strategic framework for the longer-term development of the region. The main issues were:

(1) a population increase of 4 to 5 million by A.D. 2000 arising from the natural increase of the region's 17 million inhabitants;

(2) a shortage of labour during the early seventies followed (in the late seventies and eighties) by an increase in working population needing more jobs, more houses and more recreational facilities;

(3) shortage of mobile employment (i.e. firms willing to move to new locations) to meet both the demands of the region and the needs of the Development Areas and other priority locations in the rest of the country;

(4) conflicts in the region's countryside between urban development and the need to safeguard landscape, agricultural, recreational and mineral interests;

(5) the need to provide for a satisfactory evolution of the London metropolitan region and the solution of Inner London's urgent housing and social problems which are of regional significance.

The objectives included matching population and employment growth; providing for a wide variety of housing requirements and job opportunities; making the best use of the countryside; and securing the greatest possible ease of movement within the region consistent with a good environment. The general aim was to produce a strategy combining enough flexibility for different levels of population and employment growth with enough firmness to be an adequate guide for investment decisions, and for structure plans.

The Strategic Plan itself proposed:

(1) development of a limited number of major growth areas at varying distances from London using existing or planned urban settlements as the basis for growth;

(2) redevelopment and rehabilitation in London to deal particularly with the problems of Inner London;

(3) expansion of a number of medium-sized employment centres with potential for growth;

(4) preservation of extensive areas of open country, including the retention of the Metropolitan Green Belt, and an indication of areas where priority might be given to agriculture or to the conservation of fine landscape and natural and historic heritage;

(5) a communication network to provide for traffic between the more important centres of population within the South East and between the South East and the rest of the country.

The studies of the South East confirm again – if confirmation were required – that urbanization is the core of the environmental problem. This is not only in its immediate extent and impact, but in the demands it makes on land for other uses outside the towns (such as reservoirs, airfields, pipe and wire routes, special institutions and so on, which in England may add up to 20 per cent of the land surface), and the attitudes it creates in people. Because of the great importance of urbanization, these and related issues are considered more fully in Supplements.

Overall, these considerations suggest that we need a national strategy to correct the imbalance between regions in the distribution of population and industry. Many of the present activities in and around London should be dispersed to the North, Scotland and Wales. Fortunately, regional studies show the capacity of many of these areas to develop the new cities and towns required in order to absorb populations and industry in pleasant surroundings. This would reduce congestion in communications and in industry and enable more of the best soils and areas of high value in town and country to be conserved.

INDUSTRIAL DEVELOPMENT

Whatever the wisdom shown in planning and managing the use of the land required for urban purposes, there are certain major problems which cannot be fully resolved in the present state of technology and economics. For example, the location of nuclear power stations is governed by safety factors, as well as the need for water for cooling purposes. Pipelines for gas and oil, and overhead lines for electricity, are still inevitable. Some industries – for example, mineral extraction – completely depend on physical factors. The exploitation of gas and oil under the North Sea is already having a significant effect.

Generally, large-scale industry tends to develop in estuaries for the sake of easy communications and supply of raw materials; this can be seen on the major rivers of Europe, such as the Rhine, Thames and Tees. This concentration is good to the extent that it leaves other areas free, but bad when through faulty planning it creates vast blotches on a coastline or heavy pollution.

The operations of the Central Electricity Generating Board (C.E.G.B.) illustrate some of the problems. Undoubtedly the supply of cheap power throughout the country is a great boon to people and industry. Its use leads directly to more comfortable homes and more efficient factories. The large increase in the demand for electricity over the past three decades had led to the output of the system having to be doubled.

The great new power stations required for this need vast quantities of cooling water and must be sited on or near main rivers or the sea. To save transport costs, the coal-based ones must be near the most efficient coalfields. Thus there is a limited choice of sites and this in turn predetermines the routes of the transmission lines along which the power is distributed. Vehement demands are often made that power lines should be put underground. In an average rural area a 400 kv line costs £80,000 a kilometre if it is strung overhead, but £1,000,000 if it is put underground.

The by-products of the electricity industry are also of some importance. What can be done, for example, with the millions of tonnes of pulverized fuel ash (P.F.A.) which the industry produces every year? Huge quantities are used in the foundations of roads and other works and in the manufacture of building blocks but there is still more to utilize.

The exploitation of oil and gas under the North Sea and of coal in Yorkshire in the past decade have laid the basis for a national energy policy related to the long-term use of natural resources. This has profound and far-reaching implications for the environment – urban and rural. Inevitably, problems arise over the location of sites for development and for infrastructures and these affect the landscape.

Another industry which has to construct prominent objects with a strong visual impact on the landscape is the Post Office. It must meet the rapidly rising demand for radio and television transmission as well as the phenomenal growth in all the media of communication. Over 100 towers have been developed to transmit microwave signals. These signals travel in direct lines and must have unobstructed passage for a distance of about fifty km. The towers themselves have a concrete core and are about 30 to 100 metres in height. They obviously need high ground and tend to dominate the countryside, adding yet another feature to the 'skyscape' of rural areas.

There are a number of other industries which exercise a significant influence on the countryside. Water supply is one, through the siting of its dams and the extraction of water from reservoirs, lakes and rivers. Granting the public access to, and recreational facilities in, such sites can change pressures over a whole area; fuller details are given in later chapters.

One aspect of the use of land which tends to be overlooked is that organizations often have to acquire space incidental to their primary objectives. For example, they may have to take a complete ownership of a large homogeneous area which includes land surplus to operational needs. Or it may be desirable on grounds of public safety or for amenity purposes to include 'buffer' land. The total area of this type of land held by commercial or public bodies may be around ·5 million hectares. Although it has not been surveyed, sample checks indicate that it is not fully used and should be reviewed.

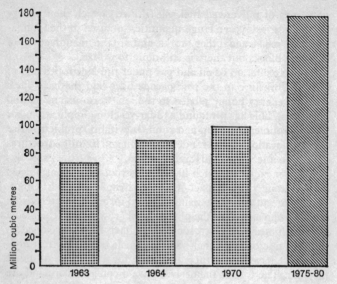

Figure 3. Sand and gravel production and an estimate of demand

These few examples show that, although industry's demand for land may be relatively small, the location, management, design and type of industrial buildings and related equipment can greatly affect the appearance of the countryside, particularly on high ground and at the coast.

AGGREGATES

The demand for aggregates (sand and gravel, crushed rock, limestone, ironstone, clays, etc.) has increased from 2 million tonnes at the start of the century to around 350 million tonnes in the mid seventies, i.e. to around 6 tonnes per person per year. The working of some thirty minerals has made it the nation's largest extractive industry, affecting over 3,500 sites (coal was producing around 130 million tonnes at this time).

The production of aggregates is essential to a good living environment; it is used for the houses, schools, roads, hospitals, shops and factories required by a larger population, which also expects the replacement of the slums and worn-out infrastructures of many of our older industrial areas. To meet these needs, around 2,600 ha of land, mainly in agricultural use, are taken each year for aggregates for the construction industry.

Total resources in Britain are adequate for the immediate future, but unfortunately the material is not in sufficient quantities where most required. Costs of movement, and land use and other constraints on exploitation, do not make the total resource a realistic basis on which to plan and so we find regional and local problems, with (inevitably) the south east of England having some of the most intractable ones.

Sand and Gravel

Probably that sector of the industry with the most widespread impact is the winning of sand and gravel. Production needs increase annually and could reach 200 million tonnes before the end of the century. Marine sources supply near 10 million tonnes, and this is important in the South East, but the many problems affecting its exploitation – adverse effects on fishing, coastlines, navigation and harbours – make it unlikely that this source can be expanded readily.

Sand and gravel, basic to concrete and extensively used for houses, factories and roads, has to be won from locations within economic transport distance of its markets. Transport costs are between 20 and 50 per cent of the final price depending on distance; a few extra kilometres can double its price. Inevitably, it becomes difficult to reconcile the urgent and increasing demands for sand and gravel with the conservation of high-quality soils and amenity.

In many localities, the workings give a frightening, often eerie look to the landscape and this has a strong effect near housing estates or in the countryside. But luckily modern equipment makes it possible for good use to be made of this industry's worked-out sites. The Sand and Gravel Association (S.A.G.A.) has issued booklets on how to tackle this work and gives guidance not only to members but also to civic bodies and societies. Already some sites have been used excellently –

they have been turned into well-managed refuse pits, fertile fields, nature reserves and playing-fields, and wet pits have been developed for water skiing, angling, wild-fowling and many other recreations. Sometimes these sites are more valuable and useful to the community now than they were prior to mineral excavation. Unfortunately, there are too many old, still derelict sites; in some localities developers and planners have failed to cooperate, and little has been done to interest the public in the possible uses of these pits.

Perhaps the problems of the South-East region will bring these issues to a head, as the nearest major sources of sand and gravel are in the middle and upper Thames area and middle Anglia, where much of the land is of high agricultural and amenity value.

The construction anticipated in the next two decades in the South East demands a greater quantity of sand and gravel. Most of it will have to be found locally, unless major improvements can be effected swiftly in the infrastructure and costs of transport facilities by road and rail and in new developments of conveyors, pipelines, or water barges, in order to provide cheaper access to a wider catchment area for the material.

Savings in transport costs are obviously not only going to benefit the prices of homes, factories and so on, but will enable the industry to undertake better restoration or re-use of sites and to respond more effectively to social and environmental considerations.

DERELICT AND WASTE LAND

The definition of derelict land used by the Department of the Environment may be summed up as follows: 'land so damaged by industrial or other development that it is incapable of beneficial use without treatment'. On this basis, there were in England, Wales and Scotland about 60,000 ha of derelict land in the mid seventies.

Despite accelerated efforts by local authorities to reclaim derelict land during the 1960s, the total amount is increasing. The creation of derelict land outpaces its redemption and so additional substantial funds to those already allocated for reclamation are required to prevent the growth of new industrial dereliction. And the problem is intensified in that the incidence of dereliction is uneven with half the derelict land in England concentrated in five counties.

A new, more comprehensive, survey of derelict and despoiled land was undertaken in 1974 by local authorities in England, under the aegis of the Department of the Environment (different arrangements apply in Scotland and Wales). This survey, which included for the first time land used for surface mineral workings and for refuse tips, is one in a continuing assessment of the problem and provided the basis for the work of the reorganized local government authorities (under the Local Government Act 1972 derelict land reclamation remains a dual function of county and district councils).

The survey revealed a total area of 43,273 ha of inherited dereliction, an increase since 31 December 1971 of 10,309 ha (though the figures are not, in general, statistically reconcilable with those in earlier surveys). It was anticipated that 5,275 ha of inherited dereliction would be restored between April 1974 and 31 March 1976. The survey showed 11,399 ha of land in use for public refuse and private and commercial non-mineral waste tipping. The total area of land with permissions for mineral working was 94,402 ha, of which 49,076 ha were currently affected by excavations and tips.

With the continuing need to exploit minerals it is obvious that, without consummate skill and care by all concerned, the total area of derelict land will continue to increase. Stringent conditions are normally attached for permission to exploit minerals, but they are often technically difficult to comply with. The planner may have the unenviable task of trying to enforce the unenforceable, for example, by requiring an operator to backfill gaping holes when no filling material is available, or insisting on tree planting where trees will not grow. However, if planning conditions are imposed for the restoration of land following excavation, the land is not classified as derelict, irrespective of its appearance and usefulness, and no Exchequer grant is available towards the cost of its restoration. So the difference between derelict and spoiled land can be crucial.

The winning of coal could lead to further waste land. More coal will be needed as the oil and gas deposits in the seas around Britain are exhausted in a few decades. More deep pits are inevitable – the go-ahead to develop the Selby Coalfield in Yorkshire (the world's biggest-ever mine) was given in 1976 – and more opencast mining is likely. Fortunately, the National Coal Board has a finely attuned organization for restoring land – every single hectare – after opencast mining. From 1960 to 1970 it restored 20,000 ha at an average cost of £500 per ha. But the spoil heaps from deep mines are another problem. About 2,000 million tonnes of colliery spoil deface the landscape. Five hundred tips are still in active use and of these about one quarter are not subject to planning control as they were in use as tips in 1948 when the National Coal Board was set up.

Increasingly, it is being realized that a blighted environment imposes severe economic penalties on the area where it occurs. As dereliction increases, the demand for new industrial floor space decreases; it deters the modern industry needed for the revitalization of the older urban areas and helps to stimulate outward migration. Some local planning authorities have set up units solely to deal with land reclamation and they, universities and regional economic councils have made valuable studies of derelict land. Planning authorities now check annually on the extent of dereliction in their areas.

Despite such increased activity and initiatives, the problem remains: how to get rid of blight and eyesores which have an effect far beyond their actual areas on the landscape and morale of people. Fortunately, something can be done about existing wastelands; what are needed most are finance and skilled staff. Inevitably, there is a shortage of scientists, landscape designers, foresters and technicians qualified in the specialized work of reclamation.

Local authorities have been urged by central government to draw up programmes for reclaiming their wasted areas.

Priority is given to the Development Areas and to the Intermediate and Derelict Land Clearance Areas in the hope of
stimulating the growth of industry. At present, where reclamation schemes are eligible for Government aid (and many of
them are not), about 85 per cent of the cost is recoverable by
local authorities in the development areas and 75 per cent in
National Parks and Areas of Outstanding Natural Beauty
(A.O.N.B.). In the Intermediate Areas and Derelict Land
Clearance Areas, grant aid is available from the Exchequer at
the rate of 100 per cent. Elsewhere reclamation schemes attract
a 50 per cent grant from Exchequer funds.

The weakness of this funding is that some local authorities
cannot find the remaining portion of the costs of reclamation.
The economic alternations, and especially the inflation, of the
seventies, with the pressure of ratepayers' associations for
economies, made this problem even more intractable. Yet
failure to reclaim is a real diseconomy, as once-derelict land is
already yielding handsome returns to the community from a
wide range of productive uses – for urban and industrial
development, agriculture and forestry, sport and recreation,
amenity and for wildlife.

Some of the research needed for effective reclamation is in
progress but it is inadequately coordinated and certainly not
yet on the scale likely to be required if, as seems probable,
world macro-pressures in the next century force Britain to
exploit minerals on a scale greater than ever seen before. For
example, if we are driven to provide our own copper, some
could be found in mid Wales but it could require the disposal
of 99 tonnes of soil, rock, debris, etc., for each tonne of copper
won. We need research on such physical problems as site and
soil conditions and stabilization, plant and animal communities and ecological processes, and into such socio-
economic issues as the recycling of refuse and wastes, transport
costs and subsidies for moving spoil, etc., into areas for re-use,
and the allocation of the costs of research and reclamation.
The knowledge and experience gained from such research
related to derelict land should be a marketable commodity of
some value and an influence for good to the world environment.

Although much further research is required on the properties of the waste products to be found on derelict land and their potential uses, enough is known to enable substantial inroads to be made on the worst areas. And while the total elimination of old disused tips may depend on new techniques to extract from them valuable minerals, such as aluminium silicates and iron oxide, there are a number of ways in which they can be reclaimed. Urban parks can be created from them as in Stoke-on-Trent (see Chapter 13). Some heaps have been bulldozed and used to fill unwanted holes. But not all of them can be moved by normal equipment; some of those in the Lower Swansea Valley require blasting. And occasionally, old quarry holes are too deep or are sited in such awkward positions that they are extremely expensive to fill in. There are also many legal problems of ownership to be overcome. Arguments over who shall develop the land after it is reclaimed, and the overlapping of local authority boundaries, render a complex task even more discouraging.

Land and water use policies should recognize the interdependence of town and country. It is absurd to let whole districts in town areas lie derelict – ignoring places like the Lower Swansea Valley and the West Midland tips and quarries makes no sense at all. And work on rural areas is no less urgent – in fact, a total renewal of our physical environment is now overdue. Unfortunately, we lack effective techniques for assessing social costs and benefits accruing from alternative policies. For example, a financial 'weighting' for the long-term value of the rural areas around Swansea for agriculture, amenity, recreation and so on, might reveal that it would be cheaper to develop the waste lands in the urban area than to take more of the (apparently cheaper) countryside. But the individual can hardly make these calculations; they require a strategic approach by an authority. And organizations of any kind should not be allowed to effect large-scale changes in land use without making some appraisal of their implications, possibly on the lines of the U.S.A. environmental impact assessment demanded from all Federal agencies.

In many ways action over derelict land offers the key to

man's intentions. So much dereliction is glaringly obvious. It
engenders squalor. At the same time, this type of land offers
fewer obstacles to the really imaginative and energetic developer – radical new techniques can be used to solve both old
and new problems. Reclaimed and put to fresh uses, derelict
sites would save good land and be a stimulus to everyone who
seeks a high-quality environment.

REFUSE

This discussion of waste land does not take into account the
great and increasing problem of how to dispose of the refuse
spewed out every day by the towns. What about surplus
chemicals and nuclear waste (by A.D. 2000 over three quarters
of all electricity in the U.K. may be generated from nuclear
power) or other major by-products of industry? These issues
need to be dealt with as part of a national assault on land
reclamation and the use of waste and by-products.

A Government Report* on refuse disposal in 1971 dealt
with the quantities and nature of refuse, and evaluated its
changing character and the current practices for disposal.
There is no single best method of disposal; whatever is adopted
should be related to local and regional circumstances. Existing
planning legislation is inadequate for the scale and character
of modern refuse disposal, and the disposal of solid wastes of all
types should be coordinated and controlled over reasonably
large areas.

So that, once again, advancing technological and planning
considerations tend to determine this important feature of
social activity. Valuable opportunities exist to relate refuse
disposal to land planning and to improve the countryside,
for example, by serving as filling material to remedy damage
done by extractive industry, or to improve natural conditions
such as unwanted marshland, which may then provide recreational opportunities.

In 1974, the Government launched a new national effort to

* Department of the Environment Working Party on Refuse Disposal, 1971, *Refuse Disposal*, H.M.S.O.

conserve national resources, to cut down waste and to promote ways of recovering and re-utilizing materials on lines set out in the Green Paper, Cmnd 5727. It also set up a high-level Waste Management Advisory Council to examine and keep under review all these issues.

The disclosures in 1972 that the dumping of cyanide had been widespread for many years led to considerable public concern and pin-pointed the urgent need for legislation to control the disposal of toxic wastes. The Royal Commission on Environmental Pollution reviewed* three issues in industrial pollution: confidentiality of information about industrial effluents and wastes – advocating more openness; the impact of new products on the environment – urging that an 'early warning system' should be adopted; and the disposal of toxic wastes on land – recommending statutory control.

These problems led to the Deposit of Poisonous Waste Act 1972 to make compulsory the notification to the appropriate authorities of the movement and depositing of dangerous materials and imposing severe penalties for offenders against the law.

Events moved so rapidly that the whole of this Act was soon replaced by provisions in the Control of Pollution Act 1974. This placed a duty on each disposal authority (the council of a county in England, and of a district in Wales, the Greater London Council, and an islands or district council in Scotland) to survey facilities and to make adequate arrangements for refuse in its area, to prepare and revise waste disposal plans on the basis set out in the Act, and to consult widely over its proposals.

The Act prohibits the disposal of waste, except in prescribed cases, other than by licence from the authority and imposes penalties for contravention. The authority must keep under review its plans and any licences it issues and has powers to reclaim waste and to turn it to productive uses, for example for generating heat and electricity.

Unfortunately, the mid seventies recession delayed the full

*Royal Commission on Environmental Pollution, Second Report, Cmnd 4894; H.M.S.O.

implementation of the Act. Authorities were, however, encouraged to get ahead with the survey and plan where they had resources to do so, and specific funds were allocated to bring the site licensing system into operation in 1976. All authorities were urged to have regard to the need for adequate facilities for all the waste to be disposed of in their areas, including that generated by industry, and to operate the new system accordingly.

DEFENCE LAND

The demands on land and water so far considered are not, of course, the whole of the picture. The Defence Departments clearly require a large area of land and water for training and other purposes, but, in the absence of a major war, this demand is diminishing. In any case, the Defence Departments sometimes help, rather than hinder, land conservation, for much of their property, like Salisbury Plain, stays in a relatively wild state, whereas it might otherwise be developed or despoiled.

In 1971 the Secretary of State for Defence appointed a special Defence Lands Committee to review the land held for defence purposes. This covered land held for training areas, airfields and ranges wherever situated, for any purpose in National Parks and areas of outstanding beauty, and along the coastline for purposes other than dockyards and port installations. Evidence was taken from the public so that the Committee should have a wide range of information on which to base its recommendations for changes in these land holdings, including improved public access.

The Committee reported in 1973 and a White Paper (Cmnd 5714) 'Statement on the Report of the Defence Lands Committee' published in 1974 gave the Government's decision on its proposals. The Government accepted in principle 25 of the Committee's 26 general recommendations; the one rejected was that to reduce from three to two the number of major airfields used for Research and Development.

In accepting the Committee's recommendations, the Government stressed the importance of a balance between the needs of the Armed Forces, for example, space and freedom to test and to train on new weapons with greater range and mobility, with protection of the environment and more opportunities for the public to enjoy its beauty. Many of the 25 recommendations have already been successfully implemented; there is widespread and improved consultation between the Ministry of Defence and official and voluntary bodies concerned with planning, environmental improvements, access to defence sites and reduction of noise. The Ministry appointed a Conservation Officer who rapidly acquired the confidence of the leading agencies in promoting environmental awareness in the Forces and practical measures for environmental safeguards and wise uses of specific sites.

The Committee made recommendations about 465 individual sites, most of which were accepted by Government. Arrangements for the agreed releases of land and improvements to access were set in hand, subject to the economic conditions. Of the major problem areas, perhaps Dartmoor is the most widely known (the Committee received more written evidence on this than on any other site) and so a special public inquiry into its use by the Services was held in 1975-6.

This major review has established general principles for use and management, of value not only to defence lands but to the entire public domain. Nevertheless, constant vigilance is required to ensure that no land is retained unnecessarily and that all its potentialities are taken into account.

Appraisal

The growing demands for land for urban and industrial development will absorb a substantial part of the land surface of Britain in the next few decades, until population growth and our expectations for material goods are brought into balance with the capacity of the environment to sustain them. As the localities suitable for urban and related development are limited great care should be exercised to secure the optimum use of all land.

But the actual total area of land to be consumed for urban development is not in itself so crucial as the choice of the sites and the manner of their development. We can afford to build houses and factories on poor land; it is unlikely that we can afford to put them anywhere else. Much more strategic planning is required nationally to create balanced regions; much more research is necessary into the problems of siting development and the use of marginal and derelict land; and much more effort must be made to apply existing and new knowledge to environmental problems.

There are, however, other uses of land and other forces at work having a substantial impact on many areas. What is loosely called the 'leisure boom' may give rise to even greater changes in some ways than those so far considered.

CHAPTER 5

LEISURE ACTIVITY

Leisure is the time for doing something useful.
Nathaniel Howe

LEISURE activity is as old as trade. All the great civilizations have bequeathed some legacy: the Greeks their theatre and olympiads, the Romans their *panem et circenses*, and Britons today still enjoy some of the deer forests and chases of the Saxons and Normans. Whenever man has had time and facilities he has indulged in some form of active recreation: hunting, shooting, fishing – the traditional trio – travel, entertainment, all have been pursued. But these activities were usually the prerogative of a few and, both because of this and the very small size of the populations, they did not affect much land, water or wildlife. Today, with vast numbers seeking holidays and outdoor recreation, and with tourism the biggest item in international trade, the impact is dramatic.

All the factors determining leisure interests – population, free time, money, mobility, inclination – have grown rapidly in the past thirty years. All European countries, especially the Scandinavian, report a great expansion in outdoor recreation. And 1975 saw the creation of a *European Sport for All Charter* by member countries of the Council of Europe – article 1 of which states that 'every individual shall have the right to participate in sport'.

Many of the traditional recreations, such as cycling, football and cricket, have declined relatively as greater wealth, time and mobility enable more varied and often expensive activities, such as skiing, sailing and golf, to be pursued. The increases have been exceptional in water sports, climbing, caving, riding and bird-watching. Camping, caravanning and motoring for pleasure have also greatly increased (over 7 million Frenchmen go camping each year); and field sports such as hunting, shooting and fishing have continued to grow steadily.

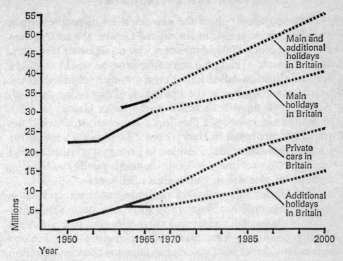

Figure 4. Trends in holidaymaking and private cars in Britain 1950–2000 (T. L. Burton)

Figure 5. Trends in holiday travel by road and rail in Britain 1950–2000 (T. L. Burton)

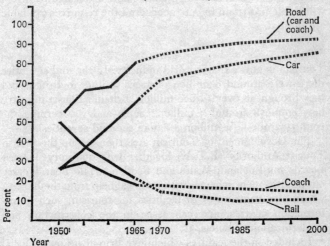

Data on page 85 show the vast numbers of people mobile and the upward trends of the related factors; the second does not take account of those numbers who travel by air transport. If the Duke of Wellington were alive now, he would no doubt feel the situation called for an even stronger remark than the one he made on seeing the first train: 'Progress be damned. All this will do will be to allow the lower classes to move around unnecessarily.' This may be contrasted with the statement attributed to Henry Ford: 'I will build a motor car for the great multitude . . . so low in price that no man . . . will be unable to own one – and enjoy with his family the blessing of hours of pleasure in God's great open spaces.'

The number of people seeking active outdoor recreation is multiplying rapidly. Since 1945 there has been a five-fold increase in coastal sailing and there are now half a million dinghy sailors, at least three million anglers, over 100,000 naturalists, and at least 50 organizations for outdoor activities.

Vast crowds take more passive enjoyment in the countryside or at the coast: over half the population makes at least one short pleasure trip during the late Spring holiday. All the indications are that leisure pursuits – both active and passive – will treble in Britain by A.D. 2000. And the resources available are limited.

Tourism

Tourism is now a major world industry. In the mid seventies there were around 8 million overseas visitors to Britain and they brought in over £1,000 million. Britain's tourist industry now employs around 5 million people and was earning the country around £4 million a day in the mid seventies.

The Development of Tourism Act 1969 set up the British Tourist Authority (B.T.A.) together with statutory Tourist Boards for England, Wales and Scotland. The Boards carry out improvement schemes with financial help from the B.T.A., which also contributes to facilities for tourism, such as information centres, and can assist in the construction and modernization of hotels.

Included in the features which give Britain its own special

appeal to tourists is beautiful countryside. Outdoor recreation and sporting holidays are growing in popularity, notably boating, pony-trekking, fishing, golfing and other open-air activities, including skiing in Scotland. It is obvious that these trends will continue to accelerate since most countries are making a determined effort to increase interest in sport.

The figures for holidays give further evidence of the pressures on countryside and coast. In the mid seventies, 40 million Britons took holidays of four nights or more in the U.K. Second holidays during a year have more than doubled within a decade and the demand for holiday services grows faster than that for most other products. In addition, it seems that the length of the average holiday is extending and more people are taking long weekends.

All these developments are placing great pressures on favoured localities – the peak of Snowdon has been referred to as the highest slum in Europe. They should be studied and their significance assessed in relation to each area's capacity to sustain them without becoming degraded. The B.T.A., in fact, urges national surveys and the preparation of a national recreational plan, to be implemented through close cooperation between the many bodies concerned. It is well aware that the shape which our environment takes is of supreme importance to the domestic holiday trade, which is the backbone of British tourism.

Facilities and Management

One of the main problems is to know what the public really wants and what it would pay to get it! The underlying trends and motives need to be investigated by the Social Science Research Council; the implications in terms of planning and commerce by the local authorities and specialist firms; and the effects on land and water by the Natural Environment Research Council. The lack of reliable information about the facilities required is one side of the coin; the other is that many landowners and planners are not sufficiently aware of the demand for facilities, nor do they understand how best to provide them. Too little is known about the returns possible from recreation.

These factors are particularly important to the recreational use of rural land. Positive management is essential to promote the multiple use of land for food, timber, sport, rambling and other activities. How vulnerable various soils are to erosion from intense recreational pressures should be assessed. The potential uses of the land – for example, for camping sites, pathways and walking – must be known, and such matters as site drainage and water disposal wisely arranged. Trees are very important to the landscaping of sites, but they must allow light through to encourage ground cover. Rotation of camp sites, climbs and walks may be necessary to allow natural renewal.

Some landowners are now denying the public access to spaces which were once open; in some cases the difficulties arise from lack of knowledge of both trends and the management necessary to cope with them. Others are infuriated by visitors' carelessness or their failure to contribute to upkeep costs. The point of the leisure boom is that a mass of people cannot enjoy, in the same places and at the same time, the pleasures that once a few enjoyed. As demand increases, so must planning and consideration for others.

Unfortunately, not enough is known about how much land is accessible to the public for recreation. Open lands managed by the Forestry Commission, the National Trusts and the Nature Conservancy Council, plus the commons, probably add up to about one million hectares.

Land available for recreation in Britain includes much of the hill and upland areas of Scotland, Wales and the Pennines. As they contain many of the National and Forest Parks and are scenically very beautiful, they also attract many tourists, as well as the ramblers, climbers and cavers who frequent them. With the development of motorways many of these areas are within weekend reach of the great cities.

Better access by road, rail and air undoubtedly contributes to the rapid expansion of Scotland's booming ski industry which will increase further as more facilities are provided (the use of artificial snow and synthetic runs may lengthen the season), and as every year many more Scottish schoolchildren get professional ski instruction. Another development is the demand for Scottish estates and sporting properties. Many overseas buyers are attracted by the excellent facilities for hunting, shooting and fishing.

The Forestry Commission prepares recreation plans for its estates in close consultation with all the many bodies concerned. It recognizes the enormous increase in pressure for recreation in its forests and seeks to develop their unique. recreational features and potential, particularly where the forests are readily accessible to large numbers of visitors from the major cities and holiday centres. As the Commission's forests occur on a wide variety of ground in many parts of Britain, they provide opportunities for many activities, such as shooting, fishing, orienteering, pony-trekking, sailing and nature study, but priority will be given to recreation for the general public wherever any conflict of interests arises.

In England and Wales all the National Parks suffer increasing onslaughts. The Friends of the Lake District Park have referred to the traffic there as 'the potential destroyer of the Lake District'. In the Peak Park there are many measures in operation to meet the vast recreational and tourist pressures from nearby cities, notably a corps of voluntary wardens. The active management it receives and its intrinsic high quality won for it the first European Diploma, awarded in 1966 by the Council of Europe. The Snowdonia Park and the Gower Area of Outstanding Natural Beauty also report great pressures. And the south-west of England, with its two Parks and its beautiful coastline, has the greatest summer holiday influx of all.

The development of seaside resorts may make a useful contribution to more positive policies for coast and countryside, particularly those of concentrating facilities and people. The wide-ranging provisions of the National Trusts for England and Wales and for Scotland make a significant contribution. County councils are being encouraged to establish country parks for amenity and recreation, and a number have done so already.

Traffic

But of all the phenomena produced by the population explosion and technology, it is the private car which is likely to have the greatest and most pervasive effect on the landscape. And this will be further intensified by shorter working hours and the trend to more and longer holidays. There could be over 30 million motor vehicles in Britain in A.D. 2000 and with over 60 million people having three days free each week (or perhaps four) the impact on coast and country could more than double that of today.

Traffic planning in the countryside is now receiving the attention it merits in view of Britain's roads being the most crowded in the world, with around 40 vehicles for every kilometre of road. This is particularly urgent in some areas of the countryside where traffic can too easily despoil and degrade.

While further study and experiments are required, it seems that the technique of 'park and ride', used in some National Parks, may be acceptable in some areas where traffic management can be paid for, but it may not be appropriate in all beauty spots, and other methods will have to be devised.

Many planners propose not only special facilities for motorists, but also motor-less zones and car-free countryside roads to enable fuller enjoyment of the countryside. The coast is probably the primary attraction for most people – for recreation, holidays and tourism. Its importance and the pressures upon it increase yearly. In the most favoured localities shortage and surfeit are common: a shortage of car parks, viewpoints, mooring berths and paths is allied to a surfeit of seasonal congestion, conflict and urban unsightliness. Fuller details on the coast are given in Chapter 12.

Water

Whether they go to the coast or stay inland, most active recreationalists need water on which to boat, canoe, dive, sail, swim, water-ski, or fish. In England and Wales 10 per cent of all households contain at least one angler. Of the near 3 million who go fishing, half are regulars, fishing weekly during the season.

Even more enjoy viewing the 'waterscape'. And this is universal. But water which is suitable for sports is, surprisingly, in short supply. Although there are altogether 250,000 ha of water in Britain, only about 80,000 ha of lakes, rivers, reservoirs, canals and Broads are in England and Wales; and not all of this is available for access or managed in a way which allows for recreation.

Of major importance for recreation is the policy of the British Waterways Board (B.W.B.) for the national legacy of 3,200 km of inland waterways and their potential as a network for pleasure cruising. The waterways have for years supported extensive recreational use, for example, angling and cruising. About three quarters of them are available for fishing and the Board and many private companies hire out cruisers. Many canals are important for science and education; some have considerable amenity value and are of great significance in the landscape. The financial aspects inevitably dominate; to use most of the non-commercial system for pleasure boating depends essentially on the annual grant-in-aid from Government. For all the B.W.B.'s operations, this reached £5·3 million in 1974. Of the total expenditure on operation and maintenance of waterways, 60 per cent was spent on the cruising waterways.

The capacity of the waterways is harnessed in a strategic plan that makes them available to clubs and individuals under agreed conditions. The plan is based on commercial factors – most people can afford to pay for their leisure – although more public money could reasonably be invested to reflect the values to society of the activities fostered and of the land and water saved for other uses.

In this context, the officially sponsored Inland Waterways Amenity Advisory Council (set up under the 1968 Act to advise, among others, the B.W.B.) believes that the overriding priority in any waterways policy based on limited public funds should be to ensure that all classes of waterways are maintained in a sufficient condition to enable their speedy development to match the demands made upon them in a more favourable economic climate. Three main needs should be met: making the waterways themselves sound; maintaining an adequate supply of water; and protecting the 'remainder waterways' including those not now used for freight traffic or cruising, for possible future development.

Inland waters are particularly valuable for leisure as many of them lie within urban areas. There is obviously a wide range of uses for reservoirs, canals, gravel pits and rivers. If suitably managed, they could meet local and short-term holiday needs. The Lea Valley and Strathclyde Regional Parks are outstanding for the utilization of poor or derelict land and water within a conurbation. More developments such as these would provide for specialized activities like underwater swimming and water-skiing. They would also help to relieve the travel and traffic problems by reducing pressures on countryside and coast. In short, what does it cost not to use these resources? Certainly, without their exploitation there will be a real loss in the quality of the environment as the leisure boom and other demands on land and water intensify.

Other potential sources of water-based recreation are the reservoirs of the Regional Water Authorities (R.W.A.s) and water undertakings, though, of course, safeguards are necessary to ensure that the quality and quantity of water are not affected. The Government encourage the authorities responsible for reservoirs to allow public access, and thus to help meet the increasing demand for boating, and other water sports. Hopefully, the official and voluntary bodies concerned strive to educate and inform and to foster positive management of water areas and good behaviour by users. For example, the journal *Water Space* and leaflets of the Water Space Amenity Commission (W.A.S.A.C.) reach a wide audience, in particular encouraging volunteers to active pursuits and worthwhile conservation and management tasks – a real leisure-in-depth.

Effects

What are the results of these pressures on water and key stretches of countryside and coast, so often inadequately planned and managed in relation to them?

One of the most serious is the erosion which takes place simply because so many people visit places of beauty and other natural attractions. It is now obvious that a given area cannot properly support more than a given number of visitors without strict control. The problems of coping with erosion by humans are great; the sheer physical trampling by walkers and pic-nickers can create lasting damage. But perhaps worst of all are the litter and refuse which mark the passage of humans and stress the need for higher standards of behaviour.

Litter anywhere is a difficult problem. It leads to insanitary and dangerous sites, pollutes water, poisons domestic animals and wildlife, and invariably reduces the aesthetic pleasures of the countryside. For example, in the New Forest over 1,000 tonnes of litter a year are removed by the Forestry Com-mission. This problem is primarily a task for the education and information services. There is no real substitute for self-discipline. This is not to deny that there is still vast scope for improvement in facilities, notably in the provision of bins in lay-bys and modern sanitation at the larger and more frequently used stopping places. But it is neither practicable on financial and legal grounds, nor desirable on siting and aesthetic grounds, to spread litter-bins over the countryside. People must learn to take their refuse home with them, where it can be dealt with properly. But for those who will not, the Dangerous Litter Act 1971 increased the maximum fine of £10 in the 1958 Litter Act to £100. The Courts, when fixing a penalty on conviction, can have regard to the nature of the litter and any risk of injury to persons or animals, or damage to property. This could be particularly important in beauty spots and amenity areas.

In sum, pollution arises from people and their cars; poorly situated and badly designed facilities disfigure the countryside; congestion causes conflict and disturbance to humans and wild-life; farmland and cattle are interfered with and forests set ablaze; water catchments are eroded; oil pollutes reservoirs; and generally the special qualities of country and coast are replaced by the least desirable of urban characteristics. Gradually wear and tear are reducing the supply of land and water for recreation. Conflict between recreational users is frequent and on the increase. The absence of suitable space and facilities for youth to 'let off steam' obviously leads to discontent and helps to produce those near-riots which make headline news. Outdoor active recreation provides an outlet for instincts, drives and emotions, as well as having social and cultural values. How should these be focused? How can a clear relationship be established between conservation of resources and continuance of leisure pursuits?

Policies and Organization

Policies for sport and recreation in town and countryside and the arrangements for their implementation came under review in the seventies. The House of Lords Select Committee on Sport and Leisure published two reports in 1973 and debated them in 1974. The Government issued a White Paper* in 1975 stating that recreation should be regarded as one of the community's everyday needs, and provision for it as part of the general fabric of the social services, with opportunities for all who wish to participate. In particular, sport and recreation should help to relieve the social stresses on many young people, especially in the big cities.

The White Paper advocated that, within available resources, highest priority for grant aid by the Sports Council should be given to recreational projects in areas of special need in towns and cities. High priority should also be given to projects intended to ensure wider use by the community of amateur and professional club facilities, and to projects aimed at extending the use of facilities by young people.

For some years local authorities may not be able to spend as much as they would wish on sport and recreation, so they are urged to ensure that the limited resources available for recreation are used in the most cost-effective way possible, making the fullest use of existing facilities with a clear order of priorities for any new facilities and the improvement of organ-

*Sport and Recreation (Cmnd 6200).

ization to avoid duplication. Better uses should be made of existing buildings, such as village and church halls and community centres, and, despite problems of staffing and caretaking, of educational facilities. The Government hoped that the Sports Council would also give priority to applications for projects aimed at ensuring that under-used facilities at clubs are made available for wider use within the community.

The independent Royal Charter Sports Council and those for Wales and Scotland were retained. The Sports Council was given a closer relationship with the Minister for Sport and Recreation and a clearer definition of its role in relation to that of the Central Council for Physical Recreation.

The Regional Sports Councils in England were replaced by Regional Councils for Sport and Recreation, covering the whole range of sport and outdoor recreational activities. Their membership reflects a balance between formal and informal recreation, and between recreation and conservation, farming and forestry in the countryside. They advise local authorities and others generally on a wide range of issues and, in particular, the Countryside Commission and the Sports Council on regional priorities for grant aid. They also promote the preparation of regional recreational strategies to ensure proper coordination of effort.

Inevitably the economic difficulties of the time diminished the substance of the White Paper and the setting of other priorities. Additionally, the Government had not then pronounced on the Sandford Report on National Parks (see page 295) whose proposals are clearly significant to leisure pursuits. The new Councils, some of which consist of perhaps 150 members, may be criticized as being too unwieldy for effective advice and decision-taking and too heavily biased in favour of 'user' interests. Much depends on how they operate – the possibility of a deadening bureaucratic structure is obvious but, given leadership and the right attitudes from all concerned, the Councils could contribute significantly to wider understanding and a healthier *rapport* between what are today often conflicting interests.

Needs

Many reports on recreation and leisure have appeared in continental Europe. Some countries have more experience of particular aspects than others; for example, it would probably repay detailed study to appraise how the land and water of Switzerland have withstood a severe impact of visitors twice-yearly without much noticeable loss of quality, except in a few localities. The leisure industry should promote codes of practice for tourists and recreationalists. Once these can be applied in all countries and more personal responsibility developed, then Europe will be on the way to the 'civilization' of leisure.

Clearly there is no easy solution. Primarily it is vital to define the requirements of the various recreational activities and to relate them to existing resources. These will include strict zoning for specific pursuits and control over the times and frequency of use. Existing resources must be allocated and managed for specified categories of use. A distinction should be made, for example, between high-density areas such as the Lea Valley, where recreation will be the main consideration; general recreation areas, such as the Solent, New Forest and Windermere, where a balance will be kept between recreation and other uses like forestry and water conservation; and high-quality areas, in which scenic, scientific or other special interests would be given priority.

In some cases the values assignable to certain areas of popular interest have been assessed. These take account not only of those factors expressed in direct charges (the entry to a historic building or a fee to fish on a river) but also of the values which cannot so easily be translated into monetary terms.

Coupled with wiser use and management of existing resources must go the planned expansion and development of land and water for recreation. Too few people recognize that human needs can rarely be met the moment that they are felt and this applies no less to leisure activities. Hence planning for leisure must become an integral task of government.

Demands should be anticipated up to a decade ahead and

areas suitable for recreation and tourism reserved, with development in them coordinated in relation to long-term objectives. In some localities recreation will have to be regarded as a dominant use of land and water in its own right.

The management of green belts, commons and national parks, the reclamation of derelict land, the use of gravel pits, waterways and canals, the creation of new facilities on marginal land, the promotion of facilities in urban parks and schemes such as the Lea Valley, can all contribute to meeting the urgent demands for recreation and tourism. Cooperation between the Countryside Commissions and the Sports Councils should help to define the social values of leisure and relate them to natural resources. However, to realize the full potential of areas for leisure activities and to avoid their erosion requires more than the provision of regional and country parks, recreational reserves, and coastline and water facilities. The pressures concentrated on such sites at peak times are too great to be sustained indefinitely with the increasing numbers of people.

Measures such as the extension of the holiday and tourist season and the strengthening of publicity, information and counselling services are essential to guide people and traffic to particular attractions or recreations at particular times. People must be helped to use their leisure more wisely to their own greater satisfaction and for the maintenance of quality in the environment. The 'House Full' notice may have to go up on occasion!

The new Regional Councils clearly need to foster more definitive surveys of the facilities for leisure, notably water, and the use being made of them now and their potential under better arrangements. Inland waters suitable and available for recreation are probably in shortest supply. Yet of the main water resources – rivers, canals, natural lakes, wet gravel pits, reservoirs and coastal waters – perhaps water supply reservoirs offer the greatest potential for development.

All these resources need to be planned on a strategic basis related to the carrying capacity of the resource under positive management and the particular form of recreation. Angling, canoeing, cruising, sailing, inland and along the coast, swimming and sub-aqua diving, and water skiing, all have differing requirements, but many can be accommodated by zonation in time and space, and good standards of behaviour from partici-pants. Unfortunately, information about demands – existing and prospective – is relatively sparse and the techniques for collecting and using it are far from adequate. Inevitably, more research is needed into the calculation of demand and supply at national, regional and local levels, the techniques of manage-ment, the relationships between various interests, e.g. intensive farming, nature conservation and water recreation, and their compatibilities, and the economics of the costs and pricing systems.

All the members of the Regional Councils can contribute to this work and especially the R.W.A.s. They have powers and duties which should enable them to resolve many of these issues for water activity in collaboration with the Sports Council and the Countryside Commissions, whose range of interests would likewise deal with the comparable land-based activities.

Appraisal: Chapters 2–5

Agriculture is undergoing sweeping changes; forestry is being expanded and serves new uses. Urban development encroaches steadily on the good land; technological impacts on the countryside are visible everywhere. And overshadowing all is the leisure boom. Despite measures for conservation, the natural environment is in peril. The land is not yet fully recognized as a vital and finite resource. Many important areas of landscape, intrinsically a natural resource, are threatened. Clear principles and policies are required – pre-ventive, remedial, anticipatory and positive – in which trustee-ship for the land must be the cardinal theme. In this, as in so many other cases, *laissez faire* equals *laissez détruire*.

National policies should ensure the maximum use of land in relation to its optimum value, based upon the capability of soil for multiple uses and other 'supply' factors. The best soils need to be conserved for cultivation and for future disposition. Land less suitable for cultivation should be managed and enhanced for such uses as forests and outdoor recreation according to its natural advantages and the part it can play in a unified landscape. Overall, more attention must be paid to improving the productivity of the land for all purposes. Even now, more than half the earth's population live on the land and obtain their living from the soil and the crops and animals it supports. Agricultural land must therefore be conserved for its own sake. It may also be necessary to assess the contribution which intensive agriculture will, in fact, be making to the renewal of natural resources. If the population explosion continues Britain and other importing countries may find their supplies of primary products diminishing rapidly by the end of this century.

Although urban development requires more land, the actual quantity is not so vital as the quality and location of the land taken and whether the development is designed in harmony with the natural environment. Obviously greater encouragement should be given to the use of degraded or low-quality land. Much more research into the impacts of technology and leisure is essential. Facilities for traffic and recreation are urgently required and must be integrated with other uses of land and water. Higher standards of awareness and respect for the rights of others are essential. These and many more measures still to be considered are needed if the optimal utilization of natural resources, on which all man's progress is based, is to be achieved.

In the long term all this is sound economics. But man is not solely an economic creature. His motivations are much wider and more complex and he responds to many other stimuli; ethics are inherent in most of his situations. He may well refuse to accept that the present pattern of land use and distribution is necessarily and automatically related to the wisest long-term use of natural resources. Whatever the basic approach, few today will question that the physical environment plays a major part in health, happiness, productivity and culture. With increasing recognition of these values, land acquires a new significance. For amenity and leisure, for solace and refreshment, for adventure and for the challenge of primitive living, land now has an even greater potential for the mass of the expanding population.

And yet it retains its pre-eminent values as a source of food, a place to live and work upon, and as a continual challenge to man in seeking an understanding of his place in the natural order.

CHAPTER 6

AIR

Away with Systems! Away with a corrupt world!
Let us breathe the air of the Enchanted island.
George Meredith, *The Ordeal of Richard Feverel*

WITHOUT air there can be no life. Without air of good quality there cannot be a healthy life. Air pollution is an old problem which has in this century assumed wide economic and social significance. Perhaps the first general realization of the new dangers came with the great London smog (smoke plus fog) of December 1952. For five days the capital was enveloped in a grey shroud. After days of spluttering, cursing and frustration the costs were assessed: over 4,000 people had died and incalculable numbers had suffered a worsening of such ailments as bronchitis and heart disease.

An average person requires over fourteen kg of air a day or about 3·4 litres every minute, and he has to take it as it comes. He would not readily stand in sewage or drink dirty water. Yet daily the individual draws 26,000 breaths, between 18 and 22 each minute, many of which – if not all in some cases – are of filthy air. The lungs of town inhabitants are usually greyish in colour; those of country people are normally pale pink.

POLLUTION

. . . this most excellent canopy, the air, . . . why,
it appears no other thing to me but a foul and
pestilent congregation of vapours!
Shakespeare, *Hamlet*

One of the major problems in dealing with air pollution is to know fully what it is. Black smoke and exhaust fumes are easy to see; it is more difficult to identify many of the potentially dangerous gases being emitted today which may not be noticeable in normal atmospheric conditions.

Air is polluted in many ways, by dust, gases, fogs and vapours, and by smokes and chemicals. In Britain about half a million tonnes of grit and ash, 0·8 million tonnes of smoke and six million tonnes of sulphur gases were discharged into the air annually in the mid seventies. The Report of the Beaver Committee* stated that this pollution cost in 1954 more than £250 million, or £5 per head, each year. Current estimates for a much lower amount of pollution put the cost at over £350 million a year.

Perhaps the classic case of air pollution today is that of Los Angeles. Over 70 per cent of the total space in the city is devoted to the car (twice the average for other American cities). Over three million vehicles crowd into the conurbation daily, releasing 2,000 tonnes of exhaust fumes and 450 tonnes of nitric acid. These often react chemically to give a lachrymatory fog so dense that the wondrous Californian sun is just not visible; it also causes serious damage to the orange crops. Even worse, perhaps, is the air of New York, whose skyscrapers trap traffic fumes, and which is also polluted by sulphur dioxide and smoke. And in Tokyo, around 150 smog warnings a year may be given, with traffic police returning periodically to their stations to inhale oxygen. Despite this, it would be misleading to blame all air pollution on industry and motor vehicles. In some areas by far the greatest source is the open fire in the home – in fact, it accounts for about 75 per cent of the air pollution in many cities.

Effects

What does it mean to be on the receiving end of this pollution? The dramatic suffocation of the London smog of 1952 is not, perhaps, so serious in the long term as the slower, daily poisoning of the human frame which insidiously lowers the quality of living for so many people. Pollution causes people suffering from bronchitis and other respiratory diseases to lose countless working days each year. Generally, the health and well-being of all individuals who breathe polluted air is affected; worse still, many are losing the taste for good air, and

* Committee on Air Pollution, Cmnd 9322.

so may never notice that yet another prime element of a high-quality environment is debased or about to disappear.

The effects on clothes and buildings are almost equally serious. Laundry bills soar fantastically in the areas of heavy industry, and wear on clothes is high; a minor phenomenon is that high sulphuric acid content in the air or smuts from chimneys cause nylon stockings to ladder. Anyone can see that the paintwork of buildings is badly affected, but not many people appreciate how much air pollution corrodes brickwork and metal too. Many of Europe's antiquities – buildings, pictures and statues – are being destroyed by air pollution, particularly from cars, in cities from Oxford to Athens. Workers in industries which produce a lot of air pollution often require special protective measures and most governments have inspectors to check on these and to reduce the pollution.

Air pollution has direct and indirect effects on plants and animals. Plants play a vital role in the 'natural balance' of life. Those containing chlorophyll take in carbon dioxide from the atmosphere and give off oxygen. Using water and carbon dioxide they convert the energy of light into chemical energy (photosynthesis) and manufacture organic substances (sugars). Being fixed by their roots, they are very susceptible to environmental factors; a reduction in their light supply because of air pollution can be serious and result in a slower growth and reduced yield. It is virtually impossible at present to calculate the real and long-term effect on plant growth of the loss of effective sunshine, but the Beaver Committee in 1954 estimated that the damage in Britain to agricultural crops alone was then £10 million a year. In some parts of Britain there is an annual deposit of over 100 tonnes of polluting matter per square km; this contains substances lethal to plant life. The layers of filth prevent photosynthesis and stop up the tiny holes (stomata or foliar pores) on and under the leaves through which the plants transpire. Many plants exposed to this treatment wither or die.

Animals derive their food from plants either directly, or indirectly by feeding on herbivorous animals. They are, therefore, quickly affected by any deterioration in the quantity and quality of their food source. Air pollution may choke the capillary respiratory passages in animals. Some of the cattle present at an agricultural show in London during the 1952 smog had to be destroyed; examination showed them to be afflicted with respiratory ailments and heart disease. The central nervous system of man and animals is responsive to even small changes in the intake of oxygen from the atmosphere but, unfortunately, not enough is known about the detailed effects in this way of air pollution. It is, however, known that ultra-violet light is excluded by smoke and this clearly has an adverse effect upon all life.

Insects, particularly bees, and mammals mainly dependent on insects for their food supply have suffered heavy casualties in many places because of specific industrial pollutants. Fundamental changes have arisen in the populations of some species as they have adapted to the changes in their environment caused by air pollution. One of the most striking cases is that of the industrial melanism of the peppered moth in certain parts of Britain and continental Europe. Two forms of this insect exist, one light and one dark. The dark species was very rare a century ago and is still uncommon in rural areas but it is today by far the more common in industrial areas. Here pollution has killed off the lichens on trees and the dark form of the moth is nearly invisible on the dark trunks. Birds thus prey more easily on the lighter variety, and have almost exterminated it in certain localities. In the countryside, the advantage is with the light form as they are similar in colour to the pale, mottled lichens. As pollution diminishes and buildings can be cleaned, the light form is returning to some older cities.

Less noticeable changes have probably taken place, or may be developing, in other species, but usually the process is a slow one. Apart from their obvious direct relationships to man, plants and animals often serve as indicators of the effects which changes in the environment are likely to have on man himself. Rainfall in areas of air pollution will pick up acids or oxides. Clearly this affects plant life; it also affects the soil and its minute flora and fauna. Large quantities of lime are regularly required in certain areas to alleviate the acidity caused by

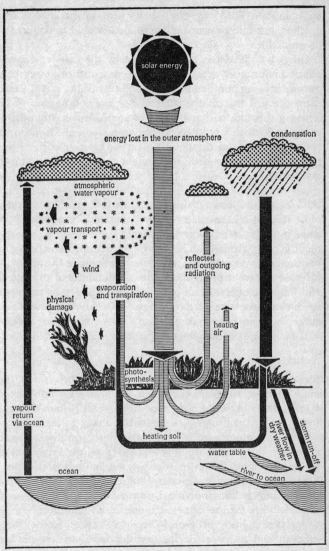

Figure 6. Dynamics of the atmosphere (B. H. Grimes)

air pollution. Study of green belts near towns and of the uplands and forests near industrial areas would undoubtedly be profitable.

Our whole planet is being affected by the massive atmospheric pollution now taking place. A vast quantity of carbon dioxide is being pumped into the atmosphere, and it looks as if plant life will use up a smaller and smaller proportion of it. The effect could, perhaps, be to create a blanket around the earth, one which would retain the heat. Such an overall rise could melt some of the polar ice-caps. Disasters such as the great North Sea flood of 1953 might then become frequent and widespread. A raising of the water level would probably result in the loss through inundation of low-lying lands and thus leave even fewer plants to deal with the carbon dioxide.

In view of all the effects of air pollution it is obviously of some importance to resolve or contain it if a healthy environment is to be achieved. The main lines of approach appear to be threefold. We must try to reduce or eliminate existing pollution, to prevent or minimize new pollution, and to control and limit the effects of all pollution which has to be accepted in the present state of technology. To achieve any success, action against the main pollutants is required on a wide variety of fronts – technological, planning, legislative and social.

Sources

First, there is pollution from the domestic fire, often the main offender. In recent years there has been some progress in setting up smokeless zones, such as those in Britain referred to in Chapter 7. Progress is affected by many factors; for example, the importance of the coal industry in the national economy, the availability of smokeless fuels, the expansion of central-heating schemes, particularly oil and gas, and district heating on new housing estates. Progress depends largely on a greater public and individual awareness and acceptance of responsibility for the domestic causes of air pollution.

As the engines of petrol-driven vehicles become more efficient and technical devices are developed to eliminate or re-use exhaust fumes individual cars will cause less pollution.

In the United States increasingly stringent regulations are being enforced from 1975 to eliminate serious air pollution by cars. Unfortunately, until every vehicle is virtually a non-pollutant, the vast increase in the number of petrol-driven vehicles on the roads is certain to increase the total air pollution from this source. In time, the better planning of cities and roads with modern traffic engineering should help to reduce its effect.

Industry has generally been responsive to technological progress and to control over air pollutants. Smoke consists of particles of unburnt carbonaceous substances left over by the incomplete combustion of fuel. This is, in effect, a measure of inefficiency; replacing the inefficient equipment often gives an improved industrial performance as well as reducing air pollution. Most of the main industries concerned, such as coal, electricity generation and chemicals, are carrying out research and technological studies to reduce pollution. Unfortunately, some major pollutants, such as sulphur dioxide from electricity power stations, oil refineries and chemical plants, cannot be controlled except at great expense. Considerable progress can be made by wise location of industry, by taking into account prevailing winds, local topography and relationship to populations. Design factors, such as shapes and heights of buildings, cooling towers and high chimneys (some are now 230 m high), are also important in helping to disperse or reduce the local effects of air pollution.

Research

In Europe alone there are over sixty research stations studying air pollution. Most of the solutions to specific problems can usually be applied in many countries. One line of study which does not, however, seem to be adequately pursued concerns the effects of air pollution on wildlife, on the micro-fauna and flora of the soil and on the ecology of the 'natural' environment as a whole.

One of the interesting developments of recent years is the study of 'air sheds'. These are zones, comparable to water catchments, which can be related to the general shape of the land. The air currents in such localities tend to come together and flow in such a way as to create a zone of distinct character. In some areas of consistent prevailing winds, there are well-defined air sheds, both in urban and rural territory. Unlike water in a catchment area, however, air in such a shed may on occasion reverse its flow and go upwards. Air sheds are also prone to 'vagrancy'. Despite these variables, a greater knowledge of air sheds, and how they can be altered, would contribute materially to environmental planning.

International

Air pollution recognizes no boundaries. This is strikingly shown by radioactive gases and dusts arising from nuclear-bomb tests and nuclear power stations. These radioactive pollutants may stay in the upper atmosphere for months and fall out anywhere on earth. With their long life they can contaminate the land and impair the health of people thousands of kilometres from the source of pollution.

One significant and only recently appreciated factor of global concern, especially for air, is the rapid rate at which new pollutants are produced and disseminated. So, in 1970, about 100 distinguished scientists and professionals met for a month at Williamstown, Mass., U.S.A., to concentrate on pollution problems of worldwide significance. This historic study* covered the consequences of pollution for climate, ocean ecology and large, terrestrial eco-systems. In particular, it examined the climatic effects of increasing carbon dioxide content and particle load on the atmosphere, and those of contamination of the troposphere and stratosphere by subsonic and supersonic transport aircraft. The general tone of a wide range of conclusions and recommendations was not alarmist but sober and authoritative; but on most issues the study called for much more research to enable society to control events and to adjust to any necessary changes. The extent of the international activity involved is briefly indicated in Chapter 21.

*Man's impact on the global environment . . ., Massachusetts Institute of Technology Report of the Study of Critical Environmental Problems, M.I.T. Press, 1970.

Appraisal

Pending developments on some of the lines indicated in this chapter, much more use should be made of the forecasting services of meteorological and climatological stations. Local broadcasting stations could provide a regular service relating the known local pollutants to current weather conditions. This would be especially valuable when inversions are expected (that is, when the air becomes warmer aloft than below) and thus there is a threat of fog. Housewives might also appreciate it! Such a service would develop a better public awareness of the dangers and problems of air pollution. To act in the ways suggested here will require not only that the public must become conscious of the dangers of air pollution but also that scientists find ways to assess the social cost and benefits of good air.

It may be necessary, in order that future inhabitants can enjoy clean air, that more of the cost is borne by long-term central government funds. As air pollution varies enormously from place to place and can, indeed, be very local, it may also be necessary for the central government to allocate money so that local authorities can meet special local problems. That these can be significant was shown by the report made in 1970 on behalf of the London Boroughs Association by the Greater London Council Research and Intelligence Unit. This revealed that in central London since 1958 smoke concentrations have decreased by 80 per cent, sulphur dioxide by 40 per cent, whereas sunshine has increased by 70 per cent and winter visibility has improved threefold. There have been reductions in mortality and hospital admissions associated with air pollution and in the response to it of bronchitics, as well as clear if less documented increases in plant types and bird species in the cities. The cost of all this has been roughly 30p per head per annum. Truly this is a great social benefit in return for very little cost.

It is essential that local government authorities regard the quality of the air as one of their major responsibilities. Such authorities can usually contribute a great deal through their various committees for public health, housing and town and country planning. They can obviously plan zones for industries by relating them to climatic and other geographic factors. They can develop district heating schemes and low-density housing or high-density flats. In particular, they can plan their towns in relation to the traffic they must withstand. Air must be 'planned' if its quality is to be ensured.

This leads on to the main goal, which is to reduce substantially and in time cut out air pollution at source. Future generations will recognize this – as with most pollution – as waste of recyclable resources. And with proper planning, particularly of energy, it should be unnecessary. The atmosphere – as with the rest of nature – is a dynamic system. It has dealt with much natural pollution – volcanoes, earthquakes, etc. – in excess of man's efforts to date by a process of continuous recycling. But this capacity to cleanse itself could be impaired, as has happened with some rivers and lakes, and this must be prevented. Hence the need to know of any substantial or potentially harmful emissions. This is possible. Industrialists, for example, could be required to report all discharges into the atmosphere as they do with those into water or dumpings on land. Increasingly, our wastes are incinerated and blown into the atmosphere; more and more we use dangerous substances with a long active life, some of which can have harmful interactions or become concentrated for too long in one place.

Man is always interfering with nature, sometimes intentionally, sometimes accidentally or unconsciously. Air pollution is obviously not intended, but that does not make its effects any less serious and man should act consciously to control it. Air pollution may, in the long term, cause an imbalance in the environment which exceeds the interferences or controls deliberately imposed by man.

CHAPTER 7

AIR OVER BRITAIN

AIR pollution has been a problem in some localities for seven centuries, since coal began to replace wood. The first law to stop the smoke and smuts in medieval London was passed in 1273. Inevitably it failed. And despite the work of John Evelyn, who, in 1661, wrote his *Fumifugium, or the air and smoake of London dissipated, together with some Remedies humbly proposed*, air pollution continued to get worse.

The chief sources of pollution in Britain are industry, vehicles and domestic fires. The general effects of these have been dealt with in Chapter 6. But Britain's air pollution confers a peculiar distinction – bronchitis – known on the Continent as the 'English disease'. It kills off five times more Britons than road accidents do. The incidence of bronchitis in the towns is much more serious than in the countryside: the death rate from it in industrial Warrington is six times that in the seaside resort of Hastings.

INDUSTRIAL

The greatest impact on the quality of our air came with the Industrial Revolution. Vast clouds of smoke and noxious fumes poured over the country and led to descriptions such as that given in the report (1875–6) of the first Chief Alkali Inspector:

Is it not true that those coming into Widnes, even from very dark and gloomy skies, enter that town with a certain awe and horror and wonder if life can be sustained there. . . . Persons told me that when they went to take up their residence in Newcastle they looked from that great high-level bridge on to the Tyne and cried in a kind of despair at the banishment from the south-west, which if not always sunny, is at least always supplied with clean air.

Air pollution was probably at its most vicious when the heavy chemical industry expanded in the nineteenth century.

The absence of any planning, inadequate technological knowledge and the 'hands-off' attitude of many industrialists led to whole localities being degraded by noxious fumes.

The worst offender was the factory producing soda. Following an official inquiry, the first Alkali Act was passed in 1863 and this laid the foundations for a control of industrial emissions as thorough as competitive international economics and technological progress then allowed. The 1863 Act and the codifying Act of 1906, on which the present system is mainly based, recognized that it is not always possible to eliminate all noxious emissions. The 1960 Act required gases to be rendered harmless and inoffensive before discharge into the atmosphere.

The improvements effected by the official Alkali Inspectorate* (coupled with the recognition that smoke pin-pointed inefficient equipment) have led to great progress. Industrial smoke is now much less of a problem. Modern industrial extraction plant can remove over 99 per cent of grit and dust. The Clean Air Act 1956 allowed industrialists seven years to replace out-of-date plants. A similar concession was given for existing furnaces in 1971 in regulations under the Clean Air Acts of 1956 and 1968. For the first time ever, the quantities of grit and dust that may be emitted from a wide range of furnaces are restricted. The regulations, which applied that year to new furnaces and made it an offence to exceed the limits, represent a significant step in cleansing the air over Britain.

Sulphur Dioxide

The main industrial air pollutant is still sulphur dioxide. Huge quantities are emitted by chemical plants, oil refineries and power stations, in fact, wherever coal, coke or oil are burned. It combines with water vapour in the atmosphere to form droplets of sulphuric acid. This occurs not only under damp, rainy conditions but also wherever industrial plants discharge large quantities of steam into the atmosphere. And at present there is no solution wholly acceptable on technical and economic grounds.

One method, used at the London power stations of Battersea

* Now H.M. Alkali and Clean Air Inspectorate.

and Bankside, is to wash out the sulphur dioxide from the flue gas before emission. This, however, makes the smoke plume cold and wet; on days when the natural dispersive powers of the atmosphere are low, it sinks to ground level and can cause serious pollution. This method is also very expensive and gives rise to water pollution.

At present, the only practicable method is to disperse the sulphur-bearing gases as widely as possible and thus to minimize any concentration. This is done by discharging the flue gas at high velocity (nearly 80 km p.h.) through a tall chimney (about 200 m). The gases thus ejected usually rise to around 600 m and spread over a large area. To disperse this sulphur dioxide pollution the chimneys should be as high as possible. Their height, which may be controlled by local authorities, should ideally be at least $2\frac{1}{2}$ times that of the nearest physical feature – building or landscape. It is, however, often impracticable to do this if there are high and low buildings packed rather closely together in the same area, and it is in such instances that there is danger of the chimney from a low building causing pollution at the windows of an adjacent tower block of offices or flats.

The high chimney policy and the Clean Air legislation have worked for Britain; although the emission of sulphur dioxide has remained fairly steady there has been a fall of 40 per cent in the concentration of this gas at ground level in urban areas. And this is despite a 10 per cent increase in population and a 17 per cent increase in annual consumption of gross energy since 1956. The Clean Air Council has estimated that, from a peak of $6\frac{1}{2}$ million tonnes around 1965, sulphur dioxide emission will fall steadily, from 5·9 million tonnes in 1970 to estimates of 5·54 in 1975 and 5·16 in 1985.

But this control of sulphur dioxide is a complex problem and depends on many resource factors. For example, coal that is low in sulphur is probably 20 per cent more expensive than high sulphur coal; heavy fuel oil can have a high or low sulphur content according to the crude oil from which it is derived, but it may have more sulphur than most coals; natural gas normally contains no sulphur; and nuclear power produces none. But each source of fuel has disadvantages – technological, economic and social – and all lead to some other impacts on the environment which may nullify apparent advantages in relation to sulphur dioxide.

Outdoor Industry

In some areas there is also serious air pollution from the brick, lime, scrap metal and other 'outdoor' industries. This can be remedied or lessened by equipment such as wet sprayers, screens and filters, but it is sometimes difficult to get the industrialist to employ them. The 1956 Act requires proof that the neighbourhood affected by the pollution is inhabited. The processes of the alkali legislation may not apply. The nuisance provisions of the Public Health Act 1936 require any abatement notice to specify the works to be done to remedy the nuisance. So progress is slow. The primary fault lies, of course, in the indifference of the public.

Control

The system of control today is based upon registration of industrial works listed in legislation (usually on criteria of size, complexity of control and difficulty of the emission problems), the requirement to use 'the best practicable means' to prevent or minimize emissions of noxious or offensive gases and upon supervision by H.M. Alkali and Clean Air Inspectorate, which has wide powers and authority for these purposes.

There are thousands of non-registered industrial premises whose emissions are subject to the control and supervision of the local authorities Public Health Inspectorate, operating under the Public Health Act 1936 and the Clean Air Act 1956. The policy and action pursued are those of the local authorities which have powers to take action to deal with 'statutory nuisances', to enforce the regulations against 'dark smoke', and to ensure that new furnaces can operate smokelessly and have means to arrest grit and dust.

The Control of Pollution Act 1974 provided new powers for local authorities and the Government's Inspectorate. The

Government took powers to impose regulations about the composition and contents of motor vehicle fuel, with local authorities being given the duty to enforce them. Other regulations imposed limits on the sulphur content of oil fuel used in furnaces or engines, except where the furnaces come under the Alkali Act, in which case it is the task of the Government Inspectorate.

The Act also enabled local authorities to undertake or contribute to research relevant to air pollution and to arrange for the publication of information about it, with powers to require, by notice, information about air pollution. These powers obviously require close cooperation between local authorities and industrialists if they are to be successfully employed. As most of the new powers are discretionary and do not involve significant public expenditure, they were not directly affected by Government economy measures in 1975, although clearly the financial problems of local authorities are inhibiting rapid progress.

DOMESTIC

By far the worst offender in Britain is the domestic coal-burning fire; it still produced in the mid seventies over 85 per cent of the smoke in our atmosphere. The majority of Britons live in small houses with small rooms heated by coal fires and the bituminous coal they have favoured gives off much smoke. Every 100 kg of coal burned in an open domestic fire pours out 2·5 to 5 kg of smoke; from a factory chimney the same amount gives only about 0·2. In 1971 domestic fires were estimated to be sending 0·7 million tonnes of smoke and 100,000 tonnes of grit into the atmosphere.

The problem is both psychological – most people like the glow of the open fire – and, again, economic. Supplies of coke and some of the treated smokeless coal fuels (usually dearer than coal) have not always been adequate in all areas. In the more prosperous South, many families use these smokeless fuels, gas and electricity, and many have central heating. This has, therefore, led to considerable progress here in reducing air pollution from domestic sources. And the benefits are far-reaching.

In the North and Midlands, the preference for coal fires is still strong. This, the proximity to mining communities, which get large supplies, and a tradition of profligate use, combine to create serious air pollution. Happily, the rapid spread of higher standards of living and the desire for up-to-date and cleaner forms of heating should have cleared up the smoke problem in these areas in a few years.

The Clean Air Act 1956 enables local authorities, with ministerial approval, to declare smoke control areas or 'smokeless zones', in which the emission of any smoke from chimneys is an offence. By the end of 1971 there were less than twenty authorities in the 'black' areas – the densely populated industrial areas which suffer most from air pollution – which had not made a start on smoke control. A Government circular (53/71) required all 'black' area authorities to review and speed up their programmes, and advised that no difficulties were expected over the supply of smokeless fuels. Although smoke control is obviously less needed in, say, a national park than in an industrial city, nevertheless the Government urged all authorities – 'black' and 'white' – to get ahead with smoke control programmes. Generally, industry has progressed more rapidly than domestic users, so that smoke emission is now about 15 per cent from industry and over 80 per cent from homes.

The Clean Air legislation of 1968 has greatly increased Ministers' powers to promote action. It widened and strengthened the scope of the 1956 Act, particularly to deal with specific sources of pollution which are more obvious with the gradual elimination of the 'smogs' and severe pollution of past decades.

Over 90 per cent of the Greater London area is covered by smoke control orders. With air as clean as in many countryside districts, Central London demonstrates the successes of the policies and measures of the past two decades. As noted on page 109, visibility between December and February is now enhanced and there is much more midwinter sunshine than a decade ago. Buildings have been cleaned and they stay clean longer. Undoubtedly, increasing material affluence has facilitated the wider use of solid smokeless fuels, electricity, gas and oil and led to this much cleaner atmosphere. And these improvements are only likely to be marginally affected by the economic recession of the mid seventies, as the increased comfort and convenience of modern methods have become part of the way of life. By the 1980s, domestic smoke should no longer be a concern to most urban communities.

TRAFFIC

The Clean Air Acts do not apply to road vehicles, which are controlled by regulations, generally regarded as inadequate, made under road traffic legislation. Pollution from motor vehicles is becoming the prime offender in many urban areas. Diesel engines, if properly maintained and operated, cause negligible pollution. Unfortunately, there are in Britain too many lorries emitting thick, black fumes and more stringent controls and enforcement are required.

Petrol engines are a most intractable problem. Their exhaust fumes contain a complex mixture of pollutants, particularly carbon monoxide. Tests by the British National Society for Clean Air have shown a high proportion of vehicles emitting more than 4·5 per cent of carbon monoxide in these exhaust gases while idling – a hazard prohibited by legislation in France, Western Germany and Sweden. Proper tuning and adjustment can ameliorate this, but so far no wholly satisfactory and economic method of eliminating it has been found. Some solution is essential on amenity grounds, because of the filth and stench, apart from possible dangers to health where there are heavy concentrations of fumes. New regulations to reduce air pollution (and noise levels) from new vehicles were introduced in Britain in the seventies as E.E.C. countries developed more controls. These measures and those of the U.S.A. should lead the world motor industry to bring this pollution under control by the late seventies.

NOISE

Noise – 'any sound, especially loud or harsh or undesired one' (C.O.D.). One man's noise is often another man's special pleasure, whether it be overloud Wagner or pop music, and unwanted and excessive noise injures. It causes deafness, stress, irritation, breeds resentment, saps energy, and inevitably lowers efficiency. Noise is today recognized as a serious personal and environmental pollutant, pressurizing everyone to some extent.

Britain has had, since 1959, the advantage of the Noise Abatement Society, an independent voluntary body which has pioneered in educational activities, lobbying for legislation, informing the public and fostering protective methods and research. Its work led to the Noise Abatement Act of 1960 and has done much to create the climate of opinion for the setting up in Britain of the Government's Noise Advisory Council in 1970 and the measures against noise in the Control of Pollution Act 1974. The Society is also active in some thirty countries and represents Britain on the Executive Council of the International Association against Noise.

The Council's chairman is the Secretary of State for the Environment, who coordinates government policy on noise. He appoints about twenty-four members, drawn from local government, industry, universities, research agencies, and voluntary environmental bodies. The Department's Noise Policy and Clean Air Division services the Council, whose basic work is done by Working Groups. These are studying noise as a hazard to hearing, noise from surface transport and air traffic, and measures to implement the 1974 Act. This introduced controls on noise in streets and from plant and machinery and gave local authorities powers to designate noise abatement zones. Local authorities are required to monitor the noise levels in designated zones and to record and control the levels.

The Council has published several reports and leaflets, including *Bothered by Noise* – a layman's guide to the legal provisions for the control of noise. This explains how individuals can act or initiate action to reduce noise from road and air traffic, noise on construction sites and in industry, general and minor noise nuisances, and noise in abatement zones. This leaflet briefly touches on the issue of compensation for depreciation value, insulation against aircraft noise and participation in planning and noise, referring on to more specific leaflets.

Two reports by the Council in 1974 merit special mention. *Noise in Public Places* reviewed the problem of abating noise which causes nuisance in public places, with particular regard to the model byelaws designed to control such noise. It recommended wider powers to regulate noise, for planning control over noise, for the control of noise from public houses and other premises covered by the Licensing Laws, to deal with amplified sound (e.g. from mobile shops, pop festivals) and the noisy motor sports and a wide range of miscellaneous nuisances.

Noise in the Next Ten Years reports on the prospect from the four major causes of pollution: road and aircraft traffic and neighbourhood and occupational noise and proposes measures to deal with them. All increasingly intrude into our lives and are, the Report considers, the products of ignorance and inertia in the past. To tackle them will need a demonstration of political will at all levels throughout the country, with strong efforts to overcome a fatalistic approach and an attitude of resignation about noise pollution.

Clearly, the work of the Council and the Society needs stronger support from everyone, with the aims of eliminating noise as much as possible at source and of inculcating in each individual the duty to be considerate.

SURVEY AND MONITORING

The Government's Warren Spring Laboratory carries out a national survey of pollution, with daily measurements at some 1,100 sites in 450 towns and in rural areas. This survey pinpoints where action is most urgently needed, promotes good planning and gives further data about effects on health. The Laboratory is also studying methods of preventing the emission of pollutants and of facilitating their dispersal in towns, although dispersal can never be a substitute for prevention. Local authorities also monitor levels of grit, dust and other solids at about 600 sites in England and Wales.

Appraisal

Britain is one of the countries most advanced in the study and prevention of air pollution. Its comprehensive statutory system is unrivalled and enables Britain to make a strong contribution internationally.

The Government-appointed Clean Air Council (set up under the 1956 Act) has an important role in dealing with most of the issues referred to in this chapter. It keeps a close watch on progress over the control of domestic smoke, sulphur dioxide levels, lead emissions from factories and alongside some motorways, pollution from asbestos, and grit and dust arrestment from cement works. Its reports and publications show clearly the problems and progress.

Much depends on the National Society for Clean Air – a powerful voluntary body which is working to abolish all forms of air pollution. It expects Britain to be smokeless within 10 to 15 years. The Society has achieved a great deal in the field of public education and has produced some excellent leaflets and reports on conference proceedings. There is now little excuse for any local authority which pleads ignorance or public apathy, and fails to put into effect the regulations at its disposal. Clearly, however, a greater integration of factors governing air pollution is needed at all levels of environmental planning and building design.

Above all, there is the major problem for the country of deciding how much it is prepared to pay and what standards the individual will observe in order to secure clean air. It is a complex problem to strike a balance in this case between the desire for clean air, which is technically realizable, and the cost of obtaining and maintaining it everywhere.

CHAPTER 8

WATER

Everything originated in the water,
Everything is sustained by water.

Goethe

WITHOUT water all life ceases. Man is two thirds water. The surface of the globe is seven tenths water. Yet men and animals still die of thirst, plants wither and deserts increase. Historically, water has determined the location of settlements and industry and the choice of routes. If anything, its influence in all these ways is even greater today. The 1960s will go down in history as years of great drought. Famine menaced the peoples of India and some African countries as crops failed without water and as populations increased. Much of the shortage was due to, or accentuated by, faulty management. Unless effective action is soon taken to conserve water and improve supplies in many countries, this century may be dominated by drought.

The mass of the peoples on this earth are profligate in their use of water, probably because so few pay its real worth. In some countries there is a proper respect for water, induced by its cost; for example, the supply of water, which will have been purified of salt, might cost in hot desert areas ten times as much as the average price in Britain; in fact, many British families get all the water they need (average consumption 168 litres per person per day) for a water rate of a few pounds yearly. Similarly, industry may also pay ten times more than industry in Britain, where the cost is very low in some areas.

Vast sums have to be spent on reservoirs and water distribution schemes in many countries, and their cost may ultimately lead to water being priced and treated as the vital natural resource it is. In fact, although so much of the earth's surface is water, 97 per cent of it is salt water. A third of the remainder is frozen in glaciers or polar ice-caps, and the minute amount left over is not evenly distributed – the temperate zones get most of it.

However, in many temperate zones the waste of water continues and rivers are polluted by the effluent from houses and industry. There are annual alternations of flood and drought, often in the same areas. This deplorable state of affairs is at last receiving some attention on the necessary scale, both in Europe and the U.S.A., mainly through the legitimate pressures arising from the vast increase in demand by agriculture and industry, and from the new range of values assumed by water as it becomes the focal point of outdoor recreation for the mass populations. In many areas the lakes and waterways now have a new significance since the development of hovercraft. They will become highways to places hitherto almost inaccessible.

These pressures and values also create more awareness of our seas and oceans. Worldwide, there is great concern over their deteriorating condition and in some areas (including the Baltic, Mediterranean, and Irish Sea) fear about the already serious consequences of their pollution, so much of which derives from treating our rivers as sewers.

SUPPLY

First, where does the water come from? The figure opposite illustrates the water or hydrological cycle. Water is evaporated by the sun, carried as vapour and clouds in the atmosphere, and condensed by temperature changes to fall as rain, hail, sleet or snow. The amount of water available changes little – only its form. The water coming out of a tap today may once have slaked the thirst of an ancient caveman or a prehistoric animal.

One of man's main objectives is to forecast and control the natural process so that ultimately the water can be directed to where it is most needed. Such power is a long way off. Effort is generally concentrated at present on conserving water and modifying its distribution and quality in order to get the right amount to the right place at the right time. Considerable resources are devoted to bringing water from remote upland

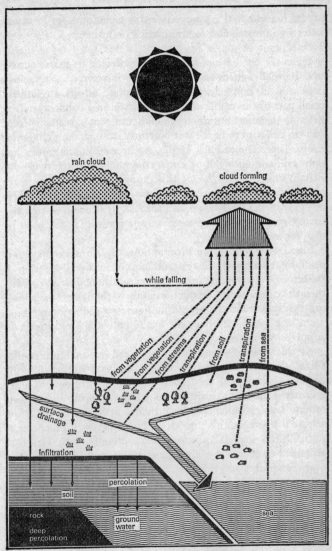

Figure 7. Water cycle (B. H. Grimes)

valleys to industrial towns, to devising techniques for re-use of water by industry and to eliminating pollution.

One point of major importance is that the *total* available water in the cycle is not substantially affected by man's activities. Rainfall figures show that man's interference at various points in the flow of water on the ground affects a relatively small part of the whole water cycle. Even in a country such as Britain, the distribution of rainfall can vary greatly – from 500 cm per annum in the wet North West to 50 cm per annum in the drier zone of East Anglia. An average annual precipitation (rain and snow) of 75 cm is common and is the figure for Britain and the U.S.A. Of this, approximately 50 cm is returned to the atmosphere through evaporation and transpiration from plants. Perhaps at the most 7·5 cm, and usually less than 5 cm, of the water remaining is controlled and used by man for water supply.

Small variations in this ground flow, therefore, can have far-reaching effects. If the ground cover is altered so that it facilitates evaporation, or the water is drained very rapidly, then the consequential reduction in the yield of water available can be crucial. On the preceding figures, a reduction of about 5 cm is a loss of 20 per cent in the potential yield for water supply of an area.

At this point both surface water and ground (under-the-surface) water are being considered. Surface water has for long been measured and controlled in varying degree but until recently insufficient effort has gone into exploring and tapping ground water, which usually provides at least half the water required by vegetation and trees. Now there are prospects of utilizing the great lakes below the deserts of North Africa. In Britain, however, very large quantities are taken from underground aquifers and this is increasing with the development of pumping schemes to tap the vast supplies of water underneath the Thames Valley.

Another important feature of the water cycle is that the movement of water in untouched rivers and natural channels is generally slower than when man has interfered – for example, with engineering works. Left to nature, water usually percolates through numerous outlets in soils, bogs, mosses, fens and woodlands. These act as sponges, retaining water in wet seasons and releasing it in dry. They exercise a moderating effect on the flow of water and enable it to make its special and vital contribution to the life cycle and the renewal of natural resources. Where man has cleared the forests, denuded the mountains of vegetation, straightened and dredged river banks and beds and provided geometrical patterns of drainage channels, then the water cascades and rushes to reservoir or sea and cannot properly fulfil its life-giving role. Furthermore it can become an agency of destruction, carrying with it the rich top-soil, leaving lower water tables (the level of the water below the surface of the land), impoverishing agriculture, silting-up reservoirs and flooding townships. Many floods of this kind occur every year in most temperate countries.

Some water authorities oppose the afforestation of their catchment areas, contending that trees transpire more than other types of vegetation and so planting them will result in a loss of water. Often overlooked are the many other benefits derived from tree cover, particularly a more stable ecology, the retention of more water in the soil and tree roots and possibilities of multi-purpose use. Unfortunately, this controversy cannot be settled by any reference to a nice, tidy balance sheet. No one has been able to work out yet the exact value of any woodland to a society nor, in particular, its role in the water cycle. Much more research is required into the effects of different forms of land use and management – especially the multi-purpose use of catchment areas and gathering grounds – on the supply of water and on the implications of such uses for the quality of the water.

At present no one knows enough about the long-term implications of draining for agricultural use ('improving') the boggy uplands from which so much water derives. The functions of wetlands – marshes, estuaries, swamps, gravel pits and other shallow waters – in the water cycle are insufficiently understood, although more people are realizing that these areas form part of the complex balance of a whole river basin. Clearly, they must contribute to the maintenance of the water table of adjoining land and perform a regulating function within the water cycle. One aspect of which there can be no doubt is their role in providing food for wildlife, and sport and recreation for man.

Flood plains are another natural feature of considerable importance. These stretches of below-river or river-level land in the lower reaches of rivers play a vital role in coping with floods. This function has greatly increased in importance over the past hundred years as overgrazing, deforestation and soil erosion in upland areas have led to more severe flooding. Unfortunately, many urban developments encroach on flood plains, which are usually accessible and easy to build on. For this and many other reasons it is essential that land planners cooperate closely with river authorities.

DEMAND

It is expected that world water needs will have increased fourfold by A.D. 2000. First, direct consumption by man is increasing at a tremendous rate, not only because of the rising populations, but because of the higher living standards to which water is the key. The purity and quality now expected of water are higher and its range of uses for hygiene and for sanitation increases daily. Authorities have to cope, too, with a quickly fluctuating demand; in Amsterdam the water authorities assess the quantity of water required in their controlled rivers by the peaks of domestic water used when television programmes finish.

Despite the tremendous increase in the amount of water required for personal and family needs, these domestic uses take only about ten per cent of the water supply. The covering-up of much of the land surface by urban development means, however, that the rain in these areas is no longer absorbed by the ground but is washed away. Expensive sewers are, therefore, usually required to avoid flooding.

Agriculture and industry are the great consumers and account for roughly 55 and 35 per cent respectively of all water used. Where water can be made available for continuous irrigation of crops it is estimated that on suitable ground it can give rise to a tenfold increase in yield. The development of large-scale, long-distance canal and pipeline projects, as in Holland, Belgium and Israel, is leading to vast and increasing demands for water. In industry, particularly for hydro-electric power and for the rapidly expanding range of chemical products, there is an almost unquenchable thirst for more water. Prodigious quantities are used; for example, the water required to produce a tonne of cement is 3,600 litres, of coke 18,000 litres, of paper about 270,000 and of artificial silk 680,000 litres. It even requires 350 litres of water to make a litre of beer! Although industry everywhere is re-using many times over the water from its processes, it is often expensive to remove impurities before re-use and to dispose of them and the polluted water.

Demand and shortages grow together. Water shortages are the product of many factors. They reflect society's failure to conserve the rainfall and direct it to where it is needed. This is an indication of faulty attitudes and economic values. Too little money and effort has been expended on, for instance, research into new underground sources, the relationship of natural features in the water cycle and methods of removing salt from sea-water (desalination).

Long-term solutions to the shortage of water require more than reservoirs, dams and *ad hoc* schemes. Water must be studied and dealt with by teams of professionals, land managers, and many scientists – geologists and pedologists, climatologists and meteorologists, biologists and botanists. These studies must be based on a thorough understanding of the inter-relationship of natural forces, and a detailed knowledge of the water cycle and where and how best to direct it for man's use. All concerned with the conservation and supply of water must appreciate the unity of the many natural features in river basins.

POLLUTION

Quality is obviously an important consideration for water authorities. For this reason, where they are unable to carry out full purification of drinking water supplies they quite properly object to animals grazing on reservoir gathering grounds and people indulging in recreational or other activities likely to lead to pollution. In practice, ground water may remain polluted for many years. In its slow passage through numerous outlets it is less susceptible to natural 'flushing' whereas a river carries most pollutants out to sea relatively quickly.

A major effort is, however, needed to reduce and, in time perhaps, to eliminate the heavy pollution of lakes and rivers which has such disastrous and far-reaching effects. Many rivers are mere open sewers, loaded with the refuse and filth of town and industries. The water is poisonous to aquatic flora and fauna and the result is desolation.

The capacity of a lake or river to cleanse itself disappears with the loss of its natural organisms. Rivers should be treated as living, interlocking systems of dissolved nutrients and elements and of plants and animals. Kept in better health, they would be able to withstand some pollution. In effect, they would 'digest' it and provide healthy water. But this natural balance of rivers has been destroyed over much of the globe.

Many famous lakes and rivers are afflicted with pollution. The Rhine is a specially serious problem; horticulture, floriculture and drinking water supplies dependent upon the Rhine suffer seriously despite the activities since 1950 of the International Commission for the Protection of the Rhine against Pollution which comprises representatives of France, Luxembourg, Netherlands, Switzerland and West Germany.

In North America the pollution of the Great Lakes, particularly Lake Erie, led to a joint United States–Canada project in the seventies to coordinate measures to combat water pollution and to restore the quality of the Lakes. A wide-ranging programme includes controls over pollution by all forms of wastes, phosphorus discharges, toxic heavy metals, radioactive wastes, pesticides and by thermal sources. Greater powers and resources have been assigned to the International Joint Commission to enable it to restore and protect water quality, and a special contingency plan has been developed to respond to immediate threats.

Many rivers are the major sources of supply for drinking water in towns. Although filtration and chlorination have reached high technical standards, they are not able to keep pace with many of the new discharges into rivers. For example, it is unlikely that the treatment processes now in use can cope adequately with all the many fertilizers and pesticides which leach through the soil on agricultural land into ditches, streams, rivers and lakes.

The Hague Water Supply uses an ingenious method for reducing pollution from river water required for urban purposes. Between 1949 and 1955 an enormous project was completed to bring water from the River Lek (the Rhine) to The Hague (Holland). The heavily polluted river water has to be cleansed of much silt and organic matter before it can be pumped through the pipeline to the city. To make the water drinkable it is fed into sand-dunes nearby from which the main water supply has been obtained since 1874. The natural filtration effected by the sand-dunes gives a much-improved and better-tasting water. The scheme replenishes the underground reserve of water, an additional safeguard when the river water is too polluted to be pumped through the pipeline or when part of the project breaks down. In addition, small lakes have been created and these have led to considerable changes in the flora and fauna of the dunes, parts of which are used for public recreation.

The cost of eliminating pollution entirely from rivers would be prohibitive at present in most countries. It should, however, be possible to reduce pollution considerably and to prevent the development of obvious new sources. Pollution can also ruin the use of water for outdoor recreation. More money should be collected from recreation and some of this spent on diminishing pollution.

Cleaner water is not only necessary for public health but also for industry, which has to have good-quality water for many processes. But much more research is essential into all aspects of the supply of and demand for water. Standards of tolerances must be established for varying uses. Financially feasible technological aids are required to prevent or reduce pollution, both at its source and in the rivers, and to help calculate the true 'carrying capacity' of individual rivers and lakes.

A further major problem in many countries is that some pollution is often difficult to trace. It frequently originates long distances away from its impact, often outside the area of the authority which has to take action. This problem of assessing the social costs and benefits of securing clean water is, therefore, usually closely related to the structure of local government.

Conflict

Shortage, surfeit and pollution of water are major issues facing society. In many localities all three occur with disastrous and costly frequency. Inevitably, authorities will have to limit the individual's freedom to waste, misuse or pollute water. These limitations are essential if posterity is to have pure water. Water has always been a source of conflict. In Britain a great body of common law has been built up from case after case dealing with individual and commercial rights. Legislation abounds in every country on the rights and obligations of riparian owners and the uses of wells and surface waters, and it will be an exceedingly difficult operation to relate these traditional principles to the measures necessary for the full development of river-basin resources.

The conflicts are spreading. In England, large industrial cities, such as Birmingham and Manchester, have met much opposition to obtaining water from Wales and the Lake District National Park respectively; in the wet South West, water shortage often bedevils the towns. On the Continent there are many areas of conflict, extending from hydro-electric schemes and polluted lakes in Scandinavia, surprisingly in the Netherlands over uses of reclaimed water, in Belgium especially over water extraction from the beautiful Ardennes, and in most other countries, including inevitably the water-short countries of the Mediterranean. In many cases opposition has developed, not only from farmers and villagers but also from tourist and amenity organizations. In the U.S.A. the major cities, such as

Los Angeles and New York, frequently face a critical situation over their water supplies. And, elsewhere, many developing countries lack reliable supplies of usable water.

Scientists, members of the professions, public servants, voluntary bodies and industrialists contend, in private and public, with members of every group on opposite sides. All profess that the common good is best served by their own use of the available water. With the increasing recreational use of water, conflict becomes more personal and cuts vertically through all strata of society. An angler on the bank needs a small space and quiet, a fisherman in a rowing boat may require ·2 ha, but a water-skier requires 20 ha and his speedboat may pollute. There are many adjustments to be made between all users if the full potential of water for recreation is to be realized.

POLICIES

Clearly a national policy is essential for all aspects of the conservation, supply and use of water. It should be part of the strategy for developing the environment at all levels. Farsighted, imaginative planning is required. What specific lines of approach are needed to get sound long-term policies for water?

Rivers should be regulated for optimal use as a whole; for example, the re-use of water *en route* to the sea is very important. Subject to this principle, water abstraction ought normally to be as near the mouth of the river as salinity allows. The piping of water from upland reservoirs is an ecologically unsound practice. It prevents the use of the natural channels of streams and rivers, and it stops the water from fulfilling many useful functions. The maintenance of flood plains must be given priority; in watersheds soil conservation practices – such as terracing, contour ploughing, multiple small-scale damming and vegetation planting – need to become part of the normal management of the land; and water-drainage schemes ought to be based on multiple-use possibilities and conservation principles. More utilization of underground supplies and new techniques of storage are required – for instance, treating or covering the water in reservoirs with chemicals to reduce evaporation.

Governments in North America and Europe now allocate large resources of manpower and money on research and development. Private enterprise is also devoting much research effort to water for industry. Few people have yet realized the flexibility in the location of industry which could result from readily accessible cheap water. This may also have a profound influence on the world economy, as at present many areas with reserves of energy – for example, oil – are short of water. With these two major resources and a rapidly expanding population, some countries could change their status within decades.

To secure and maintain high-quality water requires an expensive outlay of skill and other scarce resources. In order to bring home to the individual its real worth, charges for water – for consumption and recreation – may have to be more direct. It may be necessary to devise systems for domestic as well as industrial consumers which differentiate between different qualities of water so that, for example, people stop cheerfully using the same tap for drinking, washing and cleaning the car! If new sources are not soon available in many countries, it may become necessary to install water meters everywhere, as well as devices which automatically regulate the supply. Systems for re-use of, say, domestic water could be mass-produced for installation in new houses. Strict financial and other penalties will be necessary to prevent misuse and pollution of water.

To carry out these policies a central authority is needed which can maintain a continuous survey of available water resources and develop potential supplies. Such an authority would initiate the necessary scientific and technological research; it would establish broad priorities between domestic, agricultural, industrial, transport, recreational and other uses and ensure that its strategy is implemented. A specific task for the central authority is to develop the teams of scientists and professionals necessary for this work and to ensure that there are sufficient trained personnel for all levels of the water industry.

Regional development plans should embody measures for

the conservation and use of water. There should be close co-operation between the central organization, the regional govern-ments, their supporting authorities and the river authorities. Ideally, the best geographic and administrative unit for water conservation, supply and pollution control, is the river drain-age basin, that is, the whole territory drained by the river and its tributaries. But this will rarely coincide with the areas of local authorities; hence the need for coordination at regional level, and close cooperation at local level.

INTERNATIONAL

Under the pressure of increasingly acute water shortages, and with a high level of international cooperation, arrangements in most countries are being rapidly overhauled. Many changes have been made in Europe. Britain now has a system as ad-vanced as any in the world, and other countries are adopting similar measures. In the U.S.A. a top-level Water Resources Council guides national activity, and River Basin Commissions plan the use and development of water resources. Conser-vation legislation provides extensive Federal powers to cleanse the vast river systems and lakes of the U.S.A. and then to maintain them at much higher standards. In particular, the U.S.A. is pioneering conservation measures to establish a national system of 'wild rivers'.

Water is an important subject of international cooperation. Since 1860 over forty European conventions have been con-cluded. One of the most essential, and long overdue, was that signed in 1963 to protect the Rhine against pollution. It is not surprising, therefore, that there are numerous organizations active in undertaking research, seeking knowledge and for-mulating agreements for general observance. One example was the International Hydrological Decade, organized by Unesco, in which fifty-nine countries cooperated in a ten-year programme of research which ended in 1974. The issues studied included the balance of water at all points of the water cycle; the influence of man on water supplies; and technical research on erosion and the composition of water.

National arrangements for water are obviously of international importance in the case of the surface flow of rivers and lakes which straddle boundaries, less obvious with the movement of air masses affected by the management of the hydrological cycle. As water becomes a more expensive resource, it affects costs of production and trade. As people travel more, their needs and preferences alter and so do their value judgements about the quality of the environment and the importance of water.

Following a specialist review of freshwater pollution, the Council of Europe has prepared general principles for the conservation, supply and use of water which all member countries are recommended to adopt. The Council has also published a 'Water Charter', to put over the ideas which every citizen must be helped to understand and to act upon.

It initiated a European Wetlands Campaign from 1976 to provide a base for long-term conservation of these often underestimated and misused key areas. Wetlands comprise canals, estuaries, fens, gravel pits, marshes, peatlands, swamps and other water bodies – man-made and natural. They are biologically amongst the richest and most varied features of the environment and are of great importance to most of man's activities.

The increasing prospect that large-scale desalination will be required to augment world water supplies is yet another reason for preventing any pollution of the seas. Fortunately, an International Convention for the Prevention of Pollution of the Sea by Oil was signed in 1954. Its coverage was extended in 1962 and its rules are now observed by most countries. The convention stimulated the major oil companies to devise new techniques for minimizing pollution from tankers and pipelines but continuing oil spillages and incidents show that the problem is not yet under control.

The first major international agreement to stop marine pollution by dumping from ships and aircraft was signed by most European countries in 1972. Covering a wide range of poisonous substances and extending over the North-East Atlantic and North Sea, it points to arrangements on a world scale.

MARINE

In the past decade, there has been increasing recognition of the importance and urgency of remedying the pollution of the seas and oceans. Obviously their condition is inter-related with and dependent upon the health of rivers and lakes and the scale and quality of the development and management of coastal lands. The Mediterranean and Black Sea reveal sadly how rapidly the excesses of industry and urbanization, and chemicals used on land, can lead to severe pollution. Heavy metals damage and in some cases kill marine life. The inter-action of oil and other substances not only besmirches pleasure beaches but creates a film which affects the process of photo-synthesis and marine flora and fauna generally. Domestic sewage fouls beaches from Spain to Israel and large growths of seaweed puzzle, and sometimes frighten, holidaymakers. Other seas and parts of the oceans have their own particular permutation of such effects of misuse and pollution. The Baltic suffered for some years, but was reported in 1975 to have been 'flushed out' by clean Atlantic waters in the course of a natural cycle. Nevertheless, the pollutants must have some effects on the marine flora and fauna of the waters in which they move and it is, therefore, essential to seek to identify natural changes and those induced by man, so that the long-term implications can be understood.

The main pollutants are now numerous: pesticides and detergents from the land; effluents and discharges from industry and ships; domestic sewage; heavy metal compounds and solid objects; dredging spoil and mining; oil; and, increasingly, chemical and nuclear waste. However carefully the latter are contained there is risk in adding these long-term hazards to the increasingly diverse pressures on the seas and oceans from man's urban, industrial and leisure activities.

The resources of the oceans have been the subject of intensive research and exploration in recent decades. The discovery and winning of oil in the North Sea and off the Californian coast has attracted most attention with a lot of effort having gone into dealing with problems of oil pollution –

though more is required. The exploitation of whales, dolphins and seals and some fishing areas gives rise to much concern. Unfortunately, in the rapid expansion of ocean fisheries, much more has been done to apply modern technology to 'hunt' more fish than to research into the basic issues of biology and population dynamics so essential to a long-term sustained yield from ocean fishing.

Mineral resources in many seas and oceans are now being explored at depths thought impossible a decade or so ago. As methods of extraction from low-grade ores are continually being improved and easily accessible resources on land diminish for many reasons (e.g. shortage, political and economic factors), so the prospects of extensive sea-bed mining come nearer, with all the attendant implications for the ecological health of the oceans.

Coastal marine systems are transition zones uniting land and sea. They depend very much on watersheds, whose mismanagement or over-development can significantly affect them. Reclamation of coastal areas and barrage schemes can also exert a major influence on coastal marine systems, whose mobility and dynamic character render very expensive, and often pointless, attempts to stabilize beaches – as coastal erosion authorities and the managers of some nuclear power stations sited on the coast are only too well aware.

Nature conservationists, supported by marine scientists and leaders in the sea-sports (fishermen, skin-divers, and so on), campaigned for some years for the formation of marine parks and reserves on an international and regional basis. The International Union for Conservation of Nature and Natural Resources (I.U.C.N.) has held a number of Conferences to formulate criteria, guide-lines and objectives, as, for example, in 1975 with the Governments of the areas surrounding the northern parts of the Indian Ocean. At this the local problems, including those of the Red Sea and the Persian Gulf, were examined.

These Conferences have produced a number of agreed principles and general recommendations. The principles expound the value of marine and coastal resources, give guidelines for planning and development and set out the functions of marine parks and reserves. The Governments of the region were recommended to survey their areas, to identify sites suitable for parks and reserves, and to undertake research and monitoring; they were aided in this work by the Conferences identifying a large number of potential marine parks and reserves in the waters of the participating countries.

But marine parks and reserves are urgently needed throughout the world in order to conserve genetic resources, essential fisheries and key species and the high inter-related biological productivity of many marshes and swamps. The areas to be conserved should be large enough to contain important and representative ecosystems within buffer zones, as well as unique communities and habitats. Only a few countries so far have taken action to conserve such areas, hence the initiatives by I.U.C.N. in fostering regional conferences to select marine parks and reserves.

Appraisal

Policies for the conservation, supply and wise use of water are required at all levels – international, national and regional – with effective measures for their implementation. Particularly at regional level, these must be closely integrated with the needs of farmers, industrialists, householders and sportsmen.

Water must be studied and dealt with as a precious natural resource. This requires a systematic inventory of known supplies, research into ways to use them or to develop alternatives, and action to prevent pollution.

People should be educated and informed about the importance of water and the need for its wise use. Without such an awareness, it will be difficult to deal with the many complex problems involved, for example, in guaranteeing minimum flows of river water at certain places and times; in retaining surface water and regulating water-courses; in protecting some areas and allowing others to be used; and in constructing estuarine barrages. Above all, perhaps, people should know the causes of the floods that seasonally affect them and the droughts that imperil their industries and disrupt their daily routines.

CHAPTER 9

WATER IN BRITAIN

A RAPIDLY increasing demand for water and new pressures on all sources have led to great changes since 1945. These are intended to conserve and to make better use of the vast quantity of rain falling on Britain every year. Some estimates give this as at least 2,000 tonnes on every square km every day. First, however, what are the main features of supply and demand?

A glance at the average school atlas gives the facts. Rainfall varies from 500 cm annually in the north-west of Scotland – much of upland Britain has over 200 cm – to about 50 cm in the south-east of England. The drier areas contain a large proportion of the population and industry; in contrast, most of the areas of greatest rainfall are thinly populated. So that, although there is plenty of water over the country as a whole, it is not in sufficient quantity at the right place and at the right time. This uneven distribution affects all water policies and is a prime factor in the floods and shortages which have so troubled England and Wales in recent years.

There are many other awkward factors. Much of the evaporation takes place in the summer months, when there is usually less rain; in the south-east evaporation may exceed rainfall. With such a variation in the availability of water, storage is essential. There are, of course, lakes and man-made surface reservoirs and large areas of natural underground storage which help to replenish rivers in dry weather. The total dry weather flows (that is, the average of a few dry weeks in a dry year) amount to only a small fraction of the mean run-off of water, but they are obviously critical.

The prospective total demand for water, including re-use, already exceeds the total of river and underground flows in dry weather conditions. The main need, therefore, is for effective national policies and measures to conserve water and to distribute it to the areas of greatest demand – to move it from wet to dry areas. If this can be done and water pollution substantially reduced, the country should have enough water for many decades.

The attainment of these goals has been vastly complicated and made more difficult by man's misuse of water over the past two to three centuries. In particular, pollution has considerably reduced the amount of water usable for the wide range of interests that now demand it. Some of our rivers are absolute sewers and it would cost hundreds of millions of pounds to bring them back to a near healthy condition. The primary and most urgent need is, therefore, to control the causes of pollution and to restore those rivers which have not gone beyond the point of no return and which would confer the greatest benefit if clean. This requires stronger measures to deal with the causes of pollution and, in particular, much greater powers and resources to provide the quality of water necessary for the nation's prosperity and social well-being.

Many of the vital issues to be resolved have been dealt with in two important reports. The first was *Taken for Granted*, the report of the Working Party on sewage disposal, published in 1970 (the Jeger Report), and the second, published in 1971 by the Central Advisory Water Committee (C.A.W.C.), was entitled *The Future Management of Water in England and Wales*

The Jeger Report gave a comprehensive survey of methods· of sewage disposal and their effects on rivers and canals, estuaries and tidal rivers, and on the sea and land. To protect rivers and coastal waters from the growing volume and changing composition of sewage, a great effort is needed to control water pollution. Increasing demands from domestic and industrial users for water also require stricter control over the quality of water returned to rivers and much more re-use of water. And the report emphasized the move towards amenity and aesthetic values, with people wanting 'clean beaches and clear rivers and shining fish'. Numerous recommendations related to administration, legislation, techniques, education and research. The report urged a positive policy for freshwater quality, integrated with forward planning for water quantity both nationally and locally, and considered that the function of sewage disposal should be part of the whole water cycle.

The C.A.W.C. Report advised that regional water authorities should be established to ensure single comprehensive water management plans for every river basin and the capacity and finance to implement them fully and effectively. It gave a detailed appraisal of factors determining whether the regional water authorities should be multi- or single-purpose bodies. The Report left no doubt that the number of authorities should be reduced and that far-reaching changes were required.

And so in 1971 the Government announced legislation to reorganize water services, literally 'from the source to the tap', to cleanse the rivers, to improve sewerage and sewage disposal arrangements and to safeguard the nation's water supplies and to make the widest use of water space for other purposes, such as fishing, navigation, recreation and amenity.

ORGANIZATION

These aims were enacted in the Water Act 1973. From the former 29 river authorities, 157 water undertakings and 1,393 sewerage and sewage disposal authorities, the Act created a new major national industry in 1974. Ten autonomous multi-purpose water authorities were set up (the 30 Water Companies are continuing as independent agents of Water Authorities) to become the nation's newest and nearly the biggest nationalized industry, with nine Regional Water Authorities (R.W.A.) in England and a Welsh National Water Development Authority (W.N.W.D.A.). These are large organizations with a huge financial turnover – in the mid seventies their annual revenue was around £1,000m and capital investment programme over £600m – and they employed nearly 70,000 staff. They are responsible for water supply, water conservation, sewerage and sewage disposal, prevention of river pollution, fisheries, land drainage and the recreational use of their waters.

The R.W.A.s are based upon the main national river basins,

reflecting the geographical and natural unity of their common interests. They exercise an almost comprehensive overview of all stages of the water (or hydrological) cycle from evaporation and transpiration into the atmosphere and back to the land, through formation of clouds and precipitation as rain or snow. Although rain falls without cost from the skies, this is one of the few parts of the water cycle which does not require considerable capital outlay and expert maintenance. The collection, storage, distribution and purification demand reservoirs (expensive in cash and land use), pumping equipment, pipes for drains and water supply, plant and equipment for processing and treatment and complex safeguards for, and monitoring of, all points in the system.

The Act also set up the National Water Council (N.W.C.) as another statutory body and the Water Space Amenity Commission (W.A.S.A.C.). The Council is the national consultative and advisory body for the water services. It consists of a chairman appointed by the Secretary of State for the Environment, the chairmen of the Regional Water Authorities and ten other members appointed by the Secretary of State and the Minister of Agriculture, Fisheries and Food. These appointees have links with many of the interests concerned with water policy, including industry and agriculture, trade unions and local government.

The Council advises R.W.A.s and the Government on national water policy and promotes and assists the efficient performance by R.W.A.s of their functions in research and planning. It is primarily a consultative and advisory body and, secondarily, a provider of common services to the industry. To undertake this work, the Council has manpower and training divisions, and sections dealing with policy and technical services, testing of appliances, public relations, information, legal and financial matters and a secretariat.

W.A.S.A.C. is an integral part of the Industry. It advises the Secretary of State, the N.W.C. and the R.W.A.s on the discharge of their respective functions as they relate to recreation and amenity in England. As well as the Chairmen of the R.W.A.s, the Commission includes ten appointees reflecting the interests of major recreational and amenity bodies such as the Sports Council, the Countryside Commission (England and Wales), the English Tourist Board, and the Central Council for Physical Recreation and thus links water and recreational interests. It advises the Government on national policy and serves as an information centre, handling the latest facts and experience gained by numerous authorities in the amenity use of water in England. The relevant functions in Wales are undertaken by the W.N.W.D.A.

Other Bodies

The Central Water Planning Unit (C.W.P.U.), set up in 1974, merits special mention. It provides an independent, objective, professional planning capability at national level for the development of water resources, water quality, effluent disposal and the prevention of pollution. It keeps under review national and strategic aspects of water services, planning and operations in England and Wales, identifies likely problems and carries out or promotes related studies. It advises Government, the N.W.C., the R.W.A.s and W.N.W.D.A. and works closely with the Water Research Centre (W.R.C.) and the Water Data Unit (W.D.U.). Its programme of work includes a feasibility study of the Wash Estuary storage, Severn to Thames water transfers, water quality, re-use of water, criteria for reliability of supplies, demand forecasting and waste.

Other important agencies are the Water Data Unit and the Water Research Centre. Their functions are self-evident but their influence is sure to increase as they develop the statistics and fundamental bases for the operations of the Industry, in cooperation with Universities, Research Councils and other centres.

In Scotland, River Purification Boards (R.P.B.) set up under the Rivers (Prevention of Pollution) (Scotland) Act 1965, carry out many but not all of the functions of R.W.A.s, in particular, they lack their powers for water conservation. Other functions are undertaken by local authorities and water undertakings. The Control of Pollution Act 1974 does, however, have general application in Scotland with R.P.B.s having most of the powers of R.W.A.s for the purposes of the Act. Much will obviously depend on the reorganizations of all public sector activities in Scotland expected to follow the constitutional proposals planned to come into operation in 1978.

Finance

In view of the impact on every use of water, it is worth noting the main types of charge levied by R.W.A.s in the mid seventies. Water supply charges are for the moment still made as water rates or by reference to measured supplies and provide about 40 per cent of income. Abstraction charges may be made for direct abstractions from river and underground sources; powers for this were introduced in the 1963 Act and by now have become 'institutionalized', as have the much older precepts to cover land drainage services. Another charge covers general services – sewerage and sewage disposal, prevention of pollution, fisheries, and navigation functions; this is made by a levy on rating authorities, who collect it as a rate poundage, providing in total some 50 per cent of the income. The remaining 10 per cent of income comes from the drainage precepts and abstraction charges and some minor miscellaneous charges.

British Waterways Board

Any description of the water industry must include the B.W.B. This was established in 1963; its members are appointed by the Secretary of State for the Environment and it manages the nationalized inland waterways, owning the artificial canals but not the river navigations. These comprise some 3,200 km of waterways, mainly in England but with some in Scotland and Wales, together with their related reservoirs, docks, fleets and ancillary activities. The B.W.B. is advised on many issues concerning the amenity and leisure uses of its canals and properties by the Inland Waterways Amenity Advisory Council (I.W.A.A.C.) set up under the 1968 Transport Act.

At one point in the preparations leading to the Water Act 1973, it was intended to abolish the B.W.B. and transfer its assets to the Water Authorities (W.A.s), but this proposal was dropped. Nevertheless, the Board's assets and responsibilities obviously demand close cooperation with the W.A.s in order to optimize their values to the water system as a whole.

The Board took over in 1963 what was probably even more of a 'mixed bag' of assets than the W.A.s in 1974, with many of the canals disused or in poor condition. It is required to manage its assets with 'due regard to efficiency, economy and safety of operation' and was then to put forward proposals for their best use. Five years of urgent and intensive work, two major reports by the Board and two White Papers by the Government led to the present basis for operations set out in the Transport Act 1968. This classifies the Board's waterways into about 540 km of commercial waterways, principally available for the commercial carriage of freight, about 1,760 km of cruising waterways, principally available for cruising, fishing and other recreational purposes (see pages 156–7) and the remainder – about 960 km. The Board is required to maintain these suitably for commerce and recreation and to deal with the Remainder Waterways in the most economical manner consistent with public health, amenity and safety. Local authorities were given new powers enabling them to assist in maintaining or improving waterways for amenity purposes or to take over Remainder Waterways.

The waterways of Britain have great under-utilized potential for transport of bulk cargoes (the B.W.B. have developed for canals a form of the 'articulated lorry') and for industrial development at key locations related to its facilities. Unfortunately the B.W.B. lacks the resources to realize fully the economic and environmental values of its canals. It also requires more powers effectively to function as the nation's navigation authority for its own and other waterways.

Possibly in the further review of the Water Industry in the late seventies, it may either become a truly comprehensive national navigation authority or, more probably, the executive arm for this function of a powerful central water authority. Either course should benefit the nation and lead to the requisite powers and resources. If, however, devolution splits its

responsibilities between Scotland, Wales and, say, five governmental regions in England, then it will be essential to provide a
central capacity for the specialist staff – always in short supply –
and the coordinating strategic function so vital to the future of
the nation's waterways.

PROBLEMS AND OPPORTUNITIES

England and Wales probably have the best public water supply
system in the world, both qualitatively and in its capacity
adequately to serve more than 99 per cent of the population.
The reorganization in 1974 was the most extensive in the
history of any country. Most of the former legislative and
administrative obstacles to effective water services were
abolished, although the retention of independent Internal
Drainage Boards may lead to problems in some areas. The
system makes possible the integration of services and improved
operational management.

Leadership

Prior to 1973, long-term water planning and the necessary
research had been the responsibility of the Water Resources
Board set up under the Water Resources Act 1963. The Board
was abolished in 1974, just after publishing a strategy for the
future and its last annual report. The strategy referred to its
powerful appraisal 'Water Resources in England and Wales'
which showed how water resources might best be managed
over the next thirty years to meet the expected doubling in
demand. The Board favoured a strategy based on a mixture of
inland and estuary storage and on transfers between the
R.W.A.s, together with maximum use of ground-water and the
enlargement and change of use of some existing reservoirs. Its
Report identified many problems, but 'none more urgent or of
greater import for the future than water quality'.

The Board undoubtedly achieved a great deal in its ten
years and laid the bases for national leadership in water affairs.
The key question is where in the water industry will emerge
the leadership and dynamic so essential to Britain? The N.W.C.

is advisory; the R.W.A.s are independent agencies. Yet many of the problems of water management, such as inter-river basin transfers, demand national decisions and there is the major need for a continuing and pervasive overview of the strategies and prospects for water. Possibly the Government's review in 1976 and the many constitutional and other changes under consideration discussed in Chapter 18 will resolve this vital issue of leadership.

Financial

The financial arrangements of the industry inevitably raise criticism. In 1975, the huge increases in water charges* faced by Welsh householders led to a Government decision to bring forward its review of the charging policy and central control of the industry. As with other nationalized industries, the R.W.A.s are required to ensure that revenue meets cost. One of the problems inherited by the Industry was that charges for water services had always been too low. They had been largely concealed through subsidies by generations of taxpayers and ratepayers, probably as a relic of the public health and hygiene era of the nineteenth century. The charges were so low that, except for a few industries, there was little incentive to conserve water and to use it wisely. The quality of the assets taken over by the R.W.A.s varied greatly and sorely needed (in the mid seventies recession!) a large capital investment programme. The Industry has embarked on many projects to enable the R.W.A.s to fulfil their statutory obligation to supply services wherever needed, a duty vital to homes and jobs.

There can be little doubt that, as water becomes increasingly recognized as a major natural resource, new measures of financing will be required. These must include economic techniques to foster price elasticity in all uses of water. Charging schemes may have to be based on metering for most services – residential, industrial, agricultural and so on. Trade

* Report of the Committee of Inquiry into water charges in the area of the W.N.W.D.A., H.M.S.O. Units cost of distribution in Wales are high because of the difficult terrain and sparse population.

effluent discharges into water courses, water abstraction and leisure uses of water must reflect real costs, as should all water-related activities throughout the domain of the R.W.A.s. Quality must be paid for. The type and quantity of pollutant discharged into rivers and sewers should figure in balance sheets; maybe the costs of supply and disposal might be levied together. Transfers of water between R.W.A.s may have to be negotiated commercially, though who can assess the ultimate net benefit from the flow of a regulated river?

The Industry will need to review its principles and techniques for finance continuously in order to keep abreast of changing conditions. It could retain abstraction charges and land drainage precepts and develop metering and charges for activities, but it urgently needs money-raising techniques which are effective and as painless as possible. These not only require research and experimentation but public relations campaigns to change attitudes to water throughout society.

Supply and Distribution

The Water Resources Board has stated that the most appropriate way to convey water is through the natural river system. It saw no case for a national network of mains or national water grid to redistribute water. Such a system would divert water from rivers and be very expensive to construct and maintain. The Board favoured the further development of upland storage reservoirs in the North and West, coupled with the transfer of water in river channels, and the controlled use of ground-water storage. At the outset rivers and reservoirs should be planned for the fullest multiple use and, in particular, reservoirs should be harmonized within the landscape.

Some of the problems of water management are on a relatively small scale, though no less complicated, as in Broadland, East Anglia. One of the major needs of the growing resident and holiday population is an adequate supply of water for domestic and industrial purposes; farmers also require more water for spray irrigation. But any lowering of the existing dry weather flow of the rivers through increased abstraction would not only lower the level of the water table of the Broads and the unreclaimed fenland, but allow saline water to penetrate further into the fresh water system. As well as prejudicing water supplies, this could affect the whole character of the area.

Floods in the Severn Basin and the West Country are seasonal and involve great waste of water and damage. Clearly, storage reservoirs and control of river flows help, but much greater public support is required to implement all the necessary measures.

National Parks lie mainly in the areas of high rainfall. The inevitable need to site some water-storage reservoirs in them further intensifies recreational demand, much of which is concentrated in the drier months. The problems involved are considerable and call for the greatest regional cooperation between the R.W.A.s and the local authorities and other bodies concerned.

Sewerage and Sewage Treatment

Many of the sewerage systems inherited by R.W.A.s are overloaded and dependent upon storm overflows of untreated sewage; many are defective structurally and leak. Similarly, over half the 5,000 sewage treatment works taken over by the R.W.A.s do not meet the relevant effluent standards and this at a time when wastes are becoming more and more complex.

Many policy issues arise. Should the dangers from some flooding and the pollution from storm overflows be accepted in view of the great cost of dealing with them? Should there be a planned replacement and development of sewerage systems or should it be *ad hoc*, as required? And how will R.W.A.s and District Councils cooperate over local development and sewerage needs? In the treatment of sewage, how is sludge to be disposed of? Should industrial wastes be treated before discharge into sewers? What standards should be adopted? And over all these issues, there is the shadow of financial stringency and the problems of the bases of charging for sewerage and sewage treatment.

Quality and Pollution

The nineteenth century left Britain with some of the most heavily polluted rivers in the world. But the controls over new discharges have led to an improvement in the quality of the rivers. The capacity of rivers for self-purification means that, if pollution can be limited, the water can be re-used many times during its passage downstream, until perhaps the infiltration of salt water makes this no longer practicable. Legislation requires pre-treatment of effluent before discharge and the R.W.A.s are becoming increasingly strict in enforcing the prescribed standards. This should reduce pollution and, as the technical problems are overcome, lead to further improvement in the quality of rivers.

The Government's River Pollution Survey of England and Wales shows noteworthy improvement in the condition of rivers since 1958 but over 4 per cent of non-tidal rivers are grossly polluted, nearly 5 per cent are of poor quality, and nearly 15 per cent are of doubtful quality. The survey gives details of the causes of river pollution and the cost of remedial work, and forecasts the possibilities for improvement. The country now expects a major national drive to achieve clean rivers by the R.W.A.s with fuller information than ever before available, plus increased research and development.

All this should help to cleanse the seas around Britain. The Government must develop more effective controls over dumping and discharges at sea under the Control of Dumping Act 1974. The urgent need for a massive attack on water pollution is further demonstrated by reports of high concentrations of heavy metals, potentially harmful to marine life, in the seas off the west coast of Britain.

The Control of Pollution Act 1974 extended or introduced a wide range of controls, operations and duties to deal with the entry of polluting matter into rivers, coastal waters and sewers, with, in particular, consents being required for discharges of trade and sewage effluents. This should have brought under full control any specified underground water and all tidal waters up to the territorial limit when the main provisions of the Act relating to water came into operation in mid 1976, but the national economic problems led the Government in 1975 to defer their implementation in order to avoid the outlay of substantial capital expenditure.

There are other specific problems. Taking water from aquifers is itself an operation requiring considerable understanding of a river as a natural, ecological system which has interactions within a wide catchment area. Rivers are vulnerable to overmuch abstraction, and several, in the south-east of England in particular, reflect misuse over the past two centuries. Abstraction obviously reduces dilution and, if excessive, tends to cause similar effects to those of pollution. The river flow may change in volume and rate and thus the whole of the life-support systems of the river can be impaired. Some forms of abstraction for industrial uses or for sewage effluent treatment may also disturb the balance of the river, as for example when the water returned to the river is heated, thus giving rise to thermal pollution.

But the reverse process – of replenishing the aquifers artificially to use their storage capacity – presents problems. Once polluted or choked with sediment an aquifer might become unusable for all time. The techniques being developed are therefore concerned as much with the quality of the water as its quantity.

To achieve quality goals, R.W.A.s should consider each river as a unity. Its management needs to be corporate to achieve the comprehensive view of all things affecting a river – pollution, sewerage, sewage disposal, the level and type of uses and re-uses of water. The urgency and complexity of these issues intensifies with more and more effluent and re-use, and the financial limitations in restructuring and improving a vastly uneven but vital industrial apparatus.

Desalination

Desalination continues to be actively pursued mainly for use abroad. It is a process in which Britain has for long held the lead, British companies having produced most of the distillation plant installed throughout the world. The United

Kingdom Atomic Energy Authority, with government backing, has over the last few years carried out many experiments to improve the efficiency of the distillation process and to investigate the feasibility of other processes, including freezing and reverse osmosis. The electro-dialysis process for producing potable water is particularly valuable in countries with considerable brackish underground supplies, where the salinity does not exceed about 5,000 parts per million (p.p.m.).

In recent years the emphasis has swung from the supposed advantages of linking desalination to power stations to the undoubted advantages of operating a desalination plant, of whatever type, in conjunction with existing natural water resources. However, for desalination to be competitive in Britain, costs would have to be much lower than at present and so its use here can be ruled out until economic and technological factors change significantly in its favour. More problematical, there may be countervailing disadvantages, in terms of world energy consumption and possibly of pollution, which could diminish the value of desalination. And for the lovers of amenity coastline, a forest of desalination pipes and equipment would not be welcome.

Marine

The problems touched on in Chapter 8 are well illustrated in the rapidly growing pressures of human activities on Britain's coastal waters. The impact on marine life of development on the coastline, the continuation of unsatisfactory disposals of sewage and industrial effluents, oil spills, and gross over-use of a few once-choice areas for recreation cause widespread concern. But the causes go beyond the scope of the R.W.A.s alone and demand leadership by Central Government, if the many official and voluntary agencies involved are to work together effectively on the complex operational, legal and scientific problems to find ways of renewing and retaining healthy coastal waters for man and wildlife.

Restrictions on dumping substances or articles in U.K. waters and outside them by a British ship or aircraft were introduced by the Dumping at Sea Act 1974. Licences, enforcement provisions and measures to implement international conventions were brought in by the Act which stressed that regard should be given to the protection of the marine environment, and the living resources it supports, from the adverse consequences of dumping. An important 'Convention for the Prevention of Marine Pollution from Land-Based Sources' was reported to Parliament in 1975. By this, contracting parties pledge themselves to take all possible steps to prevent pollution of the sea.

Water Research

The development of the Industry in the countryside gives it a special interest in research on the environment and on ecological systems. The main impetus for such research is bound to come from other bodies whose primary concern is with these matters but the participation of water scientists is essential both to the research itself and the effective application of its results in water management.

The primary duty of the Industry is to supply wholesome water and its own research effort is always likely to be directed to maintaining the already high standards. This task is more onerous than might appear since the context in which the Industry operates is always changing. New chemical manufactures, new fertilizers, new pesticides and the like require constant vigilance to make sure that the potential hazards they represent do not lead to any harm to the health of the community.

Of considerable importance, therefore, is the work of the Water Research Centre – an independent cooperative research association for the whole of the water industry, from which it derives most of its finances. The Centre is devoting much effort to studies of water resources, fish and the factors which affect them, methods of water treatment, water distribution, water quality and health, sewerage, treatment of waste water and sewage sludge, and of coasts and estuaries. With the economic and environmental limitations on providing new supplies of water in future, research on re-uses of water and the treatment of waste water to higher standards is a vital part of the work of the Centre.

The bodies noted earlier – the C.W.P.U., the W.D.U. and the W.R.C. – are actively engaged on some aspects of the required planning and research. Other parts of the water cycle are being studied by the Meteorological Office, Institutes of the Natural Environment Research Council (notably the Institute of Hydrology, the Water Division of the Institute of Geological Sciences and the Marine Institute), the Government's Water Pollution Research Laboratory and the Nature Conservancy Council. But the work and studies being undertaken in Universities and industries is inadequately integrated and lacks the scale of effort to provide the answers required in the short time-scale facing the Water Industry.

Unity of Physical Features and Liaison

The separation of the canals and reservoirs of the B.W.B. from the responsibilities of the W.A.s has both advantages and disadvantages. The canals and their related waters and development can be dealt with as the composite entities intended by their constructors – this helps leisure as well as commercial carrying. But canals are significant in land drainage systems and as water supply channels and are of special importance for the best use of water space for amenity. Thus there is a need here for close and effective liaison between the B.W.B. and the W.A.s (and the Scottish Water Undertakings) as there is between both and County and District Councils whose developments affect flood plains, sewerage and sewage systems and so on. Significantly, too, many canals could become a unifying link between town and country, particularly those enhanced for amenity and leisure pursuits.

Thus, although the new Water Industry is a major advance, the unity of physical features demands liaison and co-operation on a scale and of a quality which has, so far, seldom been realized between agencies of government, central and local. In fact, the 1973 Act (Section 24(8)) enjoins W.A.s to consult with local authorities and take into account structure and local plans; and clearly the W.A.s should be consulted over many classes of application for planning permission. Hence, the possibility that, unless the new system works well, water may be put under control of the country or regional authorities with the potential advantages which that might confer for comprehensiveness and responsiveness in a newly devolved system of government.

Environmental

The Industry affects the environment – rural and urban – in everything it does. R.W.A.s have the normal responsibility to take account in the exercise of their duties of the conservation of flora and fauna and amenity and so on. They are closely involved with planning authorities and with a wide range of official and voluntary agencies.

The Industry's activities influence farming and the management of land generally. They have a pervasive effect on many habitats for wildlife, notably freshwater habitats used for feeding by a third of British bird species. Reservoirs, for example, can profoundly change the ecological balance of an area. They may open up once remote spots to active users of the countryside, and thus lead to pressures on fragile systems; in other cases, they may be constructed in areas of little value or significance and yet through a creative approach greatly enhance the amenity, wildlife and recreational interests. In turn, farming practices, such as the use of fertilizers and pesticides, and effluent discharges can and do affect lakes and rivers and change, sometimes to advantage, the flora and fauna of the waters and the surrounding countryside. The R.W.A.s have to take account of such pressures and trends.

Drainage, whether local or on a 'trunk' scale, and river management can and do shape and change the pattern and content of the countryside. For example, in south west England, the Somerset or Sedgemoor Levels are the product of centuries of man–nature interaction. But modern drainage techniques can improve the area for pasture and for arable farming and could transform the area beyond recognition. The question is

will the changes be to a well-conceived plan designed to meet
society's long-term needs?

Coastal barrage proposals, such as those explored in recent
years for the Dee, Morecambe Bay and the Wash, or the
Thames Barrage, also raise significant environmental factors.
Well planned and developed, with all aspects of multiple use
carefully taken into account, such schemes offer real opportunities to create new and exciting 'waterscapes' and landscapes, of benefit to wildlife and people. Whatever happens,
conflict and competition are inevitable, for example, between
water conservation and the conservation of the best soils or of
scientific sites, or of amenity and recreation areas.

Public Relations and Information

All the official bodies publish Annual Reports, usually submitted to a Secretary of State for presentation to Parliament,
and numerous other technical and popular booklets and leaflets.
Most of the increasingly professional voluntary bodies have a
wide range of literature and often collaborate with official
bodies in promotions, exhibitions and campaigns.

The N.W.C. publishes an authoritative journal *Water*. It
does much to give a sense of coherence and belonging to a new
Industry created from many formerly disparate parts. The
B.W.B. also publishes a journal and has a wide range of
publications including *Waterways News* – a newspaper on sale
to the public – and numerous leaflets about its wide range of
commercial and leisure facilities. Both N.W.C. and B.W.B.
produce annual reports to Parliament, which are of particular
value to professionals and others concerned in the management and use of water and to all students of environmental
affairs.

The W.A.S.A.C. publishes an attractive journal *Water
Space*, containing popularly written but authoritative articles,
and several valuable leaflets on the recreational uses of water
and the activities of volunteers. W.A.S.A.C. points out that
there are about 120,000 ha of inland estuary water in England
and Wales (as compared with 1·2 m ha of recreational land)

and that this demands sensible shared use and good management (see also Chapter 5).

Despite these excellent ventures, there is still a tremendous task ahead, if the public is to be adequately informed about the wise use of water and its enjoyment on terms which do not impair it. Perhaps the 1976 Wetlands Campaign and the projects which stem from it will help to spark the imagination of people for water as European Conservation Year 1970 did generally for conservation.

Recreation

More than ever before, water is now the focal point for much outdoor recreation. Recognition of this fact led to the inclusion in the Water Resources Act 1963 of permissive powers to enable Authorities to provide for the recreational use of their waterways. The Institution of Water Engineers publishes a booklet, *Recreation on Reservoirs and Rivers*, suggesting arrangements and standards for clubs and organizations. The water managers, who are rightly concerned with the purity of water, now accept that modern purification techniques enable them to permit certain recreations on their reservoirs, once they can be assured of the cooperation of responsible clubs.

Many voluntary bodies such as anglers' associations, naturalists' trusts, navigation and local authorities are active in acquiring interests in, and managing, stretches of water. But the legal and financial issues are complex, and practical problems in reconciling the various legitimate interests – pure water supply, navigation, drainage, recreation and so on – are great. Apart from the inherent conflict, many water-based recreations are potentially dangerous so that the authorities and clubs must pay special regard to safety precautions. Despite these caveats, it is clear that there is widespread acceptance of the recreational values of water. With the new powers and techniques, and a readiness by individuals to accept high standards of behaviour and responsibility, it should be possible within a decade to provide for recreation within the planned reshaping of all the nation's water resources.

More details of the leisure and recreational roles played by the Water Industry and the B.W.B. are given in Chapter 5. But questions of the independence and responsibilities, for matters such as grants for water recreation, arise in the relations of W.A.S.C. to N.W.C. and of the Inland Waterways Amenity Advisory Council (I.W.A.A.C.) to B.W.B. And there are inevitably problems between these water amenity interests and other bodies such as the Sports Council and the Countryside Commission. It is unlikely that any wholly satisfactory solution will emerge but the main principles of unity and comprehensiveness must be adhered to in the management of water and recreational uses should be set in such a context.

Staff and Skills

This brief summary of some of the problems and opportunities facing the Water Industry shows how much depends on the skills and integrity of its staff. Environmental codes are being developed to guide them in the complex range of interests which they have to take into account in their duties but no code can be a substitute for personal awareness and acceptance of individual responsibility. The sum of the individual's efforts is, in practice, the capacity of the Industry for the effective implementation of its duties, with all their pervasive implications for the quality of life and, in particular, the quality of the environment.

Priorities

These issues, only briefly touched upon, are but a few of the many affecting priorities in the Industry. Should more reservoirs be built or more transfer schemes developed; should more be spent on rural sewerage, on the discharge and control of waste waters into rivers, or the grave problem of coastal outfalls of sewage be tackled resolutely? How will the almost infinite local variation in the availability of services, their quality and their needs, be transformed into agreed priorities? All compete for a limited amount of resources at any one time, which usually means long deferments for those projects not of first priority. The W.A.s thus need understanding and sympathetic support, with constructive criticism, if they are to achieve the goals set for them of taking a unifying and comprehensive approach to the water cycle and the many activities of man and national conditions which depend upon it.

General

There are many other issues which merit special attention: for example, eutrophication of lakes and rivers; the problems of estuarine and brackish waters; the multiple use of barrage waters and of reservoirs (as with the great man-made expanse of Grafham Water and Empingham in East Anglia); and the pros and cons of development of existing and new canals for freight (as takes place on the Continent) – with its energy-saving values, less pollution of most kinds, and reduction of traffic on roads. For each of these, studies are in progress, groups of professionals press the particular case and lobbyists strive to alert and inform the public of what is at stake. And each issue is of significance in the water cycle and of importance to the quality of the environment.

Appraisal

A century after the Richmond Committee of 1865–7 advocated a policy of national control of water supplies, it seems that Britain is now the first country in the world to have the organization and powers, the policies and the research, and the rainfall. Much depends on the effective implementation of the Water Act of 1973 and close cooperation between the R.W.A.s and local government authorities. And the far-reaching constitutional proposals for the future government of Scotland, Wales and the regions of England must reflect the physical reality of natural resources such as water and their significance to all man's activities. Their final operational detail will have to ensure fresh decision-making processes to resolve the overuse of water and decline in its quality and the failure adequately to conserve it in the past.

Man has been writing cheques on an overdrawn account in a finite bank of natural resources. This surely applies to water perhaps more than any other of the basic elements of our natural environment. We have known for many millennia that we must look after our water or perish; we know at last, though not too late, that we must manage our water or suffer severe loss of environmental quality.

But there is still one critical weakness – the ignorance and indifference of the public. Much waste and pollution could be eliminated if there were higher regard for water as a natural resource. Much conflict could be avoided if people understood more about water's limited capacity to sustain certain uses and of the incompatibility of some activities. And people need to know more about the significance of water for all aspects of the communal environment.

Today there is no reason why rivers should not be managed on a comprehensive basis. This should be done with full regard for their natural unity and their great potential for multiple use, and with the aim of conserving and enhancing their quality for posterity.

CHAPTER 10

WILDLIFE

From Nature's chain, whatever link you strike,
Tenth, or ten thousandth, breaks the chain alike.
                    Alexander Pope, *Essay on Man*

LAND, air and water are obviously necessary to man – but is wildlife? Wildlife may, in one sense, be regarded as a measure of biological equilibrium, and is essential in the inter-relationships between all life on earth. Its reactions provide information vital to man's control of his environment and for science and education; it is economically significant in food production, sport and recreation; and it is a deep-rooted factor both in man's atavistic impulses and in his civilization.

BIOLOGICAL

First, then, to the fundamental biological inter-relationships on which all the rest are based. Plant life is the primary source of food for all animal life and is itself substantially modified by the activity of animals. The existence of both is governed by the soil and rocks upon which they live (and which, in turn, they affect) and by the climatic and other physical factors influencing the whole of the natural environment. Sunlight, air and water are necessary for soils to produce vegetation. Plant cover is needed to protect soils from erosion by wind and water and to retain water in and under the land. Animal life is essential to the growth of many plants – for example, for pollination and by preying on pests which destroy plants. Animals help to renew the soil by converting plants into excremental matter, and their own bodies turn into splendid compost when they die.

These inter-relationships are in a continuous state of change, so that although at any one point in time there may be a 'balance of nature' this phrase is misleading if 'balance' is thought of as static and not dynamic. Wildlife is an integral part of the constant interplay between the many forces of the environment, and both the competition and cooperation of animals and plants contribute to keeping equilibrium.

As science learns more about wildlife, it reveals wide scope for man's control, illuminates the penalties for inaction and highlights man's responsibilities. Often the people most concerned with management need re-educating. For example, scientists have shown that the average density of grouse on different moors depends on the quality of the soil and vegetation and its annual variations are affected by the growth of the heather. Far more effort should be concentrated on moor maintenance and burning rather than on the all-too-common destruction of predators. Investigations into the habits of shags and black-headed gulls have shown that, contrary to the belief of many fishermen, the birds do not feed significantly on commercial or marketable fish.

It seems that, generally, bounties for the reduction of pests are a most inefficient and ineffective form of control. Those awarded in the past for killing grey squirrels and common seals, and the subsidies for pigeon shoots, have usually led to the killing of no more of the population than would have died anyway from other causes. But to convince the average person involved is often a more difficult task than to get at the facts.

Many problems in agriculture and afforestation arise through over-simplification of the habitat, particularly by monoculture. Conditions are created which are favourable to a few species – for example, wood-pigeons in conifer forests – which become a nuisance to the forester and farmer. Some pests can threaten whole crops; for example, the grey squirrel imperils hardwood trees. One difficulty is that few birds or mammals are completely beneficial or harmful all the year round. So much depends on a wide range of changing factors – alternative food supplies, competition from other species, seasonal variation. Too often the wrong action is taken because predators and pests are confused. The definition of either is, of course, subjective and given from the point of view of man: many animals are both. Grey squirrels, coypu, pigeons, starlings are

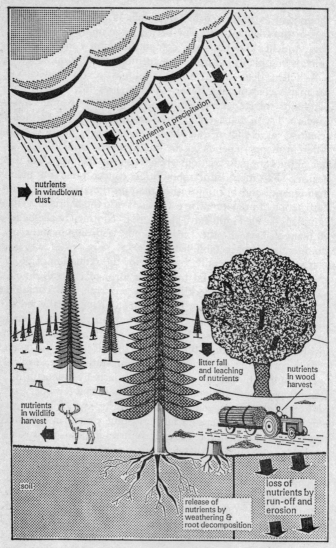

Figure 8. The nutrient cycle (B. H. Grimes)

some examples of pests whose numbers must usually be rigorously kept down; foxes, badgers, and some crows, are examples of predators whose activities are usually helpful to man. Most birds and some mammals do little harm to agriculture and forests – and many, by keeping down pests, do good.

Suitable management sometimes obviates the need for direct pest control, which is often very expensive. When action is needed it should be selective; the crops should be protected at the vulnerable time, that is, when the pest is likely to be operative, and measures be directed against the pest when it is most susceptible in its seasonal cycle. It is unlikely that, without spending far more than society can afford, any pest can be wholly eliminated.

A classic and recent illustration of an existing 'balance' being disturbed occurred when myxomatosis killed millions of rabbits. The disease became virulent in Britain in 1953 and within a few years many beautiful chalk downlands in southern England were imperilled by scrub and gorse. Some of the rare and botanically more interesting plants could not survive in competition with the tough species previously kept down by the rabbit. On the other hand – more important on economic grounds – the production of agricultural crops, freed from the depredations of the rabbit, gained considerably. During the past decade, however, surviving rabbits appear to have moved into another 'balance' within their environment, at a population level which may be similar to that of medieval times, when rabbits were reared for fur and meat.

This case illustrates how animal populations can remain stable for many years, and then have their 'balance' radically altered, with far-reaching effects. Changes can affect any type of animal. Look at what has happened to the elephants in the Tsavo National Park in Kenya, where their numbers appeared to be getting out of hand, yet now, after several periods of fair rains followed by severe drought, they seem to be stabilizing. Research on elephant population structure currently being undertaken within the Park should soon help to clarify the situation. Other investigations are being made to find out the facts and general trends among not only the elephants but other large mammals within the Park.

With the rapid interchange of ideas, peoples and materials all over the world today, there is a mingling of natural organisms which would have taken nature thousands of years to achieve. In some cases, animals, plants and minute organisms are moving across continental barriers and oceans which they would probably never have crossed without man's intervention. These changes give rise to increasing stress in some localities. Where a species of plant or animal finds favourable conditions it can spread rapidly in the absence of the restraints in its original habitat. This is well illustrated by the great spread of the water hyacinth (*Eichhornia crassipes*) which came originally from South America. In some places on the Nile it has thrown a 'blanket' across the water on which people can walk.

Wildlife is also a source of gene pools. A species may have inestimable value to science as the product of a unique line of evolutionary selection. Even the common potato – so basic to the average diet – benefits from the product of research now being carried out into species of wild potatoes. Both wild plants and animals may provide much needed strains for cross-breeding to strengthen certain cultivated plants and domestic cattle. But if man is to obtain the maximum benefit in profit and pleasure from plants and animals he must not act in ignorance. All too frequently he applies his technology without an adequate understanding of its cumulative and side effects.

ECONOMIC

Clearly there is a close inter-relationship between biological considerations and the economic justifications for exploiting wildlife for food and sport. The economic factors are more obvious as in many parts of the world local populations still depend on wildlife for their main supply of protein. The food potential of wildlife has not, however, been fully developed in most cases, although some animals, like the whale and the bison, have been so over-exploited that they are in danger of being exterminated altogether. The management of wildlife to give a sustained yield, whether for food or sport, is not yet adequately based on scientific knowledge, except for a few species in limited areas.

The wildlife of the oceans is obviously going to be increasingly important for food and to some extent for sport too. Measures for 'farming' fish instead of just hunting them, for making flour from fish and for cultivating fisheries in the sea and inland, should, in time, make a substantial contribution to the world's food and recreational needs. But the popularly imagined boundless wildlife resources of the oceans present problems of even greater complexity than do those on land.

There are the same basic relationships of plants and animals within the food chain – the algae (phytoplankton) are food for the tiny animals (zooplankton) on which larger fish feed, and so on up the scale. There are many cross-patterns of feeding and predation – for example, whales (the largest mammals) live mainly on plankton, and many of the largest fish feed on the smallest and are themselves prey for smaller fish. What is different is that the organic matter from living and dead plants or animals – so vital to renewal of fertility – falls towards the bottom in the seas, whereas it remains in the top-soil on land and is thus readily available to plants. The shallower zones off the coasts are generally high fertility areas, but in the deeper seas the fertility of the upper water is maintained by the major convection currents (shown on any school atlas). These currents inevitably lead to an uneven distribution of fertility and therefore affect the location and uses of some fisheries.

Some accessible areas offer poor catches but, for example, the Humboldt current produces rich fertile waters within easy distance of Peru. These support vast quantities of fish, notably the anchovies which provide the country's major industry of fish meal. Inevitably, the great shoals of fish attract sea birds, in fact, the largest populations in the world, and their excrement (guano) gives rise to Peru's big fertilizer industry.

Another factor is that certain fish are not yet wanted commercially. They may be thought of as inferior, or an economic use may not have been found for them. Overall, only a small part of the food required in the world is obtained from fish but this proportion is likely to change rapidly as science discovers better ways of abstracting protein from the seas. Britain is one of many countries carrying out officially backed experiments to find the best conditions for producing and harvesting large quantities of fish. The most intractable problems will probably be the result of people's attitudes and legal controversies. The fisheries of the seas have long been the subject of great conflict between nations. There are marked trends towards over-fishing in the more accessible fishing grounds. According to the International Whaling Commission, the failure of whalers to observe scientifically assessed limits threatens to wipe out many kinds of whales. This includes the blue whale, the largest animal ever to exist on this planet. Because of the low world population of certain whales, the U.S.A. decided to end its commercial exploitation of them after 1971.

Legal battles over offshore fishing rights often continue for years. Competition between fishermen is fierce and often disregards the agreed limits and seasons set by international conventions. All these problems need more top-level attention if the oceans' resources are to make a contribution to feeding the world's hungry millions.

Few fishing enthusiasts go out to sea for their sport in comparison with the enormous numbers who try their luck in rivers or inland waters. But more and more people are taking up fishing of all kinds and they are spending more and more money. In the U.S.A. one in four men and one in ten women fish for sport. At the start of the seventies around 30 million fishing and 20 million hunting licences, costing about 170 million dollars, were being issued each year. In Britain about four million rod licences are granted annually and the main associations of fishermen are very powerful. Enormous services have been developed to provide fishing tackle, boats, tourist facilities and accommodation. When river-fishing rights come up for sale they are eagerly bought by associations, whose members are often urban sportsmen. Some farmers now find that the financial return from marginal land flooded and set aside for fishing – for brown trout perhaps – often exceeds that from sheep-farming. Leasing caravan sites and selling eggs, milk and similar produce to fishermen also provide a lucrative secondary income.

On land, African wildlife presents some of the best possibilities for food production. Many species have acquired resistance to the diseases which prevent domestic cattle from being grazed over the four million square miles of the great savannahs. They have developed living and feeding habits which enable them to withstand the uncertainty of water supplies there. A striking balance exists between wild animals and plants: the giraffe browse on the trees and tall bushes, the large impala deer feed on the bushes within their reach and the small deer and other animals such as buffalo and hippopotamus feed on the grass cover. The introduction of domestic cattle has often destroyed this equilibrium without offering any long-term prospect of an equal or better one. It therefore makes good sense to farm and crop these wild animals for food. Unfortunately, African traditions – such as reckoning wealth in terms of cattle – have prevented much development on these lines. As a result, the farming of domestic cattle is leading in many places to erosion, loss of water, and a reduction in the numbers of wild animals as their habitats dwindle and are impoverished. There are, of course, many areas where conditions would support both wild and domestic animals.

Sir Julian Huxley has summed up the African position in four words: 'Profit, Protein, Pride and Prestige'.

Julius Nyerere, President of Tanzania, has said in *The Arusha Manifesto* (1961):

The survival of our wildlife is a matter of grave concern to all of us in Africa. These wild creatures amid the wild places they inhabit are not only important as a source of wonder and inspiration but are an integral part of our natural resources and of our future livelihood and well-being.

But it is not only in Africa that there is scope for farming wild animals. The kind of experiment which can be profitable has been shown by Russia; in 1900, the numbers of the beautiful Saiga bulbous-nosed antelope were down to an estimated 1,000. Following conservation measures since 1919, the population now runs into several millions and can be farmed for food. Research and management show that on land wildlife could supply us with far more food than it does at the moment. And areas where wildlife was 'farmed' could become enormously valuable for recreation. This is particularly promising for Africa, for many parts of Britain, such as the Scottish Highlands, and for poorer farming districts in many countries. Additionally, it is possible to provide for much wildlife on agricultural land. The provision of hedges, windbreaks and ponds and the retention of some wetlands would encourage birds and mammals whose economic value for sport, and perhaps for food, may outweigh their disadvantages to agriculture.

Although wildlife has always been, and still is, an important source of food and clothing, its greatest economic and social value in western countries is undoubtedly for sport. Fishing has already been referred to and the shooting of wildfowl and the hunting of game are increasingly important. As the car gives greater mobility to more people, the pleasures of the few are being avidly adopted by the masses. The field sports – hunting, shooting and fishing – are booming everywhere. Somehow we must try to conserve adequate stocks from which to take a reasonable 'harvest'. Here sporting and conservation interests should coincide. Proper management and research could produce better habitats and food supplies for wildlife, an enhanced understanding of how to maintain a balanced and healthy stock, plus 'controlled over-population' so that sportsmen could do the task normally left to natural selection.

Another need is to formulate and adopt a code of sporting behaviour to take account of humanitarian considerations and man's wider responsibilities for wildlife. To enforce such a code is more difficult. The main associations concerned have high standards but many non-members do not know them and do not always behave sensibly.

SOCIAL AND AESTHETIC

To many people the overwhelming importance of wildlife lies in its aesthetic and social values. This is revealed in the art of cavemen of 20,000 years ago and their modern descendants – the television advertisers. Many totems, taboos and rituals of tribes and nations relate to wildlife and it provides numerous rallying symbols, from the U.S.A. Eagle and the Elephant of the Republican party to the Russian Bear. Selected national birds personify protectionist movements, and a host of private societies in many countries identify their symbols of loyalty with animals and plants.

Yet today many of the wild plants, birds and other animals immortalized in art are threatened. Sculpture, painting, poetry and literature, music and many other facets of a healthy society and a full individual life would be gravely impoverished if cut off from an awareness of the animals and plants which have inspired and enriched so much of man's heritage. At one time philistines might have argued that, as few people ever have the opportunity or make the effort to see the golden eagle in Scotland, the great herds of deer in Africa or the teeming wildlife of the Amazon forests, the survival of these species was of no importance. But television has changed this. Wildlife programmes attract tremendous audiences to whom rare animals and plants are now meaningful as part of their culture. And the spread of colour television strengthens this attitude.

It is increasingly recognized that the mental health of urban man needs the refreshment and stimulus of the countryside and the joy of its wildlife. Many ascribe spiritual values to a right relationship between man and nature. Undoubtedly there are ethical and moral considerations in this relationship. Man has more and more responsibility for the fate of wildlife. Who would wish to be personally responsible for the complete elimination of a particular animal or plant which has, perhaps, been on earth for millennia? Who would deny posterity the opportunity of seeing a wide range of life forms because man is careless or fails to make the effort to save them? Yet in the past fifty years over forty species of mammals and birds of great interest have become extinct and many others are in danger of joining them. Once gone, they are gone for ever.

But conservation often necessitates culling – selective killing. The population of a species protected by man from its natural enemies and adverse environmental conditions cannot increase indefinitely without affecting its food supply and the requirements of fellow creatures within its web of relationships. So man is forced all the time to make decisions – to choose which way he will manage wildlife and which individual he will select within any species. He must act positively for all the biological, economic, aesthetic, ethical, humanitarian and social reasons already given.

CONSERVATION

Modern conservation is a dynamic, evolving concept of co-partnership between man and nature. It requires the strict management of each resource – land, air, water and wildlife – to ensure optimum value and continuity of supply. Conservation of wildlife* cannot be separated from resource management whether for food supply, forestry, sport or any of the other basic needs of man. The more that man applies his intelligence to the use of natural resources the more he will obtain satisfaction and long-term returns.

Action on many of the points of management made in the chapters on land, air and water will benefit wildlife. Proper land and water management will prevent over-grazing, erosion, waste and pollution. Application of ecological principles will enable engineering projects – dams, land reclamation, motorways – to be more in harmony with the landscape and the needs of wildlife. Intelligent use of pesticides and the increasing range of alternatives should increase food production without leading to infertile soil or unnecessary casualties in wildlife.

But more and urgent action is required for effective con-

* See the International Convention for the Conservation of Antarctic Seals, February 1972.

servation. Positive measures to ensure supplies of food, water and space for wildlife are essential. Threatened species need special consideration. Nature reserves and scientific sites must be set aside as laboratories for research. They also serve as open-air museums – to retain representative samples of habitats and flora and fauna – and as the centres for advanced education in a wide range of subjects. These national sites need to be supported by local ones so that the supply of particular species can be maintained for sport, research, and for education in schools. The habitats chosen should be large enough to be self-supporting. Ecological 'islands' – the old 'pocket-handkerchief' reserves – are unlikely to remain viable for long. Larger birds and mammals would die out and in time a community of plants and animals quite different from that intended for conservation would be left. Positive management is required to keep down pests and to prevent animals or plants from saturating and destroying their own habitats. Special regard must be paid to the power of human erosion on sites used for education and public visiting. Even the most considerate and well-behaved visitors if they arrive in large numbers can destroy an area.

In addition to legislative measures, such as those controlling close seasons and protected species, codes of behaviour are needed for all users of the countryside. A spell as a voluntary warden in the countryside could be accepted as a regular duty by citizens; continuous programmes of information and education ought to be maintained by the appropriate authorities and by the voluntary bodies concerned. Greater use could be made of urban parks for educational work and for the study of wildlife. For example, the wide scope for bird-watching in the great cities has, as yet, hardly been noticed by the schools. If more understanding and education can be encouraged nearer the urban hearth, there is a brighter prospect for rural conservation. In time, better attitudes to the use of natural resources, especially wildlife, should emerge. The higher standards of behaviour sought, and the active contribution which has to be made to achieve them, will probably help man himself to get into truer relationship with his fellows.

INTERNATIONAL

Wildlife is more and more the subject of formal action internationally by official and voluntary bodies. This is inevitable
as the ecological processes governing our biosphere become
better understood and the vital need for cooperation is recognized. The intrinsic character of wildlife and its increasing
importance to man demand the widest area of practical collaboration and for many species this is the world. Some typical
developments are noted below; more are given in later chapters.

The Convention on International Trade in Endangered
Species of Wild Fauna and Flora (the 1973 Washington Convention) started to become effective in several countries in the
mid seventies. Under the Convention a system of permits
regulates international trade in endangered wildlife. Over 370
threatened species are subject to strict controls and no speci-
mens (alive or dead) can legally be transported unless the
exporting and importing countries have certified that the transfer will not harm the survival of the species, that the specimen
was not taken in contravention of the law and that it was not
for commercial purposes.

The U.K. introduced new controls in January 1976 in order
to implement the Convention. They cover all the species of
animals and plants in the Convention and provide for export
licences for conservation purposes, to be issued on the advice
of Scientific Authorities. Full ratification of the Convention
needs the resolution of certain legal and technical problems
which requires new legislation.

The First World Conference on Birds of Prey (Vienna,
autumn 1975) called on all governments to protect them from
extinction. Birds of prey are at the 'top' of the food chain and
serve as important indicators of well-balanced healthy ecosystems. Destruction of habitats, particularly of forests, and
other human pressures, are intensified by lack of knowledge of
their ecological role. The Conference was organized by the
International Council for Bird Preservation and sponsored by
United Nations Environment Programme (U.N.E.P.), International Union for Conservation of Nature and Natural

Resources (I.U.C.N.), World Wildlife Fund (W.W.F.), the Council of Europe and E.E.C. and by international hunting and falconry bodies. It recommended that the E.E.C. should direct its members to legislate for complete protection of all birds of prey.

At the Eco-Sciences Panel of N.A.T.O. Conference in 1975 it was stated that one in ten of the world's plants is in imminent danger of extinction from man's activities. Urgent measures are required to conserve threatened plants as, once lost, they are gone for ever and (as with animals) this restricts man's future options in the potential values of each gene pool. (Point was given to this in 1976 by studies of the possibilities of the opium-free wild poppy (*Papaver bracteatum*) providing a source of raw material for the pain-killing codeine.)

World Wildlife Fund

The creation of the World Wildlife Fund in 1961 – a British initiative – was an event of historical importance. W.W.F. has become a crusade to protect, to preserve and to cherish man's priceless wildlife heritage. It is a supreme example of the right kind of international cooperation and goodwill. Its success is vital to each and every one now and to the children of all future generations.

The Fund shows that approximately 280 mammals, 350 birds, 80 reptiles, 80 freshwater fish and 30 amphibians are in danger of extinction. Additionally, 20,000 plants may be lost. These mammals, birds and plants can probably only survive if man desists from some activities which now threaten them or takes positive measures to manage them effectively. But no measures can prevent the extinction of certain of these species. Of those species which have become extinct, 25 per cent have done so because of unavoidable biological factors but the remaining 75 per cent have disappeared as a result of man's activities.

The Fund's priorities are worked out in consultation with its scientific adviser, the I.U.C.N. At present these are: to promote a global survey of conservation needs and projects; the 'fire-brigade' function of conserving specially endangered habitats, such as wetlands and oceanic islands, and threatened species, especially, for example, the great apes, birds of prey, marine turtles and succulent plants; to promote conservation programmes in critical regions, such as Ethiopia, Indonesia, Brazil; and to stimulate conservation education and training, as well as the establishment of schools for wildlife management in many parts of the world.

The Fund is established in Switzerland and is controlled by a Board of international trustees. National appeals provide the money for conservation projects of worldwide significance. Nearly twenty countries are now active through national committees. Since its foundation, the Fund has channelled over six million dollars into key conservation projects, saving several species of wildlife from extinction, making parts of the world safer for others, and conserving large areas of natural wilderness.

Appraisal

Thus wildlife is now rightly one of man's main preoccupations: to see and enjoy, to hunt and fish for sport, to remove or destroy because of crop damage, to understand and to manage – in some way most people have an interest in wildlife. The claims of wildlife on land and water and the resources directed to its conservation are considerable and must, therefore, be justified in relation to man's criteria. Although this is the view put forward here, there are those who believe that wildlife, in the grand scheme of things, has its own right of existence, perhaps, ultimately, independent of man.

WILDLIFE IN BRITAIN

CONSIDERABLE variations in the basic ingredients of climate and rock have combined to give Britain a wide range of plants and animals. For example, vegetation in the wetter parts of the country is usually lusher and, because of the milder winters, its growing period is longer than in the drier and more continental climate of the east. The type and distribution of soils are largely determined by the geology of Britain, the oldest rock deposits being in the North and West and the youngest in the South and East. The distribution of plants and animals broadly reflects these factors and some species are so directly related to them as to be 'indicators' of a whole complex of local climatic and soil conditions.

But man's long and intensive occupation of the land has led to substantial changes in the populations and, in some cases, distribution of plants and animals. These have been further affected by man's control of species in the interests of agriculture, forestry and game, and by his deliberate introductions of new species, such as the pheasant and red-legged partridge. He has made substantial reductions in the numbers of game predators – for example, the golden eagle, the pine marten and the kite.

Rabbits were one of the most significant introductions – carried here by the Normans who tried to farm them in warrens for their fur and meat. In this century coypu (known commercially as nutria) and mink were brought in for fur-farming, but as the demand dwindled they were allowed to become feral and this has created serious problems. The spread of towns has also dislodged some plants and animals from their habitats and yet has given rise to even further variety of species as adaptation and evolution continue. Many mammals, insects and plants introduced by man develop into pests, but some remain popular – like the larch and many other trees in Britain.

PLANTS

Plants may be divided into those which are seed-bearing and those which are not. In the former – the so-called higher plants – there is a further division between the conifers which carry their seeds on the cones and the flowering plants whose seeds are in the centre of the flower.

There are about 1,500 native flowering plants and about 600 introductions. The grasses, which include the cereals, provide most of the ground cover for much of the 'natural' countryside and are essential to the production of meat and dairy products. Grasslands are largely man-made and the grasses themselves are the end-product of years of intensive cultivation by man. Few other British plants are important for food, despite the seasonal enjoyment of blackberries, bilberries and nuts. They are, however, valuable reservoirs of genes and help to maintain and improve the stock of cultivated plants. Within the category of seed-bearing plants come trees and shrubs. Among the commonest, excluding the plantations of introduced conifers, are oak and ash. Trees are a major element in our landscape and serve as gene reservoirs in a similar way to grasses.

The lower plants – the seedless category – are found here in great numbers and variety. They include the fungi, such as mushrooms and toadstools; the algae, which live in water and vary from single-celled minute plants to large seaweeds; and lichens, mosses and liverworts. These plants are of minor importance for food, but may be much more significant to scientists and land managers in relation to controlling the impact of moulds, rusts and other lower plants on agricultural crops.

ANIMALS

Here the divisions are well known – the vertebrates (animals with backbones) such as birds, mammals, reptiles, fishes; and the invertebrates, the many insects, snails and other creatures without a backbone.

Nearly 200 species of birds breed in Britain, of which about three quarters are resident throughout the year. Regular winter visitors or passage migrants number about fifty species. In addition, there are over 200 irregular or scarce visitors. Birds are important for both food and sport. Grouse, pheasants and partridges are economically valuable; wild duck and geese, waders and pigeons are important to sportsmen, as well as providing a useful 'one for the pot'. At the peak of a good season there may be over one million wildfowl in Britain, of which about half are mallard. Many birds exercise significant control over mammals and insect pests, although some are pests themselves. Those that are the most nuisance include the wood pigeon and, in some counties, the fruit-eating bullfinch.

Birds are also a subject for study by scientists and naturalists and provide a unique insight into ecological factors. The changes in agriculture and forestry referred to in Chapters 2 and 3 are likely to lead to many changes in the numbers of some birds in Britain. Hedgerow birds will tend to diminish, wood pigeons seem destined to increase and the new forests should support an increasing variety of woodland birds. There may also be some more 'natural' changes, like the recent colonization by the collared dove.

The country is not rich in species of mammals, having about 60, of which 14 are introductions. About 30 types of whale and seal frequent or visit the seas near by. Certain mammals – deer, hares, rabbits – have been important for food in the past but are today more significant for scientific study and sport. Some mammals – foxes, otters, badgers – control the numbers of certain other species.

Britain has around 30 species of freshwater fish and about 50 marine, with about 20 – such as the eel – which live in both rivers and sea. They are increasingly important for sporting and economic interests and their natural range has been extended to other localities by fishermen, as, for example, the perch, pike and tench, now found in the north and west. Foreign fish have also been introduced to enrich our waters and this extends to the restocking of beds with oysters from Spain.

Of native species, Britain can claim only six reptiles – three lizards and three snakes – and six amphibians – a frog, two toads and three newts. The adder is Britain's one poisonous reptile and is hardly dangerous or numerous enough to justify the persecution it gets in some localities. The primary value of this group of animals is for scientific study.

There are many species of invertebrates in considerable numbers in Britain. For example, it has been estimated that in Sussex there may be about ·4 million spiders to the ha. But all too often invertebrates are eliminated by man in the interests of agriculture and horticulture without adequate regard to their role in the ecological web. Many of them perform vital activities in the breaking-up and re-use of vegetation; others, such as bees, are useful for pollination. Apart from the honey-bee and some crustacea – for example, crab, lobster and shrimp – these animals are not important themselves for human food, but they often have a direct impact on food production. Research increasingly reveals the significance of invertebrates as indicators of specific conditions of land and water; in this way they may lead to a deeper knowledge of management requirements.

HABITATS

By now the inter-relationship of plant, animal and habitat requires no further emphasis. The main types of habitat are obviously land and water and also waterside, which includes fens, marshes and dunes. In every town there are large areas of open space – parks, ornamental gardens, house gardens, playing fields, reservoirs, gravel pits and sewage farms – which support much wildlife.

There are many distinctive land habitats – the moorland and uplands, the downs and wolds, the lowland heaths. Although the use of herbicides has largely eliminated the buttercup from the meadow and the poppy from the cornfield, grasslands still contain numerous plants, and farmland supports a wide range of birds and insects.

Most woodlands have a rich carpet of plants and small soil animals, and a profusion of insects and numerous species of birds. Every woodland contains a series of major habitats (ground, herb and shrub, and canopy), and minor ones (rides,

dead trees, mosses). An understanding of the intimate relationships of plants and animals in these habitats is vital if the
maximum biological productivity is to be obtained from forests.

Hedgerows have long been considered one of Britain's
tourist attractions. Ecologically, their mixture of strips of
woodland, stone walls and grass verges is rich in plants and

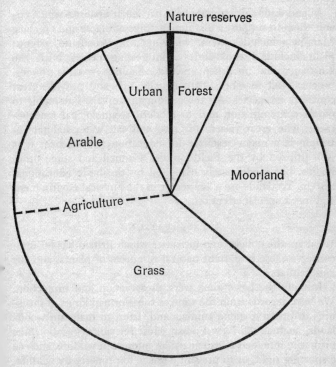

Figure 9. Habitats for wildlife in Britain (Dr N. W. Moore).
This diagram gives only an approximation of the relative areas of land
use; in particular, it exaggerates the proportion for nature reserves.
Nevertheless, it shows what a small fraction of the land in Great
Britain is set aside as nature reserves. Wildlife must therefore be
conserved as fully as possible in farmland, gardens and forests

animals, often no longer found on the fields adjoining. Although this man-made environment is relatively recent, perhaps 300 years old on its present scale, it has shown great resilience in the face of changes in land tenure and modern technology and it harbours many plants and animals important as part of a food chain or for pollination. Many reports have stressed the importance of hedgerows and farm timber to a balanced countryside.

Inland waterside habitats have particular qualities which enable them to support a distinctive range of plants and animals. Mammals include otters, voles and, in Broadland, coypu; plants include a whole series of interesting species; birds, the kingfisher and moorhen. Seaside habitats – cliffs, dunes, beaches, salt marshes – are equally rich and provide great contrasts in species. All these habitats are very vulnerable to man's contamination and to modern technological management. The great variety of fresh and salt water habitats in Britain is a major resource for education and science; it is well utilized by the Field Studies Council and some other bodies, but inadequately exploited by the basic educational system. Wetlands are a key sector in the physical environment and merit special attention.

CONSERVATION

What are the policies and measures which Britain has taken to conserve these important natural resources of plants, animals and habitats?

Initially the basic aims were preservation and protection. We have records from the time of the Norman kings of measures to preserve game animals and, later, to maintain woodlands, such as the New Forest. Most relevant legislation was primarily intended to safeguard an interest in wildlife, such as a sporting right, or to prevent damage to property by wildlife. There are in force today numerous statutes dealing with licences, burning of territory, close seasons, and poaching, as well as methods relating to game and freshwater fish, but they hardly take account of the wider considerations touched on in the last chapter.

Probably the legislation which has most reflected the increasing public interest in wildlife has been that for birds. An Act of 1869 to protect sea-birds was followed by a more comprehensive measure in 1880 and numerous specific Acts and local Orders culminating in the Protection of Birds Act 1954. This repealed fifteen previous Acts and greatly simplified the law. It laid down the general principle that, with certain exceptions, any wild bird, its nest and its eggs are protected. The exceptions are to allow for the legitimate interests of agriculture, sport, research and education. Offences against certain rare birds are punishable by special penalties. Several aspects of the law were extended by an Act in 1967.

The development of a more humanitarian approach to animals was seen in the Cruelty to Animals Act 1876. This laid down that 'no person shall perform on any living animal any experiment calculated to give pain except subject to the restrictions of this Act'. In effect, this meant that the experiment must be in the interests of science, or for saving life or alleviating suffering. It had to be carried out under anaesthetic and the person undertaking the experiment had to be officially licensed. An Act of 1954 enforces compulsory use of anaesthetics, save for very minor exceptions.

The Grey Seals Protection Acts of 1914 and 1932 are very important. The latter established close seasons from 1 September to 31 December. The population of grey seals in British waters was believed to be in danger of extinction in 1914. Some naturalists estimated their number as low as 500 but it had increased to around 37,000 in 1970. Controversy raged over the decision to vary the close seasons in order to cull a certain number of grey seal pups each year. This problem brought about the first widespread discussion in Britain of some of the ideas underlying modern nature conservation and resulted in a Conservation of Seals Act in 1970, which provides close seasons and prohibits certain methods of killing.

This is of more than national significance as over half of the world's population of grey seals lives in British waters. Grey seals number around 84,000, with over 50,000 in Scottish waters, and a large colony of 6,000 on the Farne Islands (this is culled). About 13,000 common seals are spread around the coasts of Scotland and England.

Legislation to conserve and control red deer in Scotland – the Deer (Scotland) Act 1959 – followed a widespread outcry against the cruelties and destruction arising from poaching. The Act prescribed measures to prevent poaching, provided for close seasons for red deer and other species, and appointed a Red Deer Commission to further the conservation and control of this attractive animal. An Order in 1966 laid down close seasons for roe, fallow and sika deer in Scotland. The Deer Act 1963 provides for close seasons for red, fallow, roe and sika deer in England and Wales. It prohibits the killing and taking of deer by certain weapons and devices, and introduces a 'curfew' for deer-killing (between the expiration of the first hour after sunset and the commencement of the last hour before sunrise).

The Badgers Act 1973 makes it an offence for anyone, other than an authorized person or a licence-holder, to kill, injure, take, ill-treat, possess, sell or mark a badger. The Act also provides for the Secretary of State to set up areas of special protection for badgers, after consulting the Nature Conservancy Council, and makes it the authority for issuing licences for scientific and educational purposes including collections. Unfortunately, the badger has become associated in parts of south-west England with bovine tuberculosis. This has required that it be eliminated from individual setts by cyanide gas used under strict control by persons authorized by the Minister of Agriculture, Fisheries and Food. The powers for this were included in the 1975 Act (see next paragraph), but the problems involved and the rapid spread of rabies across the Continent convinced the Government of the need to update the Diseases of Animals legislation and measures to this end were enacted in 1976. The Minister appointed a consultative Panel representative of expert and voluntary opinion to advise him on the badger problem.

Although advocated in 1947 in the famous report (Cmnd 7122) of the Wild Life Conservation Special Committee, *Conservation of Nature in England and Wales*, there is as yet no 'comprehensive Wild Life Protection Bill for Great Britain as a whole'. A significant step towards comprehensive legislation was, however, taken with the Conservation of Wild Creatures and Wild Plants Act 1975. This provides for the general protection of all wild plants against uprooting and gives specific protection to native wild animals and plants which appear to be endangered by human activities. Six animals and twenty-one plants are thus listed in two schedules to the Act. These schedules may be changed by order of the Secretary of State, thus giving a flexible means of safeguarding wild animals and plants. The Act provides some exemptions for authorized persons and that of 'reasonable excuse' for genuine errors. Measures for licensing, enforcement and publicity are included.

The National Parks and Access to the Countryside Act 1949, and the Countryside Acts of 1967 (for Scotland) and 1968 are very important to the conservation of the landscape and wildlife of Britain.

Voluntary Bodies

As so often in Britain, the voluntary movement pioneered good, practical measures. Pre-eminent is the Royal Society for the Protection of Birds. Since its establishment in 1889 it has created and managed bird sanctuaries and reserves and played a leading part in promoting legislation and education about birds. The Society for the Promotion of Nature Conservation, founded in 1912, also does much valuable work. During the Second World War it fostered a Nature Reserves Investigation Committee which provided the basic list of reserves and sites proposed in Cmnd 7122. Since then the Society has played an important part in the development of the county Naturalists' Trusts which now cover all England and Wales. The Trusts celebrated the establishment of their one thousandth nature reserve in 1976.

Other prominent bodies are the Royal Entomological Society, and the Botanical Society of the British Isles, which has produced a Code of Conduct (and a draft Bill) for the conservation of wild plants. The Wildfowl Trust (of

Slimbridge) is another voluntary initiative of great significance. The amenity and landscape societies, particularly the Councils for the Protection of Rural England and of Rural Wales and their associated bodies, are very important. Without their work much of the countryside would have been despoiled and many important habitats lost.

The Council for Nature acts as a focus for over 400 national and local natural history societies. The Committee for Environmental Conservation (CoEnCo) covers amenity, wildlife, outdoor recreation, archaeological and architectural interests, air, soil, water and noise. It provides a national organization capable of speaking to government and industry on general strategies and principles and of acting for member voluntary bodies as a whole on matters transcending individual terms of reference, as well as dealing with points of conflict between environmental interests.

The National Trusts are also active in conservation, owning many important reserves and sites.

Attitudes and Information

Undoubtedly the public is now very interested in the fate of wildlife. This derives from two broad and interacting causes: first, the increasing numbers enjoying motoring for pleasure, outdoor recreation and field sports; and secondly, the great growth in knowledge about wildlife and its significance to man which has been fostered by television and the voluntary bodies. Many people now contribute, through membership of angling societies, to the maintenance of clean rivers and lakes and to the development of artificial ponds for fishing. Others support wildfowling clubs which through their national body (Wildfowlers' Association of Great Britain and Ireland) promote research and conservation and the creation of breeding and feeding grounds for wildfowl. Many more are following the traditional field sports of game-shooting and fox-hunting.

Most people in Britain show some interest in wildlife and landscape features. But, ironically enough, this is not always an advantage – as disturbed nests, eroded paths and every littered beach can testify. This interest also leads to conflict –

for example, over blood sports or the measures necessary in some areas to restrict access in order to conserve plants and animals. How, for example, can areas of quiet and solitude be ensured for those who wish to enjoy them? How can the concept of 'wild rivers' be fulfilled if they are all to be used for recreation?

The teaching system and the public information services must obviously undertake a much more positive role in environmental education. Many educational activities can be combined with active conservation; for example, the management of a local site or green belt, the reclamation of tips and gravel pits, and the formulation of standards of behaviour. Bird study is particularly profitable and this can easily be placed on a near-professional basis by membership of a natural history society or county trust. Information services should relate measures for the conservation of wildlife to man's interests and should show their contribution to a high-quality environment.

Appraisal

In the past, change was not so rapid and there has been time for plants and animals to find an equilibrium with man. Much of man's cultivation of field and forest was compatible with the retention of many animals and plants. It has, in fact, given Britain a much-treasured landscape in which the profusion and variety of plants and animals is part of the 'natural' heritage. But today there is little time for wildlife to adjust to man's new technologies on the farm and in the countryside generally, and above all to the numbers of man himself.

Fortunately, as the threats mount, man has become more aware of the importance of plants and animals and in inevitable reaction to his own powers of destruction has developed special measures to conserve wildlife. But these cannot be enough. The great part of land and water is managed primarily for economic reasons. If landscape and wildlife are to be maintained and enhanced, then the nation must state this to be part of its policy for the farmlands. And farmers and landowners must be helped and encouraged to fulfil this policy.

CHAPTER 12

UNITIES

THE features described here and in Chapter 13 have been chosen for special consideration because together they embody almost every aspect of the discussions on land, air, water and wildlife. They show how dependent on man are countryside and coast; how little of the landscape is wholly natural; and how vulnerable it is to the new pressures arising from the population explosion. They also show how large is the scope for man's creative powers and how desperate is the need for a more responsible and comprehensive approach to environmental problems.

WETLANDS

Wetlands are usually defined as areas of marsh and water less than six metres deep. They include lakes, lagoons, gravel pits, rivers, swamps and estuaries, which serve as natural water reservoirs. To the scientist, they are a valuable and scarce resource which maintains a wide range of animal and plant life. To teachers, students and amateur naturalists, they offer unlimited scope for study and pleasure. To the sportsman, they offer fishing, shooting and sailing. Following the boom in these sports, more and more of these areas are being commercially exploited. Wetlands are also frequently the subject of limited single-purpose projects, such as drainage and flood control. For these reasons, they are disappearing faster than most other ecological systems. The following three case studies have, therefore, been chosen from different countries in order to illustrate some of the values of wetlands and the problems and needs common to them all.

The Everglades National Park, Florida, U.S.A.

The Everglades lie on the south-western tip of the peninsula of Florida. Short distances away on the east coast are Miami

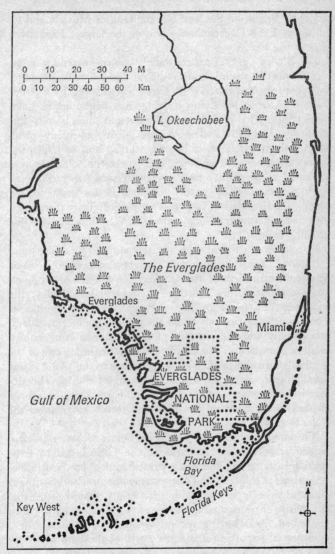

Figure 10. The Everglades, Florida, U.S.A.

and Palm Beach, on the west lies the Gulf of Mexico, and to the north Lake Okeechobee – one of the largest freshwater lakes in the U.S.A.

The Glades – as they are commonly known – extend roughly 160 km north to south and are about 100 km wide. Perhaps four centuries ago much of the area was covered by a large, shallow lake, fed by a slow-moving river beginning at Lake Okeechobee. This gave rise to swamps and small islands and conditions uniquely suited to rare plants, to many birds (among them egrets, ibis, herons, storks), and to alligators, otters, panthers and snakes. This spectacular habitat was dedicated in perpetuity by President Truman as recently as 1947. Surrounded by water – dependent for existence on water – the Everglades National Park is recurringly threatened with disaster from man-made drought. Why and how did this situation arise?

In 1947 South Florida was severely affected by a hurricane and floods. The following year Congress sanctioned a major flood-control project. This removed and got rid of so much water each year that shortage often prevailed. Today, the flood-control aspects are not, perhaps, the most significant. The drainage carried out under the project has increased land productivity and the richness of the reclaimed land, known locally as 'muckland', has led to the area becoming one of the greatest centres of market-garden produce in the U.S.A. New developments along the attractive coasts of Florida also demand more water. Large reservoirs have, therefore, been created to the north of the Park and thus further affect the water available.

The effects of these activities and a below-average rainfall in recent years reduced the area of the Glades, led to large stretches drying up, and had a drastic impact on the wildlife.

A plan for the land and the water of Central and Southern Florida has been prepared which, hopefully, should ensure that the release of water vital to the life of the National Park will be continued. And having recently stopped a proposal for a commercial jetport on a site just north of the Park, the U.S. President initiated legislation, in November 1971, to acquire

220,000 ha of the Big Cypress Swamp watershed for management as a national freshwater reserve. This is critical to the future of the Everglades National Park; it offers an adequate water supply to its western part, so complementing the 1970 Rivers and Harbors Act which does this for the eastern portion. Together, these measures should safeguard the treasure trove of natural resources in South Florida.

The economic consequences of diminishing the quality of the National Park are far-reaching and should be set against any profit from other projects. The Park attracts over a million tourists a year; loss of this income could be serious. Its waters are the nurseries of the shrimps on which a multi-million-dollar fishing industry is based and they are the spawning-grounds of the snook and tarpon and other fish in an area world-famous for its fish-sport.

The choice is not, however, between man and wildlife, nor between agriculture and fishing, nor even between food and sport. It is primarily between long-term scientific planning of the area's total resources and the aims of some limited sectional projects.

Broadland, East Anglia, England

The Broads of Norfolk and East Suffolk, long famous for their beauty and wildlife, are shallow lakes formed by the flooding of peat excavations during medieval times. Interconnected by waterways and marshy valleys, they form one of the most unusual wetland areas in Europe. There are over 40 Broads, covering about 680 ha of open water, and approximately 150 km of navigable channels.

The Broads provide the richest and most varied freshwater habitat in Britain. They are valuable fisheries and are important for duck and other wildfowl. Birds found there include the marsh harrier, great crested grebe and bittern; and plants such as the water soldier and marsh sow thistle are abundant. The surrounding marshes have been developed for grazing and tend to be dull and flat. But the view on and from the water – the 'waterscape' – and the great diversity of birds and plants make Broadland fascinating to visitors.

During this century the traditional crafts based on marshland produce, like thatching and the cultivation of forage and litter for horses, virtually ceased. In consequence, the marshes were no longer managed. Scrub grew in the open fens and dykes silted up. Many Broads moved through these natural processes and became overgrown with vegetation. Concurrent with these natural changes there has been a tremendous increase, particularly over the last two decades, in direct human pressures on Broadland. The rapid expansion of the area as a national holiday and recreational centre has led to considerable wear and tear – pollution of waterways, litter, erosion of banks and noise.

Until recent years the holidaymaker on the Broads favoured the sailing boat. Many came simply for the quiet and repose, others to take pleasure in the unique natural history, some to fish. Today the majority require motor-driven craft, with all the comforts and shore-based facilities of urban man. To meet these demands, the important and expanding holiday industry provides numerous boatyards and other facilities. Much of the pressure falls on the northern rivers owing to their easier access. Scenically and scientifically this northern part is the most important and the most vulnerable.

Outdoor recreational activities – angling, canoeing, dinghy sailing and racing – have become very popular. Recent appraisals show that there has been a three-fold increase in holiday and recreational activities in Broadland in the past two decades, and all the trends point to even more rapid development in the next twenty years.

Additionally, the waterways of Broadland are important for domestic water uses, agriculture, industry, drainage and sewerage, and for navigation. These demands, too, will certainly increase.

The *Report on Broadland* published by the Nature Conservancy in 1965 proposed a strategic plan. Its main long-term proposals were for new Broads and waterways, developed to spread existing and future pressures and to facilitate zoning in space and time of the many activities in the area. It led to the setting-up in 1966 of a consortium of the Norfolk County

Council and the River and Navigation Authorities to co-ordinate relevant policies and action and by 1971 a master plan was ready. Unfortunately, significant declines of aquatic wild-life earned the heading 'Wildlife paradise may become a desert' in the *Guardian* in 1975. And an attack of the disease *Avian Botulism* destroyed many water-based birds in the same year and led to further concern about the degradation of the area. Broadland is an outstanding illustration of the pervasive and rapid impact of man's activities on the delicate ecological balance found in wetlands.

The Camargue, South France

The Camargue, in the valley of the Rhône, is one of the most famous wetlands in Europe. It is a major link in the migration routes of Europe's birds and is a wildlife habitat of great importance, especially renowned for the rose flamingo: 20,000 or more of these beautiful birds are in the area during the spring and usually over 1,000 winter there. Resident and migrant birds number hundreds of species.

After the Second World War the production of rice for food was increased in the delta. It now covers an area of over 20,000 ha. The economy of the area is partly dependent on the rice crop and a large seasonal labour force (mainly from Spain) has been built up. Drainage channels have been developed for the rice fields and much of the irrigation water from them is drained into the lakes and marshes, raising the water level and lowering the salinity through washing salt out to the sea. Many marshes can no longer dry out fully in summer and this changes progressively the very special wildlife, which is adapted to seasonal drought and varying salinity, into more normal communities of average European freshwater marshes. The habitat of the flamingo has been reduced to a fringe of lakes along the seashore and the salt pan, covering more than 10,000 ha. These birds have so far maintained their numbers, but have had no breeding success during the last few years.

Part of the area has been a nature reserve since 1928 under the National Society for the Protection of Nature and

Acclimatization. The Government has designated the Camargue as a regional park. This covers a much larger area than the reserve and will be zoned for agriculture, forestry and wildlife. Conservationists all over Europe are eager to safeguard this unique and vital part of the European heritage. Its importance was formally recognized in 1966, when it was awarded the European Diploma of the Council of Europe, renewed again for a further five years in 1971.

Appraisal

The Everglades situation arises when one environmental problem is tackled without adequate consideration of others. Broadland reveals the vulnerability of natural phenomena and their limited capacity for self-renewal. It points to the importance of planning, managing and enhancing the supply of resources and of reconciling these with the demands made on them. The Camargue is an example of the unintended effects of man's activities. No one wishes to eliminate this marvellous habitat, yet this could well happen if it is not regarded as a unit or if people fail to realize its importance to the whole of Europe.

These cases reveal the great economic, scientific and aesthetic wealth of wetlands, which are an essential part of the ecology of river basins and serve in many unique ways to meet man's needs.

COAST

Few of the natural features of the landscape are treasured more than the coastline. This widespread interest is a relatively recent phenomenon and reflects the dominant function of the coastline today as a place for leisure and recreation. These values are becoming worldwide; the problems arising from them are common to most Western countries, and the solutions being adopted vary little in principle.

Until the nineteenth century, limited parts of most coasts served mainly to support fishing harbours, seaports and naval bases. Only a few spas had been developed for the use of the leisured upper classes. Water – salt or fresh – was not very popular. During the Industrial Revolution the coast assumed greater importance in most Western countries for both industrial and urban developments, particularly near the major estuaries. And although many excrescences blighted parts of the landscape and some beautiful sites were polluted beyond repair, remarkably little was lost. The great changes began with the large-scale sprawl of suburbs and seaside resorts during the inter-war years. After 1945 new pressures developed, many of them the result of increased leisure time. The coastline offers not only access to water but amenity, adventure, educational and scientific interest, with a sense of space and, in many places, even solitude.

But society is not yet sufficiently concerned. Suburbia-by-sea doubles its size to meet the demands for holiday, recreation and retirement. Caravans, chalets, huts and camps clutter the coastline; cars, with and without essential parking and other facilities, dominate the routes and views, and control people's mentality and activities; and all too often the rubbish visitors leave behind them contaminates the environment. This is not all. Industry still requires sites for power stations, ports and refinery centres. Developers of various kinds extract minerals from coasts, build sea walls, create barrages and continually make demands on this limited natural resource. New inventions like the hovercraft, and new sources of power like the gas from the North Sea, will lead to additional pressures on the coast. Service departments claim assault beaches, cliff climbs and testing grounds for weapons and equipment.

Most of these pressures are increasing every year. In many Western countries the development of the coast is taking place at a much greater rate than development inland. In Scandinavia the last major unspoilt coastline of Europe is already threatened. In Mediterranean countries the inevitable demands and purchasing power of tourism have created long stretches of beach camps and recreational facilities. In the U.S.A., the east and west coasts are being built up and wilderness is disappearing fast.

The effects of all this on the ecology of the coast are fairly obvious. Some habitats for plants and animals are eliminated; in others, the pressures force out certain species and may create conditions favourable to pests. Geological features are often obliterated or marred by excavations, while in some places mineral extraction and ill-considered developments lead to coastal erosion. The beaches of many large estuaries are besmirched with sewage and other pollutants. Temperature changes in the water near power stations may alter the interrelationships of flora and fauna. Barrages obviously alter the scenery and river flows and affect the ecology of large areas. Crowds disturb wildlife and disfigure the coastline. Motor boats can cause pollution; riding and skiing on some sand dunes jeopardize their stability; and aquatic sports in some areas are a new hazard to vegetation and fauna.

Policies

What is being done and what must still be done to maintain and enhance this scarce and finite resource? How can the increasing and competing claims be harmonized? What policies are required to leave some unspoilt coastline for future generations?

The first requirement is for a synoptic view of the coast as a whole, as a unique resource, whose landscape and natural features, including wildlife, merit special consideration. A second is that no development or exploitation of the coast should be permitted if it can be accommodated suitably inland, unless its long-term importance outweighs the complete loss of the resource it displaces. A third facet which policymakers must consider is that of concentration: for example, holiday camps in suitable localities which provide for the gregarious obviously relieve pressures elsewhere. A fourth requirement is that planning control for the coast should be in depth. The nearer activity is to the coast the greater the potential loss of the resource, and social cost-benefit analysis should be weighted accordingly. It is absurd to try to conserve the coast by safeguarding just those areas which are within a few hundred metres of the beach.

Additionally, there should be a continuing policy of clearance and enhancement. Modern technologies make it possible for us to undo many of the results of past abuses. Many sites can be redeveloped to meet new needs – for example, outdoor recreation – and thus relieve pressure on unspoilt areas. Positive action should be taken to create facilities for the use and enjoyment of the coast in a manner which does not reduce its quality.

The two main measures adopted to implement policies in most countries are planning and related controls, plus acquiring land or substantial and effective rights in it. Planning authorities must know what is happening to their coastline and be able to assess the needs of agriculture and industry, residence and recreation, and education and science. Perhaps most urgently needed is research, not only into the capacity of the coast to withstand the mounting pressures, but also into the trends and motives of the human population using it. The information so gathered must be reflected quickly in planning, management and development policies at all levels. The planning authority should ensure that all sections of the community are fully catered for. In particular, there must be adequate provision for vehicle routes to the coast; well-sited and designed terminal facilities for the motorist; and, without endangering the interests of landowners, effective access by foot for further use and enjoyment. The limited number of people skilled in planning and landscaping should be encouraged to work on major projects and selected areas so that they can make the maximum long-term contribution to the natural beauty of the coastal landscape.

In certain key areas, planning and controls must be reinforced by complete ownership which, in some cases, is the only fully effective long-term safeguard. This is necessary not only to ensure that the tremendous cash returns from tourism and recreation do not outbid the long-term public interest but also to provide the positive management required in the more vulnerable sites of amenity and scientific interest. Here, staff must devote much of their time to guiding and informing the public, as well as to the specific measures aimed at maintaining and enhancing local resources.

In many countries the main weaknesses are lack of public

support for measures to safeguard the coastline, and the poor environmental education of those undertaking development of various kinds. The public, somehow, should be educated not only to contribute more directly to the cost of planning and maintaining the coast as an important part of their natural environment but also to support the limitations on their activities necessary in their own long-term interest.

England and Wales

Many of the most accessible stretches of the 4,200 km of coastline in England and Wales have been under great pressure in the past few decades. Despite the safeguards and care of one of the most advanced planning systems in the world, the sixties were a decade of great concern, and many national and local measures were initiated to give extra protection to the coast. Maritime planning authorities undertook special studies of their coastal areas and the Government issued several statements of policy. The National Trust ran 'Enterprise Neptune' to raise money to acquire or place under protective covenant as much as possible of the best unspoilt coastline.

Then, in 1970, the Countryside Commission reported on the coastal heritage of England and Wales. This completed the studies made with maritime local planning authorities, the British Tourist Authority, the Sports Council and the Nature Conservancy. It related mainly to the best stretches of undeveloped coastline, from which 34 areas, extending along 1,200 km, were selected for designation as heritage coasts. Special planning and management are required to conserve scenic quality and to facilitate enjoyment by encouraging activities which rely on the natural scenery and not on man-made attractions. In 1972 the Government warmly endorsed the basic objective of heritage coasts. It did not consider that any new statutory designation procedure was required for them; the policies to be pursued should be incorporated in structure and local plans.

Much of the coast of Wales is of considerable ecological richness and is a valuable resource for education and research, as well as being in many cases attractive for recreation and leisure activities. In 1975 the Nature Conservancy Council published an evaluation of the biological, geological and physiographical features of the coast which are important in terms of nature conservation. This assessment should be of value to those concerned with planning and management, especially the maritime, county and district councils.

Many county councils acquire coastal sites as open spaces or for other special purposes, and numerous voluntary bodies, including county Naturalists' Trusts, actively promote measures to safeguard important coastal sites. All these activities have greatly enhanced public awareness of the value of the coastline. If the current impetus can be maintained and a firmer basis of knowledge provided soon, then this essential natural resource should be secured for the use and enjoyment of the far larger population of the next century.

Scotland

Until the dramatic impact and, for some, bewildering pace of the exploitation of North Sea oil, it had seemed reasonable to assume that the Scottish coastline would remain one of the great physical treasures of Europe. Apart from a few areas, distances and difficulties of access offered time to absorb and provide for the growth of tourism and small industries, given adequate resources. But North Sea oil urgently demanded sites in Orkney and Shetland and on hitherto little used or untouched mainland coasts. And so the Scottish Development Department issued in 1974 coastal planning guidelines which took account of special surveys prepared in collaboration with the Countryside Commission for Scotland and the Nature Conservancy Council.

The Department concluded that there is substantial benefit to be gained from grouping most development into zones and from restricting major development in areas where conservation is particularly important. It therefore divided the Scottish coastline into three categories:

(1) preferred development zones within which sites for oil and gas development seem likely to be appropriate and within which such development should be encouraged;

(2) preferred conservation zones of areas of particular scenic, environmental or ecological importance in which major new oil and gas related developments would in general be inappropriate, and could be justified only in exceptional circumstances;

(3) almost the whole of the west coast became a preferred conservation zone because of the variety and high standard of its scenery, and because of its ecological importance.

The guidelines are very near to being a national strategy for coastal development related to oil and gas exploitation. Plans and development control were to relate to them and they were to be drawn to the attention of prospective developers. Although cases would be processed in accordance with existing procedures, decisions by the Secretary of State for Scotland would be taken within the context of these guidelines.

EUROPEAN WETLANDS CAMPAIGN

The conservation of wetlands reveals again the inter-relationships between coastal and inland waters and most facets of environmental management. For example, the Convention on Wetlands of International Importance, especially as Waterfowl Habitat, prepared in Ramsar, Iran, is leading to the development of an international chain of habitats. The U.K. ratified this in January 1976, having already notified thirteen sites in the Convention. Of these, eleven are National Nature Reserves which depend in part on the effectiveness of national measures and in part on the quality of the local planning and management of the coast or countryside surrounding the wetlands.

Thus, the Council of Europe's Wetlands Campaign, which started in 1976, is not only important in focusing attention on the important role of wetlands, but significant in encouraging cooperation between a wide range of official and voluntary bodies – local, national and international. For the Campaign, the Council of Europe calls on the expertness of many scientific and professional bodies, notably the International Waterfowl Research Bureau and the International Union for Conservation of Nature and Natural Resources.

CHAPTER 13

UNITIES IN BRITAIN

ENGLAND is one of the most densely populated countries in the world and is short of 'suitable' land. Why, then, should so much land be wasted? Why should so much of all that is essential to a modern population be eroded away? And what land and water resources can be reappraised and dealt with in the modern manner to meet our needs? For a short discussion of these questions, three main features have been chosen – conurbation projects, open country and common land.

CONURBATION PROJECTS

The cases briefly described below illustrate the interdependence and interpenetration of town and country and of conservation and development. They cover three of the most densely populated and heavily used areas of England and Wales and show both man's capacity for destruction and his powers for creating new resources.

Lower Swansea Valley

Alongside the lively town centre of Swansea lies the valley of the river Tawe, dead and derelict, a 'lunar landscape'. Over 500 barren ha bear witness to the depredations of nineteenth-century copper and zinc smelting.

In 1961 the Nuffield Foundation, the Swansea City Council and the Government provided money for an investigation, known as the Lower Swansea Valley Project. Its aim has been to study the physical, social and economic causes and effects of this dereliction and to suggest means of rehabilitation. A team based on University College, Swansea, working with many local organizations, surveyed the area and evaluated the possible lines of action. In some of the practical experiments in the Valley several sites were cleared, considerable mounds of earth were shifted and trees planted. In the first year, out of about 80,000 young trees put in, over 1,000 were destroyed by local children. The forester in charge then undertook an intensive tour of nearby schools, explaining the project, talking about conservation and getting children to plant trees. Subsequently, few of the 120,000 trees planted were lost through vandalism.

The Project established principles and developed techniques which could be applied in other areas. Unfortunately, they are costly, and visible results are slow to appear. The legal problems arising from multiple ownership are considerable. Rehabilitating this area involves the cooperation of several Government departments and national bodies, such as British Rail, which has lines and land in the Valley, the Forestry Commission, and the Natural Environment Research Council. Locally, the City Council of Swansea, numerous private organizations and many societies are concerned.

The issues extend far beyond the Valley. Reclaiming part of the site for light industry would affect employment in neighbouring valleys where coal-mining is on the decline. Its use for recreation could relieve pressures on unspoilt countryside. The Project illustrates how necessary it is for government to comprehend the primary factors and to inject some dynamism (probably through the efforts of a consortium of public and private bodies) into removing obstacles which prevent better environments being created. A formal report on the Project was published in 1967.

Since then, good progress has been made. The restoration of derelict land has been coordinated in one part of the Valley with development projects in another. Seven reclamation schemes covering 220 ha have been completed and much of the Valley has been either landscaped or used for new development projects; part is to be a Government-owned industrial estate. Most of a 60-ha site where all vegetation had been killed by sulphurous fumes has been replanted by the Forestry Commission. Flood prevention works have been undertaken on the River Tawe and a scheme designed for controlling flooding from the River Fendrod. To resolve the problem of multiple land ownership, Swansea City Council is acquiring and amalgamating ownerships.

Lea Valley Regional Park

The Lea – second river to the Thames in London – starts at Luton sewage works. In its 90-km journey to join the Thames near Blackwall it passes through the rural land and suburbs of Hertfordshire and the built-up areas of Essex, before becoming in its last 30 km what the Civic Trust Report calls 'London's kitchen garden, its well, its privy and its workshop'. Certainly, far too much has been asked of the river and as a result it has lost its capacity for self-renewal. What was once Izaak Walton's idyllic river has become 'an ignoble stream'.

Within the river valley there lie large and small areas of land, some derelict and disfigured, some used for playing-fields and sailing lakes. The Civic Trust Report in 1964 identified sixteen separate sites within the Valley, each of which could become a park. Their area comes to 2,400 ha, most of which is unused. This compares with 3,500 ha of existing public open space in the former administrative county of London. The area of open water in the Lea Valley is 1,000 ha and exceeds that of the Norfolk Broads. The Trust's Report imaginatively proposed that these sixteen sites should be planned as a whole and developed for outdoor recreation and enjoyment as a linear park. This would unify city and country, and give the space and facilities for a fuller life to many of London's millions.

The fifteen local authorities which had commissioned this report went ahead rapidly. They obtained legislation in 1966 and soon afterwards set up the Lea Valley Regional Park Authority. It now owns or occupies around 1,040 ha of land and water and has brought into use 160 ha of water. The Park will serve up to 3 million people living in easy travelling distance and recently was visited by over 700,000 people in one year. All-weather facilities for cultural activities, minority interests and educational needs are being provided to serve all age groups, with a high degree of flexibility in their use. The Park is bringing into use for recreation derelict and formerly unused land, and is becoming a unified landscape, environmentally satisfying and attractive. The latest Annual Report of the Authority reveals an imaginative programme of development

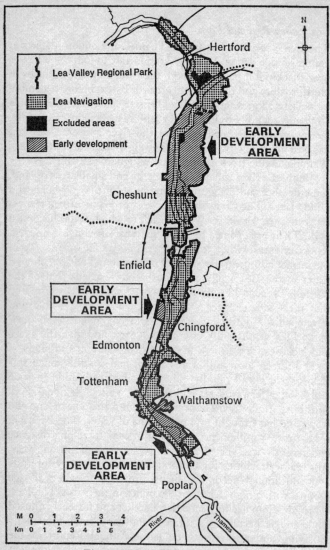

Figure 11. Lea Valley Regional Park

which is winning an enthusiastic response from the many visitors to the Park.

Stoke-on-Trent Central Forest Park: Waste Land Transformed*

A first prize-winner in the Conservation Awards Scheme sponsored by *The Times* and The Royal Institution of Chartered Surveyors is the urban land reclamation project by Stoke-on-Trent. A new and attractive, almost spectacular, landscape is being created from the city's biggest eyesores of slag heaps, marl-holes and derelict lands. Brilliant planning is turning this wasteland into a civic amenity with trees, grassed areas, recreational spots, lakes and an industrial archaeological feature – the winding gear of the former deep colliery at Hanley. This is a landmark of some significance (it has been referred to jokingly as 'Stoke's Eiffel Tower'), from where people may get a view of the changing landscape.

Stoke-on-Trent has the doubtful distinction of having within its boundaries more officially-defined derelict land than any other city in England, perhaps even in Europe. This is mainly the outcome of two great extractive industries on which the prosperity of the Potteries was based: coal, which has created black pyramids within the city; and clay marl, the raw material of the potter, which has left deep cuttings and large holes. During the past decade, colliery rationalization and streamlining of the railways have meant that many Coal Board sites have become available, together with strips of railway which often linked them. During this time, as the problem of reclaiming Britain's derelict land has become increasingly an affront to the public conscience, Government grants have increased. Stoke-on-Trent qualified for a 75 per cent grant and voted to find the rest out of Council funds.

With both physical and financial resources and the spur of a population loss to surrounding more attractive areas, the city fathers forged a master plan to clear all derelict land within ten years. Close cooperation with the National Coal Board has led to the use of their vast, giant, earth-moving machines to

* A U.K. demonstration site for the U.N. Habitat Conference 1976 (see p. 331).

mould and soften contours into agreeable shapes. Ancient pit shafts have been re-discovered and filled in so that footpaths in the park can meander without danger from subsidence. Specialists are aiding the city planners to create new landscapes for amenity and new facilities to meet the explosive demands for recreation. Near the Hanley deep pit will be a football pitch, a pitch and putt golf course, numerous playgrounds, picnic and camp sites, a water park, a riding park, and an open-air theatre, and the ambitious are even hoping for an artificial ski-slope on the remains of one of the old pit tips.

But the 50-ha forest park is only one part of the city's imaginative plan. Other projects include the use of Westport Lake for boating, fishing and other recreations and the provision of a nature study area. This involves cleansing a large area of polluted, derelict water and landscaping it. Another scheme is to turn the Clanway marl-pit into a sports arena. These areas and other park lands are being linked by greenways created from the old disused railways. These have been landscaped to provide segregated paths and trails for pedestrians, cyclists and horseriders.

These developments have fired the imagination. Children collect money to buy and plant trees and help to look after parts of the forest. An early economic effect is that, around the central forest park, house prices have increased because of the improved surroundings. And there is obviously another long-term gain to the city in the social values being created. As the dereliction is replaced by imaginative and practical projects, people will be encouraged to a new social purpose, to a new social unity in the Potteries, which will help to replace the old separatism of the six towns (not the five of Arnold Bennett) and lead to a finer sense of community. Overall, the work being undertaken here shows the unique opportunities in cities to create a sense of environmental unity. Stoke's ambitious efforts should have wide and far-reaching effects.

Appraisal

Dereliction, neglect and misuse of resources are found in all the old centres of the Industrial Revolution. They can be tackled and cleared away, as progressive authorities are showing. But of all these abuses, Britain's rivers require the most urgent action because of their far-reaching impact on land, air, wildlife and people. Of the 30 per cent which need improvement, over 10 per cent are seriously polluted. The second most contaminated large river in Europe – the River Trent – receives the sewage (its worst pollutant) of the great midland cities. It could cost nearly £200 million to cleanse it to standards set 60 years ago, yet perhaps only a quarter more to treat the sewage so that the water is almost drinkable. Although the cost may appear high, it is not as high as failure to keep rivers healthy.

These projects also reflect urban man's growing distaste for the squalor of his surroundings, and his dissatisfaction with the present provisions for aesthetic and leisure needs. Certainly they show how large is the scope for creative action, and how determined are some people and authorities to break through the fumblings and inertia arising from past and present failures. But much more civic and individual action is required everywhere if our environment is to contribute more to the quality of life.

OPEN COUNTRY

Most people today are content with being able to enjoy a view from or near to their cars or to roam short distances in pleasant surroundings. A more active few penetrate into the wilderness of mountain or moorland or ramble over unspoiled coast. To nearly all the public, such features as grasslands and heath seem a natural part of the landscape and have unity as open country. But their naturalness and unity are only in the mind of the user.

Grasslands

The chalk and limestone grasslands of England are of special importance as attractive open spaces for the urban dweller. Few appreciate that they are an artefact – a man-made creation – and that their continuance depends upon management.

Fewer still appreciate that such grasslands may be eliminated within a few years.

The development of chalk grasslands probably began after the forest clearances of Neolithic times. This interaction of man and nature is revealed by archaeological features, the barrows and camps from the Neolithic, Bronze and Iron Ages and the outlines of 'Celtic fields'. The intensive agricultural use of the cleared sites gave rise to erosion of the poorer forest soils, until lower crop yields led to fresh lands being sought. Cultivation of the valleys in Saxon times probably eased the pressure on the chalk lands and these, in time, became grasslands. For centuries, they were grazed by sheep and rabbits, particularly between the eighteen- and nineteen-thirties, and they have come to be regarded by most people as part of the natural landscape.

During the inter-war years, when the land was cheap, many thousands of acres were afforested. Subsequently, economic changes in agriculture led to the ploughing-up of grasslands and their intensive cultivation with fertilizers and modern machinery. With the great reduction in the rabbit population and the decline in sheep-rearing, in many areas grasslands have tended to pass to scrub and coarse vegetation. This can become impenetrable to walkers and disfigure or ruin the amenity of grassland. The number of plant species diminishes rapidly, and animal life changes; for example, many of the more interesting insects disappear.

To maintain these grasslands demands a new administrative approach. Many County Councils now have Countryside Committees which seek to acquire and maintain open spaces for public enjoyment; the Nature Conservancy Council and county Naturalists' Trusts also have rights over numerous grasslands. But these activities touch only part of the whole pattern of grasslands; much more action is required, nationally and locally. The policy measures should be complemented by new techniques in management, basically intended to have the same effect as grazing where this is no longer practicable. Experiments are being carried out with chemicals and with new equipment. Fresh systems are proposed to enable these lands to be incorporated on an economic basis within modern farms. The public ought to pay for the administration and management necessary. And they need to recognize that these grasslands offer an excellent opportunity for leaving some choice to posterity in the use of land.

Heathlands

The lowland heathlands of southern England provide some of the most popular open spaces; many are also commons. They extend from the Brecklands of Norfolk and Suffolk to the heaths of the South Lizard in Cornwall. To the untrained eye heaths tend to appear a uniform mixture of heather and gorse. In fact, they harbour a great variety of animals and plants and are of considerable significance to educationalists and scientists.

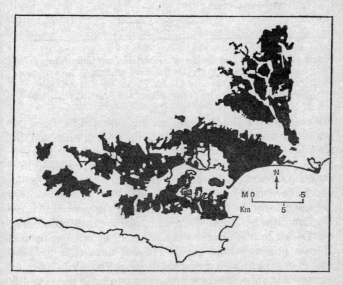

Figure 12a. The heathlands of east Dorset and of Hampshire west of the River Avon in 1811. Based on the first edition of the Ordnance Survey. The Black Down outlier south-west of Dorchester is not shown for spacing reasons

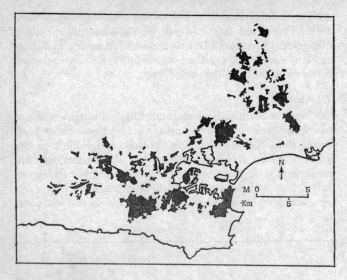

Figure 12b. The heathlands of east Dorset and of Hampshire west of the River Avon in 1960. Based on the third edition of the Ordnance Survey and on observations by Dr N. W. Moore (Crown Copyright reserved. Reproduced by permission of the *Journal of Ecology*)

For example, the Dorset heaths are the habitat of the Dartford warbler and two uncommon reptiles, the smooth snake and the sand lizard. The vegetation includes pine heath, stretches of thicket, valley bogs and grassland, as well as heathland. To maintain them as heaths requires grazing and burning, without which they would revert to woodland.

One of the most valuable studies of recent years is that on Dorset heaths by Dr N. W. Moore. Like the chalk grasslands, the Dorset heaths illustrate the influence of man on nature. Human pressures have greatly reduced them over the past 150 years. Their area dwindled from 30,000 ha in 1811 to 10,000 ha in 1960. It is now broken up into small pieces which give little sense of open country and inevitably impoverish animal and plant life.

These changes, which appear to be typical of those in other

heathlands, arise from developments in agriculture discussed earlier. Afforestation, tourism and the popularity of the area with prospective home-owners exert great pressure on lowland England. Heathland sites are also favoured for building because they are a source of gravel and sand for constructional purposes. It seems unlikely that, unless strong measures are taken, the little heathland that still survives will escape the developer for long. Parts of the areas most important to science are included in national nature reserves and require positive management to maintain their scientific and educational values. But unless the public actively support measures for conservation, it is probable that heathlands will cease to exist on any scale outside nature reserves by the year 2000.

Moorland and Mountain

As noted in Chapter 3, much of the land surface of Britain is moor and mountain; in the Scottish Highlands alone there are several million hectares. Since the Ice Age, the quality of their soils has deteriorated and bogs and peat mosses have tended to oust woodlands and grasslands. Man's activities have greatly influenced the pace and direction of change. Reduction of the original woodland cover began in Neolithic times and was intensified in the Middle Ages by Norse settlers in upland areas such as the Lake District. They cleared the valley woods, drained the swamps and opened up areas to sheep-farming and other economic development which, in succeeding centuries, gave rise to the treasured 'romantic' upland landscape.

The soil is usually too poor and infertile to be cultivated without heavy doses of manure and fertilizers, notably lime, which reduces its acidity. Much of the vegetation is heather. In those areas which are under management, this is usually burned every seven to fifteen years. Remnants of woodland and grassland on the steeper slopes testify that woodlands once extended up to 600 m. The erosion of upland peat continues, and bogs and mosses are common in the poorly drained areas. These conditions and the climate have led to the range of animal inhabitants being relatively small. They include, however, some very interesting and uncommon species, such as the wild cat (only found in the Scottish Highlands), the pine marten and polecat, and the golden eagle and peregrine.

Burning, draining and grazing are still primary activities here, with afforestation increasing in importance. Woods remove less from the soil than grazing animals, which make a continuing demand on soil fertility. Hence grazing, including overgrazing by deer, unrelated to the carrying capacity of this particular habitat, may totally exhaust the soil and leave 'wet deserts'.

Afforestation can help to prevent leaching and soil erosion, and wisely chosen trees can, in time, restore the quality of the soil. The creation of new woodlands has led to an increase in wildlife and in some areas even to plagues of voles. Some birds and mammals have returned to areas which they have not frequented for many years. Clearly, afforestation changes the landscape; in the south-west of England there has been conflict for many years over its effects on the moors. To compensate for the loss of open country, forests should be managed for their total biological productivity and planted with landscape values in mind.

There are, of course, other qualities in these upland areas. Many have important reserves of minerals; clay in the southwest; limestone in the Pennines; peat, valuable for fertilizers, and constructional rock in many localities. But above all, they hold that most vital resource – water. The peat-covered moorlands act as 'sponge-reservoirs' but ignorant management has often led to a loss of water-holding capacity, hence the toofrequent floods. In some areas, however, if man is to retain the present condition of the land, he must find a way to achieve a result similar to that from former land uses.

Jostling for importance with water supply is, of course, man's demand for quiet and wilderness, tourism, adventure and challenge. How can all these values be balanced and harmonized? In some cases upland reservoirs can provide for outdoor recreation and be blended into the landscape, but this is not always possible. Some conflict seems inevitable between the goal of retaining the best examples of 'cultural' landscapes, such as the farm patterns of the north Pennines, and that of agricultural improvement of the uplands. Some pursuits – for example, shooting and rambling – are not easily reconciled with different land uses and with each other. The climber is, perhaps, luckier, since his terrain is least susceptible to change, although in Snowdonia clubs have had to issue specific advice to prevent wear and tear on favoured climbs.

Appraisal

Most open country is largely the product of man and nature interacting over the centuries. The treasured wildness is in part artificial. And it is decreasing.

Particularly hard-pressed are the lowland heaths and grasslands near the great centres of population. Threatened, too, are the wilderness areas. A strategic plan for open country is required to ensure that heathlands, grasslands, moors and mountains are planned as part of an integrated system and to take full account of regional and country parks and multi-purpose sites. Special regard should be given to areas such as the Scottish Highlands, which are significant on a European scale.

Undoubtedly this open country is of great importance to man. It is now recognized as a vital element in his pattern of life as his needs for space are better understood. But the open country changes inexorably and will not remain open without positive management. This requires the application of proper social cost–benefit analysis. Above all, the public must be educated to understand, respect and enjoy the values of open country. The more these are appreciated, the more likely it is that money and measures will be available to continue and enhance these features of the landscape.

COMMONS

The common lands and village greens of England and Wales cover approximately ·6 million hectare, and are a major part of the uncommitted land in the country. They include woodlands and scrub, marsh and moorland, grass, pasture and arable land, and they sustain a wide variety of activities.

Common lands are unique because of their links with past forms of land ownership, customs and uses, and because of people's attitudes to them. Yet, contrary to popular belief, commons are not publicly owned; the general public do not usually have legal rights of access over them, although under the Law of Property Act 1925 they have a statutory right of access to *urban* commons for fresh air and exercise. Often records of ownership have been lost in antiquity and even those possessing rights over commons – for example, to graze cattle, to fish, to cut wood or extract peat and minerals – may no longer exercise them. Perhaps the major uses of commons today are for sheep-grazing in the north and west and for amenity and recreation in the south and east.

From 1955 to 1958, a Royal Commission on Common Land made a thorough review of commons and their report is a fascinating document of considerable social and historical interest. The Commission reported that many commons were neglected and no effective organization or management existed for them. They recommended that, subject to certain conditions, the public should have right of access for fresh air and exercise to *all* commons. One of the major proposals made by the Commission was that claims to ownership of, and to rights over, common land should be registered. This was implemented through the Commons Registration Act 1965 under which registration of common land (and town and village greens) in England and Wales had to be completed by 1 January 1970, after which unregistered rights were lost. Many voluntary bodies, led by the Commons, Footpaths and Open Spaces Preservation Society, concerted measures over registration.

A second recommendation by the Commission was that local committees should be set up to manage registered land; this requires further legislation. To give guidance on management the Nuffield Foundation and the University of Cambridge provided resources for a survey by a specially qualified team, which published a comprehensive report* in 1967. It

Commons and Village Greens, by Denman, Roberts and Smith; Leonard Hill Books, 1967.

included proposals for voluntary management schemes by local commoners, landowners and local authorities; classified commons on the basis of their physical and historical qualities; suggested principles for codes of practice relating to most uses and activities; and indicated powers required by local management committees.

One of the most imaginative schemes of the sixties was that sponsored jointly by the Freemen and City Council of Newcastle upon Tyne for a landscape master-plan for the Town Moor. This is a site of about 400 ha in the heart of the city. It is mainly open grassland used for cattle grazing by the Freemen and is owned by the Council. Although surrounded by built-up areas, it has distinct character and beauty and a wild and open aspect. The scheme proposed a major open space for Newcastle and Tyneside to function as a regional focal point for a wide range of activities. Playing-fields, golf-course, sailing facilities, car parks, cattle-grazing areas, land for a nature reserve and many other features would be blended in this multi-purpose project, which, like that for the Lea Valley, could demonstrate the principles of unity, comprehensiveness and quality.

From now on, the public is obviously destined to become closely involved in attempts to improve the quality of the environment. Because their management will affect so many people, the way in which problems are tackled on common lands will obviously receive much publicity and should, therefore, embody the best of modern thought and practice. What happens to common lands will change not only part of the physical environment but also a number of social patterns. Imaginatively handled, the management of these commons could become a matter of pride to every citizen and develop patterns of cooperation and communal action of wide-ranging application.

CHAPTER 14

PEOPLE IN BRITAIN'S COUNTRYSIDE

THE emphasis so far has been on what is happening to land, air, water and wildlife. But in this chapter the spotlight is focused on the dominant animal, the greatest predator of all – man. As already shown, it is not the amount of land man is likely to take for housing, industry and other urban uses that matters so much as where he builds and the uses to which he puts the rest of the rural landscape. These include agriculture and forestry, recreation and tourism, and the technological requirements for moving power and people.

And it is in terms of people that these uses must first be studied. What are the motives for the various activities? What are the needs of the different settlements? What do the trends suggest? These and many more questions need answering if a true picture is to be obtained of the implications of total population growth and if the main directions of change are to be detected and guided, where necessary, to socially desirable patterns. A generally acceptable quality of environment cannot be created by dreaming at a desk or on sectional and arbitrary lines. The planner should identify and understand the factors of human ecology involved; in particular, the mainsprings of an individual or group response to fresh physical situations.

One of the problems in studying the needs of rural communities is to understand the real feelings of the rural dweller. It is all too easy for the townsman to place superficial interpretations on many actions but if he does so, then it will not be possible to plan successfully for the needs of local people. To understand rural sociology it is necessary to share the experience of country-dwellers and to participate in everyday affairs. It is with these considerations in mind that a few of the major factors and trends now influencing rural life are to be assessed.

SENTIMENT

Sentiment about land is still very important. It includes the legitimate pride in heritage of a landed family, the feelings of those who make a creed of agricultural conservation, and the attachment of some workers to the land. There is much sentiment in the attitude of many townspeople – the portraits of village life on radio and television often reveal this – but frequently their feeling descends into sentimentality. Some people believe that the really lasting and worthwhile values are to be found only on the land – often underestimating the great cultural, social and economic achievements of the towns. But increasingly the sentiment arises from an understanding of how important natural things are to man, of the refreshment of mind and body which country and coast can offer, and of how towns can benefit from being set in a well-managed countryside. Sentiment is a real factor in determining the pattern and type of many rural settlements and it must be understood and evaluated if social needs are to be met.

Sentiment makes quite a number of owners disregard immediate gain as they provide for posterity by planting hardwood trees, and spend time and loving care on their property. Some still retain the approach, common to eighteenth-century landowners, of regarding their estates as settled on their families for ever and this is conducive to long-term aims in management.

Many workers could easily obtain jobs in towns where their pay packets would be bigger and conditions better, but they stay where they are because of the deep satisfaction they find in their work and the relationships they share within their local community. More and more people save so that when they retire they can move to coastal areas and to the south and west of England. And as mobility and personal affluence increase, more commute long distances from homes in the country to their places of work.

ECONOMIC FACTORS

Most landowners have to manage their estates primarily on a commercial basis. Normally they farm the land to pay expenses or provide themselves with a living. Only in a few cases as yet is income from other sources – for example, recreation – great enough to provide an equal, or higher, return.

Economic pressures are clearly effecting fundamental changes in the rural population. In the past three decades the numbers and types of machines in use on British farms have increased enormously. This and the developments and trends described in Chapter 3 demand a different type of manager and worker, one more closely akin to his urban counterpart and with a new approach to the land. Urban criteria start to prevail.

Many other changes follow from the overall fall in the 'true' rural population and in the manpower available for managing the countryside. One is the decrease in the numbers of 'lengthmen', who used to maintain roadside verges. Now County Surveyors have to employ chemicals or flail-machines, both of which tend to reduce the amenity of country roads. Many agricultural workers had a wide range of skills but the operation of machinery was not one of them. The older type of craftsman, like the hedger, is being ousted by the skilled technician, who can run a complex and valuable piece of machinery without supervision and do essential maintenance. The tasks around the farm are more highly organized and mechanized, and the farmer cannot allow casual and untrained labour to use his expensive equipment, fertilizers and pesticides. These changes, and increased mobility, are leading to the growth of a new class of specialized agricultural workers who drive in their cars to work or are ferried there in transport provided by the farmer.

Other developments include the emergence of new rural industries. Now that electricity can be obtained in almost any district, firms can set up self-contained factories wherever it seems convenient to do so. Much of this small-scale industrial development is sponsored or helped by the Council for Small Industries in Rural Areas, notably in trades requiring few resources other than skill and enterprise, for example, plastics and precision engineering. These tend, however, to fit within existing settlements and to some extent offset the decline of trades traditionally associated with agriculture.

In many upland areas and on poor land in some agricultural districts afforestation has also led to changes. In a few, it has eliminated the shepherds but in others it has arrested the decline in population and in some instances already reversed the trend. Afforestation needs skilled and vigorous labour, not only for the work in the forests but also for the ancillary industries it fosters, such as pulp mills and chip-board factories. The foresters are highly professional, with a sense of dedication; some are brought up and educated in towns. The forest workers receive special training and develop considerable skills; to use them efficiently requires continuity of employment and the facilities of well-organized villages.

POPULATION MOVEMENT

In Britain, as in almost every other country, there is a general drift of population from the countryside into the towns. There are, however, few clear-cut situations and many cross-currents of activity, some complementary and some opposing. In this context, it has been estimated by planners that well over a million people have moved into rural districts in the past two decades. The effects of reshaping transport systems, of stimulating rural industries, creating forestry-based villages, developing 'overspill' areas, and of the migrations to retirement havens and dormitories – all these tend to overlap. Problems arise where settlements are of one type; they also arise where incompatible types are thrown together. Some settlements are expanding too fast and social services have not kept pace; others are declining to a point where they are no longer viable communities.

Over the country as a whole the rural population is still declining, and the total is even lower if one excludes the immediate dormitories of the expanding towns. The number of agricultural workers in the U.K. was 976,000 in 1946 but under 400,000 by the mid seventies. If south-east England should be regarded as potentially a large urban area with parkland, then the true rural population may be thought of as declining every time anyone moves from another part of Britain to the south-east or to the towns.

Losses of 10 per cent have been recorded by some of the main 'exporting' areas which are consistently the west – Wales, Devon and Cornwall – the north-east and north-west of England, the great agricultural areas of eastern England, and the Highlands and Islands of Scotland. The main 'importing' area is the south-east with its favoured climate and easy access to London. Most retired people and commuters are to be found here. Common features of the growth and movement of Britain's population include the rapid growth of populations on the outskirts of most towns and a decline in numbers in the centres, the speed of development along the south coast, and rural depopulation.

Another important factor affecting people in the countryside is the interaction of the new towns and cities developing in the next two decades. Much will depend on their siting and planning and special attention should be given to urban–rural relationships, which will be further influenced by the placing of responsibility for town and country on the reformed local authorities. And, inevitably, the overall trends in Britain's population – will our numbers continue to grow or will they stabilize and maybe start to decline in a few decades? – affect the movement of population.

What is lacking everywhere is reliable information on which to base the provision of the costly apparatus of modern civilization. In this context one of the key features is education. Undoubtedly the inadequacy of school facilities has contributed to rural depopulation in many areas. What are the relevant standards? Some assert that below a population of 2,000, or an infant school of 50 pupils and 2 teachers, a community is no longer viable. How valid are such assertions? Until information to answer such questions is sought systematically and acted upon, the situation can only deteriorate.

EXPECTATIONS

Most people who live in the country now demand social facilities and amenities comparable to those found in towns. New types of rural dwellers and different patterns of settlements require a fresh approach in education and planning. But an even stronger demand for changes in the countryside comes from people who do not live there except during their holidays, who do not work there for more than short periods, or who go there only for recreation. These are mainly the town people – the 85 per cent of Britain's population who live on 10 per cent of the land. With their new mobility and free time, over forty million people pour into the countryside, not evenly dispersed over the rest of the land but on to the choicest pieces of coast and country. As many of the new rural populations of retired people and commuters choose to live in such spots the result is increasingly unsatisfactory for everyone. In sum, this problem is one of too many people in a few select localities, often concentrated together in too short a time.

These town-dwellers expect the countryside to include hardwood trees, hedgerows, green and golden fields, shady nooks, commons on which to play and picnic, and all the variety and detail which makes Britain's landscape so attractive. Very few of them realize that the landscape is largely man-made and requires considerable planning and management. And they are not yet ready to pay an economic price for their use and enjoyment of the countryside. Tourism is the largest earner of American dollars; outdoor recreation is big business. But neither contributes much directly to paying for the view and few of those who receive the direct benefit of visitors in a locality are involved in the management of local natural resources. Yet land must be managed to meet the new scale of leisure activities and they, in turn, must somehow be made to subscribe towards the cost of maintaining and creating an attractive landscape.

Outdoor Recreation and Mobility

The extent of these activities and their impact on land and water has been outlined in Chapter 5. Seasonal and peak congestions not only make heavy wear and tear on the natural environment inevitable but also cause new strains on people and demand many extra workers at these periods. Existing arrangements are not adequate, nor are they geared to such a situation. Inevitably this gives rise to further migrations as the popular places become overrun. These changes are taking place at a time when the impact of leisure activities on the countryside requires more creative management and more sophisticated use of the land. A new race of managers and technicians may be required to manage the landscape for amenity and recreation. All these factors must be carefully and continuously assessed and measures taken to prevent their adverse effects, otherwise they may disrupt existing settlements and the lives of the people in them.

Users and Students

Many urban people now work in the countryside to carry out technological tasks there; for example, to select a route for a power cable, a pipeline, a road or a site for a kiosk. They have to seek for their task the site or route which is technically the best and often have to modify their proposals to meet other claims, such as those of science and amenity. These people, too, must be educated to see the countryside as an entity and to understand what they can do to maintain and enhance its qualities.

Finally, in this brief survey of people in the countryside, it is essential to take account of the many teachers and children, scientists and students who make use of it. These come for short periods, usually to areas of special interest. Their numbers are increasing but, as their objective is primarily the pursuit of knowledge and understanding, they may be expected to create fewer problems than other visitors. Their activities lead, however, to the growth of centres in remote and beautiful spots and stimulate further pressures on the countryside. Stricter adherence to the many excellent codes for outdoor recreation should alleviate these problems.

No note on people in the countryside would be complete without a reference to the work of the many bodies directly concerned with it. Some have 'grass roots', such as the National Federation of Women's Institutes, the parish councils, the churches and chapels, and most have, of course, significant national status and are influenced by urban as well as rural thinking. There are bodies with specific aims, such as the Council for Small Industries, the Rural Community Councils, the county Naturalists' Trusts and many others. Any attempt to plan for the countryside must take account of all these; their participation and support are indispensable. In effect, they are part of the essential process of adult education in a modern democracy.

Appraisal

The many facets of life touched on here call for the utmost care if harmoniously balanced rural communities are to be developed. Conflicts have already emerged in many areas. Coastal resorts which rely on holiday-makers find their environmental quality diminished by sheer visitor pressure. Some areas, such as Cornwall, resent being deprived of industry just so that they may retain their character for tourism and retirement. They object to being dependent on the seasonal resources of the tourist and the slender revenues of the retired. Although many people of urban background now reside in rural areas, they are not likely to provide manpower for the management of the landscape. The fall in population of rural settlements and the changes in its composition give rise to further problems, as in smaller communities it becomes difficult to cater properly for those who do wish to stay on. More facts are required about the people who live in, work on, use or enjoy the countryside. In particular, society should know more about the purposes fulfilled by rural settlements, and take into account their capacity to remain viable as population soars during the next half-century.

If cohesive rural communities are not to be obliterated and if great waste and erosion are to be avoided, these problems cannot be left to the 'invisible hand' of Adam Smith. Much more talent and effort should be deployed in solving them.

The Development Commissioners have long argued the case for a positive policy for the countryside, particularly on social and economic grounds. They believe that it is essential to have planned development of regions subject to, or threatened with, rural depopulation and favour the selection of 'trigger' areas for vigorous action.

The human problems are critical and will be intensified in this decade. Real understanding and sensitivity are required to deal with the older farmers due to retire, the younger ones for whom fully mechanized agriculture may offer inadequate prospects, and the wives of these people, who expect living standards similar to those of the urban housewife. There are also many difficulties in encouraging participation in the planning required and in developing a truer community between town and country dwellers.

These issues would be difficult enough to cope with even if the process of adjustment to the increasing pressures of population could be gradual, but time for correcting mistakes is just not available.

CHAPTER 15

POPULATION

There is an accumulative cruelty in a number of
men, though none in particular are ill-natured.

Lord Halifax

FIRST, what is the extent of the population explosion? Is the
rate of change great enough to warrant so much debate and so
much gloom?

SCALE

The table below contrasts the phenomenal growth of recent
years with that of man's earlier history. There are now, on
average, 4 births and 2 deaths each second. U.N. projections
put the world population annual growth rate between 1970–75
at 1·9 per cent, but the Office of Population of the U.S. Agency
for International Development estimates it at 1·63. The Office

Table 2. Growth of World Population

Millions	Year (approx.)	Years taken to increase world population by 1,000 million
1,000	1830	200,000
2,000	1930	100
3,000	1960	30
4,000	1975	15

believes that an accelerating downward trend is now established, though this would still lead to a world population
around 5·5 billion by A.D. 2000. The overall impact of our
numbers on resources and living standards has already been
discussed; clearly they could eliminate most of those things
which today are considered to make up a quality environment.
And not enough thought has yet been given to the effects on

world cultures and patterns of power of the increasing disparities between races and continents.

Population projections and percentages derived from the
U.N. 'medium variant' (based on known recent levels and
trends, levels of economic and social development and
policies) are as follows:

Table 3. Population projections and percentages derived from
the U.N. 'medium variant'

(Millions)	1975	%	2000	%	2025	%
World total	3988	100	6406	100	9065	100
Northern Group	1971	49·4	2530	39·5	2930	32·3
Northern America	237	5·9	296	4·6	332	3·7
Europe	474	11·9	540	8·4	580	6·4
U.S.S.R.	255	6·4	321	5·0	368	4·1
East Asia	1005	25·2	373	21·4	1650	18·2
Southern Group	2017	50·6	3876	60·5	6135	67·7
Latin America	326	8·2	625	9·8	961	10·6
Africa	402	10·1	834	13·0	1479	16·3
South Asia	1268	31·8	2384	37·2	3651	40·3
Oceanic	21	0·5	33	0·5	44	0·5

The U.N. Concise Report on 'The World Population Situation in
1970–75 and its Long-Range Implications' should be consulted.

The world population in 1976 was estimated at over 4,000
million. The U.N. table shows there is a firm prospect of this
figure being doubled by A.D. 2025 and the table below shows
current rates of growth. Africa and Latin America lead in rate
of increase, followed closely by Asia. The developing countries
in these continents will account for about seven eighths of the
anticipated growth, although the wealthy, sophisticated U.S.A.
will have a population of almost 300 million, and the U.S.S.R.
should exceed this number. Death-rates everywhere continue
to decline and the developing countries maintain high fertility.

The next table compares the population of Europe, still the
most densely populated continent, with that of the rest of the
world. In the thirties the net reproduction rate was declining
in Europe, giving rise to serious problems. Since 1945 the rate

Table 4. Projected Rates of Natural Increase

Region	Per 1,000 per year (Birth-rate less Death-rate)		
	1970/80	1980/90	1990/2000
Africa	28·2	29·8	28·3
Latin America	28·8	28·8	26·4
South Asia	27·7	25·2	20·6
Oceania	17·0	17·3	14·9
East Asia	16·4	14·4	11·9
Northern America	11·6	12·1	9·9
U.S.S.R.	10·9	11·0	8·7
Europe	7·6	7·2	6·6

Source: U.N. *The World Population Situation in 1970* (*Summary*), Population Study No. 48.

and the total population have increased, yet the table reveals that the *proportion* of Europeans is rapidly going down.

Britain's population in 1700 was around seven million, and birth- and death-rates were high. The better diets following the agricultural revolution which began later that century and the improvement in hygiene, clothing and housing initiated about the mid nineteenth century, led to a phenomenal growth in population. The last four decades of the nineteenth century saw an increase of 14 million – or around 60 per cent. The U.K. population is now 56 million despite a decline in the average size of families from 4·5 in 1900 to about 3·1 today and if this continues the population in A.D. 2000 may well be over 63 million, although 90 per cent of those at a professional

Table 5. Comparison of Population
(*in millions*)

Year	Europe	World	Percentage of world population in Europe
1900	320	1,550	20·6
1950	395	2,494	15·8
1970	454	3,574	12·7
2000	540	6,406	8·4

symposium* in 1969 believed that the optimum population of Britain had already been exceeded then.

The population of England and Wales in 1975 had the lowest annual increase – 18,000 – since records were kept. The fertility rate was still falling and emigration was at a high rate. These trends led to requests for special studies to be made by the Population Panel of the Cabinet Office, which reports to the Minister responsible for coordinating Government policy on population matters (the Lord Privy Seal). It is, however, expected that the birth-rate may increase as larger numbers of women reach child-bearing age. The current age structure of the population appears likely to maintain its growth into the next century.

Pessimists liken the world population explosion to a cancerous growth – as life gone mad. Optimistic observers regard this century as providing an aberration in the normal balance of births and deaths and predict that, when all the developing countries have had their 'demographic revolution', numbers will return to normal – whatever that is! This view takes insufficient account of the fundamental changes noted above and the economic and social activity now taking place.

CAUSES AND IMPLICATIONS

What are the main causes of the population explosion? Primarily, it stems from 'death-control'. From 1945 onwards the birth-rate has risen in nearly all Western countries and has stayed high in Asia, Africa and South America, and the average length of life has increased. But these do not cause the great population explosion. Fertility is related to traditional values and social factors; mortality responds directly to scientific and technical advances.

It is the dramatic elimination, mainly since 1945, of the major killing and crippling diseases like malaria which has led to the great upsurge in population numbers. This process of control is itself accelerating. For example, new products have recently been marketed to relieve sufferers from bilharziasis –

* The Optimum Population for Britain, Academic Press.

a disease exceeded only by malaria in its impact on human life.

Europe really started the population explosion. It was the first continent to obtain from the application of science and industry more food and materials and better health and conditions for its peoples. As the factors which reduced its death-rate have spread across the globe, the populations of Africa, Asia and South America are growing apace. And, as in Europe during the seventeenth to nineteenth centuries, this gives rise to nationalist and expansionist trends. There are two vital differences, however, between the situation then and now: soon there will be no empty lands to emigrate to; and the conflicts between power-blocks imperil world safety, waste resources and impair the environment.

The gap between the living standards of many nations – for example, between the U.S.A.'s and India's – can seriously prejudice human values. As the disparity between the population of India and its food supply remains and as North American farm surpluses – the only substantial ones – are used up, the situation grows more menacing every day. It seems inevitable that many aid programmes will have to be linked to birth-control measures; for example, mass issues of the intra-uterine coil device (I.U.D. or loop), the 'pill' or other devices could be made, provided the religious issues can be resolved.

Population pressure is becoming a major force internationally – to some extent it is already. It may even lead to more fearful, as yet undreamed of, polarizations of peoples, dwarfing those of George Orwell's *1984* or Aldous Huxley's *Brave New World*. In fact, sheer weight of numbers could lead to a 'lemming-like' collapse of the structure of society.

The changing patterns of races must soon affect all the basic issues – living standards, social and political values, religions, governments and, of course, whether man lives at war or in peace. And clearly there can be no wise use of natural resources that is not founded upon the central issue of population planning.

Many other vitally important and urgent facets of this expansion in numbers require attention. The genetic effects of keeping alive those with organic and other disabilities which may be inherited by their children can have a profound influence on man. In nature the weak and inefficient do not survive. An increase in the number of defective humans could debase everything; the sheer weight of numbers might lead to disregard for the individual and for the environment. Foolproof methods of birth-control are imminent. Sex-selection is on the way. The implications of these products of science and technology are enormous. How will individuals and states decide on the numbers and sexes to be born? If some nations rear more children, then sooner or later others will have to have less.

There is yet another significant aspect of the vast increases in populations everywhere, namely the 'age balance' of the population. Today, under 30 per cent of the peoples of developed areas are below 15 years of age, but in less developed areas the figure is over 40 per cent and rising. Until a century ago, hardly any large communities had a life expectation beyond 35 years, but this has nearly doubled – to over 70 years – in some 'western' countries. Differences in age structure, especially between richer and poorer regions, have serious implications for priorities in the allocation of global resources and, within individual countries, raise urgent economic and social problems.

As the proportion of young and old people in populations increases, greater strain is placed on the middle age groups. The number of persons dependent on each member of the working population is rising. It might become necessary, at some future point, to cut, rather than prolong, the time spent in school or retirement. Essentially, the past two centuries have seen man's relative equilibrium and slow rate of increase transformed. Thus if man does not soon voluntarily control births he may be faced with possibilities repugnant on moral, social and religious grounds: for example, having to seek permission to have children or the use of eugenic and geriatric agents to determine the numbers and composition of the population. This may become the logical result of man's use of powers which have enabled him, so far, to flout natural processes.

Control Factors

Population issues are all-pervasive. They penetrate into the mores of private and public life. Their sources lie deep in man's basic reproductive drives, and are modified by centuries of environmental conditioning. Interference with them touches every facet of society. But it is essential, at least for some decades, to limit population numbers by reducing the numbers born. What criteria should be adopted?

The adequacy of food and natural resources is obviously one criterion. But, historically and at the present time, food alone has not proved to be a strong limiting factor in the determination of the numbers of a family or nation. In the developing countries, food supplies are all too often inadequate – for example, famines frequently prevail in parts of India – yet this is not apparently controlling numbers. In the developed countries, the rapid gains in food and affluence are still too sharp in living memory for any bald assertion of dangers of starvation from over-population to be effective. And, in these countries, it is usually the unskilled and underfed who have the largest families, and are thereby sometimes the poorer.

The quantity of raw materials available has so far exercised little effect on total population numbers. While it will do so under the pressures of the vastly greater numbers of the next century, the situation could then be altogether too urgent on other counts. It is also to be hoped that man's inventiveness in respect of materials will lead to new sources of power and protein. But in any case it would be dangerously short-sighted to imagine that population issues could be resolved solely in terms of food and natural resources. What other criteria are there?

Clues may exist in the relationship of wildlife to its habitats. Studies of wildlife, and of rats under controlled conditions, have probed into patterns of behaviour and responses. They suggest that once numbers in a habitat rise beyond a certain level social disorders and neuroses arise. Disturbances occur which may have their human parallels in the juvenile delinquency and sick violence in big cities. In the long term, an understanding of the numbers of fellow humans which people can tolerate in a given area seems vital to social harmony.

Some experts believe that several countries have already exceeded communally healthy levels of 'density tolerance'. They consider that the danger of over-population does not rest solely on the need for food and shelter, but on whether the population will exceed the limits of human tolerance towards the presence of other humans, limits which have been set by evolutionary processes over millions of years.

Research into wildlife management has shown that where man has interfered to prevent the operation of natural forces, he must control and cull. This is essential to maintain a balance of numbers in relation to food supply and living space – in particular, the carrying capacity of the available land and water. Management also takes into account the biological productive capacity of the individual and group. It is interesting to note that the selective shooting of poorer-quality animals often leads to more breeding from the younger, stronger stock who thereby have relatively more food and space. And so culling must continue.

Man has altered many of the factors previously controlling his numbers but not the basic built-in instincts and drives characteristic of his species. While it may seriously mislead, in the present state of knowledge, to draw too many parallels between wildlife and humans, it is still true that man is an animal and will tend to obey ecological principles.

It seems that, as man's numbers and congestion increase, human society too may develop a 'pecking order' like that of animals (each animal has a set place in the social pattern and cannot easily change it). Possibly a return to feudal and other hierarchical systems may emerge. And the most serious consequence of all is that, unless there is a sudden recognition of these problems by the mass of people, it may soon be too late to avoid the use of drastic methods to deal with over-population.

Perhaps further criteria may be found in the principles behind positive family-planning. In this there is usually a direct relationship between numbers of children and the capacity of parents to bring them up in a healthy and happy home. The influence of the environment is known to be great. In Western countries it often governs entry to professions; in primitive societies it determines the selection of leaders; and in most countries it is still starkly reflected in death-rates, with areas of squalor and poor natural conditions having rates well above those of more prosperous regions. Like sensible families, nations and the world must control their populations in relation to some measurements of a high-quality environment.

Some standards are capable of objective assessment, at least in broad terms. Some may be related to the capacity of land and water to sustain the pressures upon them without detriment to their long-term supply. Others will probably always be, in part, subjective, but should increasingly be based on a scientific understanding of the major processes influencing population numbers. The difficulties in defining criteria and getting them adopted are great but must be resolved if quality is to be the touchstone. Any serious attempt to improve our environment ultimately involves society in planning the use, management and development of its most pre-eminent resource – man himself. History shows that individuals can rarely be expected to think and act for posterity.

Following the savage impact of the uncontrolled entrepreneur and worker on their environment in the nineteenth century, it was inevitable that legislation for the physical planning of towns should usher in the twentieth century in many countries. Probably legislation for the planning of populations in relation to their living space and other factors will initiate the twenty-first century. More and more countries are striving to stop or limit the rapid growth of their populations, because it is clear that increases will mean a further lowering of living standards already hovering at subsistence level. Few would deny that, for the mass of the population of the world, the 'revolution in expectations' must have a hollow sound.

But even assuming that it may be possible to control or stabilize population numbers in thirty to forty years' time, there would still be great problems in relating them to resources, in meeting the expectations of the 'have-nots', in dealing with the aged and the defective, and in creating for all a healthy environment. In fact, the problems of the static or declining population might be greater in some respects than those of a population expanding roughly in relation to any increase in available resources and space. Static populations would have to face the task of making sure that the dynamic force of the younger members of society was focused where it could do the most good and of encouraging the proper levels of fecundity. The genetic effects of having an elderly population, as yet hardly studied, might be magnified in a static society. Without question, the psychological effects of living with declining numbers, of accepting massive immigration, of facing vast structural changes in industry and commerce, and of having a high proportion of aged people could be far-reaching.

The personal issues are profound and inadequately understood. The urge to propagate is basic to human activity and is the greatest single problem governments now have to face. To ask some peoples to limit their children – for example, the Red Indians of North America – would be to invite individual misery in old age (as there would be few younger people to support the elders) and extinction as a tribe. To many of the fecund peoples of South America and India it might deny the only factor of significance in a relatively short and limited existence. Even in the richer countries, notably the U.S.A., trends are now confused, as some of the most educated and prosperous citizens go in for larger families.

It is not only the total numbers of people in relation to food and space – the 'capital' – but the level of recruitment of new members – the 'interest' – that is vital to society. Population growth is now the most important factor in determining society's demands. Any adjustment in its rate would have profound economic and social consequences, interacting upon and affecting all other bases of environmental planning.

POPULATIONS AND PLANNING

The world has seen little real attempt at population and resource planning. The United Nations is now attacking the enormous and complex population problems of developing countries, so interwoven into their economic and social life. Efforts are being made to control certain major resources on an international scale, and physical planning, mainly of the urban areas, has been undertaken in most countries in the past fifty years. But there has so far been only a short period of relatively limited activity from which lessons can be drawn for the wider tasks ahead.

Despite the now obvious relationship of environmental capacity and population numbers, most physical planners have taken population and its growth as factors over which they do not exercise influence or have responsibility. They may make adjustments in the location of population – for example, over-spill plans for a town or measures to check depopulation in rural or depressed areas – but they accept general trends. Although 70 per cent of the world's population still live in rural areas not enough is known about them and their needs and problems. Each year more move into the cities and this is leading to a dramatic redistribution of population. At least it is known that most of the great urban concentrations, particularly in the developing countries, are suffering from intense physical congestion and social tension (see Supplement 1).

But in the long term population numbers must be positively related to environmental capacity not only locally but nationally. It is already clear by the criteria of common sense alone that some countries are over-populated in relation to resources, that some areas in many countries are over-congested, and that in all countries many localities are being destroyed by the pressure of numbers. People and planners must therefore accept that in the long term there is a finite amount of habitable land and water on this earth. Land set aside at one time to meet requirements for, say, open space, amenity or outdoor recreation will inevitably be needed for food production or constructional purposes within a few decades if population growth continues.

However ingenious the use of land for the basic needs of food, shelter and mobility, any land-use planning that ignores population control simply postpones the day of reckoning.

Similarly, however important and desirable, advances in agriculture which make it possible to obtain more food per hectare and developments in building which help to prevent land being wasted tend to obscure this ultimate limitation. By constant discovery and invention man has so far covered up the fact that the supply of natural resources, in particular of open land, may soon run out.

The citizens of the twenty-first century will have little room for manoeuvre. They will be faced with some very unpalatable decisions as the limits of population growth in relation to land supply are approached. Thus, to leave some choice for posterity, planners must now not only indicate fully the implications of population growth for the environment but they must also publicize how necessary it is to fight against the trends.

Population control cannot be formulated properly or translated effectively into a basis for action without full participation by citizens. Unfortunately, apathy and ignorance about environmental planning and population control are widespread. Yet if these objectives are to be served, all adults must be fully involved in their consideration, and the general aims of our communities must be appraised in all the forums of the nations and at all levels of society. Ignorance is at the root of many of society's problems. From their later years children should be educated to understand how important population control has become for each family, and to realize that the 'natural' environment can no longer survive without positive action by man to conserve it. They should realize that man himself cannot survive indefinitely on this earth, without an unacceptable debasing of standards, if he continues to multiply as he is now doing. Conservation begins with man. If man is to get a high-quality environment he has to make a vastly greater effort to understand the criteria and standards required and to translate them into effective action.

But education and encouragement – the only processes acceptable in a democratic society – will take time. It is highly unlikely that, by A.D. 2000, any significant change could be made, since a large proportion of that year's population has been born already. Furthermore, the birth-rate still shows an upward trend which may well increase in view of the high proportion of young and fecund people in the world population today.

World Population Year and Conference

The main event of the U.N. World Population Year of 1974 was the first World Population Conference in Bucharest in 1974. Although this approved a Plan of Action, it was notable for conflicting views among the 137 participating countries. The Chinese, with their 800 million, firmly deny that over-population is the world's greatest problem and assert that the earth could support more people living to their life-style. In general, there was no dispute about the basic proposition that population and poverty and development had to be tackled together. The Conference favoured national approaches, related to local cultures and interests, designed to help each individual country to work out the implications of its own population prospects and the assumptions on which they are based. As these appraisals become available, the U.N. should be able to advise on the likely resource and environmental effects, individually and collectively, and on the implementation of the World Population Plan of Action.

The Plan gives a short résumé of the world demographic situation and the main problems (migration to the cities, age structure, trends, etc.). It sets out a framework of principles to guide governments on population planning, gives recommendations for action (family planning, criteria for population policies, e.g. distribution, demographic studies, education and training and so on) and then deals with measures for implementation by governments and through international cooperation.

Despite the Chinese view, there was much support for the proposition that the earth's resources are not infinite and would be inadequate to support the population forecast for the next century, certainly on the basis of current expectations about the quality of life. The International Planned Parenthood Federation (I.P.P.F.) clearly believes that the Plan endorsed its aims to make family planning a basic human right. Overall, by setting population issues fully in the context of poverty and development and national aspirations, the Conference undoubtedly extended world awareness and probably gave a more realistic basis to the World Population Plan of Action.

Clearly, man has only a few decades in which to determine publicly acceptable standards, to get their implications understood and to initiate action on them. In this, planners and conservationists have a critical role to play. They can use their special knowledge and help formulate criteria, evaluate them in terms meaningful to the citizen, and educate those in responsible positions.

> 'Tomorrow death will be a social phenomenon for
> which we shall have to devise laws'
>
> M. Jean Bourgeois-Pichot

CHAPTER 16

PLANNING: FACTUAL

So far the term 'planning' has been used rather generally to indicate a comprehensive approach to the use and management of the 'natural' environment. In this and the next chapter the intention is to look more closely at 'formal' town and country planning. Its purpose is to create an improved environment – urban and rural; its emphasis has been, and still is, on 'town' rather than country. But modern planning aims to use wisely and to maintain the supply of all resources, including those of rural areas. Most activities having an effect on the use or development of land, air, water and wildlife are subject to some form of control. Few can be treated in isolation; they all interact in varying degree, hence, as environmental problems become more complex, the need for coordination is increasingly urgent.

Planning began in most countries in the nineteenth century with rules or prescriptions for building development directed mainly to achieving adequate sanitary and safety conditions. Much of its impetus stemmed from the realization that disease, fire and other disasters could be reduced or prevented by improving city design. But the supremacy in economic affairs of the dogma of *laissez faire*, the rapid development of great concentrations of industry and people and an era of social ferment inhibited any real progress. Italy – in an Act of 1865 – was the first to include the term 'town planning' in legislation, ten years before either Germany or Sweden.

Britain's first Act was in 1909. For the following thirty years governments sought to plan, but with little success. Most of the laws and planning schemes were thwarted because local authorities found it too difficult or expensive to acquire land. Planning, as a whole, was largely negative, impotent to control the rapid expansion of industry and quite unable to deal with such features as the growth of London and the decline of South

Wales. The history of the century to 1939 is well documented and makes fascinating reading.

The plight of the depressed areas led to the setting-up of a Royal Commission to examine the distribution of industry and population. It reported in 1940 (the Barlow Report) and recommended the creation of a central authority, the redevelopment of congested urban areas, the dispersal of industry and population and the development of a reasonable balance of industrial activity throughout Britain. These proposals and the impact of urban encroachment on agricultural land led in 1941 to the Scott Committee on Land Utilization in Rural Areas. The Committee stressed the vital need to maintain good agricultural land, and attached great importance to conserving rural amenities as part of the national heritage. It recommended the creation of national parks, nature reserves and access facilities to the countryside.

In 1942 the Uthwatt Committee examined compensation and betterment (betterment is any increase in the value of the land resulting from the efforts of the community) and advocated a drastic revision of the laws relating to them. It also proposed the formation of a central planning authority and measures for state control of development.

The three Reports inspired many of the laws passed from 1943 onwards, and supplied them with much of their practical content. A Ministry of Town and Country Planning was set up in 1943 to capitalize on the wealth of ideas available and to meet the spirit of the time. Its efforts culminated in the Town and Country Planning Acts of 1947.

These comprehensive measures were the administrative basis of the planning system until 1968. Development plans had to be prepared by each local planning authority (County Councils and County Boroughs) and reviewed every five years. The 1947 Act defined a 'development plan' as a plan 'indicating the manner in which the local planning authority propose that land in their area should be used'. These plans were to cover a period of about twenty years; they included numerous maps, written statements and analyses which described and defined the major projects in the plan.

This development plan system was very comprehensive and was also highly centralized, as all the plans and subsidiary maps had to be approved by the appropriate Minister, who held a Public Inquiry if there were objections.

Development control was generally carried out on the basis of the development plan. County Boroughs and County Councils were again the authorities responsible, with some delegation to district councils in most counties.

The detailed provisions relating to development control, most of which are still applicable, are very pervasive, especially in urban areas. Most developments – such as the erection of houses, factories, cinemas – and most changes of use – for example, houses to shops, open space to other uses – require planning permission. On the other hand, many agricultural and forestry activities and ancillary developments are outside planning control. The Ministry of Agriculture, Fisheries and Food and the Forestry Commission do, however, maintain close liaison with planning authorities.

Special amenity issues are dealt with by orders and 'tailored' systems. Buildings of historic or architectural interest are the subject of preservation orders; central ministries and local authorities employ experts to advise on the selection and maintenance of such properties. Local planning authorities may prepare tree preservation orders, and the trees specified cannot be felled except under penalty or with the consent of the authority. Advertisements – for example, on buildings, hoardings and so on – are rigorously controlled by the planning authorities with guidance from the Department of the Environment.

Many other issues are covered by special orders and procedures under supporting Acts, such as the Caravan Sites and Control of Development Act 1960. Local authorities now have a duty under the Caravan Sites Act 1968, subject to certain conditions, to exercise their powers under the 1960 Act in order to establish caravan sites 'for the use of gypsies and other persons of nomadic habit'. Additional provisions are available to control unauthorized encampments.

From 1968

Shortly after the basic planning measures had been consolidated in the Town and Country Planning Act of 1962 a major review of the system was set in hand by Government. The outcome was a White Paper (Cmnd 3333) in 1967 which noted that the system was defective with delays and cumbersome procedures, had inadequate citizen participation and was negative in approach.

This led to the Town and Country Planning Act 1968. In order to streamline processes and to concentrate effort and reduce detailed control, development plans were modified to a new form of plan consisting of two main levels:

(1) A structure plan – primarily a written statement of policy, accompanied by a diagrammatic structure map for counties and major towns only, designed to show clearly the broad basic pattern of development and the transport system. These structure plans form the main link between policies on a national and regional level and local planning. They should indicate 'action areas', i.e. areas where comprehensive treatment (development, redevelopment, improvement or a mixture) is envisaged in the ensuing ten years.

(2) Local plans – showing proposals in detail with more precise indication of the land needed, of three types:

   (a) *district plans* – to set out proposals for the whole or part of the area of the structure plan where change may take some time.
   (b) *action area plans* – showing the shape of development in those areas.
   (c) *subject plans* – for a main feature of planning such as conservation zones, a motorway route or mineral extraction.

Only the structure plan requires Ministerial approval and this may be given for the whole or part, with modification or reservations, or may be rejected; local plans only need to be 'adopted' by the local planning authority to come into operation.

Development control was improved in dealing with enforcement of planning control and in preservation of buildings of architectural or historic importance. Appeals had become a 'running sore' in the system and powers were introduced to delegate certain types of cases to selected inspectors. Other supplementary powers have been given to local planning authorities. Over 100,000 listed buildings of special historic or architectural interest receive increased protection and are covered by powers similar to those of a building preservation order.

The 1968 Act also introduced provision for *ad hoc* inquiries by special commissions into major development projects, such as power stations and natural gas installations. The Act enabled local planning authorities to delegate responsibility for certain decisions to their planning officers and required the authority not only to publish its proposals but to consult with local people.

From the mid seventies

Before the new measures in the Town and Country Planning Act 1968 could be adequately implemented, the planning system (consolidated in the Town and Country Acts 1971 and 1972 (and for Scotland 1972)) was overtaken by the reorganization of local government in England and Wales in 1974 and in Scotland in 1975. Before the reforms, there were 143 Planning Authorities in England and Wales (excluding the Greater London area which has had 34 since 1965). Responsibilities are now shared between 45 county councils (including the six metropolitan counties) and 332 district councils (8 and 37 of each authority in Wales), plus the planning boards for the Lake District and Peak District National Parks.

Counties are responsible for structure plans; local plans can be prepared by them or the districts. Under the Local Government Act 1972 the counties are required to prepare, in consultation with districts, a *development plan scheme* to allocate responsibility for making local plans and to provide a programme for their preparation. Counties have the power to determine certain strategic and reserved functions, such as mineral workings and development by the county itself, and, most important, power to approve local plans. But the districts have the primary responsibility for development control and it is assumed that they will normally prepare most of the local plans. This represents a significant shift of power to the districts and clearly gives planning a two-tier system.

Development control was the subject of a major report* for the Government in 1975. Then applications for planning permission approached the half million, with an average 15–20 per cent refused, and appeals near 15,000, of which over 70 per cent were decided by Inspectors. The Report, discussed in the next Chapter, concluded that the planning system should be made 'more rational and efficient, especially in the field of development control'.

In Scotland there were around 60 local planning authorities (a complex situation with joint authorities in some cases). Under the system of authorities brought in by the Local Government (Scotland) Act 1973, there are now 12 Regional or Islands Authorities with varying planning powers and 37 district councils which have some planning responsibilities. The Scottish Development Department basically carries out an overall planning role for economic and physical planning; this may be further extended with the advent of a Scottish Assembly (discussed in Chapter 19).

In six regions (Central, Fife, Grampian, Lothian, Strathclyde and Tayside) functions are shared between regional and district planning authorities. In the other three (Highland, Borders, and Dumfries and Galloway) and in the three Islands Authorities (Orkney, Shetland, and Western Isles) the one general planning authority handles the planning functions.

In addition to structure and local plans (prepared in the six regions by the regional and district authority respectively; both by the general planning authority) the 1973 Act provides for Regional Reports. These are discretionary to the planning authority but the Secretary of State may order them to be prepared and did, in fact, issue a direction in 1975, requiring the first Regional Reports in 1976. The Reports deal with general development policies, programmes and major regional

* *Review of the Development Control System*, George Dobry, H.M.S.O.

proposals, indicating priorities. They should provide a framework for planning and give guidance for structure plans or up-date policy trends for district planning authorities and developers. The Secretary does not formally approve or modify but makes his view on them known; these have to be taken into account in planning work.

Regional strategies had, in practice, become part of the planning system by the seventies. Eight Economic Planning Councils were set up in England in 1965; each comprises about 30 part-time appointed members with knowledge of the region and special experience of official and voluntary agencies, commerce, industry and so on. Their strategic plans are based on an analysis of regional needs, especially in terms of population, employment and industry. Each is supported by an Economic Planning Board of officials of the central government departments to coordinate the policies and interests of the departments in the region. A Council and Board operate on a similar basis in Scotland and in Wales.

TRANSPORT

Another powerful influence on the shape and quality of town and country is the infrastructure of transport. Recognition of this emerged in sharp controversy by the sixties, as the first 1,600 km of the motorway network neared completion and pressure on urban areas to meet traffic demands rapidly increased.

In the mid sixties, the Government initiated many studies, plans and policies, most notable being the White Papers leading to the massive transport legislation of 1968. The general principles of this were to make transport policy a function of local rather than central government; to unify in a plan matters relating to traffic and transport such as the local road network, investment and management; to grant-aid investment in public transport; to bring the basic network of local passenger services under public organization and control in order to facilitate its planning and rationalization; and to plan and operate public transport over larger areas than those of the existing local government authorities.

The legislation provided for Passenger Transport Authorities to be established in any area where the Minister considers that they are needed. A National Bus Company and a Scottish Transport Group were set up to bring together all public transport. New large-scale measures of government help for public transport were introduced; these include major capital grants for new tubes, monorails and the purchase of buses. Special consideration is given to rural bus services.

Local authorities in the conurbations and larger towns outside Greater London should prepare traffic and transport plans for periods of five to seven years. These must, in time, be integrated into the structure plans of the local planning authorities. (The main local authorities have also for long had important powers for the planning and construction of roads.)

In 1971, the Government announced a major expansion of the roads programme. This included the construction of a further 1,600 km of motorway to form a comprehensive network of strategic trunk routes designed to promote economic growth. To this end, the more remote and less prosperous regions will be linked with this new national network. Every major city and town with a population of more than 250,000 will be directly connected to it and all with a population of more than 80,000 will be within about 16 km. The network should also serve all major ports and airports.

In this massive development, it is intended to enhance environmental quality by diverting long-distance traffic, and particularly heavy goods vehicles, from a large number of towns and villages, so as to reduce existing noise, dirt and danger, and to free as many historic towns as possible of through trunk traffic.

The weakness of the Government's policies is generally considered to lie in the failure adequately to relate investment and the balance of effort, and the profit and pricing policies of the transport industries, to the total values of road, rail and water transport. For example, other European countries invest heavily in maintaining, improving and extending their waterways, looking to water as a means of transport which does not damage the environment or use up scarce resources of energy as does petrol/oil driven traffic. The Railways Act 1974 in a small way reflected pressures from environmentalists with its new grants towards the capital costs of private sidings and related facilities to transfer freight from road to rail. But much more strategic measures and a wide range of operating techniques are required effectively to integrate transport with full regard to its social, economic and environmental effects.

New and Expanding Towns

New Towns were officially recommended in the report of the Reith Committee in 1946. They were intended to be at a sufficient distance from London and other major cities to relieve their overcrowding of people and industry. The New Towns Act 1946 enabled the Government to designate land as the site for a new town and to appoint a development corporation to lay out and develop it with capital advanced from public funds.

In the following 25 years, 29 new towns were created, 21 in England, 6 in Scotland and 2 in Wales, and now provide for over three quarters of a million people. The first eight are in open country 20 to 30 miles from London but the three latest, to take London's people, are further afield and much larger. Elsewhere new towns serve many needs – for example, those of local industries, the developing economics of some regions or arresting rural depopulation. Most of the new towns offer attractive sites and provide employment.

Under the New Towns Act 1959, a Commission was set up to take over and manage the property of the development corporations as they end their work of building the new towns. The Commission then settles with the local authorities or statutory undertakers concerned the ownership and ultimate disposal of the assets of the corporation. These powers were consolidated in Acts of 1965 and 1968.

The Town Development Act 1952, and a similar Act of 1957 applying to Scotland, were also intended to relieve congestion and over-population in the towns and cities. The Acts encourage schemes for town development in country districts and provide for cooperation between 'exporting' and 'importing' authorities, and for financial aid both from the authorities and the Government.

INDUSTRY

Geographical and historical, as well as economic, considerations have led to an uneven distribution of industry and population in Britain. Easy access to coal, raw materials and ports helped locate the major developments of the first Industrial Revolution. Communications and power 'on tap' have enabled new industries of the past few decades to settle near the great consumer markets of the Midlands and South-East, the lowland belt of Scotland and in South Wales. Thus, as more has been expected of Government, it has had to take wide powers to secure a better balance of industry and employment throughout Britain. And these are obviously at the heart of meaningful environmental planning.

A tremendous number of changes* in techniques, organizations and priorities mark the last three decades. Following a thorough review, the Industry Act 1972 became the main legislative means for what the Government described as 'the most comprehensive and extensive programme to stimulate industrial and regional regeneration ever undertaken in Britain'. The Act provides the framework for the provision of special Government assistance, national and regional investment incentives, extended Assisted Areas, made more provision for retraining and greater mobility of labour and set up a new Industrial Development Executive (I.D.E.).

The assisted areas are the whole of Scotland, Wales, Northern Ireland, and selected parts of five English regions and the whole of the North region. In the assisted areas, a wide range of allowances and financial aids are given – aid with factories, building plant and machinery, grants, loans on moderate terms, removal grants, tax and depreciation allowances and so on. These vary according to the needs of special development

* See *Regional Development in Britain*, C.O.I. Reference Pamphlet 80, H.M.S.O.

areas, intermediate areas and derelict land clearance areas, with additional incentives in Northern Ireland.

The I.D.E. operates under a Minister of State in the Department of Industry (D.I.) with special responsibility for private sector industry generally and for industrial development in the assisted areas. It appraises and monitors projects referred to it and undertakes wide-ranging studies of industrial problems. The Minister is also helped by an Industrial Development Advisory Board. Regional Industrial Development Boards advise in Scotland and Wales and in some of the English assisted areas. Both types of Board comprise members prominent in industry and commerce and related affairs.

Special mention should be made of a key Governmental control for the location of industry, that is the requirement under the Planning Acts by which any application to erect a new industrial building or extension above a certain size* requires the approval of the Department in the form of an Industrial Development Certificate (I.D.C.). These are, in general, freely available in the assisted areas but are not required in Northern Ireland. Government has also taken direct action over the past decade to disperse its own headquarters offices and it set up in 1963 the Location of Offices Bureau (L.O.B.) to assist businesses moving out of London. It also provides, through the D.I., advanced and custom-built factories, to encourage firms to move to the assisted areas.

Rural industries are encouraged by the Development Commission with financial aid and advisory services, including grants to rural community councils and other voluntary bodies. The service is provided by the Council for Small Industries in Rural Areas in England and Wales, and by the Scottish Development Agency in Scotland and by a Unit of the Department of Commerce in Northern Ireland. Special incentives are available in parts of Scotland from the Highlands and Islands Development Board set up in 1965 and the Crofters Commission of 1955. The Board has backed fishing, tourism and small industries and has probably created over 10,000 jobs in a

---

* Outside the development areas, over 930 sq. metres in the South-East and over 1,400 sq. metres elsewhere.

decade. It has played a vital part in the transformation of many parts of the Highlands and Islands and has initiated research with universities and local authorities into the planning strategy most appropriate to the needs of the area.

The Department of Employment is generally responsible for the efficient use of Britain's manpower and for the manpower aspects of regional policy and regional economic planning. In particular it can provide, subject to certain conditions, special financial help to workers moving to a new plant in the assisted areas. New Government measures for industry through the National Enterprise Board and the Scottish and Welsh Development Agencies are obviously going to affect the location and balance of industry and so their activities will need to be carefully appraised for their environmental implications. A statutory duty to have regard to the safeguarding of the environment is placed upon the Agencies.

There is also a wide range of industries whose activities affect the environment directly and indirectly. These include the National Water Council, the British Waterways Board, the British Tourist Authority, the British Railways Board, the Ports, Airports and Airways and other development industries, such as the British National Oil Corporation. Many services, such as the National Health Service, affect our surroundings.

The E.E.C. has several measures which affect regional policies and development. They have been broadly designed to achieve more balanced development in different parts of the countries and more effective uses of resources. Since 1972 priority has been given to correcting structural and regional imbalances which might affect the realization of economic and monetary union. Funds are deployed in relation to agriculture, coal, steel, and other major sectors as well as on a geographical basis (e.g. the upland and marginal areas).

Despite some of the most generous grants and tax allowances in Europe, U.K. industry had clearly not succeeded by the mid seventies in investing adequately to compete in some world markets and to provide the nation with the economic growth sought by so many. If industrial planning plus financial and labour support do not ensure that industrialists respond to social needs, what then is required to achieve environmental goals which are of lesser immediacy to them?

Other Planning Measures

Technological developments, such as power stations, main electricity lines, and gas and oil pipelines, are subject to special procedures between the statutory undertakers and the planning authorities. The consent of the Secretary of State for Industry is also required. Where scenic amenity is involved the Secretary of State for the Environment is consulted and often public inquiries are held.

Developments by the Crown, including defence requirements of land, are not subject to formal planning control. From 1950, the local planning authority had usually been consulted, but in 1971 the Government announced a significant change. Departments were required to consult the local planning authority about any development which would need planning permission if it were proposed by a private developer. This placed government departments broadly in a position analogous to individuals, with similar requirements for publicity over applications. If agreement cannot be reached, the Secretary of State for the Environment arbitrates.

CONSERVATION MEASURES

> Conservation can be defined as the wise use of our natural environment: it is, in the final analysis, the highest form of national thrift – the prevention of waste and despoilment while preserving, improving and renewing the quality and usefulness of all our resources.
>
> President John F. Kennedy:
> Message to Congress, 1962

A number of areas shown on development plans receive special consideration within the planning system. They include National Parks, Areas of Outstanding Natural Beauty, Areas of Great Landscape, Scientific or Historic Value, Long-distance Routes and national, local and forest Nature Reserves. These provide for a wide range of interests – amenity, outdoor recreation, research, education and wildlife. Most of them were the primary responsibility of the National Parks Commission (in England and Wales only) and the Nature Conservancy, two national bodies set up in 1949. The National Parks and Access to the Countryside Act of that year contains most of the requisite powers.

From 1965, the Nature Conservancy was a Committee of the Natural Environment Research Council (N.E.R.C.). In 1973 it was split into conservation and research agencies. Research remained with N.E.R.C., becoming its Institute of Terrestrial Ecology. Conservation became the responsibility of the Nature Conservancy Council (N.C.C.) under the N.C.C. Act 1973.

The Council's functions are the establishment, maintenance and management of nature reserves in Great Britain, the provision of advice for the Secretary of State or any other Minister on the development and implementation of policies for, or affecting, nature conservation in Great Britain, the provision of advice and the dissemination of knowledge about nature conservation and the commissioning or support of relevant research. The Council also have power to carry out research which it is appropriate for them to do instead of commissioning or supporting another body to undertake such research. The term nature conservation in this context means the conservation of flora, fauna or geological or physiographical features and in discharging their functions the Council must take account as appropriate of actual and possible ecological changes. The 1973 Act requires the Council to appoint separate advisory committees for England, Scotland and Wales.

By the Countryside Act 1968 the National Parks Commission was reconstituted as a Countryside Commission, retaining its former functions and gaining wider responsibilities. In the same year the Countryside Commission for Scotland was set up under the Countryside (Scotland) Act of 1967, which gave it powers relating to access to open country, public paths and long-distance routes. The Commissions keep under review the provision and improvement of facilities for the enjoyment of the countryside, the conservation and enhancement of

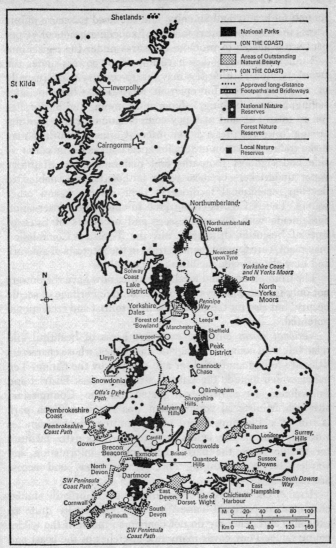

Figure 13. Statutory conservation in Britain (Crown Copyright)

its natural beauty and amenity, and the need to secure public access to it for open-air recreation. Exchequer grants of 75 per cent are available to promote measures under the legislation.

Numerous other bodies have important powers under the two Acts. Local authorities may set up country parks (usually of 10 ha or larger) for open-air recreation, which includes sailing, boating, bathing, fishing, and camping and picnic sites (of up to 10 ha), and may pay compensation for tree planting arising from tree preservation orders. Certain authorities may make traffic regulation orders for special areas of the countryside and signpost footpaths and maintain stiles. Statutory water undertakers or local water authorities are enabled to develop recreational facilities at their reservoirs and other waters. The N.C.C. is empowered to enter into conservation agreements with owners, lessees and occupiers of Sites of Special Scientific Interest. And the Forestry Commission may plant, care for and manage trees in the interests of amenity and may also provide facilities for recreation.

The Commissions and local authorities now have the powers not only for the conservation of the 'unique heritage of scenic beauty' but also for the development of tourist and recreational potential.

National Parks embrace extensive areas of beautiful and relatively wild country in England and Wales, whose characteristics are to be maintained for and enjoyed by the nation. Ten parks, which include the Lake District, the Peak District and Snowdonia, have been designated by the Commission, although Ministerial confirmation was required. Each park is run by a Planning Board or Committee which promotes work to enhance the landscape and provides extra facilities for people using the park; these include information and warden services, camping and caravan sites, and access arrangements.

Areas of Outstanding Natural Beauty are of broadly similar character to National Parks, but are not usually quite so extensive and generally do not contain so much of the wilder countryside. They cover many fine stretches of the coast and areas such as the Sussex Downs and the Cotswolds. They are designated by the Commission, but do not have a special body to administer them. The local planning authority is responsible for protecting and improving the landscape and for making arrangements for public access to open country.

Areas of Great Landscape, Scientific or Historic Value are designated by local planning authorities and depend on their readiness to seek and accept the best advice available and to show such areas on their development plans. The authorities usually require developers in these areas to achieve higher standards of design and to pay particular regard to the appearance of the landscape.

Long-distance Routes are paths for ramblers and horse-riders and are protected within the planning system. The Pennine Way was the first to be completed (in 1965); other routes exist and are being created over long stretches of coastline. The Commission handles most of this work itself, subject to Ministerial approval and liaison with local planning authorities. It can create new paths to complete a route and provide hostels and related facilities. The 1949 Act also includes further measures for access to coast and country. Local planning authorities must survey and record footpaths and other public rights of way, and they have powers to provide facilities by means of access agreements with owners or by orders if agreement cannot be reached. The 1967 and 1968 Acts also include more powers to deal with footpaths.

Nature Reserves are frequently referred to as 'living museums' and 'outdoor laboratories'. They contain habitats for the conservation of animals and plants and are areas of the greatest scientific interest for research and education. National Nature Reserves, which are the most important, are chosen and administered by the N.C.C.

Local Nature Reserves are established by local authorities in consultation with the N.C.C. Forest nature reserves are managed for research and conservation by arrangements between the N.C.C. and the Forestry Commission and certain other major landowners.

Together with *Sites of Special Scientific Interest* (S.S.S.I.s) these reserves are of much educational and scientific value to the nation and ensure the conservation of many habitats and their animals and plants. The security of Local Nature Reserves depends on the legal tenure and powers of the local authority concerned. S.S.S.I.s are, however, not safeguarded against agricultural operations or afforestation, and their interest has only to be taken into account by the local planning authority before determining a planning application.

Wildfowl Refuges, selected by the N.C.C. and wild-fowlers, give special protection to the main breeding and wintering grounds of wildfowl, although controlled shooting is permitted in some of them. They are linked in a national chain, which fits into a European pattern, and are supported by regional refuges. Although a few wildfowl refuges are National Nature Reserves, more of them are designated Sites of Special Scientific Interest; additionally, some are also statutory bird sanctuaries under the Protection of Birds legislation.

Finally, in the main categories of land receiving special consideration within the planning system are the *Green Belts*, proposed by the local planning authority and confirmed by the Minister. These were originally set apart to limit the spread of towns and to stop them merging to form conurbations (as in the Black Country) or to maintain distinctive qualities in a town, such as Bath. More recently it has been recognized that these lands must be positively managed to prevent their deterioration and that they can provide for many of the country pleasures sought by townspeople.

Conservation of clean air is increasingly within the scope of the planning system. As shown in Chapters 6 and 7, many experts consider that the best long-term solutions lie with physical planning. This is particularly important in preventing new pollution and in locating development which may pollute on sites where it can do least harm. By concentrating industry in certain zones and prescribing distances from roads and dwellings, by avoiding valleys where air pollution can be penned in, by providing open spaces and green belts, and by favouring housing and other urban development with district heating systems, the planner can help to ensure clean air. Generally, there is wide scope within the planning system for the planner to support the measures described in Chapters 6 and 7.

Water conservation affects most proposals of the local planning authority and, in turn, is materially influenced by town and country planning. The shortage of planners able to evaluate the specialized functions involved (see Chapters 8 and 9) limits the full integration of measures for water conservation into structure plans. Another problem is that of coordination between the various bodies concerned with water supply and use and the many local planning authorities. It is, however, essential that there should be close cooperation, both in strategy – when plans are made for dispersing population, relocating industry, and preparing barrage schemes – and in the more tactical detailed inter-authority joint schemes for, say, the recreational use of some local waters. It is probable that support for strategic planning of water resources and the implementation of national and regional policies can best come from full-scale regional planning.

Wildlife conservation is obviously supported by all these measures within the planning system. But many other functions of local planning authorities have a direct impact on wildlife. For example, many county councils had bird protection and sanctuary committees until their powers were altered by the Protection of Birds Act 1954; some still have them. Most councils have by-laws to control or prohibit the picking of wild flowers. The flora and fauna of roadside verges are influenced by the way in which Highway Departments carry out road maintenance. Education departments can acquire and manage sites for field studies and other outdoor activities. Many planning departments are very active – often with the help of county Naturalists' Trusts – in conserving local nature reserves and sites of scientific interest, in making tree preservation orders and enhancing the value of open spaces, green belts and amenity areas, and in reclaiming derelict land.

But the squalor of litter and refuse in urban areas and the loss of many fine buildings caused increasing concern in the sixties. The Civic Amenities Act 1967 reflected the widespread mood of the country that more positive action was essential to conserve our urban heritage. It provided extra measures to protect and improve buildings of architectural or historical interest and to conserve the character of areas containing them. Local planning authorities were also given wider powers and duties for the preservation and planting of trees. The Act introduced powers to tackle 'eyesores'; subject to certain safeguards, local authorities should remove and dispose of abandoned vehicles and provide dumps for the deposit of bulky refuse by citizens (penalties are specified for unauthorized dumping).

The D.O.E. set up a new Directorate for Ancient Monuments, Historic Buildings and Conservation Areas in 1972. The Field Monuments Act 1972 enables the Government to make payments to occupiers of land which is a field monument in 'acknowledgement' of the occupier entering into an agreement to undertake specific duties and liabilities for it. More resources were also allocated by D.O.E. to deal with archaeological features of the national heritage.

A tremendous network has been built up here of central and local agencies engaged in improving the quality of the environment. The measures set out in this chapter reveal why Britain is generally accepted as having the most comprehensive and advanced system in the world.

CHAPTER 17

PLANNING: ASSESSMENT

DESPITE this tremendous fabric of authorities and powers, British planning has disappointed. But before analysing the reasons for this, it is only fair to consider some of its achievements.

Inevitably much planning has been restrictive and the public do not readily appreciate the fine contribution it has made to the quality of the environment. Planning has saved the countryside from a great deal of thoughtless urban sprawl, unwise expansion of villages and despoliation of the countryside. Unsightly advertisements and ribbons of houses cannot now be erected to obscure the best views or create hazards for traffic.

Few of the results of planning are spectacular. Improved layouts of housing estates, faster communications, interspersed parks and greens, and better siting and design of public and private dwellings all too frequently gain no credit for the planners but only for their builders. Yet the inter-war years showed the kind of development that can occur where there is no planning control.

More obviously, new towns have been established, national parks created, motorways built, towns developed and some bad old dereliction eliminated. Planning also contributes to the provision of clean air and pure water and to nature conservation. Perhaps its main achievements, on which all the rest hinged, were the development plans, which were very much the key to the success or failure of planning.

But the achievements are dwarfed by the problems which still have to be faced. Despite the efforts of the planning network, the huge growth of population and industry in the south-east of England has continued; the blight on the older industrial areas and their centres remains; the finances of planning – the compensation–betterment problem – are still the subject of controversy; land for development is scarce and almost prohibitively expensive; the decay of the landscape and changes in the countryside under a bewildering succession of impacts are being tackled in an *ad hoc* and fragmented manner; decisions about the uses of agricultural land, the problems of living and working in rural areas, the demands of those seeking enjoyment in the countryside in their leisure time – all these are more complex and urgent than ever before.

Although so comprehensive, planning legislation has not yet proved fully adequate for the special problems of rural land. There is insufficient coordination between the many interests concerned with rural land – forestry, water, recreation, conservation, amenity and so on. Often, each one has had to prove separately that its need for a particular piece of rural land is more important than leaving that land to agriculture, with the result that some areas are being farmed which might have been more valuable to the nation if put to other, combined uses. On the other hand, there are numerous cases where best-quality agricultural land has been taken. The agriculturalist complains that little or no thought is given to the needs of farmers and their workpeople, and the prime use of the countryside, which is to grow food, is ignored.

Measures for conservation give rise to many difficulties. The farmer may find them a source of inefficiency. The industrialist, when faced with a map of these special areas, must wonder where he can develop. How can he take a pipeline, overhead cable or road through such a maze? The prospective developer sees the areas set aside as reserves and green belts as a demand on land and water which must be justified in the over-all national interest. Yet in many areas these restrictions must become tougher as, for example, over parts of the coastline.

The measures adopted for the support of industry need to be kept in force longer, for frequent changes are unsettling. Over a hundred Acts and numerous orders affecting industry have been passed in the past three decades. But within agreed strategy there should be more flexibility and selectiveness, and much more account could be taken of all the resources of an area.

Why has planning not coped adequately? Inevitably the

reasons lie in every facet of society – in laws and their administration, in the organizations and professions concerned, but
most of all in the attitudes of the people who accepted the
trends or led them.

Undoubtedly, too much was expected of planning by the
public and by those engaged in it. In retrospect, we can see
that it was both grossly unfair and naïve to imagine that the
handful of qualified planners available could remedy the mistakes and wrongs of the past, ensure that current development
did not repeat these errors, be alert to new evils and act as
prophets to diagnose trends and predict the best solutions.

People in power were also a problem. Many in central
departments or local authorities did not take kindly to being
planned, integrated, or even helped, by the planners. Inevitably consultation meant delay and often changes in their own
plans and projects. Members of old-established professions
often disdained to accept the comprehensive approach of this
new race of synthesizers.

And the people themselves? The man in the street reserved
his traditional rights: to have his cake and eat it; to grumble
about 'them' holding up development and being impractical;
to complain bitterly when a project of personal interest was
affected; and to demand better standards and services. But
would he participate in the processes of planning, through the
normal social channels? In most cases he would not! Yet to
get a good relationship between the individual or the public
and the planning authorities is crucial to the task of achieving a
high-quality environment.

Planning legislation has been, and is still, regarded by some
people as an encroachment on personal liberty. They believe it
is wrong to interfere with market forces and the interplay of
private initiative and the profit-motive. The concept that legislation can provide a framework for better living and create a
healthy environment does not yet command sufficient support.
The subject-matter of much planning legislation is technical
and complex, even to experts; overmuch has been attempted
centrally and not enough power and encouragement given to
the enterprise of local authorities.

Much modern legislation fails to treat the environment as a unity. Too many principles and policies have polarized around the attitudes of ministries and agencies. Pressure groups naturally seek to resolve urgent problems without regarding their full impact on a wide range of related issues. Undoubtedly it is a difficult operation to integrate the entire body of law relating to the physical environment. Without question, the problems inherent in coordinating the work of the modern nation-state are great and tending to increase. But they have to be tackled.

Inevitably, therefore, actions of central departments have not reflected the unity of environmental issues. Although on occasions a bulwark against misuse of power, departmental attitudes can seriously hinder effective planning. The antagonisms tend to be fiercer and more difficult to modify than those of the individuals in whom they are often focused. Also, too many decision-makers are reluctant to use the end product of modern research and survey. Their unwillingness often arises from that lack of understanding of scientific principles and distrust of quantitative data which is common to many administrators. These shortcomings affect most aspects of central administration, but they are particularly important in planning, because no environmental situation is ever static. Whether decisions are taken or not there is a changing situation, and failure to take a decision at a given time often means that desired aims can never be achieved.

Whatever the deficiencies and inadequacies of central bodies, those of local planning authorities were worse. With a few exceptions, such as the Greater London Council, until 1974 the local planning authorities in England and Wales were based on the structure established by the reforming Local Government Act of 1888. The ancient Norman counties and the large towns of the Industrial Revolution then became the major units of democratic local government. From the outset the antagonism between county and county borough shattered the interdependence of town and country and often created and intensified an antipathy between urban and rural communities. This nullified much modern planning.

A characteristic of many authorities is their (inevitable) preoccupation with rateable value; that is, the money they derive from property in their area. This is often not only half their total income but also the source of any real independence they claim. And in some localities effective planning has been rendered almost impossible by the battle for rateable values between authorities.

Many were also too small in area, and had too little money, knowledge and staff, to take account of the economic and technological demands inherent in dealing with traffic, location of industry, water, refuse disposal and sewage, and many other services. This led to the allocation of major services to *ad hoc* bodies which makes coordination and synthesis – the essence of planning and the spirit of creative development – almost unattainable.

Planning authorities would have faced immense difficulties even if they had been given a national strategy setting out principles and policies in planning and full coordination between all the agencies of central government. But they have had neither.

From the mid seventies

The Dobry Report of 1975 stated that 'the planning system has achieved a great deal', but it summed up that 'overall the planning machine is too cumbersome and complex'. It also asserted that 'it is not so much the system which is wrong but the way in which it is used' and urged changes of attitude towards a more positive and constructive approach on all sides.

The Report showed that the redistribution of functions in 1974 between counties and districts had had an uneven effect and there was an overriding need for clear division of responsibilities between county and district and a limitation of the flow of paper between the two. It stressed that the speedy production of structure and local plans is crucial and that they ought to be ready everywhere by 1980. Counties were again advised to concentrate on issues of key structural importance and to eschew lengthy, elaborate and detailed structure plans. The Report was, however, primarily concerned with development control and its proposals were mainly to streamline, not to replace, the system. Other more fundamental criticisms were being levied.

Many engaged in planning severely criticized the distribution of planning responsibilities as 'splitting the system' and believed that the increase in the number of authorities with planning responsibilities in Britain to over 500 jeopardized the future of planning. Many of the new county planning authorities are too small for the comprehensive planning needed by the new conditions and measures of the mid seventies; in some cases their boundaries continue the dichotomy of town and country; and they have lost important water services which so affect the environment. Yet the prospect of further change in the structure of government, when a period of stability is so sorely needed, puts the onus on all concerned to make existing systems work in the coming decade.

Others contended that planning did not sufficiently enough influence the shape of the natural environment and the management of land and water in rural areas. It was pointed out that measures to enhance the production of food and timber and the supply and use of water had much more effect than those of the planning system, despite the provisions for National Parks, Areas of Outstanding Natural Beauty, Country Parks and other planning designations.

Some critics held that the primary function of plans was to ensure that development was controlled wisely and that this they had largely failed to do. Zoning was alleged to be applied too rigidly and to be deficient in concept and practice. The split of the system between various forms of plan and development control was held to be unsound and its shortcomings to have been accentuated by the allocation of functions between counties and districts. More specifically, the planning system was held to have failed to provide the nation with land, especially for housing, in the right place at the right time and at the right price.

Structure plans were thought by some to be likely to go the way of development plans and be too detailed and negative. In particular, the scarcity of qualified planners and the competition for them by the much larger number of planning authorities would mean that 'orthodox' plans would take too long to produce and be out of date when complete. It was, therefore, urged that structure plans be simplified into a basic framework of facts and options and be subject to a continuous cycle of annual revisions.

Almost contrary views were voiced by some who felt that structure plans were going to be so vague and indefinite that they would not achieve their aims. Some districts appeared to be determined to produce local plans to their specification and in a way which could tend to resolve structural issues, rather than the other way round.

The processes of public participation in the formulation of plans were held to be inadequate on the one hand and yet, on the other, to be a source of serious delay and unnecessary conflict. The Dobry Report stressed the need for public involvement to be relevant, more efficient and constructive and selective, in the context of encouraging, yet containing, its increasingly considerable importance. The Report proposed a number of measures to facilitate public involvement, appeals and judicial review of decisions. It also suggested that the planning authority should have power, to be used sparingly and selectively, to require an applicant to submit an impact study on specially significant proposals. These would show fully the environmental consequences of the project and would obviously be of value in relation to public involvement. Overall, there seemed little doubt in the mid seventies that the high aspirations for public participation in planning would not be realized without significant changes in methods for and attitudes about it.

One particular feature of planning, involving plans and development control, is the Green Belt. It was being sharply attacked in the seventies, particularly outside London. From 1955 onwards it was considered to have created a *cordon sanitaire* around the major towns, which had led to potential developers or house dwellers jumping across the Green Belt and having to commute backwards and forwards. Opponents of the Green Belt saw it as an instrument of social privilege, to keep green and pleasant what only the better-off can afford. It was urged that the nation should forget about green belts and concentrate on creating green cities.

Development control, too, obviously needed substantial improvement. The Dobry Report recommended the categorization of applications into simple and difficult cases, with differing and streamlined procedures to deal with them; monitoring of applications to keep the system moving freely and concentrating on the important and complex problems; speeding-up appeals and enforcement procedures; these and many other measures to the same ends were proposed to revitalize the planning system. But late 1975 saw the Government announce that new arrangements which would place an on-going higher burden on resources could not then be introduced. A Circular was, however, issued advising the adoption of the most efficient working methods!

The two-tier structure itself poses new and special issues. The integrated character of plan-making and implementation and of development control demand close cooperation between county and district councils. The limited number of qualified planners available requires collaboration between both to deploy this scarce talent wisely. The political aspects of policy-making for plans and also of major decisions in development control and the reservation by counties of certain strategic issues, contain the seeds of severe, potentially internecine, rivalries. Wisdom and restraint, coupled with determination to achieve fruitful cooperation, are demanded of politicians and planners in county and district if the two-tier basis is not to nullify the effectiveness of the planning system.

This assessment is of the system as it has evolved over thirty years. It assumes circumstances in which planning would continue broadly on the same bases. But this is not likely to be the case. Success with the Community Land Act 1975 and the Development Land Tax and the greater use of fiscal measures could substantially alter the whole position. Developments on a world and European scale could radically transform the economic, environmental and social conditions of this island. All these would leave us with the simple aim – to plan –

and a totally new series of measures would be needed to achieve that aim.

Planners and People

To many involved in it, physical planning appeared a dull and pedestrian business. This was desperately unfortunate because planning has unlimited creative scope and requires a great capacity for understanding people. Many planners are so hard-pressed that they cannot keep abreast of the increasing demands of an exacting profession. Neither have the authorities sufficient staff of the requisite intellect and training.

Few planners are, therefore, able to spare much of their valuable working time for talking to laymen about the issues involved and for generally encouraging public interest. It is not surprising, then, that people tend to think planning is a mystique, that planners are introverted and exclusive and that they are remote and bureaucratic. Thus people fail to see how the quality of their environment can affect them, and do not grasp how they might be able to make a personal contribution to its enhancement. The divorce between planners and public is made sharper by the failure of many local councillors to lead and inspire their citizens. This is not necessarily their own fault, but often reflects the great practical difficulties which face the public-spirited councillor. And planning suffers most.

Until the necessity of planning is fully accepted and people are actively involved, it will continue to treat symptoms and not basic issues such as environmental standards and criteria. In public participation, a prime factor is that of timing – plans of the right stage must be publicized at the right time to avoid *faits accomplis*. And information must be presented suitably. Perhaps the old truism might be rephrased to read 'the public gets the planning it deserves'. But this is not really true. Today, so much specialization and expert knowledge are required that, unless all officially concerned are imbued with a belief in the vital nature of 'grass-roots' participation, the public is unlikely to get a chance either to understand what is happening or to say what it feels.

To imagine that the individual does not care would be a gross error. One of the most encouraging features in Britain today is the strength and depth of feeling about conservation and enhancement of the environment. People do care – the shortcomings and blemishes can be removed through team-work and leadership. But without question, the country is not devoting enough of its top talent to these tasks.

In Other Countries

In almost all countries planning is a function of the State. Inevitably, factors of history and geography lead to differences in planning policies and practice, but more important today is the philosophy of each society. For example, planning at national level is more comprehensive in the U.S.S.R., Poland and Hungary than in the U.S.A. and many South American countries; in some socialist countries physical and economic planning are already integrated. But few countries can equal the Netherlands for comprehensiveness and development, and yet this country is obviously of 'Western' philosophy.

At the top level in government and the professions, the work of many international associations and conferences confirms there is a common approach on principles and policies. Greater integration of economic and physical planning is sought to deal with the dominant problems of population control and distribution, and the location of industry. Strategic planning, and ways of harmonizing policies for agriculture, forestry and urban needs are emphasized. Most countries face in varying degrees problems created by urban sprawl, the pressures of traffic and leisure, the contamination of air and water, the loss of wildlife and a deterioration in the quality of the environment.

It is, however, over powers and procedures that the greatest differences emerge. Britain's comprehensive system of planning administration is the envy of many countries. Undoubtedly, it reflects the fact that this crowded island was the first to suffer the excesses of the Industrial Revolution and has therefore developed a relatively greater public acceptance of planning.

But in all countries, public support and participation appear inadequate to sustain the systems required to deal effectively with today's environmental problems.

Recommendations about these problems have formed part of the Conferences of Ministers on Regional Planning convened by the Council of Europe to deal with the main needs of member countries. These Conferences show clearly the need for cooperation in regional planning over areas which have an affinity in their climatic, geographic and social conditions, and where natural features, such as the Rhine, cut across national boundaries. It is vital to safeguard for our cultural heritage palaces, temples and monasteries, archaeological sites, national parks and great natural features, such as the Krimml waterfalls in Austria.

The Conferences also stress how certain types of regions have special problems. Frontier areas may share common environments, but divergent national population and economic policies may inhibit cooperation over their planning and development. Comparatively local action may be required here; for example, in mountain regions, tourism can usually be encouraged by relatively small 'pump-priming' of finance and services; in remote rural areas, without a base for tourism, the creation of soil 'banks', wilderness areas, and wildlife reserves may provide the viable settlements and labour force needed for long-term management. Such problem areas and those on the periphery of main economic regions require special consideration to promote the infrastructure of services and the growth of well-sited regional centres. And some of the over-developed areas, such as the potential conurbations between London-Brussels-Amsterdam or Paris-Munich-Milan, are now ripe for large-scale international planning.

If, then, powers and processes are still inadequate for modern needs in most countries of western Europe and certainly also in the Federal U.S.A., what are the changes which should be made to improve the whole position? These are the issues discussed in the three following chapters.

CHAPTER 18

REQUIREMENTS AND PROPOSALS – I

Philosophy · Principles · Government

> I have been ever of the opinion that revolutions
> are not to be evaded.
>
> Benjamin Disraeli

THIS chapter and the next consider how it might be possible
to place the structure of planning on a firmer long-term basis.
The proposals go beyond suggesting reforms merely in the
processes of planning because these in themselves will only
'paper over the cracks'. What is needed is a framework conceived differently from the present one.

PHILOSOPHY

> I repeat . . . that all power is a trust – that we are
> accountable for its exercise – that, from the
> people, and for the people, all springs and all
> must exist.
>
> Benjamin Disraeli

In most countries the State maintains law and order and seeks
to guide social development by political, legislative and administrative means. The need for the State to create a framework
for individual and cooperative effort is now taken for granted.
What is in question is its extent and detail. Planning, not only
of the physical environment but of most economic and natural
resources, is not yet wholly accepted as part of this framework.
Some regard it as a keystone of ideologies – for example, Com-
munism or Socialism – which they may abhor. Others regard
it as a factor inhibiting the free play of market forces. To some,
it is a panacea for the ills of society, an opportunity to create
their own particular Utopia or a means of imposing their own
concepts upon an inarticulate and apathetic public.

All this is particularly unfortunate because essentially planning is neutral. It is primarily a process for making a deliberate choice about future relationships between man and his environment. It is not antithetic to freedom. Where men have a choice, they usually prefer to plan their affairs. In a community, planning helps to provide the ways and means of achieving social objectives, just as in all modern industry it is a prerequisite for continued commercial existence, development and profit-making.

No one today questions the need for communal action in the field of, say, public health, or in the compilation of population statistics. But for years these were regarded as gross infringements of personal liberty and were hotly contested in Parliament, Press and Pulpit. What has not been widely enough accepted is the premise that a healthy environment requires the positive efforts of the community to create it and rules to prevent individuals or groups from marring or destroying it. It seems essential, therefore, to state some of the philosophy and principles underlying the policies and procedures suggested in this book.

The first of the philosophic issues is summed up in an extension of the old adage 'A healthy mind in a healthy body' to include 'in a healthy environment': for those who prefer a Latin tag – *Mens sana in corpore sano in vicinia sana*. If man is to achieve real fulfilment and satisfy his highest aspirations, then clearly a healthy environment is vital. The tragedies which come from his forgetting this can be seen in any of the unhealthy slums of the world. Fortunately today he is remembering it more often, as the worldwide concern about land use and conservation now shows.

Acceptance of this extended adage requires an awareness of man's creative and destructive capacities. It demands a sense of personal responsibility for curbing destructive forces and wise use of creative powers. It demands an understanding of the individual's inheritance and of his obligation to hand on to his children an enhanced heritage. Each generation should take particular care to leave its successor some scope for choice in the creation of a healthy environment.

Environmental issues need to be appraised in ethical terms.* Such an ethic embodies responsibility for the maintenance of the productive capacity of land, air, water and wildlife, for their integrity and stability, and for the aesthetic qualities of the landscape. It requires the formulation and acceptance of environmental standards and codes of behaviour, together with a constant vigilance to ensure that they are put into effect.

It is essential to make people feel that they are trustees for the environment and to infuse this attitude into all activities of the State. Conservation for posterity should become a built-in aim of central and local government. Members and officials need to develop the right attitude of mind so that they constantly seek to maintain and enhance the resources and qualities on which society depends. That this approach is not common today is well illustrated in most countries where sectional battles over land and water resources are frequent.

A danger to guard against is the philosophy of a corporate State. As many large organizations – of government, industry or workers – learn to speak the 'same language', there could emerge a system of 'package deals' which, in the long run, would be self-defeating. But once society has developed a philosophy demanding a healthy environment, based on ethics and trusteeship, planning can really become positive and purposeful, creative and imaginative. But it must be established on certain principles.

PRINCIPLES

Unity

A primary principle is that the environment is a unity. Town and country are within one society and one civilization. In all spheres – economic, social, physical and probably moral – there is clear and continuing interdependence, between those who live and work in the countryside and those who use it, and between agriculture and forestry, industry and commerce. People are concerned with one land. Most social activities, urban or rural, are enjoyed by most people at some time.

*See page 40 and Appendix 1.

The environment is a complex and interconnected system, a web and a continuum, dynamic and ever-changing. Action in one part affects others. Planning should recognize this unity of physical forces and people and seek to create a synthesis guiding changes to desired social objectives. To do this effectively, it must assess policies and developments affecting the environment not only for their impacts on natural resources but for all their inter-relationships.

Wetlands are particularly sensitive to apparently minor changes. Each part is uniquely interdependent with another. The cases studied in Chapter 12 show that their ecological balance is so delicate that any action not based on a thorough appraisal of all aspects, and a comprehensive approach to their planning, management and development, may be fatal.

And this unity embraces man.

Comprehensiveness

Coupled with the principle of unity should be that of comprehensiveness in environmental planning. Hitherto, much rural planning has been *in* the rural area – for villages, services, or minor uses. Rarely has it been *of* the countryside. Yet it needs to take account of a wide range of demands: for agriculture and forestry; for industry and housing; for traffic, tourism and outdoor recreation; and for the requirements of a changing rural population. Future plans ought to assess the capacity of the land to meet these demands. They must also recognize that people cannot withstand an indefinite increase in the pressures of city life. Again, urban and rural planning should be synthesized.

To do all this requires a comprehensive appraisal of environmental issues, particularly economic and ecological. Any future for the countryside must be based on a sound economy. Agriculture needs to be closely integrated within economic and physical planning so that limited resources are used in the best interests of society. If the nation expects rural landowners and occupiers to fulfil extra obligations – for example, to create new landscapes for general enjoyment – these must be paid for. A complementary need is to consider all developments in terms of their effects on the ecological health of the country-side and on the basis of the criteria in Supplement 1 for those living in urban settlements.

The effects of air pollution in Britain, discussed in Chapter 7, grimly demonstrate man's capacity for getting one product at the expense of many other qualities – human and environmental. Few people would question the need for a comprehensive approach if they were aware of the implications of such cases.

Quality

The third principle is that the quality of the environment is part of the heritage of the nation.

Quality has been proclaimed for years as an objective for urban areas, particularly to meet the need for environmental management of the towns in face of the all-engulfing traffic. Brilliant practical illustrations of planning for quality, which embody the principles of unity and comprehensiveness, are the Lea Valley Regional Park and the Stoke Central Forest Park.

At the same time, the quality of rural areas has been taken for granted, but it has probably altered more since 1945 than has that of urban areas. Some consider the changes of the past decade to be greater than those in the fourteenth century following the Black Death or in the eighteenth century after the enclosures. Recognition of this, and that even more sweeping changes are on the way, inspired the activities of the past 'environmental' decade.

The quality of the biosphere would be greatly diminished if there were no healthy wildlife, yet Chapter 10 shows that the world is in danger of losing the abundant wildlife of Africa just as it almost destroyed the bison of North America. The application of science and technology in Britain is inexorably eliminating certain plants and animals and their habitats, and population pressures are affecting coast and country. Yet this need not be, if conservation and enhancement of quality were accepted as a basic principle. The situation is unlikely to improve until people perceive quality as being of personal value and voluntarily act to achieve it. The individual gain will add up to overall human satisfaction, which, in the final analysis, is the ultimate test of society.

These three principles are essential if the State is to safeguard resources for the needs of future populations. What are the means of government by which they should be implemented?

GOVERNMENT AND ENVIRONMENT

Two major constitutional events of the seventies are likely to affect the shape and quality of the environment for generations ahead. These are the U.K. entry into the European Economic Community and Devolution.

Membership of E.E.C. inevitably intensifies the economic and political forces pressing towards common policies in Europe for industry and agriculture and for the marginal and hill lands and peripheral areas of member countries. E.E.C. policies will increasingly become major forces in settling the existence, scale and location of many of the activities which determine land uses and the planning and management of town and country. Measures to deal with common problems, such as pollution of air and water, will further affect these issues and the operation of our industries. Increased travel and communication of all kinds between European countries will spread ideas and techniques more rapidly. And, pervasively, there is the ultimate question of the extent and control (our biosphere can no longer allow absolute sovereignty) over these vital interests.

Devolution also raises this question of extent and control for all activities and levels of government. The U.K. White Paper on Democracy and Devolution (Cmnd 6348) made a firm commitment to maintaining the political and economic unity of the U.K. and rejected the possibility of Scotland and Wales becoming separate states. It sought to provide Scottish and Welsh Assemblies, directly chosen by and answerable to their people, which would control policies and spending priorities for very wide fields of government to enable them to bring far-reaching influence to bear in the whole physical and social environment of their countries.

These powerful trends towards closer political and economic unity in Europe and more devolution in member countries must inevitably change the balance and distribution of power for all the structures from the E.E.C. H.Q. in Brussels to the parish council or commune. The present excessive centralization and overloading of responsibilities at national level in several countries cannot survive long and remain effective under the increasing load of work arising from cooperation on a European and world scale.

The great size of many modern institutions is now widely condemned; this is particularly so in environmental issues where problems tend to be specifically regional or local in application, even though the planning and financing of some developments (e.g. North Sea oil) demand the largest possible area for coordination of goals and resources. The principle of comprehensiveness needs to be applied at each level and *ad hoc* specialized agencies reduced to the minimum demanded by the intrinsic character of the service or subject.

The E.E.C. itself must become more accountable to the people of Europe, particularly to those on its peripheries and away from any power base. It will have to redefine its relationships not only with national governments but with the many groups and interests which contend to influence its decisions. To be effective, it must concentrate on those issues which truly transcend national and regional boundaries and authority. And there must be better access to its information, decision-making processes and operations. The specific measures required to achieve these goals are outside the scope of this book, but they are of direct relevance to the care of the European environment. This demands clear and rational allocations of powers and responsibilities between the interdependent levels and effective citizen participation, both through the elective process and by means which reflect special interests.

Central government in member countries must obviously decide the broad allocation of national resources, and settle the priorities between investment and expenditure and the deployment of activities over the country. These decisions are particularly important for land and water, which are always scarce at any time in relation to the demands upon them. But to go beyond this leads to failures and frustrations. Central government should, therefore, concentrate on policies, the formulation of national standards and on seeing that the nation's intentions are effectively carried out. In particular, it should ensure that all governmental strategies, major developments and policy decisions, especially fiscal, take environmental factors fully into account. It has to develop the capacity to appraise continuously the condition of the environment and should be particularly alive to the problems such as pollution posed by technological advance. For all this, it requires a strong backing of economic, ecological and sociological research.

Central government should also ensure that the few remaining specialist official, semi-autonomous agencies or other bodies with responsibilities affecting the environment form a coherent system and are sensitive to the pace and scale of change and to current and projected needs for use and care of the environment and its resources.

Of special importance is the need to exercise as much responsibility as possible away from the centre. In this context, the essential feature of European experience in the past three decades is the need for a level of government – country, Länder or region – between central and local government. Regional authorities appear essential in the governmental structure of a nation if a synthesis of economic, physical and social issues is to be realized at the plan-making and supervisory level.

The need is particularly urgent in the U.K., where there are some twenty or so forms of regional organization in use by central government and some fifty appointed *ad hoc* agencies. These lead to numerous devices to avoid duplication and confusion and certainly lock up a lot of scarce talent in members and officers.

While there is no uniquely right answer to the allocation of powers and their reconciliation between the various levels of government, the country or region seems particularly apposite for responsibility over physical planning and environment, in close collaboration with local government. And in Britain a significant step to focus responsibility in this way was taken in the Government's proposals for devolution.

The White Paper specifies devolved subjects in which responsibility for government activities is transferred to the Scottish and Welsh administrations. Among the subjects of special relevance here are supervision of most aspects of local government, housing, physical planning and the environment, roads and transport, natural resources and tourism and some features of development and industry.

In particular, the devolved responsibilities for physical planning and the environment include the various aspects of land use – how to manage its development and control, how to coordinate land-use planning with (for example) transport planning and how to provide the general infrastructure needed for a prosperous people. The new administrations will deal with the general improvement of the environment; the rehabilitation of derelict land; all aspects of water; new towns; and the protection of countryside amenity and landscape.

These powers over land are qualified in order to provide for uniform application in the U.K. of the Community Land Scheme and to avoid economic distortions and, secondly, are subject to 'call in' by the Government if a general U.K. interest is affected. Nevertheless, the administrations in Scotland and Wales will have the maximum local freedom and initiative to determine environmental affairs consistent with safeguards for the unity of the U.K.

For England, two Royal Commissions (the Redcliffe-Maud Report on Local Government in England in 1969 and the Kilbrandon Report on the Constitution in 1973) have made it clear that some form of democratically-elected regional body is essential in order to provide effective government closer to the people. Proposals exist for various numbers of regions – 5, 8, 12 or 15. The case for coordination and synthesis at this level is particularly acute for environmental issues. The latest proposal for a regional structure – that for sport and recreation discussed in Chapter 5 – illustrates yet again the quandaries facing policy-makers and the quagmire of systems required to overcome the absence of comprehensive regional bodies – this applies to most major services.

Inevitably, there are arguments against regionalization – a further tier of government and consequent bureaucracy and costs, remoteness, lack of real community relationships, and lack of interest by the public. These arguments fail to recognize the far-reaching implications of membership of E.E.C. and devolution to Scotland and Wales. They do not really take adequate account of improved forms of communication and participation, nor obviously of the existing complex of regional bodies in England. The issue really hinges on the selection of areas for regions and the effectiveness of operation of the bodies, as compared with that of the present system.

Much relevant experience in Britain, particularly in the south-east of England, confirms that there is a practical case for an authority at regional level, to promote cooperation and cohesion between central and local government. In fact, over many years, several forms of organization have developed, one of the most successful being the Standing Conference on London and South East Regional Planning, composed of authorities within the south east, including the Greater London Council and the counties and county boroughs. Its experience suggests that a regional council should seek agreement on the broad objectives for its region and the means to realize them and would have an important role in maintaining the balance of responsibility between central government and local authorities.

There are many possible delineations of regions, depending very much on the character of the intended functions. Opponents, therefore, contend that they would lack a sense of unity as they cannot be prescribed for any homogeneous set of reasons – for example, physical geography would give different regions than would communications and so on. But regions already exist which have an ancient sense of identity and cohesion. These, in England, are older even than the Norman counties and have deep ethnographical, historical and cultural roots. Some still evoke memories of the ancient Anglo-Saxon Kingdoms – such as the Iceni (locally called 'ickennies') of

East Anglia – whose areas in some cases seem surprisingly apposite to today's needs. Giving them their own form of devolved government would soon increase their sense of allegiance.

In any event, it seems inevitable that the increased mobility and prosperity of the expanding population of the next two decades will change viewpoints and horizons significantly and it is unlikely that people who happily travel widely will be troubled by the prospect of the alleged remoteness of regions, provided that this form of government enhances their lives.

Some contend that to ensure more involvement, the regional council should be composed of representatives of the local government authorities in its area, together with people nominated from industry (management and trade unions), the academic world and from those engaged in major forms of social activities.

Others would have the regional council formed from representatives of its local government authorities plus the elected M.P.s from the area. This would focus responsibility (as well as reducing the number of elections), facilitate communication between central, regional and local government and secure more active participation by Members of Parliament in, among other things, environmental affairs. It could have parallel to it a formal consultative body representative of all interest groups which would be advisory to it. This need seems apparent at all levels of government. The non-governmental organizations already have a European Environmental Bureau in Brussels set up with the support of the E.E.C. Commission. Certainly such a system would focus much of today's concern for the environment which is frustrated and dissipated in the labyrinth of government.

Regional councils should be responsible for the general framework of population, industry and employment, for the broad planning of regional services, for all policies affecting the environment, and especially for the integration of urban and rural interests. They should be given the power and money to deal with areas of depression, sites for new cities within national strategy and for overspill within the regions, derelict land, the creation of new landscapes, and tasks beyond the scope of the individual counties and clearly not suitable for central government. The authorities would be able to take a wide view; for example, they could plan traffic and other services to clear congestion from residential areas and fine landscapes. Above all, they would be large enough and have the power to attract and keep first-class civic leaders.

The debate over devolution and the implications of government in the E.E.C. – from the E.E.C. Headquarters to the parish council – becomes further intertwined in considering the levels of government required. Some contend that there is at least one level too many and that the counties should be abolished; others would either develop the existing bodies to avoid regionalism or would restructure local authorities further. But the counties and districts set up by the reforms of 1974–5 in Britain – discussed below – will take some time to show their operational effectiveness. The argument that they should be reformed again before they can settle down and become vested interests hardly recognizes the problems of continuing effective government in today's complex and sophisticated society. And so perhaps the most compelling reason for no major changes for some time is that another upheaval in local government could bring chaos and be exceedingly expensive at a time when the nation is in grave economic difficulties.

Yet this argument only applies to England in the short term. Scotland and Wales are due to have their own administrations from 1978 and this must soon affect their local government. An interim course for England would be to reconstitute the present regional economic councils and group with them, as comprehensive bodies, all regional areas of central government and the *ad hoc* agencies. Whatever approach is adopted, some distinct timetable is vital for restructuring to ensure a more orderly handover to long-term patterns of government than has been the case in recent reforms. And now what about local government itself?

County and District

Local government employs over two and a half million people and in the mid seventies was spending on capital and revenue account well over £13,000 million a year. It provides services, such as planning, housing, education and roads, which affect the lives of its citizens during most of their daily round. Its wide-ranging activities enable it to exercise a crucial influence on the quality of the environment.

Yet interest in local government has been low, if judged by the level of polling at local elections. This is not, however, a fully adequate barometer. In certain cities, great interest has been evoked over educational changes, the impact of urban motorways and the re-development of town centres.

Local government is primarily administrative and executive, mainly responsible for implementing central government policy. It seeks the optimal combination of efficiency and economy in relation to the quality of services demanded and local capacity to pay for them in whole or in part. Judged by these criteria it has been assessed as inadequate, often unfairly. No bodies have emerged which offer better educational and political values. It is on these criteria and on the principle of comprehensiveness that local government must be maintained and strengthened to meet the challenges of modern society.

Major reorganization of local government took place in 1974/5 under the Local Government Act 1972 for England and Wales and the Local Government Act (Scotland) 1973. (Northern Ireland local government was reformed in 1973. It has a single tier structure of local authorities which carry out fewer functions than those in the rest of the U.K.) The aim of the reforms was to create a framework within which the real challenges of our time can be met so that men and women in local government can truly influence the shape and quality of their lives and environment.

In England, outside Greater London, there are 45 counties (including the Isle of Wight with a population of 110,000) of which six are metropolitan counties. These cover the main conurbations: Tyne and Wear, West Midlands, Merseyside,

Greater Manchester, West Yorkshire and South Yorkshire. They have populations ranging from 1·2 million (Tyne and Wear) to 2·8 million (West Midlands) and administer strategic functions over their areas.

The 39 non-metropolitan counties embrace rural and urban areas, retaining former county boundaries wherever possible in order to maximize traditional loyalty and to minimize administrative problems. Three new counties – Avon, Cleveland and Humberside – were formed to meet changing conditions. Responsibilities include land-use planning and transportation, the development of structure plans, and highways, traffic management and public transport.

The 'second-tier' authority is the district. In the metropolitan counties there are 36 and in the non-metropolitan counties 296 districts. These vary considerably from place to place. They range from larger towns and cities down to much smaller populations in rural areas. A local government Boundary Commission is to make recommendations regarding their final pattern. These districts have adequate scope to attract members and officers of quality. In particular, they have special environmental responsibilities, such as housing, most planning control decisions and local plans. In the metropolitan counties, where the districts are more substantial in population and resources, education and the personal social services are included in their functions.

In Wales there is a similar two-tier structure of main authorities with eight county councils in a population range of 200,000 to 400,000, and thirty-seven district councils in a population range of 40,000 to 100,000, although in both cases there are some exceptions.

Scotland's needs and circumstances obtained a somewhat different although still two-tier structure. Orkney, Shetland and the Western Isles are virtually all-purpose authorities; the rest of Scotland is divided into nine regions, although there is considerable flexibility to take account of the wide variation in the character of localities and problems. They are responsible for strategic services, including land-use planning and the use of resources; the formulation of economic policies; the development of communications and centres of population; transportation and roads; industrial development; services ancillary to major planning; police and fire services; and education and social work.

The second-tier authority is an elected district council of which there are 53. This concentrates on caring for and improving the environment, with responsibility for local planning, housing, health and several other services of a more local character, such as amenity and recreational facilities.

At the truly local level of neighbourhood or small village, it is a very difficult problem to relate direct citizen participation to a viable local government authority, responsible for any but the most minor functions. Hence, the role of the parish or community councils seems primarily to channel protests and constructive proposals in the most effective way. But in this they have great scope to develop the countervailing power of local knowledge, preference and passion against formal administration.

Thus, with the reorganization of local government in England, parish councils are being encouraged in rural areas. In urban settlements, there is need to develop a variety of bodies, community or neighbourhood, some non-statutory perhaps, specifically to promote participation by people in local affairs. In Wales, community councils, with limited but real responsibilities, are being created at the level of rural parishes and also in urban areas if local people want them. For Scotland, these are optional, depending on local wishes; any councils set up would be outside the formal government system but would be encouraged to reflect local opinion and activities.

This, in outline, is the system of local government from the mid seventies, reformed after a century of piecemeal adaptation to circumstances differing vastly from those prevailing when it was conceived in the nineteenth century. Before the new authorities were a few months old, they were subject to severe public criticism for bureaucracy and overmanning and excessive and wasteful expenditure – a backlash from the economic recession. More long-term and fundamental criticisms were that the new system was still not appropriate in area or scale to

the demands of modern services, that vital decisions affecting
its activities were taken by *ad hoc* bodies, that it lacked capacity
to administer fully the Community Land Scheme and to
finance its work locally sufficiently to retain some independence, and that there was built-in rivalry between counties and
districts.

However accurate the public comments, the world events of
the time concealed the vastness of the reforms. For example,
the number of authorities (outside London) in England,
Scotland and Wales was reduced from around 1,600 to 487;
continuity of services vital to the community was maintained,
and so on. But many of the basic problems had not been
resolved, and could hardly have been in the short time available, when devolution reopened the whole issue of the future
of local government.

The White Paper states explicitly that the Devolution Act
will not change local government structure in Scotland and
Wales. In particular for Scotland it says that it would not be in
the interests of either the Assembly or its local government to
revise radically in the next few years the new structure of local
authorities and the distribution of functions among them.
These must, however, be matters in future for the Assembly.
Nevertheless, the debate over devolution, the operation of
administration in Scotland and Wales and discussions over the
forms of regional government in England all inevitably raise
questions about numbers, responsibilities and levels of local
government – including the role of the 10,000 or so parish
councils – and make further change inevitable in a decade or so.

These structural and functional issues must be set in the
context of local government being more efficient, accountable,
sensitive and responsive to local needs. And in no field were
these qualities demanded more than in that of local government finance.

Finance

Perhaps the most critical area of immediate concern everywhere in the recession of the seventies is that of finance. 'He
who pays the piper calls the tune.' If local authorities are

to carry out their functions effectively and respond to local aspirations, then they should have a much greater proportion of their income directly from local people – their excessive dependence on the central exchequer must be reduced.

All the trends show that local government's responsibilities and expenditure will increase. Unfortunately, without significant reshaping of finance, the greater part of local funds will continue to be obtained from the taxpayer, through the central exchequer (now around 60 per cent). This is unlikely to facilitate more independence for local authorities or to free central government from many of the detailed commitments which now inhibit its capacity for strategic planning and decision-taking. If there were effective regional councils, they could be empowered to formulate and oversee budgets for public expenditure in their regions – the key to the effective implementation of regional strategies – and thus make a significant contribution to the allocation of resources by Central Government.

At present, local authorities rely on one effective local tax (the rate on property), on government grants and on miscellaneous income such as rents and local charges. The main possible categories of local tax are those on land and buildings, on income from enterprises, on consumption of goods and on the standard of living. Many in local government contend that agricultural buildings and land should no longer be wholly exempt from local rates, as agriculture is thereby subsidized. Any changes may depend on E.E.C. proposals and world trends in food prices.

The most feasible long-term increases in independent local finance appear likely to come from a local income tax, a tourist tax, and from sales taxes (an indirect tax borne by the consumer). These three are used in many countries, and have proved very effective for local revenues. But none of these proposals will eliminate the need for central exchequer grants to reduce the regional and local disparities and to deal with the special problems of some rural areas.

In 1971 the Government published a Green Paper (a basis for discussion), *The Future Shape of Local Government Finance*

(Cmnd 4741). It dealt with most proposals for developing additional sources of local revenue (although not so optimistically as the Fabian pamphlet *New Revenues for Local Government*, Research Series No. 295, published earlier that year). It also set out views on the improvement of the rating system and future central government grants – all issues which need radical reappraisal in the light of the unique opportunities presented by the reorganization of local government.

The Government had set up a Committee of Inquiry into Local Government Finance but it had not completed its task before the proposals for devolution gave a new dimension to financial issues. In the White Paper, the Government concluded that the only tax power suitable for devolution is a general power to levy a surcharge on local authority taxation – whose sources must be the same as in England. This power would apply to the rates as at present or on any new system introduced in the future, but only Parliament would be able to authorize new forms of taxation.

Finance of local government looks like continuing to be a source of serious problems. 1976 saw the imposition of the requirement of cash limits on local authority expenditure. This was intended effectively to lead to a standstill in local authority expenditure in real terms in view of the urgent economic problems facing Britain. The Committee of Inquiry reported in 1976,* recommending retention of the rating system, but favouring a local income tax to supplement the funds of local authorities in order to prevent them becoming even more dependent on central government finance. It also examined adoption of capital values as a basis for rating and a graded system of domestic rate relief to help lower-valued houses. It seemed possible that Government grants could provide for a given level of service for similar types of property and at around the same price but with local variations in standard being reflected in local rates. Whatever emerges, finance in local government is well and truly in the political arena – and inevitably determines the shape and quality of the environment.

* Cmnd 6453; H.M.S.O.

General

In addition to the reforms of central departments and regional and local authorities, advisory bodies are required for major sectors of environmental planning. Private initiative should be encouraged by the creation of development agencies to bring together functional specialists from government and commerce, the economist and ecologist, the architect and engineer, the public relations officer, the land agents and managers, the developers and so on. These could help to fuse into a harmonious pattern the various qualities essential to planning.

The requirements for research into the 'built' and 'natural' environments and the social sciences are discussed later, but one of the problems in planning not touched on elsewhere is that of distinguishing the quasi-judicial from the executive function. Some think that in time a separate branch of government will be needed to handle appeals against planning decisions.

The Law Commission set up in 1965 – to maintain a continuous review of British law – should be more strongly equipped to carry out the difficult and complex tasks of ensuring that our legislation is responsive to the rapidly changing needs of environmental management, such as pollution control, care of the oceans and traffic planning.

Appraisal

There is obviously a ferment of change about every facet of government, and there can be little doubt that to get the State to act as a trustee for natural resources and to acquire a unified approach to environmental problems requires substantial changes.

There are potential disadvantages in any form of devolution but the need to develop effective comprehensive forms of government below Brussels and Whitehall suggests that the advantages offer the greater prospect. The release of personal vigour by people determined to respond to the challenge of running their own affairs could transform many situations and activities, particularly environmental.

It is for this release of energies that one must finally turn to resolve how to combine more strategic and comprehensive resource planning with greater delegation locally and more scope for individual initiative. This question of getting a balance between the various levels of government, and between public and private initiative, and of creating a partnership in which each does what it can do best, is at the heart of all democratic government. It is particularly significant in the determination of social priorities and the policies and processes of a 'mixed' economy.

One of the State's problems in environmental management is the continuing need for reconciliation between the short-term economics of exploiting resources, which can impair or destroy the environment, and the conservation of resources which gives a greater economic return over the long term. It is essential to develop structures of government which can maintain the time-scales necessary for such planning and management.

But in terms of structure, there is no one size of area compatible with the special needs of the major services, so that there will always be some compromise. The White Paper makes it clear that, after devolution to Scotland and Wales, each part of the U.K. will have a different form of government. But its proposals are a response to differing needs and their flexibility, it states, will give renewed vigour and strength to our unity.

Probably the most appropriate conclusion here is to quote again the White Paper – 'Any change in the machinery of democratic government must bring new problems in its wake' – of that, at least, we can be certain.

CHAPTER 19

REQUIREMENTS AND PROPOSALS – II

Planning · Concepts · Issues · Means · Research

RESOURCE PLANNING

THE term 'resource planning' is used in this chapter to embrace economic and physical planning. Broadly, governments work through two main lines of policy: financial and fiscal measures controlling investment and subsidies, and physical controls over development. Regrettably, these have usually been inadequately related at all levels of government. In particular, local planning authorities have lacked fiscal and financial capacity. Most of the measures now being essayed in central, regional and local government seek to remedy this situation through a more unified and comprehensive approach to creating a better environment.

In the past, fiscal policies have often been put into effect without sufficient account of their long-term impact on the environment. But to achieve coherence in such measures is a large task. Consider, for example, the problems involved in creating a synthesis of the effects of subsidies and price supports in agriculture; tax concessions in forestry; national and local government action in water supply and use; the exploitation of minerals; the reclamation of land and the use to which it is put; the location of new towns; and the creation of traffic and communications systems. All these separate and often conflicting activities are helping to shape the environment. Yet somehow their planning, management and development must be made consistent with society's general desire to preserve natural resources.

As noted earlier, the Government's measures for investment incentives are intended to secure better geographical distribution of industry. To promote the balanced growth of regions, extra inducements are available to encourage industrial development and economic productivity. Agriculture is also helped to achieve greater efficiency and to save manpower. The clearance of derelict land by local authorities qualifies for grants (see Chapter 4) if it contributes to the development of industry.

These aids are obviously giving rise to substantial changes in the environment. For example, population redeployment and expansion of industry require an infrastructure of sites, communications and amenities. All economic and physical decisions interact. Clearly, therefore, national strategy and regional integration are required if these and other fiscal and economic measures are not to nullify much physical planning. During the past decade regional bodies and groups of local planning authorities have prepared many valuable plans, which reflect the indissolubility of economics and the natural resources of land, air, water and wildlife.

Equally, physical planning has often failed to take adequate account of real economic values. For example, to site factories which depend on vast quantities of water in the drier east of Britain may give rise to indirect social costs which might equal or exceed the benefits from other factors, such as easy access to skilled labour and communications. Policies for land and water resources should seek the maximum total satisfaction of present and estimated future needs. The optimum value of resources for specific uses must be assessed; for example, the capability of various soils for different crops. Most areas will be able to support multiple uses and the aim should be to get that combination which, in the long term, gives the best return while yet maintaining the quality of the resources.

But market forces have proved an imperfect way of moulding the environment we need and subsidies and fiscal policies are rarely assessed fully for their effects on land and water. They often fragment the unity of estates, inhibiting comprehensive management. Good quality land is developed while degraded land increases and town centres decay. Pollution costs are inadequately reflected in the price of products, thus distorting consumer choice. As society ultimately pays the cost of degradation and pollution, a concerted attack is essential to find better means of reconciling economic and environmental factors. All known and anticipated social costs (e.g. to minimize pollution, to provide funds for the use of a mineral site – the 'externalities') should be included in the price of the product, based on the principle that, when buying a commodity or developing some area, we also pay to ensure that its production does not destroy, but, preferably, improves the environment.

This inter-relationship of economic and physical planning may be simplified, perhaps crudely, into a relationship between demand and supply factors. Most immediate demands, though not all – not, for example, the community's need for leisure space – can be translated into cash terms; but to assess the cost of maintaining for posterity the required supply of natural resources is very difficult. Nevertheless the continuing nation-state has to attempt this. Somehow much more account must be taken of the long-term scarcity-value of resources as their quantity and quality tend to decline. This is increasingly important as Western civilization becomes an inverted pyramid, with the point a reducing proportion of workers (currently about one-tenth) engaged in dealing with the natural resources on which all else is based.

A major aim should be to define and assess the main alternatives that may not be implemented in the given circumstances. It is equally important to identify and evaluate the factors preventing the optimal utilization of resources and to seek to relate their cost – or the outlay required to resolve them – to those benefiting from the course of action adopted.

It is, however, essential to stress that the best economic and physical planning can only operate within defined limits. It is not possible to get a clean slate for a new blue-print environment. Past conditions and ingrained attitudes exercise a continuing influence. Despite the pace and scope of technological advances and the scale of information and propaganda, methods of land management as old as the Bible are still found side by side with chemical and factory farming. Folklore still plays a significant part in the work of many agricultural communities. Furthermore changes of policy – for example, in the type of trees planted – take generations to come to fruition and may have been superseded by new policies long before their end result is visible. As a general rule, substantial improvements to the environment take a long time – destruction is rapid.

CONCEPTS

With so much change in prospect and so many issues in contention, it is worth re-stating the goals of planning. It is primarily one of the processes by which we maintain or create a healthy and cultural environment, ensuring for the long term a balanced use and, where appropriate, development and renewal of the nation's capital of physical resources. 'Mens sana in corpore sana in vicinia sana' writ large for posterity. Planning is then concerned to give physical expression to ideas and value judgements about the quality of our surroundings. It should be seen in commonsense terms as an integral feature of the normal functions of individuals and institutions.

The factors affecting these goals are not static. Expectations of 'healthy and cultural' and the requisite standards vary considerably between peoples and places and over periods of time. The capital of resources is constantly being altered by new discoveries or inventions or by losses. Some physical features are irreplaceable – man has not the capacity, for example, to recreate an ancient deciduous woodland, a remnant Caledonian pine, an extinct plant or animal, or to replace the fossil fuels. Thus, planning on the macro-scale should become one of the means by which man makes rational use of earth's resources and maintains the life-support system of the planet.

Our physical environment is today clearly interdependent with economic and social forces deriving largely from man's activities. This leads to continuing interactions between demands on natural resources and their total effective supply and the planning process has to respond to them and cannot succeed unless it is dynamic in concept and in action.

This fundamental place of planning in modern society needs to be distinguished from the argument over its forms, methods, processes and techniques. Obviously these are important, but too often they obscure the central issue: we could

still plan for the major goals of society – say to deal with population growth and expectations, food and energy production,
and the shape of human settlements and the countryside –
and not employ any of the means taken for granted in today's
systems.

Thus, planning should embrace all the incentives and constraints open to the State – fiscal, legal, promotional and so on –
related so that one does not defeat the goals of the other (as
so often happens today). Central Government should concentrate on value judgements about the way of life – the essence of
politics – and the resource options by which these can be
guided to fulfilment. Communication becomes of ever-greater
importance to explain these issues and to foster cooperative
attitudes. Central Government should be content to take only
the major decisions, arbitrating where necessary, continually
striving to devolve and delegate to institutions and individuals,
with sensitive 'antennae' to monitor progress towards stated
goals.

It is inevitably the sum of myriad decisions, about many
large and countless small developments, that determines the
use of natural resources and the shape of our environment.
And as planning in Britain has amply shown, the greater
number of these decisions cannot, and should not, be taken at
the centre. Unless planning reflects these considerations and
the lessons of recent history, within a few years it could comprise systems without real substance.

MAJOR ISSUES

There are some easily identifiable major issues for the State to
concentrate upon in seeking to reconcile the long-term needs
of the environment and generations unborn with the pressing
politics of today. Clearly, it should safeguard the best quality
soils (and landscapes) more effectively than it does today. It
urgently needs to provide land for homes at an acceptable price
and to tackle the squalor and inadequacies of our urban areas;
to reconcile the exploitation of our resources and technologies
with the carrying capacity of the environment; to give con-

sideration to the separate elements of town and country and to resolve the serious problems of our National Parks; and to economize in the use of the limited numbers of staff capable of modern planning. And finally, how does one infuse throughout the management and development of land and water the economic, ecological and sociological knowledge emerging from research studies?

Urbanization raises such major issues of worldwide concern that it is dealt with in Supplement 1. Here it is essential to note that it is now, and looks like remaining, an almost intractable environmental problem for the next century.

Minerals

Modern technology and a wealth of underground resources combine to threaten Britain's environment. This island contains many minerals - for example, coal, chalk, clay, copper, iron ore, limestone, potash, sand and gravel, tin, and even gold and uranium. Our scientific and technical capacity to detect and exploit them has increased rapidly in recent years and is continuing to do so, while the economic pressure to utilize these resources intensifies.

One of the prime requirements is for a national policy for the winning of these minerals which takes account of the significance of their locations for other purposes, as in National Parks. Modern techniques and planning controls - if fully employed - are capable of safeguarding key areas and effectively restoring land. Some developers strive to ensure that no unnecessary damage is done to the environment and that land is reclaimed for other uses after the minerals have been won. But this is not universal. The techniques for restoration need generally to be brought to the standard of the best, and much more capacity to enforce legal and financial conditions over a long time is urgently required. Some temporary dereliction is inevitable during mining. While being kept to a minimum, it ought to be regarded as stored opportunity for a flexible choice of uses within a reasonable time-scale. Quality taken from the land in one form should be restored to it in another. This is a real challenge to ingenuity and imagination.

Technology

Technological development in the short term can destroy the environment; planned wisely on a long-term basis it can often enhance it. Modern technology now enables coastal barrage schemes to be developed and major areas of land to be reclaimed from the sea. And no environmental planning would be complete without the integration of measures to provide for traffic and leisure. Regional and local coordination of traffic is needed in relation to the national network of motorways and trunk roads now in sight of completion. In urban and rural areas, road and traffic planning and access and facilities require special care and standards if the environment is not to be further despoiled by the hordes of people surging over this island. Although the air traveller over Britain can still see lots of apparently untouched and beautiful countryside, there is a great need at ground level to plan, manage and conserve this part of the national heritage in face of the threats to it.

National Parks

In the next two decades, a real test of society's capacity for effective resource planning may emerge in the care and consideration given to the National Parks. Three features are likely to affect them dramatically: industrialization, such as potash mining on the North York Moors and copper mining in the potential National Park in mid-Wales; the flooding of attractive areas for reservoirs, as in the Lake District; and recreational pressures, generated by the increasing desire and capacity of people to escape from the cities, now facilitated by the expanded motorway network.

Fundamental change is inevitable once permission is given for industrial development in a National Park. However brilliant the landscaping, however careful the control over pollution, and however good the ancillary development, the character and status of the park will steadily diminish.

National Parks in England and Wales do not fall within the international definition in general use which relates primarily to nature conservation. This feature was noted in the report of the National Park Policies Review Committee in 1974 which gave the first major review of the Parks for twenty-five years. It saw that our Parks are unique in that they are not State-owned, not true wilderness areas and not solely for recreation, and that they have local populations and contain many competing land uses. Nevertheless, despite these interests and pressures, the ten Parks contain many National Nature Reserves and Sites of Special Scientific Interest and a substantial proportion of the total wildlife resources of the two countries.

The Committee was appointed by Government in 1971 'to review how far the National Parks have fulfilled the purpose for which they were established, to consider the implications of the changes that have occurred, and may be expected, in social and economic conditions, and to make recommendations as regards future policies'.

The Committee found that National Parks are now generally accepted, with wide approval of their statutory conservation and recreational purposes. Increased recreational use of the Parks is, however, intensifying the inherent conflict between these purposes and this is acute in some areas. Thus the Committee criticized central and local government for responding slowly to changing circumstances, allowing incongruous large-scale intrusions and being lax or ineffective over local controls and attempts to solve traffic problems.

The Committee advocated a review of development control policies, that policies for agriculture and environment should be more coordinated and that afforestation of bare land in a National Park should become subject to planning control. The design and appearance of farm buildings should be controlled through the application of the Landscape Areas Special Development Order to the whole of every National Park and farmers given assistance in selected cases to meet additional costs incurred in complying with planning decisions.

The major conflict remains over the administration of National Parks. The Countryside Commission had for some years advocated that each should be run by a Planning Board with the powers of a planning authority. The Parks now have their chief officers and each must prepare a National Park Plan. But only the Peak and Lake District Parks have their own Boards and so arguments rage over the independence of the Parks as against local control by county councils. The Committee advocated that the administrative arrangements for the Parks, under the Local Government Act 1972, should be reviewed in 1979.

The Government invited public comment on the report; its own views were made known early in 1976. It endorsed the National Parks Policy Review Committee's conclusion that both conservation and public enjoyment must continue to be given due importance and that the main emphasis must be not on negative restriction but on positive management policies designed where possible to reconcile conflicts. It also agreed with the Committee that some further powers of control are desirable and, in the last resort and in some areas, it will be necessary to give priority to the conservation of the natural beauty of the parks.

The Government endorsed, in whole or in part, the majority of the Committee's hundred or so individual recommendations. The Circular giving the Government's decisions stated that legislation would be introduced to increase the powers of the National Park authorities and that the rules governing the disposal of land under Capital Transfer Tax would be changed so that land can be offered to National Parks authorities.

Of the recommendations rejected by Government the most important concern forestry, where the administrative arrangements established since the Committee reported made the imposition of planning control unnecessary in the Government's view; minerals, where it considered that the normal planning control procedures should continue to operate; and national heritage areas, on which the Committee were themselves divided and which has met with general disapproval. Inevitably, current circumstances led to Government deciding that National Parks must be subject to whatever constraints may be necessary in the light of the developing economic situation. The overriding duty of the National Park authorities over the next few years, therefore, is to ensure that limited resources are employed with discrimination and in the most cost-effective way possible.

The Countryside Commission regretted that Government rejected the recommendations relating to forestry and to an automatic public local inquiry in the event of sustained objection to the designation of a National Park and viewed 'with alarm' the continued absence of a Government policy on mineral workings in National Parks. More positively the Commission identified ten basic requirements crucial to the future success of National Parks. These are:

(1) priority for conservation over all other National Park purposes, in order that the beauty and ecological qualities of the National Parks may be maintained;

(2) the adoption of environmental quality as the primary criterion in all matters, including roads and traffic management and the provision and management of tourist facilities;

(3) a strong presumption, throughout the whole of the National Parks, against development out of accord with their purposes and, in the most beautiful parts, a virtual prohibition to be breached only in the case of a most compelling national necessity;

(4) provision of more access and facilities for public enjoyment of differing kinds compatible with the qualities of the National Parks and related to the varying circumstances within each;

(5) the adoption of more positive management policies, including the further rapid development of adequate information and interpretive services and the strengthening of the warden services in numbers and scope;

(6) recognition of the importance of farming to the purposes of National Parks, of the need for better coordination of policies for agriculture and the environment, and of the need for measures to protect farmers from, and help them to cope with, visitor pressures, so that recreational use of the National Parks will not be at the farmers' expense;

(7) frequent and regular consultation with people who live

and work in National Parks, to secure a continuing exchange of information and experience;

(8) cooperation of all public bodies holding land in National
Parks in the furtherance of National Park purposes;

(9) consideration of public enjoyment not in relation to the
National Parks in isolation but in the context of recreational facilities of all kinds which are increasingly available throughout the countryside;

(10) the systematic provision of alternative attractions around
the main centres of population and particularly between
them and the National Parks.

Scotland does not have National Parks, although it has the
largest National Nature Reserves in Britain and extensive
areas of wild and beautiful country. In 1975 the Countryside
Commission for Scotland published its proposals to meet the
need for conservation of landscape and for opportunities for
recreation in a report *A Park System for Scotland*. This suggests a recreational system for Scotland based on a land classification pattern ranging from high to low intensity recreation
areas, from urban parks to wilderness-type country.

Four types of park are distinguished: *high density urban
parks; country parks* where people may enjoy a wide range of
open air pursuits in pleasant rural surroundings; *regional
parks*, areas of attractive landscape where recreation would be
the dominant form of land use in selected parts only; and
special parks in areas of outstanding beauty and interest which
are clearly national assets, and which would need to be managed by special park authorities to whom appropriate planning
functions would be delegated.

The Countryside Commission for Scotland stresses, however, the need to protect many other beautiful parts of Scotland. To this end it proposes that existing planning provisions
should be more systematically used and that management
agreements, which would be eligible for countryside grants,
be sought with landowners and users to maintain the character
of the area. The Government generally accepted the Commission's proposals in 1976, commending them to local authorities

as a basis for their thinking. Special and regional parks would require legislation.

Countryside

In the light of the many pressures, planning must rapidly resolve its weaknesses in relation to the countryside. No longer should large rural areas and green belts lack a conscious policy for their use and enhancement. Without a more positive and creative approach to the needs of the land itself and of those living and working in the countryside, there is every prospect of squalor and degradation.

To realize the potential of the structure plan requires a broad evaluation of numerous uses of the countryside, such as agriculture, forestry, landscape, wildlife and open-air recreation. This needs the efforts of many professions and sciences, and the harmonization of the activities of many organizations concerned with specific resources, such as the Ministry of Agriculture, Fisheries and Food, the Forestry Commission, the Nature Conservancy Council and the Water Authorities. And to apply the action area concept to specific parts of the countryside requires more detailed and precise assessment of resource zones and their suitability for a wider range of activities.

The distinctiveness of town and country should be recognized and not confused by their interdependence. The countryside contains forces and values of special significance, particularly to urban man. The farmer himself must expect to become a land manager with a wider range of functions than solely that of food production, if he is to meet the changing requirements of society. He requires training and obviously economic support. One of the financial instruments is management agreements. Under these, the farmer might be recompensed for any cost or loss of profit arising, for example, from not being able to use certain chemicals or to plough some grassland, or being required to undertake some positive work such as planting hedgerows; that is, activities not within normal 'commercial' management.

MEANS

To apply the principles of unity and comprehensiveness to land-use planning obviously requires reform in the structure of central and local government on the lines discussed in the last chapter. But certain major dichotomies have to be overcome.

One is between 'planning' and 'management', which, as just noted, particularly affects the countryside. A sound planning framework facilitates wise land use and practices; good management, whether in town or country, can truly translate plans into a living, meaningful environment. A second is the false antithesis between town and country. There are, and will remain, clear differences and needs, as already explained, but the inter-relationship and interdependence of urban and rural areas increase. To help unify them comprehensiveness needs to be built in as instinct to, and the life-blood of, the administrations in Scotland and Wales and regions in England. The Scottish Office, in fact, already provides some of the necessary 'overview' of environmental affairs, as the Secretary of State is the Minister for planning, agriculture and forestry; additionally Scotland has also the advantage of the 1972 report of the Select Committee on Scottish Affairs which provides the first comprehensive examination of rural and urban land use in a country.

Another urgent need is to resolve the dichotomy in the State's means of planning for its environmental resources. That of 'town and country' planning, stemming in England from the Department of the Environment and local planning authorities, has appropriate goals, but is based overmuch on constraints. More important, it excludes many of the activities of agriculture, forestry and other rural uses affecting over 80 per cent of the land. The second set of means are those used by the Agricultural Ministries and the Forestry Commission – of subsidies, incentives, free advice and so on. These are employed to guide land managers to meet given objectives, primarily single-purpose goals of food and timber production. These means are, on the whole, effective over much of the land and so the shape of the countryside increasingly reflects their operation.

So in the forthcoming historic constitutional changes, it is essential to unify resource planning at all levels of government. Central government should bring together the formulation of policies and top-level administration of land and water, so far divided among various ministries. Executive functions such as food and timber production, housing and roads should either be the responsibility of special agencies, if the intrinsic character of their work demands it, or be devolved.

Those agencies retained on a U.K. or Great Britain basis would be reorientated to the determination of strategies and standards, to provide highly specialized services, and to carry out those things whose nature requires the larger area or which are of U.K. concern. A central ministry for environmental affairs could then concentrate on becoming the supremo for planning and management for town and country, with the emphasis increasingly placed on the greater use of incentives and guidance rather than constraints. (The Scottish Development Department has demonstrated the way in which guidance from the centre could build up to constructive, comprehensive strategy for the environment with the issue of a dozen excellent guidelines in 1975 in its Planning Advice Series; these embraced agriculture, forestry and fishing, the countryside, nature conservation, sport, recreation and tourism, coal, electricity, and economic and demographic guidelines.)

Corporate planning is essential at each level to ensure the teamwork of specialists necessary to deal with environmental issues, with clear definition of responsibilities to free planning and management from internal dissension. And corporate and structure planning need to be closely related if the one is to facilitate the realization of the other and if, in turn, structure plans are to lead to meaningful and effective local plans. Throughout, a much greater input is required from the social sciences, particularly over the identification of community goals and accountability to them in the planning process.

This realignment of functions requires many reforms and

new measures. The plans themselves – national, structure, local – need to be flexible formulations based on constantly updated information about resources, qualities, options and goals – long- and short-term. Development control needs to be closely integrated with them so that it increasingly becomes a realization of the plans. All this demands systems of communication and storage of data on a scale hardly contemplated outside the international industries. Yet these are today practicable. They are also essential if development is to take place rapidly when resources and circumstances permit and still remain within a long-term framework designed to safeguard the natural resources of good soils, clean water, minerals, wildlife and landscape, and the best of our architectural and industrial heritage.

Fiscal incentives should be applied much more in town and country. To provide the money for these, radical action is required to redeploy the nation's resources on to basic needs. Today, there are numerous means by which individuals could be helped and encouraged to own and/or manage their homes for their lifetime; housing allowances and subsidies have for long operated in a sector where capacity to contribute adequately towards actual costs is no longer a significant part of the budget for many people. Apart from the value of the increase in personal responsibility for improvement of the environment, the finances thus freed could be used to eliminate the slums and to encourage development – private or public – to create better living conditions for the mass of our people. And there are many other sectors where current subsidies by the State act against the long-term real interests of the individual, the community and the quality of the environment. They bring to a head the wider questions of how the pursuit of equality can frustrate a number of other equally vital – and, long term, probably just as fundamental – goals. The essence of all these issues is the balance between concern for today's generation and the heritage saved for the future.

There are still other issues. Much of the planning talent of the nation is locked up in constraining action; the past few decades have seen a slump in the stature of the architectural profession. These are serious issues. The remedies lie in a positive promotional approach to development. Local authorities should offer well-planned infrastructures on sites chosen to utilize the vast areas of waste, derelict or poor urban land and the fringe areas of towns. And with this should go a wide range of imaginative designs for properties of all kinds. Obviously charges should be made for these services but related to the community goal to foster such development and to encourage ready resort to such services.

These county and regional services should be backed by the powerful Agricultural Development and Advisory Service (A.D.A.S.) with new terms of reference embracing long-term social and environmental goals and scope to advise not only over the countryside but for some land within town boundaries. And the wealth of ability in the talented Governmental Planning Inspectorate should be used with that of A.D.A.S. to foster a coming together of the best of planning and management, to achieve essential land-use goals and the maintenance of the environmental qualities desired by society. Both would play a significant part in contributing to or advising upon Environmental Impact Assessments for selected major developments – public and private.

The constraints – some are inevitable – should apply over those areas where better soils could be affected or costly infrastructures required if development were to go ahead. Additionally, a developer would be told that in certain cases he would pay much more for basic services with the possibility of restrictive legal covenants on his operations. Constraints would also arise in the adjustment of fiscal measures designed to foster food production. Obviously it will be the primary use in many areas, but there are usually compatible uses. Over most of the land multiple uses are physically possible and usually desirable. Hence incentives would be related to maintain and enhance environmental and social values.

The net effect of such measures would be to give real prospects of achievement to developers – public or private. Backed by the provisions of the Community Land Scheme discussed in the next chapter, they should lead to a much more dynamic system, more responsive to change and the needs of society than hitherto. They should further be reinforced by action to use and manage land in the public domain as an exemplar of environmental quality. There should soon emerge a coherent system of planning, related to newly-defined functions of government, which would increasingly be comprehensive and unified by complementary measures.

RESEARCH AND SURVEY

Knowledge is required for all these tasks, much more than exists at present. Research is essential not only into the distribution of resources but also into their quality and quantity. New techniques and methodology need to be devised. Research into systems for classification and inventory is necessary for all physical factors. And much study of personal and social motives and attitudes is long overdue.

Millions of people now go into the countryside; what is the real nature and impact of their activities? How will these develop? For example, should outdoor recreation be regarded as a use in its own right? How will the country-dweller respond to these developments and what changes are needed in economic and social policies? Not to answer such questions will inevitably result in changes desired by no one; to answer them requires much more knowledge than at present exists about the physical environment and about the behaviour and attitudes of people. In turn, people need to know more about the processes of government, especially planning, if they are to participate fully. All this demands research and surveys – sociological, economic, ecological.

The Land Utilization Surveys in Britain describe current uses. They need to be complemented by thorough classifications and inventories of soil capability and the possibilities for multiple use; the Canada Land Inventory is an example of one line of approach. These assessments of resource potential should be processed and stored regionally and nationally by computers. Such data banks would provide a much firmer basis for decision, speed up development and facilitate a concentration of effort on the enhancement of 'key' areas. Comprehensive inventory of all features of interest is required. Work of this kind which has already been done in Britain and the U.S.A. shows that these are often grouped together in zones or corridors. The planning process could, therefore, provide for more effective control over them; and the executive arm of local government – perhaps a special committee – ought to have responsibility for their conservation. The voluntary bodies should be encouraged to participate fully in this work. With suitable measures for effective communication between all sectors of society, such research and survey could give zest, meaning and depth to the quest for a high-quality environment.

A particular sector for intensive effort by professions, sciences and universities is that of techniques for economic assessment. These are required at all levels: for example, nationally, to assess the full implications for the environment of price supports, subsidies, taxes and tax concessions, systems of site values and land levies and a host of macro-economic factors; regionally, to quantify more effectively features such as investment incentives, location of industry and airports, and the costs of reducing environmental contamination; locally, to encourage people to pay more towards the creation of the town or countryside they enjoy. But whatever techniques emerge – and social cost-benefit is as yet in its infancy – they are unlikely ever to eliminate or quantify wholly the aesthetic, ethical and emotive criteria which are an inherent part of land-use policies and actions.

It is important that most of the research and survey necessary for the shaping and creation of a new urban landscape should be in parallel with that for rural planning. Data collection, the deployment of manpower, the capacity of the construction industry, commuting, people's choice of residence and surveys of land use – these and many other fields of 'urban' research are all interlocked with the economic, physical and sociological material relating to the 'natural' environment. Urban planners have to decide, on the basis of their research into resource demands, where certain types of development should be located, taking care to consider all the while how the maximum benefit to the whole society can be obtained. This approach is equally relevant to rural planning and can best be developed by integration of research at the outset in both regions and counties. But it is also essential that there should be close liaison over policies and techniques at national level between leaders of the professions and sciences and of the research and development institutes concerned with the environment.

CHAPTER 20

REQUIREMENTS AND PROPOSALS – III

Land Ownership · Zoning · Standards

THE past two chapters have set out guide-lines and measures for action. This chapter is concerned with three issues of great topical and yet continuing interest – land ownership, zoning and environmental standards.

LAND OWNERSHIP

The intention here is not to advocate any ideal solution or to give a comprehensive picture of this vast and complex problem, but to indicate some of the most interesting features and current developments.

Few people can discuss land ownership and betterment without emotion or prejudice. It raises a host of technical problems and the only point people generally agree upon is that there is no solution wholly acceptable to everyone. Proposals to resolve these problems vary enormously. At one extreme are the people who favour complete public ownership; at the other are those who seek complete freedom.

Some favour annual taxation of site values or a scheme to return to the community part of the extra value created by its actions, especially by planning decisions. Those who oppose interference with the free play of market forces in land transactions overlook the fact that complete freedom in the use of any natural resource is against the interests of the State; history – long past and recent – has amply proven this and the inadequacy of the collective 'wisdom' of the market, particularly in relation to land. Additionally, in very few sectors of the modern 'mixed' economy is there untrammelled bargaining, and land especially is subject to restrictions of one kind or another. In some situations its qualities give it all the features of an effective monopoly product. It therefore requires special consideration, not least because few people now question that the wise use of land is vital to a healthy society. This inevitably brings in criteria of ethics and social justice.

Complete public ownership is no panacea. There are about 2·5 million hectares of land in Britain owned by public authorities; decisions still have to be taken about the planning, management and development of this land. Conflicts rage, not only secretly in 'corridors of power' but openly in public, at inquiries and in the press. Often a decision based on the facts of a case is baulked by someone pleading a higher degree of 'public interest' or being more expert in the 'committee game'. Sometimes the major disputes over land and water use are between public bodies with the landowner a third party living under the threat of compulsory purchase from either side. Experience in countries where most or all of the land is owned by the State, as in Russia, does not suggest that public ownership, in itself, resolves conflict. And when the State makes an error of judgement, its effects are usually widespread.

Whether public or private, a landowner is still faced with many of the same problems. Economic considerations obviously come into play at the outset, but the town and country planner should initially assess the potential of the resources available and their capacity to sustain heavy demands without becoming debased. Obviously, private ownership and market values of land affect public decisions and social priorities. But these are not thereby rendered insoluble and market value may, in some cases, give a better 'yardstick' than the often subjective assessment of relative public interest. Although the power of a landowner may have political and social repercussions, it is little different from that of the organized 'lobbies' of other pressure groups.

If the primary aim is to determine the long-term optimum use of natural resources, then the fact that in the process some people make money from land is inevitable; society's concern is to keep this within reasonable limits. Critics rail against betterment and the unearned profits of the land speculator, and forget about 'worsement': sometimes land becomes less valuable through the action of the community and this may be serious, especially for the individual landowner.

Some traffic facilities, such as flyovers and airports, impair privacy and create noise; an arbitrary line on a map may enable one person to develop and make a large profit while another, refused permission or finding his land is zoned for a purpose of lower value, will sustain a loss. In justice, there should be some transfer of cash here, as most social action consists in redistributing wealth on one or other principle of equity or need. In practice, the complications of such a concept would probably render it unworkable. Additionally, the continuous changes in British land values and the various planning provisions make it even more difficult to assess whether any such 'worsement' or 'planning blight' has occurred on any appreciable scale.

The financial system established by the 1947 Planning Acts was intended to resolve the problems of compensation and betterment. All development rights in land were taken over by the State, and before anyone could develop he had to pay a charge to do so – in effect, to buy the right to develop. In practice, the system failed. The development charge was abolished in 1953, and the Central Land Board set up to administer it was disbanded.

The system operating until 1967 was based on legislation of 1959 and 1961. It provided for the landowner to receive the value he could expect to get for his land in a private sale in the open market if there were no proposal by any public authority to buy it. As most development requires planning permission, it was specified that, for assessment of compensation, permission would be granted for development or uses prescribed for the land in the development plan.

Land Commission

Yet a further attempt to resolve these problems was made with the Land Commission Act 1967. This sought to secure that a substantial part of the development value created by the community returned to it. A second objective was to ensure that 'the right land is available at the right time' for the implementation of plans. To achieve these aims the Land Commission was set up in 1967. It had wide powers to acquire land compulsorily and by agreement, on the basis of its market value less a proportion of the development element in that value.

The Act aroused strong feelings, mainly against its methods rather than the objectives. By 1970 few politicians or experts of any persuasion denied the desirability of the community taking a proportion of betterment as an essential element of social justice. But the central criticism of the Commission remained that its justification as an instrument for taxing betterment in land had disappeared with the introduction of the capital gains tax. And so the Government abolished the Land Commission and provided a system whereby development value realized from land transactions is dealt with through normal taxation of profits and capital gains.

Community Land Scheme

From the experience with the Board and the Commission, three main premises have been derived on which to base this scheme.* These are:

(1) the key to positive planning and to a successful attack on betterment problems is acquisition of land by the community;

(2) a central agency is too far removed from people and from those responsible for planning decisions;

(3) an inflexible scheme can only be self-defeating.

Thus, the Government sought to set up, through the Community Land Act 1975, a permanent means by which the community could control the development of land in accordance with its need and priorities and acquire the increase in the value of land arising from its efforts. The acquisition and disposal of development land, for example, for houses, shops, factories (not for agriculture and forestry) is mainly the responsibility of local authorities in England and Scotland. In the Principality it is entrusted to a Land Authority as the special circumstances in Wales require a different organization.

Land to be acquired will be that requiring development or

* See *Community Land – Circular 1. General Introduction and Priorities*. D.O.E. Circular 121/75, 3 December 1975.

redevelopment generally not more than ten years ahead. Needs will be monitored as part of a five-year rolling programme as local authorities build up their land banks. With the passing of this Act, objection to the principle of public acquisition of development land will not be an appropriate ground of objection to an individual compulsory purchase order. The Act does not enable the Secretary of State to disregard objections made on the ground that the *development* for which the land is required is unnecessary or inexpedient.

The ultimate basis on which the community will buy all land will be current use value. This is rather a more generous concept than that under the Land Commission Act and includes value attributable to any unsuspended planning permission in force at the time. There are some transitional arrangements, as well as permanent exemptions from acquisition as, for example, for buildings or other operations required for the purpose of agriculture or forestry.

Complementary to the Community Land Act, the Government introduced a 'development land tax' to be generally payable when development value is realized on disposal or development of land. The effect of these measures is to ensure that the community enjoys the full value created when land is developed – in essence, development land will be municipalized.

The Act came into force in April 1976. Before then, authorities had to set up land acquisition management schemes between the counties and the districts. By May, the Government required from authorities their first five-year rolling programmes in which they were required to give clear indication of their intentions and the cost.

Many objections were raised against the Act. Some were on practical grounds, namely that local authorities had been given a near impossible task, compounded by the economic problems of the mid seventies. Nearly 14,000 more staff would be required to bring the measures fully into operation; many of these would have to be highly professionally and technically skilled. The competition for planning staff between county and district following the 1974/5 reorganizations might be repeated at the expense of the tax- or ratepayer. And there is the long-term problem of determining relationships and responsibilities between the two tiers. Certainly, the inhibition of the private developer would demand from local authorities qualities of initiative and entrepreneurship hitherto foreign to their nature. It would, therefore, be vital to ensure clarity of purpose and action between the authorities over development.

More basic objections are that adjustments to the existing development gains tax would be a simpler, less cumbersome and less costly way of securing betterment to the community. The application of 80 per cent and ultimately 100 per cent development land tax would stultify private development and – in the absence of adequate enterprise from the town and county halls – soon negate planning; certainly the experience of the system set up by the 1947 Act indicated that this was a probability.

More specialized dissent came from local authorities generally over the Government's intention to take a share – initially 40 per cent – of any profits from municipalization. And local authorities in Wales felt strongly against the different arrangements there and the detrimental effects they might have on their own responsibilities for planning and management.

With so much more land likely to enter the public domain, including that from arrangements under Capital Transfer Tax, it is vital that governmental agencies of all types plan, manage and develop their land much better than happens at present. And systems need to be devised to prevent the strife over land between agencies, departments and committees of government which inhibits wise use and wastes scarce talent.

Devolution also has implications for the operation of the Community Land Act. As already noted, the U.K. Government reserved responsibility to ensure that it should apply uniformly. But if effective regional authorities were in existence now, wider powers, including financial, could be vested in them and the Scottish and Welsh administrations to encourage development where it is most needed. This should, of course, be within a national strategy.

By extending the opportunities for more revenue and the

area of financial responsibility, it should be possible to make progress with environmental renewal, particularly in urban areas, in which Britain lags behind many other European countries. This problem is also acute in the cities of the U.S.A. and there too stems largely from problems of land ownership and financial capacity. And in France the Government is faced with similar problems, both in its plans for devolution to regions and in its measures to stop land speculation.

Despite the objections and the problems to be overcome, there is little question that, in principle, society expects betterment to be restored to the community and, in practice, land banks are essential to the planning and management necessary to create a high-quality environment. These should, if handled sensitively by local authorities, give builders greater assurance of land supply and less need to lock up much of their capital in land for future development. And the public ownership of development land – if intelligently administered – should ensure positive planning to the benefit of the community.

It is to be hoped that some measure of political agreement over these issues will soon be achieved in Britain. Without it, planning will continue to be bedevilled and the quality of the environment will suffer.

ZONING

To explain fully all the concepts included in modern resource planning would need several books, but as zoning is the subject of many new ideas it is considered here. To survive, a concept must evolve and adapt to meet changing circumstances. Ideas about zoning well illustrate this process. In its basic form, zoning is the defining of an area for specified purposes. It started as a rough, rule-of-thumb guide in the early town plans; now it has become an integral part of all planning, including that for traffic.

The word 'zone' rarely appears by itself but is usually accompanied by some other term which indicates the use or activity assigned to a particular area of land or water. In urban areas there are zones for industry, obnoxious trades, education and open spaces, housing, public services and for clean air. Frequently these are intermixed. In the older towns this is usually due to inadequate planning and the result is often unsatisfactory. Where mixed zoning occurs in new towns it generally takes advantage of the inconspicuous nature of modern light-industry buildings and other facilities: for the sake of compactness and convenience small factories are placed in or near residential areas. Often zones permit several compatible uses.

Zoning based on activity and function is now practised in some towns, with environmental areas, set within a network of highways specially designed for the free flow of vehicles and for safety. Pedestrians and traffic are separated. Sufficient data exist to specify zones for some natural resources, such as for most minerals, and these are now usually kept free from development which might prevent future exploitation. Other forms of zoning are the green belts, National Parks and the measures described in Chapter 16. Zoning has been used over countries as a whole. Already some people talk of England as becoming one big city, with zones for parkland and other uses, and with access to wilderness areas in Wales and Scotland.

The greatest long-term value of zoning is its contribution to the creation of a high-quality environment, particularly in the countryside. Here it should be applied on a regional scale, as in Germany and Holland, to provide the framework for the sound management of natural resources and the aesthetic and functional development of the environment for work and for relaxation. Regional authorities should relate economic needs to major resources for agriculture, forestry, urban development, water, minerals, science and recreation. They could specify 'growth' zones – that is, areas where investment and development might be concentrated.

Within regional plans, the new county could define smaller zones, special landscapes, sites for intensive recreation, countryside 'treasures' and other features contributing to the economic and ecological quality of its area. To keep some flexibility and to facilitate forward planning, the effects of zoning need to be continuously monitored on a regional basis. Models should be devised to project the impact of change on an area for, say, five to seven years ahead. Data about the main components of a region or town could be stored in a computer, together with a range of criteria for formulating alternative courses of action. As changes are noted, they should be fed into the computer and the plan reassessed accordingly.

The more that zoning can be applied to an inventory of classified resources, the more likely it is to be successful. Much land is already classified on the value of its soil and other features for agriculture and forestry, and on the basis of ecological factors for natural systems, wilderness areas, 'wild' rivers, and wildlife.

A Nature Conservation Review (N.C.R.) of Britain has been completed by the Nature Conservancy Council and the Natural Environment Research Council drawing on the help of universities, specialists, and voluntary bodies. The N.C.R. brings together extensive ecological data about the nation's natural habitats and wildlife, evaluated according to their scientific importance for nature conservation. Sites of the highest quality are designated Grade 1; these are of national and sometimes of international importance. Grade 2 sites are also of national importance but either duplicate the features of related Grade 1 sites or are slightly lower in quality. Around 700 Grade 1 and 2 sites – the 'Key Sites' – cover nearly 1m hectares. Thus, the N.C.R. contributes a basis for a national policy for safeguarding sites and a guide for scientists, planners, landowners, administrators, politicians and others concerned with the planning, management and use of land.

Zones for air sheds may become definable like water catchments. Mineral deposits are well defined. Much of the 'bad' land – derelict, twilight and so on – is also well known. These assessments could be correlated and then similar information about all the other main features of the environment added to them.

Inventories of this kind have been carried to a very advanced stage in Canada and the U.S.A. In Wisconsin, a State larger than England, survey teams have already mapped its natural and man-made features of interest. The maps reveal a network of 'environmental corridors' which can be traced back to the Ice Age. Inevitably, man settled in them and subsequent developments by man and nature have intensified their values. These 'corridors' are often notable for their pure air and water and have become zones of quality. This in turn helps to determine planning policies. Today even the forest and land patterns in Wisconsin are linear. Inevitably, the conditions are very attractive to would-be developers and to tourists and recreationalists.

In Britain there are also identifiable zones of high quality – the various National Parks, large stretches of the coastline, the Broads, the Gower Coast, the Cairngorms and many other attractive landscapes. Detailed survey in certain counties in England reveals smaller 'resource zones', comparable to the Wisconsin 'corridors'. Several may be found in a typical English county. Within them there are specific features of interest – archaeological, scientific, historic, landscape and so on – usually protected in various ways by official and voluntary bodies. Some local planning authorities have undertaken 'character' surveys of selected localities – Cornwall, for example, has examined Polperro. The experience gained in these should help further appraisals and conservation of quality.

Stricter control and higher standards for development should obviously be applied in such zones and localities. This would, of course, intensify the differences between resource zones and other areas. As locations of relatively poorer quality thus become more obvious, agreements about their development – for example, by industry – should be reached more easily and quickly; or, in some cases, special remedial treatment could be arranged. Developers would welcome the greater certainty arising from the clear identification of the main resources and their zoning. The planning authority could make available in appropriate zones large areas of land for relocation of industry and dispersal of population. Development clearly needs to be encouraged, say, in parts of Scotland and Wales, and doubtless expansion in the south-east of England would be very strictly controlled.

Other examples of large-scale zoning may be seen in the

development of the new and expanding towns already discussed. New dispersed cities of sub-region size are favoured by some planners, with buildings and countryside intermixed and the whole reflecting the importance of the car in modern life. Other proposals include the creation of clusters of four or five villages of a few thousand people around existing centres, such as market towns. These and linear cities are held to be better than the gradual congealment of the conurbations into vast, amorphous cities.

Preference for the concept of corridors was shown in *A Strategy for the South East*. This made far-reaching proposals for corridors of growth based upon major lines of transportation leading from London to new cities, which could become counter-magnets to the capital and be large enough to promote two-way flows of traffic. Between the corridors would be country zones, where good agricultural and amenity land would be more positively safeguarded than at present.

Proposals for care of the countryside include more intensive management of National and Country Parks and green belts; the safeguarding of wilderness areas; the enhancement of air and water zones; and the multiple use of land reclaimed from dereliction or from the sea. The coastline is being zoned by many countries as a major natural resource. Great scope exists for zoning small areas of land or water. For example, certain parts of a lake may be allocated to different activities – field study, angling and boating – this is zoning in space. Or an area can be let for different functions at separate times or seasons – zoning in time. These methods can obviously be combined.

More such zoning, particularly on water, is needed for recreational activities. Its success depends largely on the co-operation of the individual and this is usually best obtained through clubs. Liaison to promote these objectives provides an excellent basis for planner–citizen relationships. It facilitates the most efficient use of the limited supplies of land and water in suitable locations, and thus gets to the heart of the problem of maintaining the quality of the rural environment.

ENVIRONMENTAL STANDARDS

For over a century, public health, housing and factory standards in Britain have been codified in regulations and by-laws. Although still valuable, they are relatively clumsy and are not always relevant to contemporary needs. In recent decades standards have been prescribed for many social activities; for example, the area of playing-fields is related to the number of schoolchildren. But so far the rule books offer little guidance about standards for the carrying capacity of land and water, for wildlife, or for man. These should be related to performance and need and based on ecological and sociological research. They must be formulated as soon as possible if planning is to become fully effective.

Population

To relate population to environment optimally may well be the greatest technological task of the end of this century. It involves national and individual factors such as family planning, selecting space for work and play, and the problems which arise when a high proportion of the population is either very young or very old. It requires the efforts of many professions and sciences, with information on economic trends, technological change, the physical capacity of resources and, above all, on the wishes of people.

The Royal Commission on Environmental Pollution emphasized in its first report in 1971 that any comprehensive understanding of the problems of pollution must take account of the much larger issue of population. The Select Committee on Science and Technology, reporting in 1971 on 'Population of the United Kingdom', stressed the need to study the inter-relationship between population and such major factors as food supplies, natural resources, economic growth and the environment. It recommended that the plans of the main Departments of State should be appraised in the context of population policy and that the effects of population levels and their consequences should be publicized.

The public sector in Britain (that is, the nationalized industries, defence departments and so on) accounts for about forty per cent of the national output and twenty-five per cent of the manpower. It should be required to estimate the resources it needs to support different levels of population. To these projections could be added those of international companies and the larger private organizations. County planning authorities should provide estimates of the population they can 'import', or, in some cases, should 'export', on the basis of yardsticks specified by central government.

Decisions about many technological projects have to be based on estimates of what the market and developments will be like in twenty years' time. Those taking them have to make some assumptions about population and resources, nationally and for specified localities. For example, the Agricultural Research Council has planned some research on the assumption that Britain will need at least twice its present net production of home-grown food by A.D. 2000. In turn, all these planners, whether fiscal or physical, can contribute when the criteria required for population numbers are being determined. Bringing together such estimates, and relating them to resources and trends, should give an overall figure for population. This could then be used for national strategy: broad allocations of population between main areas could be indicated to serve as a basis for structure plans. Regions would prescribe in more detail the population numbers for the counties.

Research is urgently required into criteria for assessing the balance of working, travelling and leisure time in a community and the needs for open space and outdoor recreation. Once standards can be properly formulated and generally accepted, they should be used for evaluating the population appropriate to any area.

An optimal population should obviously be one in which individuals are able to realize their potential within socially acceptable forms of organization (see Supplement 1 on Urbanization). It ought to help lessen or eliminate some of the causes of stress situations, such as disease, pollution and famine. And of the main determining factors in our numbers, none is more basic and long-term than the carrying capacity of the environment and the interrelated processes of human ecology.

Natural Resources

Some urban planners argue that agriculturalists have conserved land at the expense of the town-dweller, who consequently suffers lower standards of housing and amenities. But the farmers can retort that once the first-class soils are built on they are lost for ever and that science cannot economically upgrade poorer lands to the productive quality of the best.

Arguments of this kind should no longer be necessary. As discussed earlier, we already possess the scientific and technical means to categorize land and water in terms of soils, agriculture and forestry, minerals, recreation, amenity and so on. We should use these evaluations much more and relate the quality, location and potential for improvement of land and water to known and forecast demands, now so often focused through national and local bodies. The criteria then are relatively simple and are based on a conservation approach. Further possibilities should emerge from ecological studies of the renewal of natural resources.

Standards are required for air. Conditions vary widely. Some authorities are very progressive and are well ahead with their programmes for preventing pollution. Others lag behind. Similarly, standards for water for consumption and use need to be made mandatory, perhaps with a short period of grace for those areas where major reorganization or re-equipment is necessary.

The environmental zones and 'treasures' discussed earlier must also be regarded as natural resources. Experts in the various bodies responsible already have criteria but these need to be codified for wider acceptance and use. National legislation and local by-laws exist for the protection of many animals and some plants, but (except in a few cases – for example, birds) they are generally inadequate. There is available, however, expert knowledge on which standards could be prepared, if the contribution of flora and fauna to the quality of the environment were generally understood. Much more education and information would be required to secure wholehearted acceptance of newly devised standards and of the higher level of behaviour necessary to implement them.

Pollution

The establishment of standards beyond which levels of pollution should not rise has attractions but inevitably has disadvantages. In its favour is the argument that nature can and does cope quite effectively with some pollution and that to seek a 100 per cent purity in, for example, our industrial operations would be expensive in manpower and materials. But a standard may deteriorate into a licence to pollute up to its limit with the price passed on to the consumer in the product. And the 'polluter to pay' principle used by the E.E.C. can also amount to purchasing a right to pollute. The main argument is often that as society pays in any event – from the costs of pollution or the costs of preventing it – society might as well decide what it wants and enforce it.

And here there are real practical problems. The basis of the standard is difficult to determine – what concentrations in what situations for how long and with what effects on which creatures! There is the complex problem of deciding where to draw the line in the pervasive – and often international – impacts of most forms of pollution. From local authorities to international bodies, these questions are further compounded by the difficulties of survey and monitoring and the technical capacity of men and equipment available to do this. Nevertheless, even the British Alkali and Clean Air Inspectorate approach of the 'best practicable means' involves some evaluation, however individual, of what is acceptable and what is not. Hence there are implied standards.

Materials

Standards are also required for the intelligent use of most materials, such as sand and gravel and other aggregates, to ensure that the poorer qualities are used wherever practicable and that the best deposits of natural resources are not exploited wastefully. But in these, as in all cases, standards and principles cannot be applied rigidly – they should be guide-lines, not straitjackets.

General

Many outdoor recreation activities are paid for directly – for example, the angler pays for the lease of a river and water-ski clubs for the use of a lake. The owner obviously follows the practice of charging what the market will bear and doubtless sees to it that the source of his income is properly maintained. But for many outdoor recreations this arrangement is not yet possible. Classifications of land and water for recreation have been mentioned earlier. Development plans include measures for the improved care and use of these areas in relation to the numbers of people visiting them. Some planning authorities who seek to maintain spaciousness and solitude have already decided not to allow gregarious facilities, such as cinemas, dance halls and marinas, in certain localities.

The Noise Advisory Council pioneers in a vital field – human capacity to sustain certain modern pressures. Among the new measures it has fostered to deal with noise are the creation of noise abatement zones, which inevitably depend upon agreed standards.

Modern traffic management depends upon criteria for relating the amount of traffic allowed in a town to the quality of the urban environment; these are just as necessary for rural areas. In some localities, such as National Parks, volume of traffic, speed and engineering considerations should be subordinated to the needs of amenity. In others, traffic can be segregated to allow for the enjoyment of walking, bicycling and horse-riding.

Appreciation of design is mainly subjective and often depends on local tradition and preference. The standards proposed, say, for estate layouts, street furniture and landscaping should, therefore, relate primarily to functional efficiency. In this the British Standards Institution (B.S.I.) has developed many widely agreed standards. The Royal Fine Arts Commission (R.F.A.C.) has for long advised on urban design and has many criteria. The Central Electricity Generating Board (C.E.G.B.) has formulated several standards for its massive constructions. All these should form guide-lines which could, in time, be used when considering the whole environment.

But most important is the possibility of using modern techniques of social survey to assess individual reaction to various qualities in the environment from street furniture to landscape. These are being used by authorities such as the C.E.G.B. and the British Tourist Authority, and from the picture that they give a valuable code could be built up to complement those of the B.S.I. and the R.F.A.C. These codes should also indicate where levels of aesthetic appreciation need improving in the schools and professions.

There are many other fields where criteria are required. One is time. Often it is the vital factor: when, say, an industrialist is trying to organize a new development, when a struggling community is in danger of losing its younger members, when an area is being eroded. If the time required for the implementation of a plan is not to render it out of date before it is completed, then economic and physical planning must be highly anticipatory. In particular, planners must resist the temptation to seek perfection. Trying to achieve this can inhibit citizen participation.

The implications for environmental planning of all standards ought to be fully worked out and kept under constant review by ministries to ensure their responsiveness to change. Criteria should be disseminated through the information services and subjected to a continuing dialogue in society.

Appraisal: Chapters 18–20

Planning as envisaged in this book embraces all resources in a strategic sense. The issues touched on in these chapters are intended to indicate the spectrum – from philosophy to processes – for action. It is widely recognized that to design an environment for the twenty-first century demands extensive changes in the structure, functions and operation of central and local government in most countries.

It is vital that these changes are based not only on stated philosophy and principles but also on a psychological appreciation of how people behave in situations of power. Lord Acton's dictum 'Power tends to corrupt, and absolute power corrupts absolutely' is reported to have been modified by one African leader to 'Power is enjoyable, absolute power is absolutely enjoyable'. Whether this is wholly true or not does not really matter. Common sense dictates that there must be a system of checks and balances running through all forms of government. This is particularly vital in planning. The expertness required, the long time-scale, the scope for arbitrary judgements, the idiosyncrasies of taste or form and the certain fallibility of planners – these and many other factors confirm the need for maximum delegation and fullest citizen participation.

The best solution, therefore, seems to be to create a streamlined central government and to put it at the head of an administration in which centralization is opposed on all fronts except policies and standards. Many powers now lodged at the centre could go to democratic regional authorities, who should concentrate on strategy and the planning of services, leaving all possible implementation to the appropriate local authorities. The principles of unity and comprehensiveness must be stressed at all levels, otherwise specialization may lead to fragmentation. This is also important for the citizen. Too many people now function and enjoy themselves effectively in only one or two ways – as managers, workers, recreationalists and so on – and not enough as whole persons. So another aim here is to strengthen those organs of society, especially Parliament and local government, which represent the citizen. In this way the developing threat of the corporate State may be avoided.

The way to rouse people's interest is to give them more personal responsibility and scope. People must grow to expect their environment to be both beautiful and functional. Physical planning, in particular, offers a great challenge to planner and citizen alike, since most of its measures are revealed in the visual character of the environment. It is in the State's best interests to encourage the maximum personal effort by every citizen; it is both good government and in the long term good economics. Common acceptance of policies depends primarily on common involvement. Success here could lead to a great release of individual energy of lasting benefit to the nation.

CHAPTER 21

INTERNATIONAL

The art of life lies in a constant readjustment to
our surroundings.

Chinese Proverb

INTERNATIONAL influences – whether economic, ecological
or social – have an enormous if often uncomprehended effect
on the life of the average man. Since the time of the Roman
Empire, with its legal code, and the establishment of the
Roman Catholic Church, with its canon law, the institutions
of the Western world have always had an underlying unity.
This common heritage has not been substantially affected by
the political changes of the intervening years. There has been
a broadly similar approach to the physical environment which
has led to a distinctive European husbandry of natural resources. There are inevitably differences of emphasis; for
example, the Germans excel with their forests, the British
are great protectionists of birds, while the Dutch tame their
waters and use every hectare of land.

In Europe there are in force numerous conventions between
countries on social and political, economic and physical
standards. For example, in politics, some countries accept
the compulsory jurisdiction of the European Court of Human
Rights. In this court a citizen may even complain against his
own government. Conventions reflect the increasing sense
of unity which animates leaders and pervades policies in all
sectors of European life. In land planning, the trend is towards selecting large regions to facilitate comprehensive
planning of all resources. For air, several European top-level
meetings have revealed widespread agreement on the policies
to be adopted and the action to be taken. For water, there are
numerous arrangements to deal with the major rivers, like
the Rhine, and with catchment areas that overlap political
boundaries. For wildlife, a comprehensive network of practical

measures includes, for example, agreements on legislation for protecting birds and a wildfowl refuge system which covers most of Europe. Throughout these main fields there is close cooperation between the experts of many countries and a striking agreement on fundamental aims.

Trends and current problems reinforce this unity. The impact of outdoor recreation and tourism on European coastlines and wilderness areas demands urgent action to conserve them as part of the European heritage. From Norway to the Mediterranean, governments are seeking to control development along coastlines and to encourage and enforce higher standards of behaviour from visitors. This work is strengthened by cooperation between governments, particularly in the Council of Europe* and other European agencies. These organizations have formulated agreed principles for action – one of the most important, for instance, is on the use of pesticides. They cooperate in education and pool much of their information. In 1966 the Council of Europe awarded its first Diplomas to the Peak District National Park in England, the Hautes Fagnes Reserve in Belgium and to the Camargue in France; by 1976, thirteen had been awarded.

In all these European activities Britain takes a prominent part. Although historically the forms of cooperation have varied, Britain has always been a part of Europe intellectually and socially. Now these links are strongly reinforced by political and economic moves towards a strategic unity.

European culture has, of course, spread over the world. Much of what has taken place in Europe has been repeated, with variations, in the U.S.A. and many other countries. But the emergence into world affairs of numerous Afro-Asian countries has created complex situations. Most of these countries have few or only superficial roots in the culture, social mores, law and religion of Europe and have very differently based systems.

The developing countries contain about eighty per cent of the world's population and this percentage is increasing. And

* See publications issued by the Information Division of the Council of Europe.

they have by far the greatest part of the fifty per cent of the world's population suffering from hunger and malnutrition. In such circumstances, their priority must be food production. For these reasons and the social ones just noted, Africans may adopt criteria for the management of their great herds of wild animals different from the European conservationists, who regard them as part of the world's heritage. In Asiatic countries the potential long-term dangers to people, soils and wildlife through misuse of persistent organochlorine pesticides are outweighed in the short term by the need for increased food production.

Nevertheless, despite these basic differences, a much greater degree of world unity is developing. This stems from the recognition that now disease and pestilence – the ancient controls over population numbers – are being eliminated, the danger of over-population is the dominant threat to mankind. Everywhere governments are concerned about the multiplying pressures on food supply and natural resources. As the biologists uncover the importance of territory-consciousness in the forces motivating animal behaviour, man's need for adequate space also becomes apparent.

Environmental issues affect almost every activity. For example, the management of British nature reserves provides information of direct value to Africa and many other parts of the world. The drier countries, who have experimented for years in an effort to find new conservation techniques, can now advise a wet Europe facing serious water shortages. Contamination by radio-active gases and dusts and traffic fumes, oil pollution of the seas, control of ocean fisheries, the effects of space programmes, and other environmental problems require action on an international basis. Perhaps meteorology offers the greatest scope, the most promise, and the most complexities. If weather can be controlled on a large scale, then the potential for good and evil may exceed that from the development of nuclear energy. But without close international cooperation and control, anarchy could rapidly prevail.

A further powerful force for international unity (although

also a possible source of contention) is the revolution in expectations. With the great increase in communications, particularly the spread of films and television to the market-places
and bazaars of the East, people see the living standards of the
West and want the luxuries for themselves. These expectations
are also reinforced by the desire for more economic democracy,
a factor underlying incomes policies in Europe. The complex of
motives towards unity includes fear of disease from inadequate
public health measures, religious and humanitarian beliefs,
and, of course, the traditional strivings after collective defence
against the current potential aggressor – real or imaginary.

The interrelationships of economics and the physical
environment, the political and social factors, the problems of
conserving resources for future populations, all combine to
throw up common problems and needs which can best be
resolved by cooperative action. It is not surprising, therefore,
that there are already over seventy international organizations
concerned with the conservation of nature and natural resources. Probably there are even more involved in town and
country planning and air and water problems. The latest
edition of *The Yearbook of International Organisations* lists
over 200 inter-governmental and nearly 2,000 non-governmental organizations, in over 4,000 agencies, covering almost
every aspect of human endeavour.

Overshadowing them all, of course, are the United Nations
and its major agencies, notably the Food and Agriculture
Organization (F.A.O.) and the United Nations Educational,
Social and Cultural Organization (U.N.E.S.C.O.). F.A.O.
launched its 'Freedom from Hunger' campaign in 1960 and
has prepared an Indicative World Plan for agricultural development; all its activities affect the physical environment.
U.N.E.S.C.O. promotes the discovery and spread of knowledge across the world and exerts an increasingly significant
influence on environmental affairs.

International bodies obviously provide a meeting place
for the exchange of ideas and experiences. They stimulate work
towards solutions to common problems. They formulate agreed
standards and codes which become part of the social fabric of

the countries adopting them. They promote training and education and the dissemination of information in a whole range of subjects. Both within national programmes and in special international centres, they plan and carry out important research programmes. All these activities justify international cooperation.

In the past two decades international projects on environmental issues included the International Geophysical Year; the International Hydrological Decade; the United Nations Development Decades (the second started in 1970); and the recent International Biological Programme. The periods for these exercises reflect the great time usually required to obtain results in environmental affairs and the complexity of the problems involved.

Many independent professional and voluntary bodies are active in international affairs, exerting great influence on governments. For example, a voluntary body, the International Council for Bird Preservation, has made and is still making a vital contribution in the convention governing oil pollution of the seas. The International Union for Conservation of Nature and Natural Resources (I.U.C.N.), whose members include governments and voluntary bodies, is playing an increasingly important role in the conservation of natural habitats and in environmental education. The World Wildlife Fund has already been mentioned (see Chapter 10). The David Davies Memorial Institute of International Studies pioneers new fields of cooperation in international problems: the Institute has, for example, brought together members of the legal profession and the environmental sciences, and has initiated studies to prepare the basic material for conventions.

The Council of Europe's pioneer work in European Conservation Year, 1970 – the first in the world – was uniquely successful in its two main objectives: to get decision-makers to take account of the environment in their work, and to involve the public. The Council also sponsored the second European Population Conference in 1971, promoted European Architectural Heritage Year, 1975, and launched the European Wetlands Campaign in 1976.

Also largely European are the Organization for Economic Cooperation and Development (O.E.C.D.) and the North Atlantic Treaty Organization (N.A.T.O.) which have expert committees working on special environmental problems, particularly pollution. And, of course, the European Economic Community is also fully committed with its environment programme; its first priority is to reduce pollution and nuisances, the second deals with conservation and environmental education, with studies on the ecological effects of modern agricultural techniques.

The U.N. itself has promoted major world conferences; on the environment (Stockholm 1972), population (Bucharest 1974), through F.A.O., on food (Rome 1974) and on Human Settlements (Vancouver 1976).

The Stockholm Conference led to the setting up of the United Nations Environment Programme (U.N.E.P.). This has its Headquarters in Nairobi and under the guidance of a representative Governing Council funds a wide range of environmental projects and researches relating to the management of terrestrial ecosystems and the oceans. It is responsible for Earthwatch to monitor pollution and other factors bearing on environmental quality and runs certain international environmental information and monitoring services.

References have been made in earlier chapters to the Conferences on Population and Food. The Habitat Conference on Human Settlements in 1976 was in many ways a successor to Stockholm, bringing together the many lessons learned since then in terms of principles for cooperation, the role of international bodies and the contribution of individual nations. It dealt in particular with the growth of cities, problems of land ownership and tenure, housing, transport, planning and public participation.

All the 'family' of the United Nations are very active. The European Economic Commission of the U.N. is deeply committed in many aspects of pollution control and environmental management. U.N.E.S.C.O. made a significant start in 1968 with its Biosphere Conference and its own major programme 'Man and the Biosphere' is well advanced in promoting research designed to provide practical answers for decision-makers involved in the interactions between natural systems and man's activities.

The Inter-Governmental Maritime Consultative Organization (I.M.C.O.) is developing more conventions to control traffic on the oceans. The Food and Agricultural Organization (F.A.O.) and the World Health Organization (W.H.O.) are very active on a wide range of issues, W.H.O. having initiated a worldwide recognition and warning system for pollution of air, water, fauna and soil. The World Meteorological Organization (W.M.O.) has organized through its 133 member countries a world network of weather stations as 'regional air pollution monitoring stations'. And all these and many more world agencies will be undertaking specific programmes during the U.N. Second Development Decade to 1980.

International conventions completed in the early seventies included the Conservation of Antarctic Seals, International Trade in Endangered Species of Wild Fauna and Flora, Wetlands of International Importance, and the Prevention of Pollution from Ships. Draft conventions under preparation were the Conservation of Islands for Science and the Protection of Marine Species and Migratory Animals. The Convention concerning the Protection of the World Cultural and Natural Heritage came into effect in 1975. U.N.E.S.C.O., with advice from I.U.C.N. on criteria and guidelines, is compiling a world heritage list of areas and monuments and will tell the public of those in danger.

Polar bears in the Arctic were given almost complete protection by an agreement signed in 1973 by Canada, Denmark, Norway and the U.S.A., and by the U.S.S.R. in 1976, when it came into force. This first treaty between the five Arctic States should lead to further cooperation over conservation in the Arctic.

An 'Asian Plan of Action on the Human Environment' was adopted in 1974 by the U.N. Economic Commission for Asia and the Far East (E.C.A.F.E.). This plan seeks a wide range of action by governments in E.C.A.F.E., including the designation in each country of a central agency to give full weight to environmental considerations.

The Baltic – the largest body of brackish water in the world – is now protected from pollution by a comprehensive treaty signed in 1974 by the nations on its borders.

There are also a great many bilateral and regional measures; for example, the United States and the United Kingdom signed in 1971 'a Memorandum of Understanding' to exchange experience on many subjects, including community and regional planning, construction technology, housing management and finance, citizen participation, programme evaluation techniques and legislation.

Such activities infuse into the work of politicians and professionals a better understanding of the measures needed for environmental management and help to ensure that, in time, many of today's urgent problems will be resolved 'in the normal course of business'.

All these activities are emphasizing at every level, from international to local, the interdependence of living things and their relationship with land, air and water. These environmental issues and the increasing knowledge about them are providing a firm and lasting basis for a strategic approach to achieving a high-quality world environment. Everywhere the development of regional groupings – in Europe, in North and South America, and in Asia – confirms the trend to unity. Cooperation at this level is facilitating and stimulating activity on a world plane. Everywhere experts recognize the need to pool resources, especially those of human talent, in the attack on common problems.

Of vital day-to-day importance is the need for international frameworks, standards and agreements, to seek optima in the use and allocation of the world's resources, notably food, timber and minerals. The maldistribution of resources will probably be the dominant problem of the twenty-first century.

It may well be that two to three centuries of industrial revolution will appear a mini-period in the cultural advancement of man and that in time many of society's existing structures will be found inadequate. Increasingly, internationally determined criteria will become widespread for many facets of our lives and for the management of our environment as man recognizes that society involves the whole world.

The seventies emerge as the decade in which man got to grips with his responsibilities for planetary management. The primary need is rapidly to translate the newly-kindled world awareness and all the plans and recommendations into tangible results through the activities of central and local government, industry, the professions and the voluntary bodies. Much depends on the follow-up by the U.N. and its specialist agencies, on direct cooperation between countries and on effective national programmes.

The tendency to fragment the human dilemma into separate tasks – environment, energy, food, population and so on – gave way rapidly in the seventies to a realization of their close inter-relationships, with special importance attaching to a synthesis of environment and development. The new approach had as its key word eco-development, with poverty as its primary target. As noted in Chapter 1, this had been dramatically asserted by the Prime Minister of India at Stockholm; the concept continued its pervasive influence in Bucharest and Rome. Perhaps the clearest expression of the problem came from the U.N.E.P. and U.N.C.T.A.D. (U.N. Conference on Trade and Development) meeting in Mexico in 1974. The Declaration then made at Cocoyoc asserts that the world's primary problems arise not alone from population numbers and shortage of resources but from maldistribution within economic and social systems no longer relevant to the world's needs. And the Cocoyoc Declaration stresses the fundamental ecological principle of diversity in advocating more self-reliance by individual nations. This itself is consonant with the international cooperation demanded by the basic nature of our common problems.

The rapidly growing number of international conventions is clear recognition of the 'one world' concept – that our environment does not stop at any shore and that its physical realities are determined by international economic, political and social forces.

There is today a world renaissance. The development of a worldwide and instant system of intercommunication is stimulating a world cosmos of ideas. The re-emergence into world affairs of the ancient civilizations of the East, the restlessness of the new nations, and the product of two millennia of European culture, are combining to create fresh and dynamic human and environmental situations. To all this Britain has a substantial contribution to make, perhaps most of all in the development of standards and in the creation of a public both informed and articulate.

CHAPTER 22

CONCLUSION

> Whatever makes the past, the distant, or the future, predominate over the present, advances us in the dignity of thinking beings.
>
> Samuel Johnson

To achieve a continuous improvement in the quality of the environment demands perception, education, economic strength, research, plus policies and administration geared to the right aims. A process of constant appraisal and adjustment is necessary, for as the scope of existing imponderables is reduced new ones will arise. Fresh discoveries will bring fresh difficulties – and will always do so. As Goethe said, 'Every solution of a problem is a new problem.'

PERCEPTION

Of first importance is the capacity to perceive the essentials of society's existence, to be able to analyse the factors that create and enhance the environment and to relate these to the contemporary situation. If people are to understand, they must be offered ideas which widen their horizons; ideas to excite them to an awareness of a deeper purpose in their living and to a new relationship within their environment. The challenge is to find and capture these ideas and to put them over with the *élan* to hold and inspire people.

Although much remains to be understood, we do have a sufficient basis of knowledge and ideas to make it possible for us to create a new fabric for man and his physical environment. All the time we must remember that man is both part of nature and yet able to influence its processes; that he, like other animals, needs space and repose; and that all his actions have far-reaching effects on other living creatures.

Man has made vast changes on the earth with relatively primitive tools and limited knowledge. What is he going to achieve with the vast power now at his command and the explosion of knowledge under way? Here it is important to note that, while between 1840 and 1940 man created better food, clothing, housing and hygiene for millions, he also contaminated the land, air, rivers and sea and eliminated much wildlife. Now we believe that he need not have done so, that in the next century greater progress can be achieved without the accompanying despoilation, and the old dereliction and waste can be cleared away. Such a creative approach requires perception of the significant and lasting features of the national inheritance. These are, of course, inter-related. As understanding increases, more values will be identified and cherished.

People must know the implications of their tastes and preferences: for example, that consuming vast quantities of newspapers and magazines imperils the forests; that veneering furniture requires the chopping down of certain trees; that growing speck-free fruit and vegetables needs the use of chemicals; that using certain types of indestructible plastic involves special methods of refuse disposal; that an open coal fire leads to air pollution; and so on. People cannot both demand a product and oppose the means of getting it and the damage it may cause. Knowing what lies behind the chosen product is not, in itself, enough. People must be helped to develop some criteria so that they can evaluate alternatives and can judge what shortcomings may be due to plain mismanagement.

EDUCATION

Such levels of perception demand an alert, educated and participating citizen, responsive to the environment and conscious of his responsibilities to others and to posterity. He must have much higher standards of education and information and a highly sophisticated level of awareness. It will take time to achieve this state, but a comparison of, say, the civilization of 1914 with that of today suggests that it can be done.

People need varying depths of knowledge to carry out their aims, but everyone needs some understanding of the 'natural' environment – even the people who see the country only at weekends. It is particularly important that the decision-makers in government and commerce, all the workers whose activities affect the countryside, scientists and teachers, and members of the professions who plan, manage and develop the land should appreciate the forces at work there. To educate them to do this will require a new approach in the schools. Children must learn respect for other forms of life and that caring for their environment is essential to their own personal status and to a proper enjoyment of their heritage. This must start in the schools.

> All who have meditated on the art of governing mankind have been convinced that the fate of empires depends on the education of youth.
>
> Aristotle

Aristotle would, doubtless, apply this to the fate of environments. Children should be taught the scientific facts about natural processes and the role of such major elements in the landscape as agriculture and forestry. Education should make full use of the countryside as an outdoor laboratory or classroom, on the lines developed by the Field Studies Council. Where this is not practicable (say, for primary schools in a large urban area), city parks can be used and waste land and school gardens developed imaginatively, as pioneered by the National Association for Environmental Education, to give real scope for the teacher and child.

In all this activity the aim should be to stimulate inquiry into the factors governing the environment and the interactions between it and man. Man's powers and responsibilities and his capacity to alter and re-create society need to be explained. To these ends, the importance of the teachers' role must be recognized, and the positive and creative character of education encouraged. Refresher courses with other professions and cooperation with visiting or part-time teachers from industry and agriculture, science and the land-linked professions, should help. Councils and societies for environmental education also have a major role to play.

But formal education can never be enough. The levels of

adult awareness at any time will always lag behind those of the leaders in educational and professional knowledge. So the educational process must be continuously reinforced by a sustained campaign of information, as undertaken so successfully in European Conservation Year, 1970. This should interpret and disseminate national policies, persuade people to learn about new developments, and encourage a wider involvement in civic affairs, particularly those concerning the enhancement of the environment. To achieve these aims will require new interpretative skills* and measures to maintain better inter-communication. Television has a great capacity to stimulate, but the most vital need is for sustained 'follow-up' in all media of information.

Clearly education and information on this scale, while increasing a nation's will to create wealth and a better environment, itself costs a good deal of money, and this fact reminds us inexorably that economic factors can never be ignored.

ECONOMICS

You take my life
When you do take the means whereby I live.
Shakespeare, *The Merchant of Venice*

Prosperity is essential to the objectives proposed in this book. A hungry man has his own priority – food. Economic considerations are one half of the environmental equation – the other is ecological capacity. Any worthwhile national economic plan must invest a proportion of the resources available in the maintenance and enhancement of the environment – in effect, the real capital of the nation. Land is still the primary source of food and raw materials – only one per cent of the world's food comes from the sea – and this will remain so for some time. Conservation of the best soils and pure water is vital to future prosperity.

The unthinking acceptance of economic growth solely in terms of material goods threatens many environmental qualities and uses up fossil fuels and other resources on a vast and

*See Supplement 5.

increasing scale. This need not be, provided we work on ecological principles, with materials recycled in varying time-scales of use, and with economic growth redirected to embrace the overall quality of life. Official support for these views came from the Organization for Economic Co-operation and Development (O.E.C.D.) in a major report* in 1971. It stated that economic growth *per se* is no longer a sufficient overall objective and that it should take second place to improving the quality of life. It considered that further interventions in the operation of the market economy† will become necessary and that science and technology should be guided in radically different directions.

To achieve the economic expansion necessary to meet the rising demands of a growing population and to relate this to environmental and resource capacity demands new measures. There are some hopeful long-term pointers in the work of multi-national corporations. As some of these have greater longevity than many governments, as their managerial talent seeks to maintain their future, as they diversify and become more independent of single markets and products, so they realize the need to adopt a conservationist philosophy.

To rise to tomorrow's challenges, industry will have to solve some special problems: the need to relate its capacity for vast economies of scale with the allocation of resources by governments; that of communication internally within its own 'empires' and externally within the communities where it operates; the need to anticipate the possible social consequences of its inventions before they are applied on any substantial scale; and, perhaps most difficult, the achievement of a rapport between its power élites and those of governmental and international agencies. If industry resolves these problems, then the mobility of its ideas and practices could become a significant force for international unity.

The Trade Unions, which represent many people in lower-

* *Science, Growth and Society. A new perspective.* Report of the Secretary-General's *ad hoc* group on new concepts of science policy (O.E.C.D., Paris, 1971).

† See also 'Pricing for Pollution', p. 378.

income groups who are least able to escape from environmental degradation, must become involved and demand and work for pollution-free products and better environments.

The use of all resources is competitive, both in quantity and quality. The choice in quantity is more widely understood than that in quality. But when the resources to plan good towns, clean air and pure water are assessed, it will be obvious that some other desirable goods must be forgone. This elementary economic premise is, of course, subject to the qualification that dirt and dereliction are often symptoms of inefficiency and their removal might also cut costs and wastage of resources. Generally, however, quality costs money and must be a conscious choice.

RESEARCH

Science is organized knowledge.
Herbert Spencer

Research is required into all these economic issues if imaginative new landscapes and industrial progress are to go ahead together. The primary need is for research into the real cost of a given result in terms of the benefits obtained – social cost–benefit analysis. It was used in the decision to go ahead with the Victoria underground line in London. The line might not be economic in terms of passenger fares, yet the value to society of reducing congestion and saving time outweighs the direct costs.

Pesticides are another case for cost–benefit analysis. Too wide a use is made of them without considering whether, in fact, the loss from pest damage actually justifies the outlay. Taking account of side-effects and accumulating environmental contamination, there is obviously a *prima facie* case for fuller research into the economics of their use.

Techniques are required for assessing the costs of the unintended effects of industrial development; for example, the damage done by river pollution could be evaluated and part or all of the cost of remedying it placed on the originator. This would lead to a truer assessment of production economics and perhaps to a more realistic deployment of resources. If the real price of obtaining congestion-free cities, clean air, pure water and fine landscapes can be assessed, then society may make a better choice of priorities. Ways and means of getting people to pay more directly for a particular use or activity must be devised. This applies to outdoor recreation and to the enjoyment of country and city parks, coastlines and wilderness areas where management is necessary to maintain the quality of interest. In some cases the only practicable levy may be on the taxpayer and/or ratepayer. But the more that use and enjoyment can be paid for directly and related to people's capacity to pay, the more likely it is that the money will be forthcoming to manage and enhance the environment.

The social aspects of a high-quality environment are, perhaps, even more elusive than the economic. In Britain the Social Science Research Council covers the relevant fields and has a major contribution to make in evaluating people's attitudes to given situations, in assessing trends in human activities and in determining, with ecologists, the values of repose and space to the individual. Too little is known about the social functions of environmental features, such as forests, wetlands, open country, and the individual need for and response to them, or about the effects of concentrating people into cities, towns and holiday camps.

The impact of policies and practices is not always known or understood. The dynamic flows and the long 'production' scales of environmental processes are not appreciated by most people, including many concerned with the planning and development of land and water. Inter-disciplinary teams are needed to study the components of environmental situations. Laboratories are required in which models can be created and studied to find parameters and to detect relationships. Once criteria and methods have been established, techniques must be developed to exploit them. Countries know too little about environmental contamination; of the capacity of land and natural resources to sustain given demands and about what tomorrow's trends are likely to be; of how to detect and develop resources for the future; of how to maintain a continuous audit of social change; about how to control and direct the knowledge explosion; and of how to communicate to all types of people an understanding of man's environment and of his responsibility for it.

Although so much research is still necessary, enough is already known to make a substantial improvement in society. But policies and administration and *all* decision-taking must be more scientifically based. It should not, however, be assumed that even with all available knowledge there could or should be policies to cater for the detailed planning of every resource. The variations in the major factors involved are too enormous; for example, population numbers and settlement, agricultural productivity and its relation to world trade, capacity for industrial exports, the disposition of national and individual wealth, the motivations for leisure – having so many variables means the scope for error is wide. The economic forecasts published before Budgets amply demonstrate this. What is avoidable, however, is the failure to diagnose the long-term national interest. Nor is there any excuse now for not settling criteria or publicizing the results of scientific research so that people can evaluate the possible courses of action. The real aim is to provide for continuing research into policies affecting the environment, to make a determined effort to bring them into harmony and to create a synthesis for further advance.

ADMINISTRATION

> Government, even in its best state, is but a
> necessary evil; in its worst state, an intolerable
> one.
>
> Thomas Paine

Many people oppose planning while contending for the benefits which only planning – of one form or another – can provide. Car-owners want better roads and traffic conditions, yet they often impede the controls necessary to produce the flow which will help all drivers. Farmers are annually locked in negotiation with ministry officials to get subsidies, grants and other aids vital to a healthy agriculture; these must be planned and administered, yet at many stages there is often bitter opposition. Commerce states a preference for competition and itself plans rings, monopolies and so on, seeking government interventions if conditions become 'unfair'. Above all, many individuals abhor the thought of population control while demanding the fruits of medical and social service which make it necessary. They take for granted the social planning all around them which has helped man to eliminate diseases and many of those other checks that, so far, have staved off the rigour of Malthusian correctives.

The paradox is that, without population planning, the rapidly increasing pressures could be too much for land, water and man himself, and so lead to panic followed by more and more government regulation. It therefore seems better to control births, to agree on a strategy of choice for numbers related to activities and agreed living standards, than to become subject to the regimentation of the *Brave New World*. This means a clear understanding of the choices available and the priorities on which resources are to be deployed. So a social plan is required to weave together resources, ideas and people and to provide the basis for a continuing appraisal of priorities.

Such a plan for all the nation's resources must be in broad terms and initially would be a synthesis of the policies of the national and regional economic plans, the county development plans and those of major industries and services. As the central and regional inter-disciplinary teams of planners, economists, ecologists and many other professions gain experience, so central government ought to take the initiative and give clear guide lines. A strategically planned and positively encouraged use of resources reduces the need for detailed regulation. For example, family planning and allowances could be related to population objectives, and agricultural and industrial economic policies should reflect the community's need for a 'social' landscape.

Much more self-government needs to be encouraged. Central government must concentrate on strategy and ensure that there is real *delegation* to regional and local authorities and effective *devolution* to officers. Land users and owners ought to participate in the processes of decision. Associations and clubs, such as those for recreation, should educate and inform their members, be responsible for their behaviour and participate in the shaping of the environment. The processes of decision-making need to be the subject of continuous scrutiny. They should be more widely based and yet more expeditious – not incompatible objectives with modern techniques.

PREDICTION

> . . . the one fact about the Future of which we can
> be certain is that it will be utterly fantastic.
>
> Arthur C. Clarke

Logically, the first prediction is that in the twenty-first century Europe will become a single unit for strategic planning and administration. All over the world regional 'blocs' are evolving and nowhere faster than in Europe, not only in the economic field but also in the whole range of social activities. In a Europe planned as a physical entity, the Scandinavian coastline, much of Scotland, the Black Forest, the Alps and many similar areas would receive priority for conservation and enhancement.

Perhaps most of England and Belgium would be accepted as primarily industrial; possibly southern Sweden would be the location of half a dozen new cities, each of a million population taken from the overcrowded areas of Europe. The planning of six new cities would call for new patterns of thinking, for no country in the Western world has so far attempted anything on this scale. Development for six million means deliberately setting out to create a new environment for more people than at present live in the whole of Scotland.

With the development of techniques like atomic blasting, vastly more nuclear power, and underground sources of oil and gas, it should be possible to create landscapes on a European scale. Resources could be developed in a vast and excitingly imaginative way – agricultural zones could be related to the value over centuries of the best soils and climatic conditions, fish farmed in barrages created for water supply, and hydro-electric schemes combined with new motorways.

More knowledge of the environment should lead to measures for elimination of ailments like bronchitis, which are associated with particular environmental conditions. Great scope exists for the detection and control of illnesses related to the mineral and other content of soils. Biogeochemistry has already found some areas which are conducive to cancer or heart problems. Preliminary indications relate these to a wide range of environmental factors, including soil. Perhaps planning will exclude certain activities or uses from such areas or require the dangerous conditions to be remedied before development takes place.

Computerized inventory and processing of all resource information will have become an accepted feature of man's relationship to his environment. Research will increase in importance; its role in decision-making may be extended to promote the examination of basic assumptions and personal prejudices. Decisions should thus be based more on facts and known preferences and less on vague intuition. Although the imponderables will always count in respect of physical issues, many could be eliminated in the twenty-first century. Design-awareness centres will be an accepted 'institutionalized' part of the educational process as the public-health values of a high-quality environment are accepted.

As more is learned about the diversity and quality of intelligence and man's potential for increasing it, so it may be expected that environmental conditions will be improved to enhance this most vital of all resources. The population pressure itself becomes the source of new qualities and quantities of human ability, provided that its growth is related to the development of man's intellect and his resource productivity, and that it is always borne in mind that he may have to occupy this planet for millions of years.

But optimism is denied by the assessments and forecasts made for the Club of Rome in its project* on the predicament of mankind. This stresses the critical world situation arising

*'The Predicament of Mankind'. See *World Dynamics*, J. W. Forrester (Wright-Allen Press, Cambridge (Mass.), 1971) and *The Limits to Growth*, D. Meadows (Potomac Associates, 1972).

from the many complex interactions between industrialization and depletion of natural resources, and between populations and food shortage, pollution, war, stress and disease. It forecasts a marked deterioration in material standards of living of western nations and contends that many of the proposed remedies may be self-defeating. The Club seeks to identify and implement policies* which will enable the world to make an orderly transition from a growth-based economy to an ecological equilibrium.

These aims received strong support in January 1972, when the British magazine *The Ecologist*, vol. 2, no. 1, launched *A Blueprint for Survival*. This proposed the formation of a movement for survival based on a new philosophy of life in harmony with the environment. It prescribed a comprehensive programme for the long-term stabilization of society based on self-regulating systems and self-supporting communities.

Albert Schweitzer, too, was pessimistic. He said: 'Man has lost the capacity to foresee and to forestall. He will end by destroying the earth.'

How then to conclude? In such a vast field and with so much at stake, it is perhaps most important to emphasize man's responsibility, and to stress the challenge he faces now.

RESPONSIBILITY

> . . . every interest is partly conservationist and
> partly destroyer.
> > H.R.H. The Duke of Edinburgh

Is man responsible? The Book of Genesis and the Epistle to the Hebrews certainly state that man has dominion over all nature, because he is made 'in the image of God'.

Does man really have such powers? Until this century the subjection of all things to man has been potential – never actual. Today, his powers are enormous. Science has become the mainspring for the exercise of vast control, whether based

---

*The President of the E.E.C. Commission (Dr Sicco Mansholt) put forward proposals in Spring 1972 based broadly on a similar approach.

on religious, humanist or other beliefs. What evidence is there that man has the capacity for this supreme responsibility?

Surely everything points the other way. Man has not to date acted responsibly. His arrogance as an urban species, disconnected from and unaware of his interdependence on nature, the lack of humility betrayed by all classes of society – these hardly demonstrate his responsibility. And the results confirm that he does not live wholly wisely nor look after the interests of living creatures. The evidence of environmental contamination is widespread: wildlife extinguished, air and soil poisoned, land eroded, waters polluted and other natural resources (coal, oil, metals) wasted. This is not a single major problem but the result of myriad acts of thoughtlessness or ignorance. Each individual pollutes and each pays: as taxpayer, ratepayer, consumer, or by suffering from pollution, squalor and lost opportunities, and from a diminished or poor-quality environment.

It took millions of years to form the present reserves of oil, gas and coal, and centuries to create the top-soil on which life depends. The pace of man's growth and the pervasiveness of his activities threaten to exhaust these resources and many other vital features of the environment unless he makes radical changes in his life style.

But will not man develop new powers to resolve these problems? Will not his venturing into space open up fresh vistas of unprecedented expansion? For a certainty man will develop new powers but whether he will have them in time is in doubt. The pace of change is so rapid, his population explosion and activities so great, and the psychological problems of expectation so deep in the mores, that his present civilization may collapse under economic and ecological pressures. And even if he does export himself into space, the likelihood that there are stars capable of sustaining some life may well lead him into conflict with another species, perhaps one which will not tolerate man fouling his habitat wherever he goes. Man should know more about himself, his attitudes, limitations and capacity, and about the earth he lives on, before he seeks to populate other planets.

Luckily, the activities of leaders in all sectors of society give hope that man is responding to the challenge of his powers. Most social institutions – governments, churches, professions – recognize that man is responsible for the environment. Professional and social groups now press their demands for action and themselves make a more active contribution. Governments, both nationally and internationally, devote an increasing part of their effort to maintaining and enhancing the environment. A few are pioneering research into the discovery and production of resources for the future.

Probably the weakest points in the chain of social responsibility are at the level of the operative in a particular industry and of the citizen who feels his only duty is to grumble. Once the individual has accepted his obligations, then, indeed, the 'Age of Responsibility' will have arrived. Thus at the centre of all this – present or future – is man. He cannot abdicate responsibility for using his creative powers to guide the evolutionary process. He must seek stability and challenge in a new relationship within his environment and a new rapport between leaders and people.

Challenge

> A state without the means of some change is
> without the means of its conservation.
>
> Edmund Burke

Historically, the Renaissance is seen as a time of great intellectual activity and change in the systems of ideas. New movements emerged which charted the course for centuries. This present era may qualify as the start of a new Renaissance. Everywhere there is a ferment of thought, a consciousness that ideas are on the move, that the world is an exciting place to live in. The capacity of man to communicate is intensifying the rate of interpenetration and interaction of all ideas. Men and nations are being transformed. And there develops a great unitary cosmos of thought, which becomes itself a force of global significance: 'One person with a belief is a social power equal to ninety-nine who have only interests' – J. S. Mill. Even if only one hundredth of tomorrow's population is needed to get the right policies working, that will still be a great number of people with beliefs! But it is necessary to create in all an awareness of their stake in life and to encourage their contribution to it. That in itself is one of the ideas which may later distinguish this Renaissance from its predecessor.

To accept responsibility and to have ideas is sterile without action. Man must get the measure of the challenge. Its *pace* now is breathtaking. It took a thousand years to transform the forest and swamps north of the Alps into fertile farmlands; to change the west of the U.S.A. took only fifty years. The *scale* of the challenge is fantastic. The next forty years will see the creation of human settlements greater than in all recorded history and far exceeding those which now exist. In this, man must fulfil certain prime objectives: he must eliminate poverty; create a healthy environment; and provide for posterity. It will require insight into the continuing processes of adaptation, competition and reconciliation between man and the environment, between man-made and natural systems. Environmental change must be seen as a continuum, as a constant interaction between all elements of the environment in a three-dimensional web. Man has the great advantage of being able to look at the whole and to influence both the interaction and the continuum.

If these aims are to be realized population growth must not continue indefinitely out of relationship to natural resources. Their use must increasingly reflect their finite capacity; our expectations for material goods and our economic growth will have to be founded on wider values, embracing healthy land, clean air and pure water; the ecological unity of our biosphere must become the basis for our planning and management; and major war, pandemic or other large-scale disaster will have to be prevented.

Probably of equal importance is whether the values of western society, with its undue emphasis on materialism, are compatible in the long term with the conservation of the earth's natural resources. The developed countries need to guard against the arrogance which has led them to export unthinkingly their technology, forms of urbanization and other characteristics. They should cultivate more humility in relation to the mores of different societies. The developing countries may find it unwise to copy western systems and, hopefully, will realize that in their cultures they have a great deal to offer in the implementation of a grand design for the future of this planet.

All this adds up to the need for different life-styles based on a healthier human ecology. This should embody a true partnership between leaders and people; it must encourage each individual to accept responsibility, to articulate his ideals and to seek to achieve them in cooperation with his fellows. Democracy must become real in political terms and extend into economic and social fields. This is vital to counteract the obvious dangers for the individual, as the powers of society, through the State, industry and organizations of one kind or another, are increased. A central problem of the next century may well be the reconciliation of personal liberty and democratic action with the power of the State. As man obtains more power to control his environment so he must exercise greater vigilance over its use.

Above all, if men are to maintain the earth as a healthy place in which to live, they have to face up to an urgent spiritual and ethical challenge. They have to replace their ancient carelessness with genuine love for the seas and the land. They have to transcend preoccupation with their own times and assume responsibility for the environment they bequeath to future generations. Only through such a revolution in attitudes will they be willing to pay the costs and do the work needed to tackle effectively the management of our planet.

Failure in this context could lead to vast unrest and human suffering, and perhaps the debasement of people. They might then even look back nostalgically to the glorious nineteenth and twentieth centuries!

Success in strategic planning, by people, for people, now and for posterity, could open the way to a 'Golden Age' for man. But time is running out. It is not on the side of man. Awareness, passion and an urgent determination to act are required of every one of us.

A CREED TO PRESERVE OUR
NATURAL HERITAGE

*Extract from President Johnson's message to Congress,
February 1966*

TO SUSTAIN an environment suitable for man, we must fight on
a thousand battlegrounds. Despite all of our wealth and knowledge, we cannot create a Redwood Forest, a wild river, or a
gleaming seashore.

But we can keep those we have.

The science that has increased our abundance can find ways
to restore and renew an environment equal to our needs.

The time is ripe to set forth a creed to preserve our natural
heritage – principles which men and women of goodwill will
support in order to assure the beauty and bounty of their land.
Conservation is ethically sound. It is rooted in our love of the
land, our respect for the rights of others, our devotion to the
rule of law.

Let us proclaim a creed to preserve our natural heritage with
rights and the duties to respect those rights:

The right to clean water – and the duty not to pollute it.

The right to clean air – and the duty not to befoul it.

The right to surroundings reasonably free from man-made
ugliness – and the duty not to blight.

The right of easy access to places of beauty and tranquillity
where every family can find recreation and refreshment –
and the duty to preserve such places clean and unspoiled.

The right to enjoy plants and animals in their natural habitats – and the duty not to eliminate them from the face of
this earth.

These rights assert that no person or company or government
has a right in this day and age to pollute, to abuse resources, or
to waste our common heritage.

The work to achieve these rights will not be easy. It cannot
be completed in a year or five years. But there will never be a
better time to begin.

Let us from this moment begin our work in earnest – so that future generations of Americans will look back and say:

> 1966 was the year of the new conservation, when farsighted men took farsighted steps to preserve the beauty that is the heritage of our Republic.

I urge the Congress to give favorable consideration to the proposals I have recommended in this message.

(signed) LYNDON B. JOHNSON

THE WHITE HOUSE
  23 February 1966

ENVIRONMENTAL ETHICS

To live up to this creed you need qualities of:

Integrity   to infuse ecological precepts and a true environmental ethos into your life-style.

Humanity   to share the earth's resources more equitably with all life on earth today and tomorrow.

Determination   to arrest pollution and squalor and to promote quality in your surroundings.

Judgement   to choose wisely between competing and conflicting aims and values in order, with humility, to promote the trusteeship of society for the environment.

ROBERT ARVILL

SUGGESTIONS FOR ACTION

SOCIETIES

1. *Check* whether your local Planning Department has an up-to-date inventory of the natural resources of your area. Assess the role of these resources in local civic life and whether they are fully and wisely utilized. Ask your Councillors and Planning Office staff to explain the proposals in the Development Plan and, in particular, to show whether local natural resources are adequate for the next ten years, and until A.D. 2000. Check what is being done to ward off threats to them or to fill in gaps.

2. *Initiate or support action* with your local authority on practical works, such as surveys and pilot projects, fund-raising exercises and educational activities. In particular, help your authority to deal with:
   (i) canals, wet gravel pits and other waters, woodlands and commons which can be developed for field studies and recreation;
   (ii) derelict, degraded or waste land which can be reclaimed for other uses or landscaped;
   (iii) survey of, and perhaps measures for clearance of, derelict buildings and installations, and abandoned cars in your neighbourhood;
   (iv) measures to diminish air and river pollution locally;
   (v) measures to prevent local floods or droughts;
   (vi) cooperative schemes with local landowners and farmers to enhance the condition of roadside verges, areas of access, etc., and to secure more responsible behaviour in relation to them.

3. *Allocate in your programme* a number of sessions every year for lectures and discussions on topics such as:
   (i) the quality of your local environment; in particular, the design and condition of its buildings, the pollution of its land and water, the availability of open spaces,

       environmental standards and measures to improve your surroundings such as tree preservation and planting schemes, and the management of local commons;

(ii) population numbers and control;

(iii) rural and urban settlements – their inter-relationship;

(iv) conservation of wildlife and landscape;

(v) standards of responsibility and consideration for the enjoyment of coast and country;

(vi) the work of bodies such as your County Countryside Committee (especially over the 'treasures' of your locality), the Regional Council for Sport and Recreation, the other local voluntary organizations;

(vii) publicity and public participation in planning and management of your local environment.

INDIVIDUALS

4. *Check that:*

(i) you and your family know the country code and any special safeguards expected of you at the coast and country you normally frequent for recreation or holiday;

(ii) your family does not waste water and that your house and car do not pollute the air;

(iii) you do not misuse pesticides in your garden or allotment;

(iv) you and your family always place litter in a bin or bring it home.

5. *Support:*

(i) one or more of your local voluntary bodies in measures to enhance your neighbourhood;

(ii) activities such as: National Society for Clean Air; The Noise Abatement Society;

(iii) measures to inspire the environmental education of your family, friends and local people.

6. *Undertake:*

(i) voluntary wardening to prevent vandalism and to encourage enjoyment of your town and country under arrangements made by your authority and/or society;

(ii) lecturing, leadership activities or other appropriate measures with local youth organizations.

URBANIZATION

URBANIZATION now has far greater influence than ever before. A worldwide process, its impact may be found almost everywhere. United Nations' statistics show that, within about three decades, over half of the world's much greater population will then live in urban settlements. This is a profound change, perhaps a vital landmark in man's history, and must affect him and his environment in ways at present incalculable.

Throughout history human settlements have evolved in close relationship to topography and resources. Until a few centuries ago, settlement patterns were mainly determined by agriculture, fishing and mining, water and defence. Towns and villages developed as business and market centres to serve a hinterland. In Europe, from the time of the Renaissance, the rich built large dwellings in the countryside and moved between town and country. Most of this urbanization developed on a scale and at a rate of change which enabled it to be harmonized with the natural environment.

Situation and Trends

With the advent of the Industrial Revolution and accelerated population growth, the situation changed dramatically. Urban centres grew and new ones multiplied. England became the first really urban country about a century ago. In the past 200 years, about 1,600 cities of over 100,000 population have developed in the world. Many of these are densely populated and lack the facilities to satisfy even the barest needs and aspirations. This vast concentration of population continues. It is primarily based on people migrating from farms to cities, a movement which accelerates in developing countries and which is encouraged by governments in developed areas to get the immediate benefits of intensive productivity. But increasingly this concentration results from the total growth of population, which is often greater in urban than rural areas.

There is a fundamental difference between cities of the nineteenth century and those of today in the developing countries. The latter offer better health and opportunity and their facilities lead to a lower mortality, but they still retain their pre-industrial fertility rates. Families with five or six children are common in African and South American cities and show that these people are still motivated by long-standing attitudes. And even if the fertility of the people now in the cities declines substantially, this is likely to be offset by further improvements in longevity. Furthermore, migrants from the rural 'reservoir' normally start with a higher fertility than that of the established city dweller. All these demographic factors will probably lead to continued growth of the cities.

In Asia, the classic tragedy is Calcutta. It has around 12 million people today and may have anything between 30 and 60 million people within a few decades. Yet its conditions are already beyond belief. The poor of Calcutta lack the most elementary needs of even the lowest standard of living. At night over half a million poverty-stricken people lie in its streets, and each morning corpses are carted away. Pollution is widespread – some of it from the burning of dung. The recent catastrophic floods and internal strife show the dangers facing the world community.

In Africa in 1900, around $1\frac{1}{2}$ million people (1 per cent of its total population) lived in cities of 100,000 people and above; now the figure may be approaching 40 million, perhaps 16 per cent of the total. This suggests a rate of increase of the population of the larger urban centres at about 7 per cent per annum when the total population itself grows by about 2·3 per cent per annum. One of the most serious results is that of urban unemployment, particularly amongst some of the young people. Another is that of inadequate capacity for the organization and management of these rapidly emerging industrial cities.

South America had the largest rate of population increase in 1970, overall 2·9 per cent. As well as coping with the clamant needs of a large population, several countries face the desperate pressures of rapid urbanization in the next 15 years; for example, Brazil must provide for 3·2 million and Mexico 1·8 million extra people in their towns and cities. The problems are intensified by the disparities between areas of great density and the extensive unsettled land which cannot be developed without the large resources which these countries do not possess.

The rate of urbanization is relatively faster in the still largely rural developing countries. These, too, have the most rapid increase in population. Here the city acts like a magnet, appearing to offer escape from the subsistence level and drudgery of rural life. It also provides the opportunity to raise living standards, and the possibility of greater social mobility.

But the developed countries already face a second phenomenon – the drift from the cities to the suburbs. Here, the aim is often to seek relief from the pressures of urban life while keeping some of its advantages – to gain the best blend of town and country. This movement usually hastens the decay of city centres and intensifies pressures on surrounding countryside. And the spread of great cities on coastlines and in strategically placed lowlands becomes more and more obvious.

IMPACTS

This pace and scale of change, particularly of urbanization, has significant consequences for man and his environment. The individual is often rootless in the city, lacks continuity with people and patterns of behaviour, and faces the problem of survival in a harshly competitive yet increasingly interdependent world, out of touch with the rhythm of the seasons and the relationships of work to food and shelter. Too often the long-standing problems of rural life – illiteracy, under-employment, boredom, squalid conditions – are transferred to urban areas where they become 'writ large' and explosive. Too often the result is 'culture shock', whose character and processes are not yet understood. And the cities themselves become life forces with their own special needs and problems, having an impact on the environment far beyond their immediate location and leading to indifference and acceptance as people become inured to squalor.

Many urban areas, in developed and developing countries alike, are now characterized by sprawl. They lack coherence in form and function. The social cost of all this – services and facilities, minimizing pollution and coping with transportation and congestion – is high. Slums concentrate in definable geographical districts to become ghettoes with unhealthy, debasing social conditions. Unplanned suburbs spread into transition zones – areas where rural land has effectively gone and refuse tips, car cemeteries, hoardings and petrol stations proliferate.

In developed countries especially, urban expansion encroaches upon rural land. The material needs of town-dwellers lead to demands for greater productivity from agriculture and to more pressure on the better soils. One of the increasing forms of intensification is monoculture in agriculture and forestry, which is sometimes accompanied by degradation and erosion of soil. Conditions develop which lead to more and more use of chemicals for fertilizers and to control pests. Often fundamental ecological balances, which have adapted themselves over centuries to traditional systems of agriculture, are disturbed and become unstable.

The mechanization and chemicalization of agriculture require better roads to make areas more accessible and to achieve quick transport between farms and towns. Water supply, drainage, electrical power (with its pylons) and telephones (with their poles) are required. Farm buildings take on an industrialized aspect and often lose their harmony with the landscape.

But the city also has its own 'entrails' or infrastructure. Roads and railways link cities and ports; power lines and communications make a wirescape across the countryside; pipelines convey oil, petrol and gas; and massive power stations dominate the skyline. The land is pock-marked with holes as minerals are gouged out to provide the raw materials for the physical structure of urban life. Activities located outside the cities include obnoxious trades, airports, reservoirs, and prisons and other institutions, which, in developed countries, such as England and Holland, may occupy another 10–20 per cent of the land surface. Thus, the countryside surrounding the towns increasingly becomes less rural.

Slums, squatter and shanty settlements provide the living conditions for a large proportion of the population of the developing world – both urban and rural. The poorer agrarian countries have a rural density five times that of the industrialized countries with potential migrants in numbers too large for the cities to take in addition to their own natural increase. So they get squatters by the million, not only in cities but in rural areas.

These bad environments affect not only their nations but increasingly the world as a whole, as can be seen from the example of Calcutta. In many developing countries, people in these low-quality settlements are becoming the majority of the population – in some cities this is the position today. It is also inevitable that for many decades these conditions will not only continue but intensify.

Thus, the earlier assumptions that urbanization was an un-qualified boon, and that modern economic processes and growth were dependent upon it, have been questioned in the light of these increasing adverse impacts. With its disruptive contri-bution to the population explosion, the pollution of air, land and water, the spread of unemployment and the problem of ghettoes, urbanization has become the core of our social and environ-mental problems.

As there are more and more of us, and less and less unspoiled land and water, no country can afford to continue these wastes and failures. Everywhere growth is largely unplanned, unrelated to society's needs and long-term values, and insensitive to long-term ecological factors. Man must recognize that the environment – town and country alike – is now largely man-made and take full responsibility for its condition and its capacity to meet the needs of future generations.

PROPOSALS

But attitudes to and comprehension of the problems differ greatly. In most western countries people still demand urban values together with the qualities of a 'natural' environment. But the two thirds of mankind living in the developing countries and those in the world's slums are less concerned with these values and qualities than with their struggle for the necessities of life. Over-riding demands in most of the world's swelling cities are for an infrastructure of clean piped water and drainage, and better dwellings and basic social services.

And it is on this simple and priority basis that the problems must be tackled. Shanties and squatter housing meet vital and urgent needs; they are the only cover some people are likely to have throughout their lives. They provide for people who would otherwise be on the streets; give facilities to help migrants into the city to adapt; lead to some employment and some form of shelter; and facilitate the emergence of social and communal life systems. It does not, therefore, make sense to bulldoze them away until resources are available to provide better facilities. The effort should be concentrated on providing the elemental infrastructure.

Unfortunately, the worst areas are usually the least able to find the resources required. Most of the conditions in these areas are beyond the capacity of conventional 'western' housing clearance schemes or development programmes to remedy. And the capital-intensive techniques of the developed countries are only likely to exacerbate the problems, especially for the poorer people. So new approaches and methods are urgently required.

The need for low-standard though basically sound dwellings should be accepted, and effort concentrated on essential resources for them and their infrastructures. Intensive labour should be used in developing countries wherever possible, as for many their largest resource is unskilled manpower. Somehow this has to be utilized, at the appropriate market rate of daily wages if possible. Development, too, should be decentralized. United Nations' observers report that many of the people living in slum settlements have shown remarkable ingenuity in improving their living conditions, despite enormous obstacles, including opposition from official and voluntary institutions to the existence of these low-quality settlements. So the energy and capacity of the people in them should be harnessed within programmes of urban development and renewal.

The provision of local roads, power stations, drainage and hygiene facilities, irrigation pumps and canals, local industries, schools and hospitals is urgent everywhere. The standard at which these should be provided will obviously vary considerably, but the prime need is to ensure that these parts of the infrastructure are capable of future development and do not inhibit renewal of dwellings and other facilities as standards rise. Thus they should be planned on a long-term basis, despite the urgency of the need. Some students of urbanization contend that in the past two decades most of the available capacity of urban infrastructure has been 'used up'. To meet even the minimum requirements of the urban population of the year 2000 requires an increase of the rate of construction to almost 40 times that of the past century.

But most efforts, particularly in the developing countries of South America, will be frustrated unless backed by measures of land ownership reform and acquisition to provide adequate land for development. And resources for this and the dwellings and infrastructures needed will have to be provided internationally if the world environment is not to suffer a disastrous cancerous blight in the next century. All this inevitably involves political leadership and judgement.

Common political weaknesses are that too few leaders are

fully aware of their personal responsibility in shaping and creating the environment in which their peoples live. This leads to the absence in many governments of a ministerial focus of responsibility and of a strategic framework for environmental affairs. These gaps inevitably lead to inadequate care of our common environment at international level and to wasteful use of the earth's patrimony. They are revealed in a failure to plan for natural resources; lack of strategic land-use planning, especially to provide a comprehensive network of viable urban and rural settlement; speculation in land to a degree which inhibits national and local planning; inept and insufficiently science-based management of land and water; faulty economic systems and distribution of resources; inadequate control over, or unwise use of, technology; and a general failure to provide the leadership, and to develop the cohesion and cooperation between sectors of society, which a modern approach to the care of our environment demands.

Other serious problems are the lack of continuity of the normal political administrative systems, particularly in an electoral process of four to five years, and the inadequacy of operating within annual budgets. Thus, where specific development agencies are set up they should have a 'rolling programme' for finance and implementation which will operate over several years. This should include the capacity to combine investment in basic services with the provision of incentives to stimulate industry and production and the ability to take a comprehensive approach to the formulation of policy, its planning and the execution and operation of projects. Procedures for disbursement of public finance should be related more to the entrepreneurial function of the agency.

With world resources to back them and land made available, development agencies should be set up in critical areas. By planning their policies for economic growth, especially for towns and cities, in the light of the experience and lessons learned, for example, in the detailed and sophisticated planning of the U.K., the land reclamation and settlement planning of the Netherlands, the construction of over 400 new towns in the U.S.S.R., work on regional development in Turkey, and new settlements in India (of course adapted to their particular circumstances), developing countries could obtain many of the benefits of urbanization without its pollution and shortcomings.

It would be a significant development if, through international cooperation, new 'model' cities of various types were built in key areas of the world. Renewal of many existing urban settlements is urgently required. Much can be done now to separate incompatible land uses, to segregate traffic, to zone buildings more rationally and to create foci for community activities. This kind of work needs to be pursued concurrently within national strategies, particularly to avoid a flight from old to new areas.

The dominating factor is that, in the next three or four decades, the sum of all urban settlements on earth today will have at least to be doubled to accommodate the inevitable increase in population. (And this takes little account of the demand to raise standards. Even in 1971, two out of every five houses in Britain needed to be replaced or improved.) Governments should, therefore, stipulate that all development should be assessed at the outset for its environmental implications and, in particular, that sound landscape plans should be a prerequisite for most projects. These aims demand clearer definition of social goals, continuing research and a valid theory of urbanization.

RESEARCH AND THEORY

The first critical area is that of the way in which decisions are taken, especially about investment, and their implications for urbanization – its growth and renewal. This is vital if we are to improve on the present unsatisfactory results. Secondly, much more must be known about the kind, timing and manner of investment in infrastructure, especially how to finance the development required, where to invest, and the size levels beyond which further development has disadvantages outweighing the advantages. We also need to determine the particular types and patterns of urbanization which should be encouraged in various countries and at various stages of growth.

Criteria for development standards require urgent research, especially the important 'minimal' infrastructures and the bases for 'self-help' by migrants into the cities.

Research should be undertaken into the qualities people seek in urban settlements, the dynamics of growth and evolution of urban forms, the technology of development and the demands of traffic and leisure. New methods for the integrated planning and management of town and country are needed which will recognize and provide effectively for the three major functions of rural areas: the primary one as the resource-base for agriculture, forestry, minerals and water conservation; for activities which are essential to but cannot readily be located in urban areas; and increasingly, for recreation and leisure in developed countries. All this kind of research should, of course, be inter-disciplinary, blending economic, ecological, social and cultural expertness.

If society is to have an effective policy for urbanization – whether in the continuing short term for temporary develop-ment or for longer-term goals – it must have verifiable theories to explain and guide the processes bringing about the organiza-tion of society on a regional and national environmental basis.

Commonly argued theories are those of 'primacy' and 'rank-size distribution'. The primacy theory shows that there are two main types of settlement within a nation or area; the one is a powerful city and the other a small rural town or village. A severe disparity between the two usually tends to increase, with the cities becoming magnetic for people and continuously taking the bulk of a nation's wealth, while the rural areas tend to stagnate and become poor. The rank-size pattern is found in the more developed countries. For example, in Europe there is a wide range of medium-sized towns which provide a link between the extremes of the metropolis and the village. There is also a complex series of services and social patterns linking in sophisticated ways the various levels in the ranking order. The rank-size system appears to provide a more balanced distribution and tends to reflect both more mature and more equitable societies.

But the data and correlations are challengeable in these and other theories and, regrettably, there has been inadequate dia-logue between academics and decision-makers, to whom few theories appear realistic and helpful in meeting the urgent requirements of urbanization.

CRITERIA

Perhaps the most radical social policy would be to accept that within half a century or thereabouts the best qualities of urban life will be the goal of most people. Such a policy should seek to 'get ahead' of the drift from the land by diverting available resources into the development of strategically planned settle-ments and relating these to the management of rural resources. Society should plan constructively for the variety and number of urban settlements needed to fulfil human aspirations, which might, hopefully, in time, be based on the following criteria:*

(a) A healthy environment with adequate and safe housing, clean air and pure water, parks and open spaces, agreeable streets and minimized noise and other disturbing elements.

(b) A variety of economic opportunities with healthy working and living conditions, job security and fair rewards.

(c) The opportunity for each individual to realize his role as a member of an identifiable community, by participation in social, political and cultural activities.

(d) Recognition of and provision for human needs at all stages of life.

(e) The scope for social and economic mobility, learning and cultural enrichment, and creative use of leisure time.

(f) Well-designed buildings and spaces, and continuing the cultural heritage by preserving buildings and areas of architectural and historic significance in appropriate settings.

(g) Access to places of natural beauty and wilderness.

CONCLUSION

The time-scale for the creation of new urban settlements gets less and less as our demands for the benefits of urban life multiply. What we require most of all is a new approach towards urbanization, recognizing it as a prime determinant of the quality of the physical environment, bringing it into balance with natural phenomena, and promoting its values for socio-economic planning and regional development. At last we have the technical capacity to determine the shape and quality of our surroundings. Have we the courage? International and national action now await mainly the political will to provide a healthy and satisfying environment for all life on earth.

*See U.N. Symposium on the Impact of Urbanization, June, 1970.

PARTICIPATION AND VOLUNTARY BODIES

PARTICIPATION means sharing from the outset in making decisions about the things for which we care, which affect us and about which we can do something. As society becomes more complex and its pressures mount, so many more citizens wish to have a direct say in local affairs, particularly in those which affect their environment. And this is good. It will help to use the enormous reservoirs of human energy and goodwill in work for the community.

Inevitably, some of the impetus for participation in environmental affairs springs from fear – fear of pollution, fear of the unknown implications of our numbers, powers and expectations. And growing awareness of the issues at stake reinforces this concern. Everywhere among people who care, we face a barrage of questions. How can we get the dynamic resolve to clear away the degradation of the first Industrial Revolution? How can we eliminate the squalor of our own towns and the misuse of resources which are such an affront to our dignity and intellect? How do we avoid the unnecessary costs of economic growth and prevent any new lasting spoliation? How can we prevent the big mistakes, like the oil spillage from the *Torrey Canyon* and the poisoning of the Rhine or the myriad neglects and thoughtlessness of each of us? Above all, how can we change the attitudes which regard care of the environment as incidental to our activities?

PEOPLE

Who are the people who already participate? By and large, they are the middle classes and probably even a minority of those who could and should participate.

Aristotle said

. . . that the best political community is formed by citizens of the middle class, and that those states are likely to be well administered, in which the middle class is large . . .

They have the greatest access to information about the issues at stake and the alternatives possible. They are the main source for the large number of nominated posts on the hundreds of committees which shape our lives.

Their position is reinforced by their capacity to cope with complex environmental issues and their skill to manipulate, choose, and influence decisions. Thus there is a danger that participation could give even greater influence to members of the largely middle-class societies. Some corrective to this may be that

the greater the change in the structure of the society or organization that a governing group is attempting to introduce, the more likely the leadership is to desire and even require a high level of participation by its citizens or members.*

So, as the pace of change accelerates and the sheer pressure of our numbers and demands threatens to ruin much of our environment, the need grows apace for those in power at any level to inform and educate the average citizen to an extent never before conceived.

We must identify the many and varied wants of an increasingly diversified society. The 'general public' is largely a fiction; yet for posterity its hopes and fears must somehow be understood and taken into account. A special problem is how to reconcile the clamant demands of youth in creating its own style of environment with the judgement, capacity and experience of older people, and help them both to develop a finer perception of their distinctive contributions.

If people are to participate effectively, those holding power will inevitably have to forgo some of their privileges and choices. Additionally, unless they govern in a true sense of stewardship directed at maximum public involvement, the smouldering discontents in society may erupt more widely.

VOLUNTARY BODIES

Most of the effective existing participation in government and social affairs today is by voluntary societies. These tend to specialize in certain fields in which their members are often qualified either by profession or by hobby and thus usually have strong motivation.

*S. M. Lipset, *Political Man*, page 180, Heinemann, 1963.

It is in the context of what society expects of the State, and the means by which other social aims are formulated and pursued, that voluntary bodies are so important. The form and functioning of most democratic governments are, tacitly at least, based on the assumption that they will be advised, helped and criticized by the specialist knowledge of interested parties. This view reinforces the recommendation of the European Conservation Declaration that governments should encourage and support the effective operation of voluntary bodies. In 'western' society these cover most facets of our physical surroundings. Their range is wide and their membership large and varied. But most of them owe their existence and development to one or more of the accepted mainsprings of voluntary effort. These are:

(1) to satisfy individual and social urges and aspirations to be active for the good of the less fortunate or for the community. This encourages the exercise of initiative and can release much latent human energy. Together these values enhance the freedom of the spirit.

(2) to achieve public recognition, consent and support for minority interests and acceptance of the right of the minority to persuade the majority to a given line. These values are inherent in the freedom of association and expression in a democratic society and emerge in positive and practical ways in the pioneering of new ideas and standards.

(3) to provide a further means by which individuals may collectively participate in decisions and plans affecting their environment and living conditions.

(4) to provide an essential complement to the functions of the State and to serve as a 'watchdog' and pressure group. History shows the continuing value of these functions; present trends reveal increasingly powerful and arbitrary central government in many countries.

BRITISH VOLUNTARY BODIES

Britain has a vigorous tradition of voluntary service, enriching and giving depth to most facets of social activity. But the greatest development of voluntary bodies has come about in the last 150 years. In the nineteenth century they were mainly concerned with alleviating poverty and improving the lot of the 'working classes', as the conscience of enlightened and more favoured individuals was affronted by the hardships of the Industrial Revolution and realized its limitations and those of State action.

In the twentieth century voluntary effort has been more widespread and now extends to almost every field of social endeavour and human interest. In recent years, a notable feature has been the activity of the associations whose aim is to conserve and improve the environment. Rarely a day goes by without Press, TV and radio reporting upon some environmental problem in which voluntary bodies are fulfilling their primary roles of initiators, 'watchdogs' and foci for action beyond the formal consensus of the official Establishment.

The criteria determining environmental quality are made up of many values – economic and scientific, aesthetic and ethical, traditional and new. These are based very much on personal ideas and standards and are inevitably more 'open-ended' than those of quantity and more susceptible to a wide range of approaches. It is not surprising, therefore, that to conserve and enhance the infinite variety of the countryside – its wild creatures and landscape – there have arisen numerous societies with diverse aims.

In Britain, there have been two main streams of activity: one stemming from the countryside as a unity – beauty in the mind of the beholder – drawing much of its inspiration originally from the romantic poets, such as Burns, Scott, Keats, Wordsworth and Shelley; and the other deriving from an interest in natural history and the pursuit of scientific knowledge which owes so much to Hugh Miller and Cromarty, and Gilbert White and Selborne. Latterly, both streams have been reinforced by man's desire to escape from the trials of existence in town and city, particularly in the pursuit of leisure outdoors, and, perhaps, by even more fundamental forces underlying the pressures of populations, which in many countries are already exceeding what is healthy for man.

LOCAL AUTHORITIES AND PLANNING

How can a local council balance the often conflicting claims of the many pressure groups it meets? How can it be sure that the claims of a voluntary body or group really reflect the majority views of its members rather than those of a ruling caucus? There is no ready-made answer to these questions. The main hope is that in public debate on the issues at stake the council will find the genuine balance and where the community interest really lies. But good government is never easy and it will always be difficult to weigh the many interests and factors found in most environmental problems.

The local authority possesses so much information relevant to local affairs that it has special obligations of trusteeship to its people to get the best ideas accepted and implemented. *Ex parte* statements and biases must be identified, freely acknowledged and given appropriate weight according to their source. To achieve this we need a continuous open dialogue at various levels of society, based on the simple premise that good government is our business and requires us to be active and dedicated to it.

We should attach the greatest importance to the development of new forms of local government, particularly at the 'grass-roots' level. We need social organizations much closer to people and with a great diversity of functions and areas, to tap the special interests and enthusiasms of the individual. Localities can vary from groups for streets, wards or villages, to the existing parish or proposed common councils. They can be tailored to subjects and functions and varied with the time-scales of projects.

The classic British report on Public Participation in Planning – *People and Planning** (published 1969) – is essential reading. It describes the conditions of the new and more effective partnership to be developed between planners and people:

We want the paper of the plans to come to life; and to come to life in a way people want. The essential requirements are that the planning authorities should act openly, and that the public should react constructively to the facts and ideas put before them. There must be give and take; and the preparation of plans, which are only the first step towards the improvements we all seek, must move on smoothly and with reasonable speed.

Two main themes run through the report and its 47 detailed recommendations. They are:

(1) that the flow of information from planning authorities during preparation of the new structure and local plans should be continuous – through press (especially local papers), radio, TV, exhibitions, public meetings, leaflets and other suitable publicity media – to create conditions for open well-informed public debate; and

*H.M.S.O.

(2) that the processes of consultation and participation should be disciplined by a timetable with set pauses for consideration of public reaction to prevent debate becoming endless, with people given full opportunity to react and planning authorities taking positive steps to help them to do so and to ensure that they know the results of their representations.

Authorities should, therefore, constantly help their citizens to match aspiration with action. They must stimulate experimentation, particularly in the personal services, before settling, if at all, on any formal pattern. All this will require much improved regular liaison with universities, churches, chambers of commerce, voluntary bodies and other social groups, if the authority is to hold effective public forums and to get results on significant issues. In most areas the liaison required is extensive and there is an urgent need to rationalize arrangements with and between voluntary bodies if talent and effort are not to be dissipated.

Government circulars on publicity and public participation in development plan proposals have been issued. They stress that authorities should 'carry the public with them', and give guidance on the methods and techniques, time factors, stages, organization, and education and information required.

NATIONAL

This emphasis on participation at local level should not obscure the need for participation at other levels, particularly those where strategies are formulated and big decisions made. To ensure that these are soundly based and reflect the hopes of citizens in the area requires greatly improved systems of communication – horizontal and vertical. All the existing forms of cooption, liaison and the communication media must be employed and new methods developed. The authorities may need to provide an independent service or organization by which citizens can use modern techniques, including TV and local radio, to put forward their views, individually or in groups, and, when necessary, to oppose those of the authority. Without penetrating communication and effective participation, the 'top' authorities will inevitably become bureaucratic and remote.

Yet experience also shows that the more societies and interests that participate the more likely are their aims and values to conflict or compete with each other. But society's growing complexity demands greater harmonization among many separate decisions. Thus, participation and comprehensiveness may themselves be in opposition, with adverse effects on decision-making. Participation is sometimes confused with self-protection on the one hand and unwise responsiveness on the other. So participation, advice and consultation should not be allowed to impair responsibilities for management, once policy has been settled. The line of political and official responsibility for governmental affairs should be strengthened rather than weakened. All this adds up to a delicate balance, with the authority and planner tip-toeing precariously along a tight-rope which some will be trying to cut. But this makes the real challenge. A possible life-line is that as choices and their implications are brought into the open there may be more support for the authority from the intuitive commonsense of the average citizen.

International

European Conservation Year, 1970, is the classic example of participation on the international scale. It evolved logically from the widespread and increasing concern for the environment all over Europe. It had two main objectives: to get decision-makers to include in their policies and activities the need to conserve and enhance the environment and, secondly, to inform and encourage all Europeans to play an active part in caring for, and improving, their coast and countryside. It involved nearly 30 countries and numerous international bodies. From princes and premiers to societies and citizens there was unlimited teamwork and individual effort. Probably a quarter of a million practical measures were undertaken and these have led to many more activities. But above all, the educational work should give fine results during this decade.

Conclusion

In sum, participation *could*:

(1) offer an outlet and satisfaction for individual urges and aspirations, especially the love of locality and country which so many people still have;

(2) be anticipatory and timely for worthwhile decisions and produce tangible results within an individual's lifetime;

(3) be infused into the normal activities of society and be widely beneficial as a form of leisure in depth;

(4) be a challenge to the citizen to continue his education, especially about human ecology and environmental processes;

(5) show that government, central and local, is only part of society and create a healthier relationship between leader and citizen; and, hopefully,

(6) lead to a new ethos for man, his powers and expectations.

These are large issues, but healthy people should be responsible for maintaining a healthy environment. If we delegate that responsibility without check or balance, without active care, then we diminish ourselves. This is a specific justification for voluntary bodies. To be involved or not is one of our most important choices.

POLLUTION – A SUMMARY

1. POLLUTION – the presence in the environment of substances or forms of energy deriving from man's activities in quantities which have, or may have, harmful, offensive and unwanted effects.

2. Pollution arises from three major forces:
   Population – our numbers increase by approximately 2 per second (4 births less 2 deaths).
   Technology – which is inadequately based on ecological precepts (e.g. recycling) and works insufficiently with and through natural processes.
   Expectations – for material goods, which outstrip the capacity of the earth's resources.

3. Pollution affects all the elements on which life depends:
   Land – by chemicals used in agriculture and forestry; through the by-products of industrial processes; by solid wastes from urban settlements, farms and industry; and by particles and gases from home and factory.
   Air – by domestic smoke; by fumes, smoke and grit from industry; by motor-vehicle exhausts; by radioactivity (which may affect all the elements); and by noise.
   Water – by sewage and industrial effluent; by run-off and leaching of chemicals from farms and forests; and by oil pollution.
   Wildlife – by ingestion of poisonous substances and destruction of habitats.

4. Principles to govern the approach to pollution include:
   Prevention is better than cure – such as monitoring the movements of oil tankers and employing 'load-on-top'; building-in environmental assessments at the earliest stage of any development.
   Guilty until proved innocent – any new substance introduced into the environment, or the proportions of one found naturally which are significantly changed by man, should

be assumed to be a pollutant until shown to be harmless or its consequences acceptable.

Polluter should meet the costs of his pollution – this requires action to incorporate at the outset preventative measures, to insure adequately to provide remedies in case of accidents, and, by including such cost in the price of a product, to give a truer indication of real prices and thus of the choices for society.

No freedom to pollute – the consumer should not be given the choice to pollute or not, where this can reasonably be denied him by government or industry.

Positive management – as well as always seeking to use 'the best practicable means' available, the aim should be to move away from a solely preventative approach to the conservation and creation of values by positive management. This requires systems to detect the unexpected and to deal with accidents, together with the capacity to answer effectively the following questions:

(a) What can we now authoritatively say about particular pollutants?

(b) What gaps in knowledge limit confidence in the assessments we make of them?

(c) How can we improve the data and our understanding of their significance so that better assessments may be made?

(d) What programmes of research, monitoring and action are needed?

(e) What are the main features of the national and/or international action needed to bring pollution under control and the most appropriate timescales?

5. Pollution is indivisible in the sense that man shares a common biosphere, and action in one part tends to affect others. Yet it is particular and often local in its impact and in the measures required to deal with or eliminate it. Action is therefore required over a wide spectrum:

International: the provision of a common framework, especially for industry, by declarations, agreements and standards; the coordination of methods to combat pollution and the sharing of knowledge to prevent or eliminate it, plus concerted action to deal with such special common problems as:

Climate – research into and prediction of effects of pollu-

tion, especially carbon dioxide from fossil fuels, particles in
the atmosphere and air transport.

Ecological – evaluation and control of technological impacts,
notably persistent pesticides, mercury and other toxic heavy
metals, oil in the seas, nutrients in inland and coastal waters
(especially eutrophication) and wastes from nuclear energy.

National:

Legislation – to apply internationally agreed measures and to
specify standards of control and performance for industries
and professions.

Economic – incentives to encourage the use of non-polluting
equipment in home and factory, to facilitate the treatment
of wastes and the reduction of accidents, and penalties
for failure to meet society's standards.

Research – into technological processes (e.g. to re-use
sulphur dioxide economically in oil refineries) and ecological factors (e.g. to assess the most responsive natural
systems and the effects of man's activities on them).

Education and Information – to develop in the public and
decision-makers personal concern and responsibility for
care of the environment.

N.B. Many of the developing countries urgently need more
food and material goods and might accept some pollution if
this were part of the price to be paid (for example, many crops
depend on widespread use of persistent pesticides).

Local: most local authorities have some powers for action.
These include local by-laws, economic sanctions, town
and country planning controls, and especially education and
information to foster individual action against pollution and
for creative local improvements.

6. To combat pollution effectively and to ensure wise long-term
care of the environment, most countries require:
(a) a central ministry, department or agency, led by a powerful politician, to exercise general oversight over major
environmental issues.
(b) a central decision-making group to assess the costs and
benefits of strategic developments and policies affecting
the environment, to concentrate advice on pollution and
ecological criteria for development, and to provide continuous oversight of the state of the environment.

(c) an assessment of environmental impact to be submitted with every application for permission to develop land or to produce a new chemical, with the costs of non-conservation brought into account.

7. Pollution, in some form or other and to some extent, is always likely to be with us. The main needs are to identify and monitor the primary pollutants, to determine their medical, ecological, economic and social effects, and then to contain these within levels which are not only safe for survival but fully appropriate to the quality of life expected.

8. Pollution cannot be dealt with in the long term on a remedial or cosmetic basis or by tackling symptoms; all measures should deal with basic causes. These are determined largely by our values, priorities and choices. Pollution thus poses the question of choice between three things: economic growth; the carrying capacity of the environment; and the rights and freedoms of individuals. To resolve this choice requires a revolution in attitudes.

PRICING FOR POLLUTION

Summary of Hobart Paper 66

(1) The better method of confining pollution as near as possible to socially optimal amounts is by charges (taxes) on the amount of the environment 'used up' by pollution than by direct government control.

(2) Pollution charges (taxes) would improve the allocation of resources. Yet they are opposed by authority, which uses taxes that distort allocation, and illogically by industry which usually prefers pricing to direct regulation.

(3) The rejection of pollution charges by the (majority of) the Royal Commission on Environmental Pollution was based on intellectual error.

(4) Pollution is caused by private industry, semi-government corporations and by government itself, local or national, in capitalist and communist countries.

(5) Pollution is an 'external' diseconomy that does not enter into the costs of its producer because he does not have to pay for it. The task of the economist is therefore to devise

the best way of inducing the polluter to economize in 'using up' the environment.

(6) Scarce goods carry (positive) prices. Pollution is a 'bad' (it 'consumes' the scarce environment) and should carry a negative price – a charge (tax) to discourage pollution and encourage the discovery of methods to reduce it. Pricing the environment is the means to conserving it.

(7) Since the environment – like labour and raw materials – is 'used up' in production, the rational objective is not 'no pollution' but 'optimal pollution'.

(8) There are qualifications to this principle, the chief of which is the effect on the distribution of income. The object of equalizing income is at the root of most policies that mis-allocate resources, e.g. in housing, nationalized industries, agriculture, overseas trade. But pollution charges would not necessarily be borne by people with the lower incomes, any more than the costs incurred by alternative and less efficient methods.

(9) Charges (or some other price-mechanism system) would be cheaper than direct regulation and hence result in less pollution for any given use of resources to combat pollution.

(10) Direct controls tend to be uneven according to the variable anti-pollution fashion. Like all taxes, charges would be independent of fashion.

WILFRED BECKERMANN

Reproduced by courtesy of The Institute of Economic Affairs, London.

THE CANADA LAND INVENTORY

A Guide for Resource Planning

THIS is a comprehensive survey of land capability and use. It is specifically designed as a basis for land-use and resource planning for agriculture, forestry, recreation and wildlife. The area covered embraces about 2·5 million square km, including all of the Atlantic provinces and the settled portions of Ontario, Quebec and the Western Provinces. By 1970, the programme was complete in the Maritime Provinces and Ontario, with a large number of maps available for each sector in the other provinces.

Mapping is carried out at two scales. Maps at a scale of 1:50,000 are used as the basic documents for planning; these can be obtained from the provinces. With the exception of present land use, the data are generalized, plotted on maps at a scale of 1:250,000 and published by the Department of Regional Economic Expansion.

The Agriculture Maps show the varying potential of an area for production, with classes indicated according to the soil capability classification for agriculture. The mineral soils are grouped into seven classes which indicate the degree of limitation imposed by the soil in its use for mechanized agriculture. For example, class one soils have no limitations – class seven soils are unsuitable for agriculture. The thirteen sub-classes indicate the kinds of limitations that individually or in combination affect agricultural land use. These are, for example, adverse climate, erosion damage, salinity, excess water and so on. These maps can be used for a whole range of purposes – for decisions on land improvement and farm consolidation, for land-use plans and for land assessments.

The Forestry Maps are based on the national classification system, rating the land in its natural state without improvements such as fertilizer and drainage. Again class one – the best land for tree growth – and class seven – land which cannot yield timber commercially – represent the extremes.

The Recreation Maps also have classes ranging from class one – with very high capability for recreation – to class seven, with a low capability. The basis of this classification is the quantity of recreational use that the land can attract and with-stand without undue deterioration. A wide range of sub-classes on the map covers most interests, including angling, camping, viewing and family boating.

The mapping of land capability for waterfowl uses a seven-class system developed with the aid of the Canadian Wildlife Service. This is related to the quantity and quality of food, and the protective cover and space available to meet the needs for survival, growth and reproduction of waterfowl. A similar system is followed for wildlife ungulates.

These maps are applied in the land-use planning process. They provide valuable guide-lines for planners by identifying the most suitable uses for lands in terms of their physical capability. When they are integrated with information on mineral and water resources and the economic and social determinants of land use, then the planner rapidly obtains a clearer picture of the best ways in which demand on limited resources can then be met in harmony with natural capability, and he also learns where conflict is most likely. The need for such plans becomes urgent with the great pressures of our populations and changing technologies.

FILMS AND THE ENVIRONMENT

FOR several generations film has been one of the great mass media. It has had a profound and yet inadequately studied effect on people everywhere. There can be few of us today who do not consciously or unconsciously owe some of our attitudes to the impact of the film.

For fifty years the cinema was the great focus for films. In the past decade or so, certainly in western countries, television has become more dominant and is now the source of much of our mass 'pop' culture. The cinema, on the other hand, has broken up into many cultures, all more individual and diverse. It has educational and travel films, industrial and commercial films, sex and 'underground' films, and in many of these specialized sectors it is now the *avant garde*.

The influence of the cinema on current affairs has been almost wholly eclipsed by the recording of actuality by television, whose power to shape opinion (using film extensively) has increased to such dimensions as to cause concern. In this way, film has increasingly greater significance and potential and its use requires much more understanding and thought than has so far been given to it.

Capacity

Film can inform people in an entertaining and dramatic way about the realities of the physical world. It can help us to understand and to respond to natural processes and the rhythm of the seasons and to appreciate the primitive drives and instincts which man has inherited but which now need to be set within our cultural environment. More knowledge and more concern about our surroundings are essential. One of the most effective ways in which these can be developed is by using films to expose to man the consequences of our actions for other living creatures and the natural resources on which we depend.

Film is able to reveal natural processes, such as the opening of a flower bud and the interrelationships of living creatures, which would not normally be visible to the average person. It can identify the artistry of pictures and sculpture and the architecture and craftsmanship of buildings in town and city.

Often such revelations initially lead to a sense of awe and wonder, but slowly and very surely, they are cultivating a more environmentally 'literate' person, able to obtain new pleasures from the sensitivity to the world around him which film can help to foster.

The penetration into the interdependence of man and his surroundings makes more and more evident the new kind of world emerging, and that which we could create. This is an awe-inspiring prospect. But a logical consequence of our capacity to communicate knowledge and ideas is that it presents us with new choices. Thus, the film itself must accept responsibility for evoking involvement and attitudes based on understanding and love of our environment. And films must be able to do this honestly and entertainingly.

As we detect the causes of environmental problems and anticipate their outcome, so we must inform and educate, and the film comes into its own immediately. As it becomes necessary to influence decision-makers – politicians in particular – and the public, we need clarity of exposition about our complex environment. Here the film can help greatly. But it must use modern techniques and develop new insights if it is to succeed and promote perception and participation in these crucial issues of our time. The environment will change with or without us. We should seek to guide that change in desired directions. To do this, we must infuse an ethos – to conserve quality – into all functions affecting the environment; agriculture, forestry, urbanization, industrialization and leisure. If we fail to do this, then many of our activities will simply be cosmetic – doctoring blemishes on the face of our overcrowded planet. And the opportunity, to which films can contribute so much, is to show the scope we have to create a high-quality environment. This is a great challenge.

Audiences

One certain thing about audiences is that their numbers will increase inexorably. This is due not only to the growth in the world's population, especially in urban settlements, but also to the massive growth of environmental education. The increasing awareness of the importance of natural processes and the need to understand our environment better if we are to do more than survive, will undoubtedly ensure vast audiences.

Finance (advertising, production and distribution costs)

and other elements of the film-making process will dictate a constant search for majority audiences, especially from TV. But the factors of total growth should increasingly lead to more specialist and minority audiences and facilitate greater scope for diversity in the production of films for them, especially for those dedicated or committed to environmental causes. Here one aim must be to ensure adequate distribution and availability in other languages to optimize the intrinsic universality of appeal and message of environmental films.

Their dramatic and entertainment quality for mass audiences has to be very high to compete with that of alternative programmes; their standards must equal those of the best on the many subjects seen on TV and in cinemas. Furthermore, new methods of penetration are required to get through to audiences increasingly conditioned by the daily diet of world crises in news bulletins. In the face of pressures from all the communications media, new methods are needed to give and maintain a sense of responsibility for, and identification with, the environment.

Audiences usually dislike overt propaganda and being too obviously 'educated'. Conversely, as people become more and better informed, the appetite for information presented in an acceptable manner – especially artistic excellence – increases, and this is nowhere more so than in environmental subjects. So the main need with audiences is to have the sensitiveness of contact which will create an empathy with the individual, whether in the cinema or at home, to enable him to recognize the reality around him, and accept sympathetically, though critically, what the film puts over.

The interests of the layman should not be underestimated. There are few subjects which, if treated properly, do not command broad popular appeal. Problems have to be dealt with in human terms. The emphasis needs to be on the present – what is being done – and the immediate future – what can be done – rather than on the remote past or some science-fiction distance ahead which may be meaningless to the normal audience. The range of the average citizen is also being extended by the vast educational revolution of recent decades, especially the growth of interest among young people in environmental affairs. And the result is a young citizen actively concerned in a wide range of interests with time to devote some personal effort to them.

The film for cinema and TV is well equipped to deal with many of the urgent questions of today. It can dramatize and create awareness to an extent not readily available to other techniques. It increasingly utilizes a wide range of modern equipment and directly connects with today's youth, whose aptitude for technology usually exceeds that of their parents. Youth often challenges the use to which technology is put, especially in an environmental context, but does not hesitate to make wide use of the capacity of modern gadgetry to reflect a sense of poetry and an insight into the inner spirit of so much of the world around us.

One major type of audience increasing in all countries of the world is that of children at school and adults continuing their education. This will be further extended by the technological developments of closed-circuit TV and cassettes. These and the demand for knowledge are very important and must surely be basic to long-term planning of the use of environmental films.

Material and Presentation

Films should be positive in style and tone, and abstract and mechanistic terms avoided. They should deal with the ever-present factor of fear and our environmental problems in terms of the challenges they present to man to create new and better surroundings. Judgement is always required to distinguish between the needs of an evolutionary process and the opportunities which may emerge from a new leap forward, and this ability is required in the production of films. Some of the most successful films have made a deliberate point of immediate contrast between urban and rural conditions and between squalor and beauty.

One problem is how to reveal the reality of man's personal responsibility for the situation without undue pessimism – to give hope and show the opportunities open for creating new and finer environments. Again, if films are to have wide audiences, even if specialized ones, they must not concentrate on developed countries as against developing countries, nor should they be so local as to be parochial. Neither can they be so international as to lose relationship to a personal or grass-roots situation. This is difficult. How can something which is relatively ephemeral lead on to underlying principles or more permanent values to society without blunting the cutting edge of a film?

These considerations demand high professional standards in all phases of production and a wide range of training and education. And in almost every aspect of the film-making process more research and survey are required. More needs to be known about the kinds of approach which have the most effect on audiences, about their motivation and mainsprings. But the types of interests and the responses to different material and forms of presentation are not yet studied significantly, particularly for environmental films.

More needs to be known about the techniques of film production appropriate to varying levels of maturity and intellect – how many ideas can people of different intellects take at one time? More understanding is obviously needed of the levels of stimulation for given audiences, of their capacity to distinguish a reasoned case from polemic, particularly in the presence of powerful pictures, and of the impressions people have at the end of a programme. Armed with such information, it should be possible to avoid the over-simplification which leads to distortion of meaning or the elaboration and technical detail which so frequently diminish the successful impact of a film. More positively, it should encourage original and unconventional techniques. And for all these issues, the reality can only be achieved through direct audience research.

Themes

Themes covering the environment can be summarized readily under population, industry, resources, urbanization, wildlife, leisure and organizations. A well-balanced series should probably reflect all or most of these categories, although in each case they lend themselves to a unity of approach which could have worldwide relevance.

In films about population, we should show the relationship of man's numbers to his life-style and the quality of the environment. We need to explain the implications for the earth's 'carrying capacity' of the number of children in a family being solely the responsibility of the individual and of the right and freedom of everyone to enjoy a high-quality environment. The contribution that family planning can make to man's happiness in a personal sense should be put over, and, for developing countries especially, the point made that parents need no longer have large families solely on an 'insurance' basis to support them in old age.

With industry, we should spread the basic point that it must conserve in the modern sense. It is responsible to shareholders, customers and public, and ought to maintain its resource base if it is to fulfil these responsibilities in the long term. Industry, as a whole, should therefore work on ecological principles, such as those of recycling and re-use, and diversify to produce stability. It should strive to eliminate waste or pollution of any kind. A special problem in industry is that of the small firm. How can the big corporations help them to conduct their operations on a conservationist basis? And what about the trade unions? Surely it must be shown that the individual worker, especially in the towns, is the one who suffers most from pollution! If resources are to be wisely used and pollution diminished, his activities on factory floor or farm must be fully backed with a sound knowledge of our technological capacities and understanding of their implications. And modern industry contains many fascinating processes suitable for films for which there is a wide public audience, apart from their obvious capacity for training and for use in schools. These are the sort of challenges which films could handle dramatically and excitingly.

Films about natural resources are relatively easy to make, and rarely lack interest, whether in the excitement of drilling for oil, the awe-inspiring power used in strip-mining for coal or iron, the control of oceans and rivers, or the conservation of clean air. All these carry potential for stimulating films, in which we can infuse ideas about wise use and long-term maintenance of stocks, so that these become accepted and build up into an ethos of resource conservation.

And in view of all the pressures and significance of Urbanization (see Supplement 1), a great effort is required from film-makers to illuminate the opportunities for the good life in well-planned towns and cities, to reveal the qualities of our architectural and historic heritage to be conserved, and to demonstrate the scope for an active citizen to care for his surroundings.

Wildlife films are now commonplace in TV and cinema. Zoos, aquaria, stately homes and their parks, and very many members of naturalists' trusts bear testimony to man's interest in wildlife. The globe offers an almost unlimited range of subjects and spectacles – the splendour of great herds of animals in Africa, the grace of massed flights of birds, the effortless agility of porpoises, and so on. Many films have reached high standards and many series have shown the importance of this theme.

Leisure is an enormous theme. But today it is often a euphemism for under-employment, for misuse or non-use of a potentially great resource. Facilities relating to leisure are relatively inchoate. In particular, many of those responsible, as well as the masses enjoying their leisure, fail to realize the pressures they place on the environment, which is often the immediate facility enjoyed, as well as the 'backcloth' to all outdoor activity. Films on leisure can be both entertaining and educational. They can widen people's horizons and help them to get much more out of life, as well as to become environmentally literate. As more time becomes available, and often more money and facilities, so people wish to 'spread their wings' and to take on new activities and they develop hitherto unsuspected talents. In this process, the film has played and will play a great part.

And, finally, one of the major themes to be tackled is the role of environmental organizations in society. Films can help people to look at their agencies and institutions (official and voluntary) in a critical but constructive manner. Often such films are necessary for training and informing personnel in the large state and industrial corporations, but, if handled intelligently, they can have a wider audience and facilitate community education. There are many international organizations concerned with the environment (see Chapter 21) and a large number in most countries, so that there should be ample scope for such films.

Within such broad themes, one of the main needs is to diagnose well in advance issues of increasing future relevance. Another is to facilitate and promote continuity in the subjects dealt with. One way of overcoming transience in the film medium is to develop interrelated series with parts allocated to illustrations of practical follow-up work which may be undertaken by community groups.

Sponsorship

In the production of films, differing motivations of official and industrial sponsors are very significant. The strategy of production needs to avoid overt propaganda, advertising, 'whitewash' films and blatant claims. These can not only impose limitations on films which otherwise could be of high intrinsic merit, but rebound adversely on their sponsors. Obviously it is difficult to get sponsorship entirely without 'strings' but sponsors should be helped to realize that they usually gain far more from giving the producer clear, enlightened guidance and then the fullest artistic freedom within stated aims. And an effort must be made to persuade sponsors, who are often competitive, to cooperate in developing an integrated series, so that the always limited funds and talents available can be given the continuity needed for a comprehensive coverage of environmental subjects. Production to high standards requires the backing of 'centres of excellence', which can provide a briefing service for environmental material.

The cost of equipment – camera and laboratory and so on – makes it difficult for some who would like to be active in this medium. Inadequate finances have meant that many films have not been completed or have failed to reach the screen. Nevertheless, some of the great film achievements in the past decade have been produced by talented and dedicated people financed 'on a shoe-string'. These are finding many separate and sectional audiences all over the world. And where equipment costs can be met by young people, so their wide-ranging interests will burgeon into a new flowering of films of many kinds and this will certainly include many about environment. In several countries of Europe, local groups and societies have developed a capacity to produce such films. If a common stock of facilities can be provided and some guidance and encouragement given to such bodies – especially by trade unions – then the number and type of audiences which cinema and TV films about the environment can reach can be rapidly extended.

Conclusions

These final considerations lead to the need for an international focus for environmental film-making, to maintain good communications between professional environmentalists and those dedicated to films, as well as with possible sponsors.

It would provide rapid contact (the 'switchboard' concept) with, and support for, centres of excellence, with information on the sources of film and sound, with expert advice on techniques and subjects, and with guide-lines for those involved. It would also maintain 'antennae' over the issues briefly touched on here and could ensure a continuing review of the film–environment relationship. It might also, in time, promote some rationalization and economy of effort in environmental film festivals, prizes, awards, studentships and fellowships.

But the overriding objective of an international focus should be that of a 'catalyst', to promote the role of films in environmental management – a goal to which the film can make a truly creative contribution.

ENVIRONMENTAL IMPACT ASSESSMENTS AND STATEMENTS

THE U.S.A. National Environmental Protection Act (N.E.P.A.) 1969, which set up the Council on Environmental Quality (C.E.Q.), required any agency of the Federal Government proposing legislation or planning to undertake an action significantly affecting the environment to file an impact statement with the Council. The intent of the Act is given in Section 101: 'The Congress, recognizing the profound impact of man's activity on the inter-relationships of all components of the natural environment . . . declares that it is the continuing policy of the Federal Government . . . to use all practicable means and measures . . . to create and maintain conditions under which man and nature can exist in productive harmony, and fulfill the social, economic and other requirements of present and future generations of Americans.'

Section 102 (2) (c) of the Act specifies that Environmental Impact Assessment (E.I.A.) must cover five points:

(1) the environmental impact of the proposed action;
(2) any adverse effects which cannot be avoided should the proposals be implemented;
(3) alternatives to the proposed action;
(4) the relationship between local short-term uses of man's environment and the maintenance and enhancement of long-term productivity;
(5) any irreversible and i rretrievable commitments of resources which would be involved in the proposed action should it be implemented.

An E.I.A./E.I.S. (Environmental Impact Statement) should give a detailed description of the development proposed, supported by as thorough as possible an appraisal of existing knowledge, factors and trends relating to the environment to be affected and of the changes likely to arise from the development. The Act calls for statements only on major actions with significant environmental effects, thus seeking to avoid wasteful preparation of E.I.A. 'Major' and 'significant' are relative terms, but the C.E.Q. issues guidelines, which give weight to the overall, cumulative impact of one or more actions. In fact, the process of deciding whether an E.I.A. may be required is itself a means of alerting the public.

As many Federal agencies' programmes involve a number of individual yet interdependent actions, the Act can often be implemented more effectively by preparing a single statement on the programme as a whole, rather than by filing E.I.A. on each action. Where more than one agency is involved, the one with the primary responsibility may prepare the E.I.A. or the agencies may together prepare an overview statement. The E.I.A. is, of course, intended to let the public know the facts and judgements *before* permissions are given and developments started. It must be circulated by the agency to the public and to appropriate Federal, State and local environmental agencies at least ninety days before the proposed action, and revised with all comments in the final statement at least thirty days beforehand. The responses of the agency have to be published and are tested at the public hearing and there is the fullest disclosure of the implications of any impending decision. In its responses, the agency has a duty to consider opposing views and to discuss alternative courses of action; these must satisfy the courts, if necessary, that adequate analysis of them has been made, with 'trade-offs' balanced in the context of environmental and other public values.

Responsibility for the decision on proposed development remains with the Federal official who administers the programme and prepares the statement – it is not transferred to the C.E.Q. The Council has sought to make Section 102 self-implementing, so that environmental factors receive proper attention without needing frequent intervention by itself or the courts.

By the mid seventies, around 6,000 E.I.S. had been prepared on a broad range of actions, particularly in the energy field and on air and water quality, land use and forestry changes. Although the Section 102 only applies to Federal agencies, nearly half the states had modelled their systems on it with California in the lead in applying it also to private projects. The technique had been tested and upheld numerous times in the courts and had by then become a vital weapon in the armoury of the U.S.A. environmental movement. And, significantly, the court had awarded legal expenses in some cases to citizen groups bringing N.E.P.A. lawsuits for acting as 'private attorney general' in vindicating an important public interest. Internationally the E.I.A. technique has been used to prepare statements prior to the conclusion of conventions, for example, for dumping wastes at sea, for pollution by ships and for endangered species.

These uses of Section 102 led to many countries, including Britain, assessing its possibilities for improving their decision-making processes over major projects affecting the environment. Obviously, E.I.A. does not provide a crystal ball to reveal all the direct and indirect effects, long and short-term, on the environment of physical, economic and social activities. The 'trade-offs' in values forgone for those in prospect are subjective and often difficult to make and for large-scale developments are often settled by political considerations.

Considerable efforts are now being made in the U.S.A. and elsewhere to improve the quality of E.I.A. and E.I.S., especially in forecasting, not only for ecological factors and trends, but for legal and economic and other non-physical issues. The secondary and individual effects of projects are being identified more thoroughly, both to enable them to be more effectively assessed and to clarify those which are crucial to the decision. Better timing of the E.I.A. and its processes and streamlining and size of E.I.S. are undergoing rigorous examination. Means of following up and monitoring projects are required so that their effects and the forecasts and evaluations can be tested and experience consolidated and extended.

As the U.S.A. does not have a planning system and measures, including the constraint powers, like that of Britain, the E.I.A./E.I.S. should not be bodily transplanted like so many other transatlantic imports, but used on an experimental basis for a few selected projects to gain experience. An existing clause in the 1968 Planning Act, providing for *ad hoc* inquiries by special commissions, could probably be used. E.I.A. should be programmed rapidly to provide successive approximations of intent and implications to be improved and clarified, with appropriate public participation, prior to any final comprehensive report being revised and then submitted to the deciding authority – if the project has survived all the stages! Not only developers – public or private – but the specialist *ad hoc* agencies, planners and scientists, citizen groups, journalists and politicians – all involved in E.I.A. – require a positive approach. They will not only have to defend proposals constructively, exploring their virtues and shortcomings, but to compare them honestly with the pros and cons of other options. Difficult as forecasting is for E.I.S., this capacity to appraise objectively and to respond fairly to criticism is likely to prove the critical test in its long-term success.

Critics of E.I.A./E.I.S. make many points against the technique. It is important to take account of these so that the E.I.S. does not appear a panacea or become a substitute for hard thought and painful decisions. Obviously the sheer amassing of more data will not, of itself, give better forecasting; judgement is required to weigh up probabilities. And many environmental affairs are local or unique and defy extrapolation. There is also the eternal difficulty of getting people to act in advance of catastrophe. Most regulations, for example, governing transport derive from post-mortems on accidents, the causes of which had been foreseen. Sceptics also question whether people will pay the price of E.I.S. and face the costly delays alleged to flow from it. They contend that as economic pressures force people back to basics, their priorities change and those of the environment deteriorate. These points overlook changing values about the quality of life and ignore the fact that many decisions are better for openness, challenge, and reassessment. Pragmatically, the inadequate numbers of professionals skilled in systematic inter-disciplinary work and with the necessary breadth of comprehension will limit the use of E.I.S. to really significant or major projects. Hence the suggestion to deploy some of the Government Planning Inspectorate and the Agricultural Advisory and Development Service on this work, together with experts from the specialist agencies. This, in itself, could be of benefit to the whole planning process. It would also be very educative for the public and far from giving the 'lobbies' runaway cases – as some fear – should increasingly induce critical respect and understanding, with more responsible participation.

E.I.A./E.I.S. are with us. The Scottish Development Department made a start in Britain in 1974 with guidance to its planning authorities on appraisal of the impact of oil-related development. A U.K. Government report on the system was published in 1976. The European Economic Community is actively developing possible applications. In the Southern Hemisphere, New Zealand* leads in seeking social and physical

* The appraisal of the environmental impact of governmental policy for New Zealand's beech forests in the 1975 book *Rush to Destruction* by Graham Searle, is of special significance in that it makes the assessment at the vital policy stages rather than the later ones of public inquiry into implementation.

environmental audit on all major development projects before granting approval. Multi-national corporations employ consultants to prepare for them E.I.A. in advance of major projects. Public concern and disquiet over large-scale activities and their feelings of impotence in the face of 'juggernaut' developers – official or private, national and international – cannot be ignored. If E.I.A./E.I.S. can help to dispel these feelings, it will be worthwhile in key cases. Britain is in a ferment of change: devolution, reorganization of all levels of government and of services such as water, new planning processes and techniques, legislation to enable the community to acquire development land and to secure betterment, fiscal measures affecting land such as capital transfer tax and a possible wealth tax, more land in the public domain and greater urgency to synthesize planning, management and development. In all this, E.I.A./E.I.S., judiciously employed, could be a valuable tool in a new approach to creating a high-quality environment.

THE TOURIST INDUSTRY AND THE ENVIRONMENT

THE Tourist Industry is increasingly of world-importance, with a great potential for good or ill, in the inevitable reshaping of the environment. Unfortunately, there is far too little visible recognition of this truth. Much resort development for tourism on the coastlines of the world demonstrates thoughtlessness and lack of standards; the ancient towns and cities and their historic buildings wilt and decay under tourist pressure and are often diminished by new buildings, out-of-character and scale; great landscapes are blighted by excrescences and sprawl; and pollution from people penetrates everywhere.

All this obviously cannot be attributed to tourism. To make sounder choices and to exercise wisely our responsibility for environmental management require better and continuous education and information at all levels of society. It requires a contribution by the Tourist Industry, which should strive to ensure the wise use and management and enjoyment of attractive coastline, beautiful countryside, historic buildings and charming towns and villages. It cannot – neither in economic terms nor in its own enlightened self-interest – allow the insidious destruction of these assets. Management for tourism and care of town and country are complementary, and, in many cases, necessary to each other. The Tourist Industry should therefore accept a share of responsibility now for the carrying capacity of the physical heritage and the creation of new features of quality in the environment.

There are no easy answers in this work. It is a long, hard haul which involves overcoming inertia and apathy in many sectors of society and too often indifference from the public. What guidelines are available, when experience shows that a fine plan for one resort or city may be wholly inappropriate in another situation?

Requirements

Environmental Impact Assessment (E.I.A.)

The Tourist Industry needs to possess at most levels the ability to assess the environmental impact of tourist activities. This kind of assessment is now becoming an accepted task for major projects by modern industry. It calls for expert advisers with regular survey and monitoring of key tourist areas and routes. To be effective, a keen environmental awareness should permeate the Industry. And this demands tour organizers and guides and other staff systematically trained to assess the tourist-carrying capacity of cities and resorts.

E.I.A. should embrace the beneficial and adverse implications of tourism for the town, resort, village or landscape affected. It should analyse tourist activities, defining their impact in its varying intensity in space and time (seasonality, etc.) and propose courses of action and alternatives based on the widest possible experience. It should acquire the character of an 'operational audit' on the general health of the Industry, with especial reference to the tourist–environment interaction.

A combination of alert environmental awareness throughout the Industry, backed by professional and specialist support, should soon facilitate the setting-up of 'clearing-houses', to disseminate information on impacts, carrying capacity and the management of people and places. The experts in support would produce publications on all these issues, with guidelines for most of them, especially for behaviour, education and enjoyment. And backing up the experts and 'clearing houses' would be task forces to help resolve particular problems in important locations.

Planning and Management

The Industry should seek to forecast tourist demands in relation to the environmental features as far ahead as possible, with the 'desire' lines of tourists expressed in geographical terms and the options they reveal carefully assessed, so that areas potentially suitable for tourism can be reserved in cooperation with local authorities. Development can then be coordinated in relation to long-term objectives and plans. This is important for the financing and timing of investments on infrastructure and for deciding the size levels beyond which further development has disadvantages outweighing the advantages. This forecasting ability should be reinforced by the preparation of specific guidelines and of operational techniques for town and resort planning, design and management. Good planning can increase carrying capacity for tourism. Zoning of defined quality areas of land and water, the development of high density locations, and the incorporation of the needs of tourism at the very outset of any proposals can achieve much economically. Whatever methods are adopted, zoning in space and time is essential.

Other specific considerations include the selection of sites with favourable climatic conditions and scope for effective communications. Access to pure water, good winds, distance from marshlands, capacity for sewage and the normal infrastructure for any town should be thoroughly evaluated. The balance and compatibility of land uses – existing or proposed – need much thought, as does the harmonizing of development with landscape qualities; for example, roads should not only be safe and functional but provide, by contrast or harmony, new vistas and tourist interest. These factors of location and the planning framework should be set within a regional context, so that access to places of natural beauty and wilderness or to facilities for energetic and noisy pursuits can be enjoyed without detriment or undue restriction.

To do this requires sound knowledge of those features contributing to the quality of an area – the special landscapes, sites for intensive recreation, countryside treasures, nature reserves and sanctuaries, buildings of artistic, architectural or historic interest, and caves, archaeological, geological and other attractions. In sum, a 'heritage inventory' is essential to the effective planning and development of an area. And where the heritage is deficient in desirable features, then the plan should provide for the creation – as far as possible – of these values. This could embrace open spaces, public parks and gardens, woods, water areas, individual buildings of distinction and town areas of character. In general, in the development of towns and resorts, incompatible uses should be separated, traffic segregated from pedestrians, buildings zoned to create centres of quality for community activities, and much more insight shown in reconciling development with the natural constraints of land, air, water and wildlife.

In the detailed development of tourist areas, it is essential to maintain and improve rights of way giving access to seashore, mountain, lakeshore, riverbank, or other place of natural beauty of recreational utility. Derelict sites or other land should be reused for many purposes, such as car parks, seating and playing facilities, tennis-courts, shelters, toilets and playgrounds. Forgotten or polluted stretches of rivers and canals can be refurbished for water sports and amenities. The active recreation component of much tourism depends on water areas, land-needs often being for linear, scenic routes, or foci of interest.

Communication systems should, therefore, always be related (or 'networked') so that people can circulate easily by various forms and most essentially by foot. More facilities such as 'park and ride' are required. In new or redeveloped areas, footpaths, pedowalks, travelators, horse-riding and cycling facilities and viewpoints should be incorporated, in association with car and bus parking locations, in turn linked to air and rail termini. Fine squares and streets, historic buildings and other prime qualities of an area should be kept free from vehicles by such positive provisions. Where these are not readily available, controls become inevitable and this in turn demands more information and persuasion. The overriding point to recognize is that the best qualities of town and resort are, at any given time, not only finite but depreciating if not actively managed.

One of the features of active management of the environment, if tourism is to be regarded as a land use in its own right, is sharing of the environmental resources of town and country between various interests. Only so many can enjoy a location without harming it, whether this be a seaside town, a country park or the Seychelles. There is over much concentration on a few areas of great excellence – visually and historically – as in the case of Jerusalem and other parts of the Holy Land. The Industry faces the challenge of finding and creating more values. Town centres and buildings of good character and design could be enhanced by adding, in appropriate situations, distinctive contributions of quality from our own times. We must, too, find new uses for old buildings (such as the *Paradors* in Spain) and new techniques of harmonizing modern materials and styles with existing features of quality.

Cooperation and Liaison

The expansion of tourism is often promoted and subsidized by countries for a wide range of political, economic and social reasons. The Industry needs allies in government (central and local), the professions and voluntary bodies; environmental activity offers an excellent continuing basis to cultivate them.

The U.S.A. Travel Industry for the Environment Council
(T.I.E.) has, since 1972, brought together representatives of
travel, tourism and the hotel industry, of major environmental
organizations, and of State, Federal and overseas governments,
into one group with the following objectives, to:

(1) encourage travel-tourism industry members to involve themselves in long-range government environmental and outdoor
recreation planning;

(2) develop selected programmes to support government field
programmes;

(3) encourage business–industry exploration of the growing
opportunities in outdoor recreation–environmental preservation.

But to make these objectives meaningful demands initiatives
by the Industry in cooperation with the many sectors of society
actively concerned with the environment. In addition, the
Industry needs to pioneer, initiate and develop new and old
facilities and ventures to cater more for the increasing range of
minority pursuits. For example, in Britain, there are the numerous arts of the Arts Council, the eighty sports of the Sports
Council, the wide range of supporters of the Historic Monuments and Buildings Directorate, the depth and scope of the
official and voluntary nature and amenity conservation bodies
and so on. More original items are needed, such as the 'Three
Senses' Nature Trail for blind people, more farm parks and
trails, the Rickshaw bikes in car-free zones, more uses for *son et
lumière*, more urban trails, and the wider use of the great wealth
of parks in the existing towns and resorts of Europe. Tourism
can also help to stimulate local crafts and customs – not as
kitsch – but as a real expression of local individuality and as a
contribution to shared cultures.

These possibilities have a common aim – to extend, enrich
and diversify the enjoyment of the tourists by encouraging
them to the right place at the right time. In structural terms,
the Industry requires networks of liaison, organized at varying
levels with the main bodies affected by or involved in the tourist–
environment relationship.

Education and Information

An overriding requirement is public support. Quality and wise
use must be paid for, but it is more economic to strive for them
than to allow our physical heritage to diminish. So every

opportunity should be taken to promote new insights into the planning and layout of towns and resorts, their buildings, street furniture, the facilities of reception areas, car parks, kiosks, and to develop a form of education for leisure in depth which enhances peoples' enjoyment and their concern for their surroundings. Thus, a massive interpretative capacity is needed – not, of course, to be provided alone by the Industry, but to be shared with other bodies concerned with the quality of our surroundings.

Obviously, the Industry must anticipate and respond to changing standards and preferences. In resorts, town and countryside, there is an ever-increasing demand for better standards in the strict control of new construction in old towns; the building of roads to by-pass historic centres and charming villages; the removal of unsightly outdoor advertising, cables and wires and other blemishes; the elimination of litter and ugliness; and the introduction of more trees and flowers in towns and villages. In all these issues the Tourist Industry can take the lead with local authorities and other industries and commerce.

An increasing range of specialized tourist interests depends on the quality of the environment – ornithological, botanical, archaeological, photographic, etc. – and the Industry caters more and more for them. While these once-minority interests will increase and ramify further, it is essential that there is much more research into the sociological and environmental aspects of tourism, especially to learn about the implications of changing life-styles and of peoples' sources of enjoyment. Without more realistic data on situations and trends, the Industry would miss many real opportunities.

Maps and publications on a national and international basis need to be organized for fresh, well-balanced itineraries. These should be made available well in advance of tours, with recommendations as to how prospective tourists can equip themselves with knowledge, through, for example, local societies, before they go on tour and thus get much greater benefit and enjoyment from visits to historic spots, seaside resorts, nature reserves and so on.

If leisure is not to be a euphemism for misuse or under-employment of time, then new dimensions of culture and activity are required to enrich the human personality. This is a formidable challenge to the Tourist Industry. If it can also develop participation from tourists towards the wider aims envisaged, it may find that the contribution is not only in finance but in other forms of benefit to the Industry.

THE PLANNER

> . . . logic and learning and all mental activity . . .
> have been understandable only as a process by
> which man puts himself *en rapport* with his
> environment.
>
> Norbert Wiener, *I am a Mathematician* (1956)

There are many types of planners: the economist who helps to formulate the national economic plan; the specialist who plans the programmes of nationalized industry or a major private concern; and the scientist or professional who plans natural resources. All of these obviously have to take account of many issues. But they do not have to cover the whole range of social, economic and physical factors, which is the task of the town and country planner. This planner has, in fact, to comprehend all the factors which make up the total backcloth to life. He must not only know the requirements of his own profession but also appreciate the contribution to planning of other professions and be capable of creating a synthesis of related concepts and data. The planner should be in frequent contact with universities and research councils and be aware of scientific knowledge bearing on land and water resources. He must understand and use assessments of the ability of land and water to sustain, without detriment, the uses to which they are put.

About half of the 5,000 members* of the Royal Town Planning Institute are engaged officially in central and local government. The heads of the major departments directing the preparation of development plans and town maps are the key figures. These really do have to apply to the environment the principles of unity, quality and comprehensiveness.

About twenty per cent of qualified planners are engaged in private practice, many as consultants. They employ similar methods to those of their official colleagues. Although not all have the resources of the major local planning authorities, their greater freedom from official and routine commitments enables them to make a valuable contribution to the thought and practice of planning. A number of these consultants are undertaking plans

*Fellows and members (including legal); plus 4,000 students.

for new cities and towns, such as those mentioned in 'New and Expanding Towns' in Chapter 16.

Most planning on any scale is carried out by teams which include people skilled in many professions – architecture, estate valuation and engineering, for example – and sciences such as economics, geology and ecology. Their leader aims to synthesize the main elements emerging from the work of the whole team. Members usually have the training and capacity to seek out and to identify those issues on which a judicious contribution can be crucial in creating a good three-dimensional environment. In effect, the planner develops a special quality likened to sophisticated 'antennae'.

But still more professional cooperation is needed, particularly with the knowledge emerging from the environmental and social sciences and from international activities. The in-service training and education of the planner – from whatever basic profession – must be organized to enable him to keep abreast of the rapidly increasing and changing knowledge relevant to his work. To extend awareness of each other's role and needs and to promote cooperation over the common knowledge and skills required for effective management of the environment, the Professional Institutions Council for Conservation (P.I.C.C.), embracing all the main professions, was set up in 1971, under the aegis of the Royal Institution of Chartered Surveyors.

Different requirements are needed at the three main levels of government. At national level, the planner must be able to identify the relevant principles, to apply them to complex masses of information, and then to formulate strategy and policies for the nation. At regional level, he should contribute to the shaping of national policies and be able to prepare a strategic plan to take into account the special characteristics and resources of a region. He is also required to plan for population policies; the distribution and development of industry; communications; regional services, such as water and drainage; major landscape features; and generally to bring into balance with human needs the economic and physical resources of the region.

At the level of the county authority, the planner is increasingly concerned with the detailed design of the environment. He should work out more fully the policies of the region. He must prepare plans to implement them and to deal with any issues not covered in the regional plan, including policies for the smaller towns and villages. He also organizes the procedures for the control of development in his area.

One of the most important problems facing society is that of relating its human talent to its priorities. This is particularly so in environmental planning. Many qualities are obviously required for this exacting work. To those of first-class judgement and a sense of political issues must be allied the discipline of many professions and sciences. The intellectual requirements for planners are obviously high, and the qualities of dynamism and persuasiveness are scarce. With so few fully qualified planners to take on this important work it is essential to place them in key positions. Hence the significance of experiments with unified staff.

Perhaps most vital, the planner should understand the reality of people's lives, have a feeling for the wide range of standards and scope for personal choice needed for human satisfaction, and accept the probable impossibility of resolving all conflicting aims and values. He can only succeed if he gets on with people, communicates well with them, and is acceptable to a wide range of his fellow-citizens.

The planner's task is to spear-head man's response to human impacts on the environment. To do this effectively requires readiness to accept great responsibility, to make decisions, to argue a case with those concerned – publicly if necessary – and to lead, persuade and inform.

REVIEW

NOTES are given here of:

(1) some developments subsequent to the submission of the text to the printer;

(2) some current statistics;

(3) some features not ready or appropriate for inclusion in the main text.

U.N.C.T.A.D. IV

The U.N. Conference on Trade and Development was set up as an organ of the U.N. General Assembly in 1964, with over one hundred and fifty States as members. It seeks to evolve policies to influence the external trade and payments of all countries, as well as the economic development of developing countries.

Its fourth conference took place in May 1976 in Nairobi in the midst of the greatest world economic upheaval since the Great Depression of the 1930s. Global economic disequilibria, severe inflation, and general recession demand penetrating and critical examination of the fundamental causes and worldwide collaboration to resolve them and to develop a system which takes account of the basic issues discussed in Chapter 1.

Unfortunately, the conference was marred by the inadequate response of the developed countries to the Manila Declaration of 1976 by the developing countries. This urged positive action over commodities, industrial development and credit facilities. Essential elements in its proposed integrated programme included buffer stocks for certain commodities and a central fund to protect producers against inflation. After a month of debate and work, a compromise proposal emerged to bring some stability to the fluctuating prices of eighteen raw materials – details will be negotiated at a conference in 1977.

The pervasive and fundamental character of the U.N.C.T.A.D. problems were confirmed by reports in 1976. The World Bank *Atlas* revealed that growth in *per capita* incomes in the rich countries continued to outpace that in the poor nations, of which several have had negative economic growth over the previous five years. A book by Erik P. Eckholm of the World Watch Institute showed that the agricultural resources of Africa, Asia and Latin America were steadily shrinking and unable to support their populations under the pressure of rapid deforestation, desert encroachment, destruction of mountain ecosystems and the waterlogging and salination of irrigated lands. This situation becomes even more critical as only three countries in the world – Australia, Canada and the U.S.A. – are still net exporters of food. Canada's exportable surplus is sufficient only for about seven million people and Australia is in process of becoming a net importer.

The Commonwealth Development Corporation decided in 1976 to concentrate its new commitments over the next five years preponderantly in the poorer countries and into renewable natural resources projects. It contended that continuing recession has left the poorer developing countries in a desperate state of poverty and their future is unspeakably grim.

In sum, unless new 'one-world' relationships can be developed, rising expectations can only lead to bitter and deepening frustrations – and men and environment everywhere will suffer.

ENERGY

Forecasts in 1976 suggested that there could be a world shortage of uranium within two decades, unless substantial new deposits can be found to meet projected plans for the expansion of nuclear power.

LAND

U.N. Conference on Desertification, August 1977

Projects being developed in relation to this conference include global reviews of the processes and causes of desertification and plans to combat it; case studies on critical problems such as cold winter and warm summer deserts, salinization and waterlogging; and the development of fresh approaches to managing natural resources in arid and semi-arid areas.

Sudan

A Sudan Government-sponsored expert reconnaissance shows that its desert is extending southward about five km annually. Sand is also being blown ahead of the shifting desert and in some areas is affecting agriculture.

E.E.C. *Common Agricultural Policy (C.A.P.)*

The C.A.P. is widely criticized for the effects of its systems of intervention in agriculture such as the 'mountains' of beef, butter and fruit and 'lakes' of milk and wine but all too little attention is given to the implications of the man/food environment equation. And the failure of Europe to contribute powerfully to the needs of the developing countries extends the negative environmental dimensions of C.A.P.

More particularly, the F.E.O.G.A. (Fond European Orientation Guarantee Agricole) scheme of the E.E.C., which provides grant aid of up to 80 per cent of costs for farm improvement schemes, including land drainage, in excess of £100,000, is of increasing environmental importance and is intensifying the pressures on wetlands in Europe.

U.K. *Agriculture*

Data published by the Government in 1976 confirmed that, in the mid seventies, the nation's farmers and fishermen were producing over half of all food eaten in the U.K. Home production generally provided around two-thirds of the total value of supplies of 'indigenous-type' products grown in the U.K. About two-fifths of food imports were of products not normally grown in the country.

Agriculture *(Miscellaneous Provisions) Legislation* 1976

This legislation extends the definitions of 'disease', 'animals' and infected areas given in the basic Diseases of Animals Act 1950, in order to strengthen the capacity to deal swiftly and effectively with diseases.

U.K. *Forestry*

The 1975 survey of Dutch Elm disease by the Forestry Commission showed that the total number of dead or dying trees had reached 5·6 million. The trend is expected to continue and to lead to the death of about half the elm population in the survey area. The movement of *all* elm timber into and within highly affected areas is prohibited unless the bark has been removed.

U.K. *Urbanization*

A report by the Department of the Environment in 1976, 'British Cities: Urban Population and Employment Trends,

1951–71' confirmed increasing urbanization in Britain. The dominant trend is 'accelerating decentralization', as the commuter hinterlands spread and the population of the larger and older cities declines.

U.K. Airport Expansion

Concern increased in 1976 over the implications for regional planning and transport and the environment generally of the steady growth of Heathrow, Gatwick, Luton and Stansted airports, following the abandonment of the proposal for a third London airport at Maplin. The Government was urged to produce its airport strategy for the rest of Britain, that for London being the subject of a Consultation Document issued in late 1975. This issue demonstrates again the need for a comprehensive environmental approach in decision-making at all levels.

AIR

Concorde

Commercial supersonic flights started in 1976 with the inauguration by British and French airlines of Concorde schedules from London to Bahrein and Paris to South America, and a limited scheduled service to the U.S.A.

At the U.S.A. Department of Transportation hearing into the necessary applications for the Concorde service in January 1976, the Environmental Protection Agency (E.P.A.) recommended they be denied because of significant environmental impacts. These would be increased noise perceived by the people living under flight paths of the Concordes as they take off; increased air pollution in the vicinity of the airports; possible deleterious effects on the earth's ozone layer that could increase skin cancers by allowing more ultra-violet radiation from the sun; and a wasteful demand on limited fuel supplies.

Both in Britain and the U.S.A. the immediate major complaint was about the effects on people of Concorde's high noise level. In 1976 a report for the Local Authorities Aircraft Noise Council held that it would pose a significant hazard to people living near to London Heathrow airport. The E.P.A. contended that Concorde's noise would be twice that of a Boeing 707 and four times that of the Boeing 747 and the D.C.10.

WATER

E.C.E.

The U.N. Economic Commission for Europe (E.C.E.) was preparing guidelines in 1976 for the future planning of water resources in Europe and North America.

I.P.O.D.

The International Phase of the Ocean Drilling (I.P.O.D.) programme was in operation in 1976, with Britain, Japan and the U.S.S.R. participating. It is initially investigating the deep sediments at continental margins. These researches have already shown that the sea floor is, in some areas, rich in minerals.

U.N.

'Water – vital resource for life' was the theme for World Environment Day 1976 (5 June). The call for action at all levels from individual to world organizations was timely, with the U.N. preparing for its World Water Conference in March 1977. This will assess the world's water resources and needs, examine the potential and limitations of technology, formulate policy options and develop proposals for action.

Marine

The International Union for Conservation of Nature and Natural Resources (I.U.C.N.) initiated in 1976, with financial support from the World Wildlife Fund, a programme to accomplish more effective conservation of marine species and habitats through encouragement of government action and the development of favourable public attitudes. Activities in train include surveys of existing and potential marine parks and reserves and critical habitats, and action over threatened species.

Water Organization and Charges in Britain

A full review of the water industry in England and Wales was initiated by the Government with the publication in March 1976 of a widely distributed consultative document. Views were invited by the end of July so that the Government's final decisions could be announced in the autumn.

The consultative document focuses on two major issues – the general structure of the industry and the charging policies it should follow. On the former, the Government propose to re-place the largely advisory National Water Council with a broader-based strong National Water Authority, with increased powers and functions relating to the planning and execution of a national strategy for water. It would become responsible for the Water Research Centre and the Central Water Planning Unit. The broad structure of the industry, and, in particular, the independent status of the regional water authorities, would, however, remain largely unaltered. The long-term future of the regional water authorities would be examined in the context of possible regionalization in England.

On charging policy, the Government propose to introduce a measure of equalization of charges for domestic supply, on the basis of an interim scheme which will pool the cost to the water authorities of financing debt incurred up to 31 March 1976 and redistribute it on the basis of a common cost per unit of supply. The broad effect will be to reduce the range of average household bills in England and Wales.

The consultative document also suggests the possible merger of the British Waterways Board with the proposed National Water Authority as a first step towards setting up a National Navigation Authority. Apart from the operational advantages, this would lead to the introduction of a uniform registration and charging system and a national navigation code, so that boats could pass all along the waterway system on a single licence and be subject to the same regulations from one part of the system to another.

The Government also announce their intention to integrate the twenty-eight private water companies in England and Wales with the regional water authorities 'as soon as practicable', as they stress their view that the water industry as a whole should continue to be financially self-sufficient and should operate with-out subsidy, and that transfers of water and other services should be on a non-profit/no-loss basis.

Two omissions of significance from this latest review of the water industry are the absence of proposals for Scotland and for internal drainage boards.

As in many spheres of governmental concern, Scotland needs to simplify and streamline the allocation of responsibilities be-tween Central Government, water and river purification boards and other authorities. The powers and effectiveness of the system for water conservation, supply and use must be strengthened if needs and opportunities are to be realized in the next decade. This should be a priority task for the Scottish Assembly.

Internal Drainage Boards, of which there are over three hundred in England and Wales (in Scotland the Regional and Island Councils exercise these functions), are virtually autonomous bodies representative of local farming and water interests. They are largely responsible for field drains, intermediate water courses and larger drains (over 30,000 km) so that their policies and operations to achieve higher agricultural efficiency are of especial importance locally and, in sum, can be of wider environmental importance. By persuasion or direction (the Water Authorities have power but rarely exercise it), the activities of the Internal Drainage Boards should be made much more sensitive of and responsive to modern approaches to the planning, management and development of the natural environment.

Paying for Water, a discussion of economic and financial policies for the water services, was published in spring 1976. Water will have to cost more, according to this review by the National Water Council. This is largely necessary to find the finance to renew and replace the country's capital equipment – dams, mains, treatment works, sewers and sewage plants – much of which was created in the last century. The gross replacement cost of the assets of the water authorities in 1974–5 was in the order of £15 billion.

This important part of the total water problem was given new urgency in 1976 by the 'Great British Drought' of that year (water reserves were 40–60 per cent down in many areas of Britain). This, and similar conditions in other countries, increasingly suggested major climatological changes, with rainfall and winds altering to an extent which affected agricultural production, water for industry and domestic consumers, and the environment generally.

WILDLIFE AND HABITATS

Elephants

The mid seventies saw worldwide concern over Kenya's illicit trade in ivory. As world demand soared, poachers profiteered, killing elephants in such numbers that conservationists feared that the elephants would not survive much more than a few decades.

Wildlife Conventions

The Endangered Species (Import and Export) Bill enabling the Government legally to ratify the Washington Convention was expected to become law before the conference of participating countries late in 1976. The Management Authority (the Department of the Environment), responsible for the effective implementation of the Convention, and its three advisory Scientific Authorities (the Royal Botanic Gardens, Kew, for plants; a specially-appointed expert Committee for Animals; and the Nature Conservancy Council for general conservation policy) were by then fully operational.

Under the Wetlands Convention, nine countries have so far nominated seventy-nine wetlands, covering over two million hectare, the U.K. list comprising thirteen. Another eight countries are in course of ratifying the Convention. I.U.C.N. has already compiled a directory of wetlands of international importance in Europe and North Africa, and this will be extended to other parts of the world.

Threatened Plants

The I.U.C.N. Committee on *Threatened Plants* (run by the Royal Botanic Gardens, Kew) has begun work on the first of its programme's three elements. These are:

(1) survey and evaluation, in which an index of threatened species is compiled and centres of endemism, particularly those most at risk, identified;

(2) action, in which the most appropriate measures for each case are identified and developed as a project;

(3) public awareness, in which public support and concern for threatened plants is aroused.

It has compiled a list of rare and threatened species for all Europe, except the U.S.S.R., to be published late in 1976.

Save the Jungle – Save a World

This major campaign launched by the World Wildlife Fund, with the scientific backing of I.U.C.N., sought to raise two million dollars by the end of 1976 to promote ways of living with the tropical rain forests and using them wisely, and to establish and help maintain national parks and other protected areas in the major regions of tropical forests.

Wildlife and Farmers in Britain

The Government's Agricultural Development and Advisory Service reported in 1976 – 'Wildlife Conservation on Semi-Natural Habitats' – that farmers were sympathetic to wildlife and would welcome specialist advice about its conservation on their farms. This finding is particularly important, as the future of wildlife in Britain must largely depend on the management of the 80 per cent of the land surface in one or other form of agricultural use.

Rabies

Rabies increasingly made news in 1976 as its sylvatic form spread westwards across the Continent, mainly through infected foxes, at about fifty km a year. Some experts predicted that it would reach the Channel within two years. If it should reach Britain, it would have serious implications for wildlife and for people.

Loch Ness, Scotland

Reports of 'sightings' and photographs of phenomena in Loch Ness excited international interest in 1975 and 1976 as scientists wondered whether the reports justified the view that the Loch was inhabited by 'monsters'. If there were to be a wild creature in the Loch in need of protection, it would be possible, *inter alia*, to invoke provisions of the Conservation of Wild Creatures and Wild Plants Act 1975.

Broadland, East Anglia

The Nature Conservancy Council launched a three-year research programme in 1976 to find out the main causes of the decline in the aquatic plant and animal life of the Broads.

Dorset Heaths

Surveys in the mid seventies show that since 1960 the loss of heathlands (two-thirds between 1810–1960, see page 208) increased to four-fifths.

U.K. PLANNING

Plans

By spring 1976, of twenty structure plans submitted, four had been approved; fifty-one were in preparation and due by April 1978.

On average, 20 per cent of applications for planning permission was being refused. Appeals were running about 12,000 annually with 70 per cent being decided by Inspectors.

The Dobry Report

The Government issued advice (Circular 9/76) to local planning authorities on improving their development control in the light of the review by Mr George Dobry, Q.C., with the aim of assisting all authorities to reach the standard now set by the best.

The Government, having earlier rejected most of the main recommendations put forward by Mr Dobry (Circular 113/75) – largely on grounds of cost – drew special attention to his conclusion that '. . . it is not so much the system which is wrong, but the way in which it is used'. It stressed the need to eliminate delay and laid down guidelines:

(1) to make sure that applicants can acquaint themselves easily with local planning policies;
(2) to grant planning permission unless there is a sound and clear-cut planning reason for refusal;
(3) to consider whether more applications should be delegated to officers for decision and whether the planning committee meets often enough;
(4) to exercise control over design detail with the utmost discretion and not attempt to improve acceptable design;
(5) to lose no time in agreeing a development control scheme if there is not one in force.

Additional observations were given on publicity, on planning applications, monitoring of numbers received and improvement of enforcement procedure.

Planning Control over Mineral Workings

The Government Committee on Mineral Planning Control advocates that county planning authorities should give high priority to this work and should employ expert professional staff exclusively on it. The (Stevens) Committee proposes numerous measures to improve the operation of the present system, including a new class of planning application called a mineral application, with powers to review every five years the conditions (other than size and life of a working) attaching to a mineral planning permission. The Government decided to consult widely on the Committee's recommendations before coming to its conclusions.

Environmentalists are concerned at the Committee's proposal that exploration should be permitted development and disappointed that it did not recommend financial guarantees to cover restoration (to be reviewed after ten years monitoring), but welcomed the new procedure to remove the profit incentive to illegal working.

Land Utilization

Dr Alice Coleman, Director of the Second Land Utilization Survey of Britain, contended in 1976 that planning practice today was now actively promoting the misuse of land that planning was designed to resolve, for example, in allowing more sprawling development and a serious rate of loss of farmland. She advocated a drastic revision and simplification of the planning criteria and system, in particular proposing five major classes of environment: townscape, farmscape and wildscape – to be conserved; and 'Rurban' and marginal fringes, to be converted into one or other of the 'scapes'. To support this approach the Survey – to be published in 1977 – provides a precise analysis of land use under carefully differentiated categories. It also reveals the disturbing fact that Britain has 1,085 sq. km of waste land and scrub in and around urban areas.

Conservation

At mid 1976 there were thirty-three Areas of Outstanding Natural Beauty, amounting to some 1·5 m hectares, and one hundred and fifty Nature Reserves, covering 120,000 hectares.

Green Belt

The Countryside Commission inaugurated a three-year experiment in management of the 'urban fringe' in 1976. The project area covers 210 sq. km of green belt in Hertfordshire and the London Borough of Barnet, a typical 'no-man's' land of uncertainty in overall responsibility and inadequate harmonization between its variety of uses.

London – Deployment

The economic and social effects of the fall in London's population by nearly a million to just over seven million and the loss of almost half a million jobs in manufacturing industry impelled the Greater London Council to review its policy in 1976 for growth areas in the Strategic Plan for the South East and for New and Expanding Towns.

Significant economic and social changes since the Plan was prepared must obviously be reflected in the resource and investment needs of the capital, especially such areas as the docklands, *vis-à-vis* growth areas. The designation of any more London-related New Towns would appear to be detrimental to resolving London's problems, as would, probably, a continuance of more relocation of London's citizens in Expanding Towns.

GOVERNMENT

Wealth Tax

The Wealth Tax proposed in the Government Green Paper of 1974 was postponed by the Government in 1976.

Development Land Tax

This came into operation in 1976, initially levied at a rate of 80 per cent on the development value exceeding £10,000 realized from the sale or development of land, subject for a time to a reduced rate of 66⅔ per cent on the first £150,000. Owner-occupiers are, within limits, exempted.

Devolution

The Government announced in May 1976 that it would introduce a single combined Bill into Parliament in the autumn to give devolution to Scotland and Wales. Responsibility for the Scottish and Welsh Development Agencies will go to the devolved administrations, subject to guidelines by the Government. It seemed unlikely that there would be any action taken for some time on devolution in England.

Rural Economy

The Development Commission, which advises the Department of the Environment on use of the Development Fund set up in 1909 (and replenished annually by Parliamentary votes) to benefit the rural economy, has a new remit from the Government to intensify its work to stem rural depopulation and to regenerate the rural community in areas suffering from it.

Transport

The Government published its consultative document on transport policy in April 1976. It recognized the pervasive effects of

transport on town and countryside in advocating higher priority
to the effects of transport decisions on the environment. Specific
proposals could affect heavy lorries (held not to pay their way
against environmental costs), railways (not considered to offer
much gain environmentally by taking freight from road), and
roads (priority improvement at sensitive and congested places).
The Government proposed to set up a National Transport
Council, representative of the main interests, to become a
national focus for monitoring developments and to consider new
ideas and proposals.

POLLUTION

E.E.C. Objectives and Standards

A major clash on pollution policy in the E.E.C. emerged late in
1975. The Community seeks, first, to lay down scientific and
technical criteria about each pollutant, secondly, to set quality
objectives for air and water, and, thirdly, to prescribe measures
to control pollution. The U.K. opposes uniform standards of
emission controls and would not commit its industries to them,
as they do not take account of the variations in the capacity of a
locale to take in pollutants and deal with them naturally, without
damage. The U.K. believes that uniform standards would waste
resources and in some areas would be too high and in others inadequate. The U.K. therefore argued that the E.E.C. should set
objectives and leave members to achieve them in accordance
with local conditions.

After much deliberation over these issues, the Commission
decided on a compromise over the disposal of toxic wastes including the discharge of certain dangerous substances in rivers and
seas. From 1976, the E.E.C. sets both uniform emission standards and quality objectives for each 'black list' substance (the
more dangerous ones) leaving it to member countries which method
they adopt. Member States will establish programmes to reduce
pollution from a 'grey list' of less dangerous substances.

In the case of lead in petrol, the U.K. Government announced
in spring 1976 its aim progressively to reduce the maximum
content of lead in petrol in order to be in harmony with the proposed E.E.C. standard of 0·40 grams per litre.

Nuclear Power

The nuclear power industry in Europe faces the prospect of

storing underground large quantities of nuclear waste by the eighties, because of the serious shortage of equipment to reprocess it. This, the U.K. Government's decision to receive nuclear waste from Japan and the dumping of 6,700 tonnes of low-level radioactive waste in the deep Atlantic in mid 1976 are of increasing concern to environmentalists.

Mediterranean

At the Barcelona Conference in 1976 called by the United Nations Environment Programme (U.N.E.P.) eighteen countries bordering the Mediterranean agreed on urgent measures to reduce, eliminate or prevent pollution of the Sea.

Pesticides

The U.S.A. National Academy of Sciences published a major report in 1976 on the increasing problems arising from the widespread use of pesticides. It points out the dangers as genetic resistance to pesticides increases and calls for more research and more effort to provide alternative technologies, including integrated pest management. It considers that much more information is required about the vast scale of pesticide uses in the U.S.A. – and that, as the tasks of pest control become larger over the next decade, agricultural production could suffer.

Oil

U.N.E.P. and the petroleum industry hold a seminar in March 1977 to assess major aspects of the effects of the industry on the environment and of solutions to remedy environmental hazards.

U.K. 'Air Pollution Control: an Integrated Approach'

The standing Royal Commission on Environmental Pollution in 1976 recommends in its fifth report that a new control body should be set up to deal comprehensively with all forms of pollution, whether gaseous, liquid or solid, from those industrial processes which present technologically difficult pollution problems.

The proposed H.M.P.I. (Her Majesty's Pollution Inspectorate) would take over the much-criticized Alkali Inspectorate and be part of the Department of the Environment. (There would be a separate H.M.P.I. for Scotland and special arrangements for Wales.) It would be backed by new legislation, with additional powers of enforcement, and would set national guidelines for separate industries which would be flexible according to local conditions. The system would be made more comprehensible and be much more accountable to the public.

Control of Pollution Act 1974

Dumping of dangerous or poisonous waste was brought under control from mid 1976 by regulations made under this Act (see D. of E. Circular 55/76). Unlicensed dumping carries a penalty of up to five years in prison, plus an unlimited fine. County and Metropolitan Councils, the G.L.C., and the District Councils in Wales have to license all waste disposal sites having first consulted the water authorities.

The D. of E. Central Unit on Environmental Pollution reported in 1976 that when peak production of North Sea oil is reached, about 2,000 tonnes of oil will be discharged as contamination even under the best operating conditions. It stresses the need for the development of continuous monitoring and research into the environmental effects of such oily wastes.

INTERNATIONAL

European Architectural Heritage Year 1975

Some one thousand delegates from more than twenty-five European countries – Ministers, parliamentarians, officials and planners of central, regional and local government, representatives of independent specialist and citizen groups and professional societies – approved a Declaration in Amsterdam in October 1975 reflecting a new attitude towards Europe's architectural heritage and calling for joint action to protect it.

Europe's Environment

The second conference of European Ministers of the Environment took place in Brussels in March 1976 under the aegis of the Council of Europe. The conference developed further the programme of work on the conservation of the natural environment set in hand in Vienna in 1973. It endorsed the conclusions and recommendations of the European Technical Conference on Leisure and Nature Conservation (June 1975). Their main aim is to reconcile economic development with the protection of the environment and a series of measures has been designed to achieve it, particularly in relation to coastal regions, lakes and rivers; mountain regions; and densely populated regions.

The E.E.C. produced its second Environment Action Programme in 1976 for the period to 1981. This concentrates more on the conservation of natural resources and waste. The E.E.C. continues its established work on pollution and is initiating measures to help developing countries to facilitate international cooperation and to foster more research and dissemination of information.

PROSPECT

Objectives

The Science Council of Canada has adopted as its primary focus the concept of the 'Conserver Society' – that is one opposed to waste, favouring re-use and recycling of resources, questioning consumer demand, and seeking diversity in measures for stability.

Monitoring and Assessment Research Centre

This centre, set up in 1976 at Chelsea College, London University, started a two-year study into the type of international early-warning systems needed to safeguard food supplies and the environment from pollution and to combine conservation of resources with good agriculture, animal husbandry and industrial production. The centre is financed by grants from the United Nations Environment Programme and the Rockefeller Foundation.

FURTHER READING

Students should consult *The Environment* (Readers' Guide no. 1, Library Association, Public Libraries Group) and contact the Librarians or Information Officers of the national and international bodies referred to in the text (their addresses are in public libraries) who will readily provide a wide range of their own material and thereby also further sources for reference and study.

INDEX

(not including Supplement 9)